JERUSALEM IN HISTORY

JERUSALEM
IN HISTORY

EDITED BY K J ASALI

OLIVE
BRANCH
PRESS

ACKNOWLEDGEMENTS

The idea of writing this book was first suggested to the editor by Mr Muhammad Ibrahim Kamal of Beirut and Mr Awni Dajani, for whose support, along with that of Dr Albert Hourani, the editor expresses his gratitude. Financial support towards the cost of writing the book was made available through generous donations made by Mr Kamal and, at his initiative, by several friends and Jerusalem lovers. The donations made by Muhammad Kamal, and by Faiq Abu Khadra (Riyadh), Samir A Aweidah (Dubai), Bassim Azzam (Dubai), Abu'l Huda al-Taji al-Farouki (Washington), Shaikh Muhammad al-'Isa (Jedda), Wa'il al-Khairi (London), Hassan Yabrudi (Dubai), are hereby gratefully acknowledged.

The Editor

NOTE ON SPELLING

This work is the result of co-operation between nine eminent scholars from various academic disciplines. As such there may well be some variation in the method of transliteration adopted, although every attempt has been made to standardise this where possible.

The system used for the transliteration of Arabic spelling is the one devised for the *Encyclopaedia of Islam* with minor modifications.

PHOTOGRAPHIC ACKNOWLEDGEMENTS

The publishers gratefully acknowledge the assistance of the Palestine Exploration Fund in the preparation of illustrations for this book. They also express their gratitude to Peter Dorrell for permission to reproduce plates 1-8, 11-24, and to the Controller of Her Majesty's Stationery Office for permission to reproduce the Crown copyright map on page 66. All attempts to trace the copryright owners of the photographs reproduced as plate 9, plates 25-28 and fig. 14, from H Kendall, *Jerusalem: the City Plan,* London, 1948, have been without success and anyone with a claim should contact the publishers.

First American edition published 1990 by

Olive Branch Press

An imprint of Interlink Publishing Group, Inc.
99 Seventh Avenue
Brooklyn, New York 11215

Published simultaneously in Great Britain by Scorpion Publishing Ltd.

Library of Congress Cataloging-in-Publication Data

Jerusalem in history / edited by K.J. Asali. — 1st American ed.
Bibliography: p.
Includes index.
ISBN 0-940793-44-X
1. Jerusalem—History. I. 'Asalī, Kāmil Jamīl.
DS109.9.J459 1990
956.94'42—dc20

89–16000
CIP

ISBN 0-940793-44-X
Printed and bound in Great Britain

Contents

CONTRIBUTORS

H J Franken

Hendricus Jacobus Franken, born in the Netherlands in 1917, studied Theology and Semitic languages in Amsterdam and Leiden and gained his PhD in Old Testament Studies at Leiden, where he became senior lecturer on Palestinian archaeology. He has excavated at Tell Deir 'Alla, Jordan, and in Syria and has written several books and articles on archaeology. He developed new approaches to ceramic studies in archaeology and later became head of the Dept of Pottery Technology in Leiden. Emeritus professor since 1984, he is at present preparing publications on Deir 'Alla and the Jerusalem excavations of the British School of Archaeology in Jerusalem.

G E Mendenhall

George E Mendenhall is Professor Emeritus of Ancient and Biblical Studies at the University of Michigan where he taught from 1952. He has been active in archaeological and philological research in Jordan, Syria and Lebanon since 1955. His most recent major work is a decipherment of *The Syllabic Inscriptions From Byblos*, Beirut, 1985, which proves that in the Early Bronze Age the population of the Eastern Mediterranean regions of Palestine and Lebanon spoke and wrote a language that was an ancestor of Arabic.

J Wilkinson

John Wilkinson is a Canon of St George's Cathedral. For nine years he was at St George's College, Jerusalem, teaching history on short courses, mostly to foreign clergy and undergraduates. He is interested in the texts of Christian pilgrims to Jerusalem and has published English translations of all the texts from 333 to 1187. He was Director of the British School of Archaeology in Jerusalem from 1979–84, studying early Christian churches. A Fellow of Dumbarton Oaks, he continued his research at Tantur (Jerusalem) and is now writing a book on the design of early churches.

Abdul Aziz Duri

Professor Duri was born in Baghdad in 1919. Since 1969 he has been Professor of Islamic History at the University of Jordan, Amman, and was formerly President of the University of Baghdad (1963–68). His special field is Islamic Economic History. His doctoral thesis (University of London, 1942) is entitled: 'Studies on the Economic Life of Mesopotamia in the 10th Century AD'. Prof Duri is the author of several books and articles. In 1986 he was awarded the International King Faisal Prize (Saudi Arabia).

Mustafa A Hiyari

Mustafa A Hiyari gained his PhD in Islamic History at the School of Oriental and African Studies, University of London, 1975. He is currently Professor of History at the University of Jordan. His main areas of research are the tribal history of the Arab world, the *thugūr* or border areas between Byzantium and the Islamic Caliphate, and the Crusader period. He has published and edited a number of books and articles on these subjects and on 'Abbāsid administration.

Donald P Little

Donald P Little is Professor of Arabic and Islamic History at the Institute of Islamic Studies, McGill University, Montreal. He has been Director of the Institute since 1982. A specialist in the historiography of the Baḥrī Mamlūk period, he gained his PhD in Islamic Studies at the University of California, Los Angeles, in 1966. His recent books include *A Catalogue of the Islamic Documents from al-Haram ash-Sharif in Jerusalem*, 1984, and *History and Historiography of the Mamluks*, 1986.

K J Asali

Dr Asali is a native of Jerusalem. He received his PhD from Humboldt University, Berlin in 1967. At present he is engaged in research on Jerusalem at the University of Jordan. From 1968 to 1983 he was director of the Jordan University Library. During the last 10 years he has written six books on the Islamic heritage of Jerusalem, and many articles and papers. In 1982 he was awarded the Prize of the Kuwait Foundation for the Advancement of Sciences.

A Schölch

Prof Alexander Schölch was born in Mosbach (Germany) and educated at the University of Heidelberg. His doctoral thesis, *Ägypten den Ägyptern*, 1972, was greeted as one of the most important books on the modern history of the Middle East. Later the interests of Prof Schölch gradually moved towards 19th and 20th century Palestine. In 1981 he edited *Die Palästina Frage (1917–1948)* and in 1983 *Palästinenser in Israel*. His last published work, *Palästina im Umbruch*, 1986, is a masterly study of the development of Palestine in that period. The last post held by Prof Schölch was at the University of Erlangen where he was appointed in 1984 to the newly established chair of Modern Middle Eastern Studies. The tragically early death of Prof Schölch in August 1986 is a great loss to Middle Eastern studies in general and the history of Egypt and Palestine in particular.

M C HUDSON

Michael C Hudson is the Director of the Center of Contemporary Arab Studies and the Seif Ghobash Professor of Government and International Relations at Georgetown University. He received his PhD in political science from Yale University. He is the author of several books, including *Arab Politics: The Search for Legitimacy*. His 1968 study of Lebanese politics, *The Precarious Republic: Political Modernization in Lebanon*, has been reissued recently by Westview Press. Dr Hudson is a member of the editorial boards of the *Journal of Arab Affairs* and the *International Journal of Middle East Studies*.

PREFACE

A universal and comprehensive work on the history of Jerusalem is long overdue. Although several excellent books have been written and published on special epochs or themes, the whole field of research still needs the concentrated efforts of scholars – to investigate different specific aspects of the history and heritage of the Holy City – so that an authentic and universal history of Jerusalem may be accomplished.

The present work is an effort in that direction. It is a general presentation of the history of Jerusalem in all periods. Although it is an outline, it is hoped it will lay the foundation for a major and comprehensive work.

Students of the history of Jerusalem, in all periods, are confronted with two kinds of difficulties.

In the first place they realize that there are many gaps in the history of the Holy City which have to be bridged, many ambiguities, and a host of problems relating to historical facts which have to be clarified and solved.

In the second place there is the all-important aspect of 'objectivity' in the narration of historical events and their analysis. This difficulty is a natural one in the case of a holy city with the stature of Jerusalem, where the claims of the adherents of three world religions, Christianity, Islam and Judaism, met and clashed.

The sanctity of Jerusalem has in more than one sense made its history. Loved and adored by hundreds of millions throughout the world and through the ages, Jerusalem lived through times of glory during which it was built and embellished on grand and impressive scales. Yet for the very reason of its unique place in the eyes of the faithful, Jerusalem was, in other times, to suffer terribly. It was several times razed to the ground and its inhabitants annihilated. But each time Jerusalem was destroyed it was destined to rise again. The history of Jerusalem is a mixture of glories and catastrophes.

In almost all cases powerful religious feelings were present in the shaping of events, very often artificially generated and channelled to serve worldly ends.

But when religion is manipulated, the disasters of fanaticism will be always at hand; in such cases historical reporting suffers most and its pages will be wide open to bias and prejudice. Such a situation arose several times in the history of Jerusalem.

In the last one hundred years a vast amount of literature has been produced about Jerusalem embracing all aspects of its life: history, geography, archaeology, religious significance, culture, political case, economic life and urban development, etc. The volume of writing has increased immensely in recent years, especially after the Israeli occupation of a part of the city in 1948, and of the whole of the city in 1967. A large part of this literature was evidently part and parcel of a political campaign designed to justify a specific end: the transformation of Jerusalem. As a result of the constant flow of this type of literature the perspectives of whole peoples were dimmed.

Under these circumstances it was felt imperative to contribute to remedying the current situation by trying to represent a balanced and authentic picture of the history of Jerusalem, an objective history, which aims to help people understand and form an independent opinion about the history of the city.

In order to achieve this aim, it was thought best to resort to international co-operation in which several scholars from many countries would join in efforts to write the history of Jerusalem, each in his special field of interest. Thus an international team was set up, comprising eight eminent scholars from seven countries, namely, the USA, Canada, Great Britain, Germany, Holland, Iraq and Jordan, in addition to the editor.

The contributors accepted very kindly our invitation to enrich the book with the fruits of their research on the history of Jerusalem. Each one presented a picture of Jerusalem in the specific period on which he has been working for a considerable time. In this book they have all put the fruits of their research within the reach of scholars and the reading public at large. Their contributions are supported with illustrations and maps.

Our thanks are due to each one of them. It is hoped that their common efforts will, as I said earlier, lay a sound foundation for the great history of Jerusalem, and be a good prelude for future work on the most sacred city of mankind.

K J Asali

CHAPTER I

Jerusalem in the Bronze Age 3000–1000 BC

H J Franken

INTRODUCTION

The history of Jerusalem in the second millennium BC is the history of a period from which hardly any historical documents have survived. Since there is very little real historical information about the early stages of the city, one might call this chapter the protohistory of Jerusalem. Most information about the city's earliest history dates from later times and is not of a strictly historical nature. What is historically known about Jerusalem in the Bronze Age can be said in a few words. But the concept of history needs not only to refer to the physical fate of a town in the past, but also to the origin and growth of the 'meaning' which the city acquired at later times. The fact that there was a settlement in the Bronze Age which was given the status of predecessor to the Holy City at a much later date justifies that in this chapter the conditions that gave rise to these later developments are described as part of that early history. Some ideas about Jerusalem as a spiritual centre of the world may very well go back to the time before the fortress of Zion was captured by David. Many of the so-called well-known historical and archaeological facts from the Jebusite settlement are not true facts but rather reconstructions based on texts that are ill understood, because they are not clear or not complete, or on excavations that have revealed remains whose historical function is difficult to describe.

We shall have to deal with all these various kinds of evidence in an analytical way to see what their value is for any historical reconstruction. Unless we proceed in this chapter in this cautious way, describing the nature of the evidence at our disposal and attributing the evidence to its own branch of oriental research where it primarily belongs, such as philology, religion, etc., we run the risk of constructing a panoramic view of the ancient city of Jerusalem which suggests far more than there ever was. This has happened too often in the past. Rather we shall weigh the wide range of literary and archaeological material at our disposal for the reconstruction of Jerusalem's 'protohistory' and early history by analysing the nature of the sources in their own perspective to see what real historical information they potentially contain. In general there are two main sources: the literary and the archaeological source. The literary sources are of a purely linguistic nature or of an historical, quasi-historical, or, in most cases, religious nature. The archaeological sources are unfortunately restricted to a minimum of useful information, almost inversely proportional to the intrinsic importance of the history which they supposedly reflect. In every case we will find that no 'evidence' can be taken at its face value.

It is difficult for readers who are not acquainted with the 'grammar' of scholarly interpretation of texts to understand why what often seems to be a simple fact or something which seems 'to say exactly what it is' is not taken at its face value. But in fact such texts are never taken at their face value; not in the scientific world and equally not in a religious world; nor in an archaeological context where one has to admit that archaeological interpretation still often lacks the rigorous framework which a grammar puts on the interpretation of texts. Many religious texts dealing with pre-Israelite Jerusalem contain information which is valuable for the understanding of the nature of Jerusalem in the Bronze Age. Much less do these texts help us either to reconstruct history or to locate events connected with the history of the town. Whereas there is a host of stories about ancient Jerusalem, many of which are almost as old as the Bronze Age walls of the city, we have to deal with this body of ancient information in a concise and strictly scientific way. Only then will it be possible for the reader to find the historical truth about Jerusalem's early past and at the same time appreciate the intrinsic value of the world of myth that sprang up around it. Myths often contain very useful information about the past, but unfortunately it is the nature of myth that history is heavily concealed by it. Myth was an extremely valuable way of transmitting the truths of life of a pre-modernistic age, and it is only when we lose our feeling for the nature of myth that it becomes dangerous to mankind. Myth can be interpreted in various ways and the story of Melchizedek, king of Salem, will be used to illustrate what in a sense is also true for the stories about Jerusalem in the

Bronze Ages.* Whoever understands the creation of myth in the past will easily understand the nature of modern myths that have sprung up around Jerusalem in this day and age. A most striking feature about the myths that originated from Jerusalem is that many of them seem to date from its protohistoric period, as will be shown in this chapter. Transmitted as they were by the Jewish and Christian religions on to the present day, they were created and nursed in Jebusite Zion on the Ophel hill.

THE NATURE OF THE EVIDENCE

Readers not acquainted with modern approaches to the study of ancient historical, literary or religious texts, or of the systems of interpretation of archaeological finds may find it helpful to read a short introduction to the study of such fields. This chapter is entirely based on such critical studies. We shall mention literary, archaeological, religious and historical research.

The Literary Evidence

All ancient written information about Jerusalem in the Bronze Age is primarily of a literary nature. This is also true for any religious information which is found in the Scriptures. Literary information is naturally studied by linguists. Here philology has the first word and at this stage of the study of the text, other ancient Near Eastern languages are often used besides Hebrew to arrive at a philological interpretation and translation. A good deal of all Old Testament studies is concerned with the study of the Hebrew text itself. The next step is the interpretation of the written text and here more often than not the date of the text is discussed first. The question then is, which is the *Sitz im Leben* of the idea that is expressed, in which time did it play a role, or for what purpose was it made part of the text? In general, the information dates from long before it was written down and was only preserved in the texts because it served some purpose of the writer. The results of such studies often give reasons to read and translate the text differently from earlier scholars and translators. One of the most debated questions which such interpretative studies produces is that of the historicity of the subject.

* Quotations from the Bible are taken from A Jones, ed., *The Jerusalem Bible*, Reader's Edition, New York, 1968.

Can Melchizedek be considered as a person who once lived, and did he indeed give a blessing to Abram? The answer to such questions by different scholars is often composed of a combination of different approaches. They apply a critical approach in accordance with the main stream of textual studies and they 'balance the evidence' against their own religious convictions. This seems quite a legitimate procedure in view of the fact that very often no amount of philological or phenomenological effort can produce the 'ultimate' or conclusive answer. There is always room for fresh interpretations and there is always a chance that new epigraphical material will be found which forces us to revise our interpretations. But scholars who agree fully that a given interpretation of a text is acceptable may still disagree on the point of its value for historical reconstruction of 'what actually did happen' on the basis of, for example, their religious convictions.

The history of the Melchizedek interpretation is a good example. When it was first discovered that the Pentateuch (or the first five books) of the Old Testament was a very complicated composition of different sources (Kuenen-Wellhausen school[1]), Melchizedek was no longer considered to have been a historical person. De Vaux argued that in the light of archaeological finds one could not draw such a conclusion and others followed him in this opinion.[2] But archaeological evidence is even less fit to be taken as a reliable witness of the life of Bronze Age man in Palestine, unless such evidence consists of inscriptional or epigraphic material, such as monumental inscriptions, clay tablets and writings on pot sherds. The name of Melchizedek does not occur in any archaeological record.

The 'schools' to which the various writers belonged or belong, or the religious background, which so often gives shape to the final conclusion of an author about what happened in the past, helpful as it may be in producing solutions to certain difficult problems, are beyond the reach of scientific historical reasoning. As we shall see, it is beyond the power of modern historical reasoning to deny that Jerusalem as a town existed in the 3rd millennium BC if someone 'believes' that it did. Albright once declared: 'There can be no question whatever that Jerusalem was inhabited during the last centuries of the third millennium . . .'[3] Such statements are common in literature up to the present day. The evidence on which Albright based his opinion is now seen in a totally different light and all the evidence we have at present disproves his statement. But can we disprove it? Being unable to find traces of such a city is not enough to demonstrate that it did not exist. Suffice it to say that we have no literary or archaeological evidence which points to the existence of Jerusalem in the 3rd millennium BC. Literary evidence, when properly translated and understood, tells us what the ancient writer wanted to say. Whether what he wrote was historically true is altogether a different question.

The Archaeological Evidence

The history of excavation in and around the Holy City demonstrates that excavation of walls and other archaeological remains is only at the base of archaeological work. When excavations started in the second half of the last century there was only one way to interpret the finds, i.e. by applying the historical knowledge derived from the writings of Josephus and from the Bible to the ruins. Questions such as where to locate the city of the Jebusites were hotly debated after fragments of walls had been found. These finds were usually made in restricted areas. Pottery dating in those days could only be done for fairly late periods, such as the Roman and Byzantine, but stratigraphic research was lacking entirely. Macalister and Duncan summarized the work that was done up to 1925,[4] but all the dates of important structures excavated by them later appeared to be demonstrably wrong or could not be verified for lack of reliable dating evidence. Yet they managed to fit all their finds and many of those of their predecessors into a historical sequence which was entirely derived from the literary biblical sources. Recent work in the same area is such that one either dates the finds provisionally because the dating material (pottery) has not yet been properly studied,[5] or one gives dates on the basis of the same material[6] before publishing the evidence. Of course it has become easier now to establish in which period structures were built, but it is, for instance, not yet possible to say with certainty on the basis of pottery analysis whether the features date from the time of King David or King Solomon. Here again the text of the Bible often plays a decisive role in the reconstruction of the building history of the site. The general tendency in the archaeology of the area to fit things in with what we know, things which by themselves cannot be historically interpreted, is understandable but has often blocked the way to fresh interpretations. It is obviously extremely difficult to study ruins and analyse structures primarily for their own sake, and not to jump to conclusions before these ruins and structures have been completely described and studied. The ruins of Jerusalem are not self-explanatory and cannot be compared with, for example, ruins with inscriptions such as those found in Egypt, or ruins containing historical archives such as those found in Syria and Mesopotamia. The way to go about cases such as Jerusalem is to compare finds with those from elsewhere that are already well-dated by their association with inscribed objects from Egypt.[7] This method implies that there will always be some uncertainty not only where dating is concerned, but also in the interpretation of the nature of a given structure. We shall for instance see that the Jebusite city wall discovered in the sixties can only be supposed to have been built in the 18th century BC, and that the duration of its active life is rather uncertain.[8]

The Religious Evidence

This evidence is also a potential source of historical information. Much ancient cultural and religious material has been preserved in the text of the Old Testament. It was used by the ancient writers of the Old Testament to reconstruct the history of the Hebrew tribes or to remind the readers of Yahweh's great deeds in the past. But often they seem to have quoted ancient written or oral sources, from which they took what was strictly needed, while leaving out information that would be rather essential for us to have if we are to find the right historical interpretation. Thus in the story of Melchizedek we meet the name of El-Eljon, the high god, of which Melchizedek was the priest. It can be explained from a religious point of view why this name was preserved but we can hardly quote the New Testament to explain the historical origin of this priest: 'he has no father, no mother or ancestry' (Hebrews 7:3) or that of El-Eljon. We are not dealing with historical information in this case but with religious interpretation. In each case where reference is made in the texts to the Bronze Age site of Jerusalem we have to see what the context of the reference is, how fragmentary it is and what can be relied upon to reflect some historical, cultural or religious aspect of the Jebusite settlement. It can hardly be expected that the Old Testament contains shreds of information dating back to the Middle Bronze Age (*c.*1900–1550 BC), let alone earlier periods.

The Historical Evidence

True historical evidence concerning the early history of Jerusalem can only be found through 'weighing' the literary and archaeological information available to us at present. History or historical time is preceded by prehistory and protohistory. The distinction is in some cases rather an artificial one. History is taken to begin at the time that there are literary documents about people and places. In that sense Jerusalem may have entered history at the time of the execration texts. It did so surely in the Amarna period. Archaeological non-literary finds cannot change this date for an earlier one. If this chapter deals with the early history of Jerusalem it should include its pre- and protohistory, or at least the evidence about human occupation of the site which cannot be indicated by historical labels, be they ethnic or otherwise. The name of the hill in the 3rd millennium BC and before has not been revealed by inscriptions, although it had become clear through chance finds and excavations that people have been there and temporarily lived there or were settled nearby from Palaeolithic times onward. It is fairly certain that the water source or sources in the area always attracted hunters and other food gatherers as well as early farmers and shepherds. And if there is no evidence of human presence in the area for certain periods it should not be forgotten that in the times that elapsed since the first human visitors came to the area the surface on which they walked had either long since been washed away by erosion or buried under the debris of many subsequent cultures. And this is symbolic for the historical evidence about Jerusalem in the Bronze Ages. Most of it seems to have been washed away with time, but some of it is still there to be dug up, both out of the soil and out of an enormous accumulation of later spiritual 'deposits' left behind by the human mind

THE LITERARY EVIDENCE

The Name of the Site

The oldest occurrence of the name Jerusalem is in the collection of the so-called execration texts that were found in Egypt. In 1925 H Schaefer bought in Luxor 251 sherds, most of which showed a very old hieratic script. Later more sherds were bought. From these sherds about 80 dishes and vases could be restored. In that way also the texts were made legible. Only a year later K Sethe published these texts in Berlin, with a translation and commentary.[9] Several times Sethe found a word which he transcribed 'Awšamm' and which he read as 'urusalim'. Some scholars had their doubts about this reading but most of them were impressed and convinced by this rendering of the texts. Initially they were dated to the last centuries of the 3rd millennium BC. They are now usually ascribed to the period of the XIIth Dynasty and more specifically to the reign of Sesostris III (1879–1842).[10] This later date also caused a change in the interpretation of the use of these texts. They are the so-called execration texts in which the names of countries, towns and rulers are mentioned which were cursed because of their real or potential evil intentions or deeds against Egypt. It was thought at first that these curses were supposed to have magic power against all those enemies which Egypt was not able to control with military power.[11] However, the new date puts these texts in a period in which Egypt exercised power over Palestine and Syria, and therefore 'the text is not referring to historical reality, but to the dogmatic belief in universal domination by the Pharaohs, according to which every human being, wherever he might be, must submit to him and owed him obedience.'[12] Therefore they cannot be used to determine the extent of the empire that belonged to the XIIth Dynasty nor do they point to weakness on the part of Egypt. The execration ritual was 'a routine matter and not an exceptional measure imposed by circumstances'.[13] Twenty countries are mentioned in the earliest texts and thirty princes. Amongst them is Urusalim and two of its princes. Here we meet for the first time the name Salem, Salim or Shalem. Salem has been identified as the name of a deity, and 'uru' probably means 'has founded'. The name is considered to be of Amorite origin. The first mention of the name of Salem in the Bible is in Gen. 14:18 where Melchizedek, king of Salem, is mentioned. It is not at all certain that this Salem is short for Jerusalem. The identification of the two names occurs first in Ps. 76:2 and is followed by Josephus (*Ant.*I.10.2). But Eusebius seems to locate Salem in a village east of Nablus where he thinks Abram and Melchizedek met each other, and Jerome identified it with Salumnias, 8 miles south of Scythopolis. It is possible but by no means certain that these different interpretations of the location are merely caused by the fact that Salem sounded like another place which the authors happened to know. Rather one may think of a problem the ancient 'theologians' had with the blessing of Abram by a non-Israelite king whose god was not the god of Moses or of Abram. Skinner in his commentary on Genesis quoted Gunkel: 'The scene between Abraham and Melkezedek is not without poetic charm: the two ideals [Grösse] which were afterwards to be so intimately united, the holy people and the holy city, are brought together for the first time: here for the first time Israel receives blessing from its sanctuary.'[14] But although many scholars accept the identification of Salem with Jerusalem, there is just no definite proof. Salem could be related to Shechem instead of to Jerusalem.[15] Peter eliminates Melchizedek completely from the story of Abraham's blessing, which could leave 'Melchizedek king of Salem' out of any context.[16]

Especially since the town or the fortress of Jerusalem of the Jebusites did not have any specific religious value in Israelite thinking before it became a religious centre for them during the united monarchy, such ancient shreds of information may have attached themselves to any story related in the Bible by association of the sound of the name or even less traceable aspects. If and where they did so, we can be sure that the value of their survival is not primarily historical but symbolical, or of a religious nature. The Melchizedek episode was mentioned because it might contain a very ancient reference to the city of Jerusalem. Firmer evidence comes from the so-called Amarna texts, which were also found in Egypt. Tell el-Amarna used to be the site of a Bedouin village situated on the ruins of a town called 'Horizon of Aton', Achet-Aton, which was founded in 1370 BC by the Pharaoh Echnaton. Amarna is situated in middle Egypt on the eastern bank of the Nile, about 300 km south of Cairo. In 1887 documents from the archives of Amenhoteb IV were found there, consisting of letters written in cuneiform on clay tablets.[17] Six of them were written by King Abdiḫiba of Jerusalem and in others Jerusalem is mentioned. From these letters it can be deduced that Palestine was divided into small city states that were only united by the power the Egyptians exercised in the land. But when the Pharaoh failed to maintain order amongst his vassals the latter tried to enlarge their territories at the cost of their neighbours, while at the same time complaining in their letters to the Egyptian court about all the injuries they had to suffer from those neighbours. In that time the area possessed by the king of Jerusalem was not so small because it bordered on the land of Gezer in the west and Shechem in the north. In the case of the Amarna letters we are dealing with a situation which can be called historical because these documents were written at the time of the events which they describe and the towns can be located on the map. The king of Jerusalem was not very successful because he seems to have lost his allies in the end; he even lost control over the direct route to Egypt. The name of Urusalem is secured for this period (first half of the 14th century BC) and there is little doubt that it referred to a royal city situated on ed-Dehurah or eẓ-Ẓahūrah which is known in the west as the Ophel hill south of the Ḥaram. It is suggested in the Old Testament that Jebus was used as a name for the 'Jebusite' city of Jerusalem (Judges 19:10) but it is unlikely that Jebus is a real name used in pre-Davidic times. Some names are known indicating certain parts of the hill on which Bronze Age Jerusalem was situated. Ophel for instance may be an ancient name which is interpreted as 'fortified hill' or citadel of a city. It may have been in use already to indicate the Jebusite fortress.[18] The name is also used in the case of Samaria and other cities. Sion and the stronghold of Sion may also have been in use to indicate the Jebusite fortress or citadel (2 Sam.5:7).[19] While these names could have been used by the Jebusites, this is very unlikely to be the case with the name of Moria (Mōriyyāh) which in Jewish and Christian tradition is the site of the Solomonic Temple of Jerusalem and is used to indicate the site where Abraham was told to sacrifice his son. But Gen.22:2 mentions 'the land of Moriah', which in Samaritan tradition was near Shechem but is often corrected into 'the land of the Amorite' which is Palestine in general. If we assume that the name is a corruption and that 'the land of' hardly justifies the traditional interpretation as a place of sacrifice 'foreshadowing' the choice of the temple site by King Solomon, we will find ourselves dealing with a religious tradition rather than historical information.

The Personal Names

Several names of rulers of Jerusalem in the Bronze Age have already been mentioned. The earliest mention is of two 'princes' in the execration texts: Yaqir-'ammu and Saz'anu. Their names were identified by Albright[20] as Amorite names. In this period people of 'Amorite' affiliation inhabited Palestine and Syria[21] and the name 'Amorite' survived in biblical times. The language was West Semitic and is often called Canaanite.

Melchizedek, who is traditionally so strongly connected with Jerusalem and Abraham, cannot be dated in history. Ideally he is dated to the time of Abraham but here we meet with the same problem. Abraham must be dated to the earliest dated texts about him or earlier. Although there are many attempts to date this period by archaeological means, or by comparison with written sources from Northern Syria or Mesopotamia (Mari), the results remain hypothetical.[22]

With Abdiḫiba, king of Jerusalem in the Amarna period, we are dealing with a historical person. He claimed to be faithful to the Pharaoh but slowly saw his kingdom dwindle after initial success in combatting his neighbours in the south. Thus Suwardata from Kilti (=ḫirbet qīlā south of Jerusalem?) wrote in a letter to the Pharaoh: '. . . Labaja (from Shechem) had taken over towns. He is dead now but another Labaja is Abdiḫiba and he takes our towns.' Another letter states that the king is fighting the Sa.qaz or habiru, a name which first suggested that these enemies were the Hebrews. The name 'Ḥiba' is also part of a name found in Sam. 23:32, which belonged to a soldier in David's army, Eliḥiba, 'my god is Ḥiba' and Ḥiba was a deity of the Hurrians. In the Bible two names of kings have been preserved: Adonibezek (my lord is Bezek) and Adonizedek (my lord is Ṣedek). The latter was king of Jerusalem and the former a king who went to Jerusalem to die. It has been thought that the two names refer to one king, but it is possible that Adonibezek was associated with the city of Bezek between Sichem and Beisan. Adonizedek was king of Jerusalem in the days of Joshua, according to Joshua 10:1-15. He organized a coalition of five kings of small city states and was defeated by the Israelites. But the story poses a number of problems to the interpreters, because there is obviously a confusion and possibly two different tales of campaigns of Adonizedek have been put together. It is also possible that the two kings are not contemporaries, Adonizedek having lived much later than Adonibezek. And according to the text Adonizedek did not lose Jerusalem at all on that occasion.

The Population

The Amorites

In ancient and modern literature several names of people are mentioned who inhabited Jerusalem or were somehow in contact with the town. During the Middle Bronze Age Jerusalem had probably an 'Amorite' population. This can only be deduced from the two names that are preserved in the execration texts and from the name of the town itself as being Amorite. The Amorites made their appearance in history (which means in literary documents) during the IIIrd Dynasty of Ur at the end of the 3rd millennium BC. Occasionally there was already mention of them in earlier texts. In

Mesopotamia these people were called Amurrū (Akkadian) and Martu in Sumerian. At that time their homeland was Syria with a centre probably in the Orontes valley where they were organized in kingdoms but also at least partly led an unsettled life. They became a threat to the Mesopotamian kings and *c.*2000 BC Sumeria was invaded by Amorites led by the king of Mari. Kenyon's identification of the Early Bronze/Middle Bronze Age people who put an end to town life in Palestine from *c.*2300 BC may be correct. There are no written documents to prove it. Revival of city life is due, according to Kenyon, to new incoming people into Palestine *c.*1900 BC whom she identifies with the Canaanites.[23] From the historical records found in Mesopotamia it appears that the name of Amurrū is of northwest Semitic origin.

It may be assumed that the Semitic language was spoken in Jerusalem in the Bronze Age. Whether the inhabitants in the Middle Bronze Age were descendants of the first wave of immigrants in the last quarter of the 3rd millennium BC or from the second wave cannot be decided.[24]

The word 'Amorite' is also found in inscriptions from the 1st millennium BC and in the Old Testament. There are no Middle or Late Bronze Age texts from Egypt or from Mesopotamia and Northern Syria in which the term Amorite is used for any part of Palestine or Transjordan. But biblical sources from the 8th century BC or later refer to the Bronze Age population as Amorite, for instance in stereo-typed lists of people: Canaanites, Hittites, Amorites, Hivites, Perizzites, Girgashites, and Jebusites. Assyrian sources from the 8th century BC incorporate also in 'the land of the Amorites' for the first time Palestine with Israel and the Philistine cities, Moab, Ammon and Edom. This does not indicate a change in the population either in the Bronze Age or in the Iron Age but rather an evolution of the meaning of the word 'Amorite'. For the Assyrians it meant 'the people in the West' and for the Old Testament writers 'peoples that used to live in the mountains.' In a similar way it seems that the word 'Hittite' lost its historical context and became more or less synonymous with 'Amorite' in the 8th century. Both words pointed to the inferiority of people thus indicated. In Ezek.16:3 the prophet applies this to Jerusalem: 'Your origin and your birth are of the land of the Canaanites; your father was an Amorite, and your mother a Hittite.' This is not to be read as a historical description of the origin of the city but as a negative opinion about the behaviour of the inhabitants at the time of the prophet.[25]

The Hyksos

Between 1700 and 1580 BC the Hyksos ruled in Syria and Palestine as well as in Egypt. Very little is known about the background and the nature of these invaders, who were called by the Egyptians 'Rulers of Foreign Lands' and by Manetho 'Shepherd Kings'. Manetho was an Egyptian priest and scribe who lived *c.*300 BC. It is often thought that the Hyksos were the architects of a special type of defence system. This consisted of enclosures of extensive rectangular areas with walls of 'terre pisée' piled up in layers on top of which a mud brick wall was built. This defence system is found both in the north at Carchemish on the Euphrates, northeast of Aleppo, and throughout Syria and Palestine as far as the Egyptian Delta.[26] But it appears that after the Pharaohs of the XVIIIth Dynasty had expelled the Hyksos from Egypt and Syria to the Euphrates, another type of name of local rulers in the whole area is found. Noth has noticed that 'after the Hyksos period we find an upper class in Syria and Palestine in which especially Hurrian as well as Indo-Iranian names are not uncommon.'[27] There is no archaeological evidence of the existence of a Hyksos defence system in Jerusalem, which would have been taken as a sure sign of the takeover of the city by the Hyksos. Neither is there any sign of the presence of pottery types in the Middle Bronze Age ruins of Jerusalem that can be confidently dated to the Hyksos period. In fact pottery from the 17th–15th centuries BC seems to be entirely absent. The Hyksos maintained themselves from the beginning of the 15th to the middle of the 14th century BC east of the Euphrates in the kingdom of the Mitanni which had a predominantly Hurrian population. The influence of the Mitanni in Palestine can be traced in the Late Bronze Age and it may have affected Jerusalem as well.

The Jebusites

In the Amarna period Jerusalem was inhabited by Jebusites. In the Bible the Jebusites are considered to belong to the Canaanites as distinguished from the Amorites (Gen.10:16), who supposedly inhabited the city in the Middle Bronze Age. Their presence in the town at the beginning of the Iron Age is well attested in the Old Testament. King David captured the 'fortress of Zion' and it may well be that this did not refer to the town proper but to the acropolis on the north side of the town. It would seem that once the fortress of

Zion had been captured the town itself was defenceless and became automatically part of David's property. There is no mention anywhere that the Jebusite population of the town was expelled. As already mentioned above, Jerusalem was a city state in the Amarna period consisting of a centre and land with towns bordering on the land of Shechem and Gezer. Slowly this property had to be given up and in the 11th century BC the border between the land of the tribes of Judah and Benjamin ran through the valley of Hinnom. The Jebusites not only occupied the city of Jerusalem but also the countryside. Judges 1:21 refers to a situation in which Benjaminites and Jebusites lived together. 'As regards the Jebusites living in Jerusalem, the sons of Benjamin did not drive them out, and even now the Jebusites are still living in Jerusalem with the sons of Benjamin.' In the same chapter of Judges, vs 8, it is stated that the sons of Judah attacked and conquered Jerusalem, killed the population and then burned the city down. But since in vs 21 it is suggested that the tribe of Benjamin did not manage to take the city and only mixed with the original population, the statement of vs 8 does not reflect a historical fact. It was not until King David captured the city that it fell into Israelite hands.

The Habiru

According to the messages sent by Abdiḫiba, king of Jerusalem, to the Pharaoh at Achet-Aton (Amarna), the Habiru were invading his lands.[28] The fact is mentioned here because after these Amarna letters had been published it was often suggested that the Sa.qaz or 'Apiru' were no other than the first Hebrew descendants of Eber (Gen. 10:21-31) entering the country under Joshua. It is now known, however, that Apiru refers to groups of people who were unsettled and had mostly lost their freedom. They could be found anywhere in the Near East. But the name could also be used to indicate groups of people who behaved like Apiru or like marauders and highway robbers. In the case of the enemies of Abdiḫiba the Habiru may even have been a tribe trying to penetrate into Jerusalem or which had been displaced from somewhere else. Whoever they were, they did not succeed in conquering the land around Jerusalem or the city itself and there is no point in speculating on an identification with any of the known Hebrew tribes.[29]

THE ARCHAEOLOGICAL EVIDENCE

Structures from the town in the Bronze Age have only been properly identified by recent excavations on eẓ-Ẓahūrah.[30] With regard to the Bronze Age and the Early Iron Age the great works by Vincent[31] and Simons[32] are outdated, although they have not lost their importance as surveys of archaeological work done up to that date. Vincent and Kenyon have paid much attention to the earliest occupants of the site and its immediate surroundings.

Here follows a short survey of archaeological and prehistoric finds in and near the city. At the time these discoveries were made very little was known about the prehistoric context to put them into proper perspective. At present far more is known since subsequent finds enable us to estimate the dates and to describe the cultures to which they belong.

Palaeolithicum

In the Beqa'a, a valley southwest of Jerusalem, flint tools were already found in the last century, which eventually (1933) were brought to the notice of Breuil. Neuville, assisted by Stekelis, made excavations and found tools *in situ* which they attributed to the Acheulian industries. No human remains were found but the site was obviously a station for Palaeolithic hunters.[33] Some people connected these finds with the 'Palaeanthropus Palestinensis' of the Carmel.[34] The opinions about this 'Palestina Man' have rather changed in the course of time. According to Vandermeersch he is related to the Cro-Magnon people rather than to the Neanderthal Man, which could mean that Palestina Man was at the base of a large part of the population of West Europe after about 35000 BP [Before Present]. Both Cro-Magnon and Palestina Man belong to the group that at present is named Homo Sapiens.[35] It is not known whether Palestina Man migrated to Palestine or developed from an earlier stage in the area itself. The Beqa'a's deposits may represent many thousands of years.

The find of these flint tools gave rise to the assumption that the name of Rephaim, mentioned in Jos. 15:7-9 as being a valley, part of the border of the land of the Judah tribe near Jerusalem ('south of the mountain of the Jebusites') still preserved a very old tradition about the Palaeolithic people of Palestine. Especially it seemed that the description of the skeletons found at Skhūl and elsewhere as being comparatively large played a part in this assumption. The Rephaim were a giant aboriginal race known in Israelite folklore and said to have lived in Canaan, Moab, Ammon and other places (Gen. 15:20 etc.). There is no point in trying to identify Palaeolithic man with these stories, no matter how old the stories may be.[36] Stories about giants inhabiting the world after its creation are found all over the world. They seemed to find their origin on the one hand in tales about the origin of the megalithic monuments in many parts of the world, which were told when there was no longer any traditional link with the people who erected these monuments, and on the other hand in an equally widespread belief that in primaeval times human beings not only lived longer than became normal later on, but also were larger and more powerful. This was the situation after the creation of the world and this ideal state of affairs will return in the last days of this creation. This is the myth of the *Urzeit und Endzeit*.[37]

Early Bronze Age (3200–2000 BC)

The pottery ascribed by Macalister to the Neolithic period has now been identified as Middle Bronze Age cooking pots.[38] Some caches of pottery from the Early Bronze Age were found by Kenyon. Shiloh in his area E I found two small structures which on the basis of a preliminary analysis of the pottery was assigned to his stratum 21-20 = the second half of the 4th millennium BC, which is the end of the Chalcolithic period and the beginning of the Early Bronze Age.[39] Kenyon discussed a period which she called the Proto-Urban period in Palestine after the Proto-Dynastic period in Egypt and the Proto-Literate Age in Mesopotamia. She mentions a tomb from Ophel containing pottery from that period and dating to the last centuries of the 4th millennium BC. This stage precedes that of the founding of the Early Bronze Age towns in the country.[40] There are, however, no traces to indicate that this development took place at Jerusalem. After the first tablets from Tell Mardich (Ebla) south of Aleppo in Syria had been published, some scholars claimed that Jerusalem was mentioned in the texts from the middle of the Early Bronze Age. But this is now considered to be 'wishful thinking' and archaeologically there is nothing to support such an interpretation.

Early Bronze–Middle Bronze Age

Kenyon worked out on the basis of her excavations of the cemeteries at Tell es-Sultan (ancient Jericho) that the end of the Early Bronze Age civilization was caused by incursions of nomadic tribes which were associated with the Amorites.[41] Towns were destroyed and not built up by these tribes who are best known by their cemeteries that are found at many places. Kenyon called this period the Intermediate Early Bronze–Middle Bronze Age after the First Intermediate Period in Egypt. Others prefer to call it the Middle Bronze I period. One tomb of this period was found by Warren and during her excavations in Jerusalem Kenyon dug another eleven tombs belonging to the same group on the Mount of Olives. No sherds of this period were found on Ophel but the tombs are clear evidence that at the end of the 3rd millennium 'Amorites' were living nearby in the Kedron Valley.

Middle Bronze Age (2000–1550 BC)

Structures that undoubtedly belonged to a town of the Middle Bronze Age were found by Kenyon in 1961 well down on the eastern slope of Ophel.[42] Above the city's main water source, east of a rock scarp, a 2 metres thick wall was found running from south to north. It had a re-entrant angle on the north side and disappeared under a much later town wall built higher up the slope. Pottery was found in the space between the wall and the rock scarp which can be dated to the 18th century BC. Shiloh found the continuation of this wall further south in his area E I.[43] Pockets of pottery from the same period were found higher up the slope with a few fragments of structures by Kenyon, who demonstrated that north of the line where the Middle Bronze Age wall supposedly ran up the slope of the hill to the west there was no trace of Middle Bronze occupation. Soundings made west of the crest of Ophel in the direction of its southern limits caused her to conclude that the wall ran along the west side of the crest to the south and on the east side halfway down the slope back to where she had already excavated part of the wall. The line of this wall along the east slope allowed the inhabitants access to the spring through a shaft which was first explored by Warren and later by Vincent. In case of a siege they would not have to go outside to fetch their water. But the steep slope inside the wall was not inhabited it seems, or only where rock ledges were wide enough to be built on. How long this city lasted is not known.

Neither Kenyon nor Shiloh found any pottery that could be dated to the 17th–15th centuries BC. Kenyon assumed that the wall still stood as a defence wall when David conquered the city *c.*1000 BC, because no other wall was found that could have served in the Late Bronze Age or the beginning of the Iron Age.

We have no means of telling where the palace of the king of this city stood. In Roman times the crest of the hill served as a stone quarry and in the area where Kenyon cut her trenches all building remains were removed from the rock surface by the Roman stonecutters. Only buildings from after that period have survived.

Late Bronze Age (1550–1200 BC)

The earliest remains from the Late Bronze Age preserved in the excavated areas date from the 14th century BC.

If the results of Shiloh's area G are combined with Kenyon's squares A II–III, which partly overlap, we find a huge Late Bronze Age structure which must have served to enlarge the area on the crest of the hill. It is still within the boundaries of the north wall of the Middle Bronze Age town, since no Late Bronze Age remains were found to the north of that line. Kenyon describes this structure as follows: 'The original nucleus consisted of a fill almost entirely of rubble, built in a series of compartments defined by facings of a single course of stones built on a batter. . . . They lean back to the north against a spine, . . . to the north of which the batter is in the opposite direction. One must visualize the process as a series of adjoining pyramids built up to produce a platform. The whole structure in squares I–III was retained to the east by a north-south wall parallel to the slope. This wall was much more substantial than that which divided the compartments of the fill, but much too slender to take the thrust of the massive fill; . . . It is, however, clear that it had been supported on the downhill side by a lower terrace, of which most of the evidence has been removed by a later terrace of the Iron Age.'[44] Kenyon thought that this and similar structures served as terraces 'on which houses of a more civilized type could be built.' She was led to think this because she excavated houses of the 7th century BC on the existing top surface of the structures. Subsequent excavations by Shiloh brought to light that before these houses were built a stone mantle covered the Late Bronze structure, which went up to the crest of the hill. Unfortunately none of this mantle was manifest in Kenyon's trench I. Because the 7th century houses were built after the 'mantle' had lost its function and were dug into it, they were naturally situated on the remains of the Late Bronze terraces. However, originally these terraces went up much higher and it seems now that the stone mantle served the same function as the terraces. It not only enlarged the building area on the crest of the hill, it also served the purpose of defence of that area in the Iron Age. Kenyon's suggestion that the Late Bronze structure represents the 'Millo' mentioned in 2 Sam. 5:9 becomes more plausible if it not only served civilian purposes but also military ones.[45] Later kings paid attention to the Millo which must have had some vital function. Kenyon's impression that everything that was built on the terraces from the 14th to the 7th centuries BC had collapsed because of a structural weakness of these terraces is a conjecture which can no longer be sustained. It is more likely that the defensive function of the Middle Bronze wall was taken over in the excavated area by this Late Bronze stepped structure. What Kenyon considered as a series of collapses of terraces in her trench I that ran down the eastern slope of the Ophel hill and in which she found the Middle Bronze town wall is not a series of gradual collapses. In this respect it is also important that she found no traces of the stone mantle constructed in the Iron Age and covering the Late Bronze structure. A study of the field notes of her excavation which was recently made in Leiden has suggested another explanation. A very heavy 6 metres wide town wall built late in the Iron Age parallel to the Middle Bronze wall, but slightly higher up the slope, which retained the earlier buildings to the south and the north of the excavated trench, had collapsed exactly where trench I went down through it. This collapse or breach in the wall must have happened when the wall was under construction or soon afterwards. Above that breach in a straight line up the hill the stone mantle, the fill underneath it and buildings south of the remains of the Late Bronze structure slid down when support from the town wall failed. Traces of the stone mantle have now also been identified to the south of the trench. There was very heavy erosion right on the spot where Kenyon excavated. This may explain why she only found dating evidence for the Late Bronze terraces in the period when they were constructed in this area. It all went down right from the crest of the hill into the Kedron valley. This illustrates the problem which Nehemiah encountered when he attempted to inspect the state of the city's wall and gates at night time (Neh. 2:14).

The Water System: Warren's Shaft

When Kenyon started her excavations on the Ophel hill she was convinced that 'full command of the only available water supply, the Spring Gihon, must have dictated the position of the town walls of Jerusalem on the eastern side, . . .'[46] Her excavation on the eastern slope just above the spring revealed that the rock shaft which had been explored by Warren in 1876 came to the surface in the area walled in by the Middle Bronze wall. Vincent found sherds in silt layers which he attributed to the Canaanite–early Israelite period and it seems likely that the shaft was in use in the Late Bronze Age. This shaft is not a tunnel in the rock with steps that go down in a straight line to the spring. There is first a descent with steps in the rock, then a relatively gentle gradient along the zig-zag track ending abruptly at a shaft which goes vertically down for about 15 metres; then the shaft goes through the roof of a horizontal rock-cut channel which is level with the spring and is fed by it. Shiloh has pointed out that a series of natural karst clefts, tunnels and shafts were utilized and integrated into the water system, which explains its irregular appearance.[47] This means that there may always have been the possibility of going down to the water through the clefts and fissures in the rock but that stonecutters in the Late or even Middle Bronze Age made it easier to pass through.

THE RELIGIOUS EVIDENCE

The Religious Background of the Jebusites

In modern scholarship it has become customary to relate many aspects of the Israelite religion during the first three centuries after the capture of Jerusalem by David to the Canaanite religion. This is especially the case with the ritual practised in the Solomonic Temple. Both the prophet Nathan who blamed David for taking the wife of his army commander Uriah and also forbade him to build a temple and the priest Zadok who was in charge of the ritual after the inauguration of the temple were supposedly Jebusites. Studies of the influence of Jebusite rituals on the religious institutions of the Solomonic Temple in Jerusalem are based on more general studies of the influence of Canaanite beliefs and rites on Israel.[48] It should be stressed that there is no written evidence concerning their religion from the Jebusites themselves, nor direct evidence from other sources from that time. It has been deduced from the general Canaanite environment in which the Jebusites lived that their language was Canaanite or a Canaanite dialect and that their beliefs were of the same nature of those of the Canaanites. Our knowledge of the Canaanite world was greatly enlarged when the numerous texts found at Rash Shamra, ancient Ugarit, were deciphered and interpreted. One of the most striking results was that many of the suggestions about Canaanite spiritual life being incorporated in formal and less formal religious practices in Israel were confirmed. That is to say, Hebrew words and expressions which scholars suspected had a religious meaning appeared to be connected with the cult ideas in the Canaanite language. In other words, far more ancient religious ideas were hidden in the texts of the Old Testament, especially in prophetic and poetic literature, than had been anticipated and the question was raised whether such expressions still had a religious meaning in the Hebrew text of the Old Testament. The Hebrew word for 'sea' is also found in Ugarit, but does 'sea' in Hebrew poetry indicate a deity as it does in Ugaritic? It is clear that the main problem was not solved when these texts were found. There are different approaches to the problem. One may say, for instance, that the Hebrew tribes only learned about agriculture after they had penetrated and settled in the land. Therefore all Israelite laws, rituals, festivals, songs, proverbs and the like, connected with agriculture, were borrowed from the 'Amorites' and 'Canaanites' who lived in the land before they came.

There are, of course, other possible answers. One is that the Hebrew tribes were basically formed in the land and therefore they did not have to borrow anything from their countrymen. Another is that their background was similar to that of the Amorites and Canaanites and that they arrived in the land with sufficient knowledge of agriculture and agricultural religious institutions which they developed in their own way. It has already been pointed out that there is no unambiguous light from the existing texts. Texts can be interpreted in different ways and it depends on scholarship and on the question of which 'school' or 'generally accepted assumptions' one adheres to, as to which meaning is given to the texts. The approaches may vary considerably. Most famous for a long time was the 'Myth and Ritual' school. Numerous religious phenomena were described which were said to have been derived from religious and cultic texts from all over the ancient Near East. Well known is the theme of the death and resurrection of the god, which caused the land to 'die' from drought and to revive when the rains came. Such myths and their exact words did not, of course, literally say that they were concerned with the drying earth or its return to life after the rains had come. They were interpreted as meaningful because they were connected with certain festivals of the agricultural calendar and were therefore supposed to have given people hope of an end to the drought when the god rose from death. Thus the performance of the ritual would have created the desired results in a magical way. But in modern studies this lack of obvious self-interpretation opens up the possibilities of devising various meanings and also connections with various rituals. Such debated themes are, for instance, the general, world-wide danger of chaos gaining domination over the world, the control by the gods over death and destruction, the fertility of the land, the livestock and the human race, or the identification of king with god, town with centre of the world, or sea with the netherworld.

Some scholars have found reasons to believe that some of the general themes, which were also found in the Canaanite religion, have played a role in the Jebusite religion. The themes were supposedly taken over by the Israelite king and after the temple was built they were acknowledged by the Jerusalem priesthood. From there they became part of the Israelite religion in which they were slowly transformed into a monotheistic pattern. If these scholars' assumption is correct, the general Canaanite religious substratum refers to Jerusalem in pre-Israelite times. Their evidence is texts dating from after the takeover by King David, and dealing with his time and that of his successors, the time of the Babylonian Exile, or later. Such texts can also be found in the 'early' Books of Moses, the first five books of the Old Testament, as well as in later historical, poetical or prophetic books. The attempts to reconstruct the Jebusite religious heritage from Israelite sources are often based on one aspect that is in general historically acceptable to modern scholarship, namely that at the time of the great prophets (8th–7th centuries BC) the Israelites had many religious, economic and social traits in common with the Canaanites, not so much because of their contacts with them, but that they 'recognized' the Canaanite concepts as being similar to their own spiritual world. It is clear that scholars who depict the early Hebrew tribes as landless uprooted vagabonds will not agree with this concept. What is probably very difficult for the reader to grasp is that such scholars often quote the same texts to build their theories on as those who think that the Hebrew tribes took over part of the general Near Eastern cultural heritage of the

Early Iron Age. But this accentuates the fact that the evidence of all these reconstructions is derived from literary studies and not from historical data and that the decision of what is accepted hinges on scholarly background and spiritual education. It is for this reason that only a selection is given of the proposed Jebusite religious phenomena that can be reconstructed from the biblical texts which often date from centuries after the takeover by David.

Stolz has reconstructed a certain number of themes that he argues characterized Jebusite religious practice.[49] The religious and ritual themes Stolz deals with are the battle against chaos, the battle against the nations (both well-known themes in the prophetic and poetic literature of the Old Testament), the far-away god, El, god of the city as creator and high-judge, and other gods of the city such as Salem. Then there is strong evidence, according to Stolz, that in Israelite times Jerusalem was considered to be inviolable, but it is debated whether this idea existed as early as the Jebusites, or whether it is later.

It was often thought that Zadok, the priest in Solomon's temple, was transferred by David from the Jebusite temple.[50] If so, Zadok would undoubtedly have continued to officiate in the new temple following his own centuries-old rituals. It has also been suggested that Benaiah, the captain of David's royal guard, came from pre-Davidic Jerusalem and was a Jebusite. Thus there would have been enough links with the Jebusite past after David had taken over the city. Jerusalem became the symbol of heaven in Christian belief. This symbol was derived from the idea that the world had a centre, often said to be the navel (omphalos) of the earth. The question has been raised whether Jebusite Jerusalem was already considered by its inhabitants to be the navel of the world.[51] Terrien has given an elaborate description of the myth in its relation to Jerusalem. '. . . the Judahites have adopted from the Canaanites of ancient Jebus the belief that the site of Zion was related to the navel of the earth. Solomon's temple is built on a rock which is the earth-centre, the world mountain, the foundation stone of creation, the extremity of the umbilical cord which provides a link between heaven, earth and the underworld. It therefore becomes associated with the cosmic tree, the garden of Eden, and, at a later time, with the new Paradise, the heavenly Jerusalem.'[52] Terrien has pointed to an analogy that exists between the myth of the omphalos in Greece (Delphi), at Shechem and at Jerusalem. He thinks that the Nehushtan, the bronze serpent which was removed from the Solomonic Temple by King Hezekiah (2 Kings 18:4), belonged to a Jebusite shrine. He argues that the 'Sea of Bronze' which was installed in front of the temple by Solomon symbolized the association of the Jerusalem temple with the underworld, the abyss and the myth of the Edenic rivers. This may not have been an element that was derived from the Jebusites but the idea behind it was certainly part of Canaanite beliefs and therefore possibly also of the Jebusite religion. All we can say is that much of the Jebusite religious inheritance was accepted and transmitted by the kings of the house of David through the temple cult, but the question of what was directly taken over from pre-existing Jebusite practices remains a matter of conjecture. It has been suggested that Araunah who sold a threshing floor near Jerusalem to David was himself a Jebusite king of Jerusalem. Araunah is a Hurrian word which also occurs in Hittite and refers to a ruler. Such suggestions rather illustrate the ingenuity of Old Testament scholars than the possibilities of arriving at firm historical conclusions. We may, however, confidently accept that the change of power in Jerusalem did not create a great revolution in the Jebusite cultic inheritance and practices, and therefore we have much general information about their religion.

King Solomon immediately introduced non-Yahwistic cults into the newly built temple for his foreign wives (1 Kings 11). This is in agreement with the practices of kings in the ancient Near East. It should not be taken as an indication that this was acceptable to those tribal members who upheld the Yahwistic religion. In modern thought the Mosaic or Yahwistic religion is not supposed to have been closely related to general Canaanite practices. Whatever it was that was transmitted from the Jebusite cult in the Solomonic Temple cannot be taken as being on the same religious level as the essential elements of Yahwism in the first centuries of the 1st millennium BC. On the contrary, the case of Jebusite religious material playing a part in the later cult practice of Jerusalem has to be taken as foreign to Yahwism and caused by the change from a tribal federation into a state with a king who behaved like all other kings did.[53]

The Gods of Jebusite Jerusalem

Names of deities that were definitely connected with Jebusite Jerusalem have been preserved and scholars have added other names to the list. Here we mention Salem, Zedek, El and Ḥiba.

Salem

Salem, whose name is assumed to be preserved in the name of the city, is considered to have been its patron god. The name has been explained as 'evening star'. In one of the letters of Abdiḥiba to the Pharaoh mention is made of 'the capital of the land of Jerusalem, of which the name is Bit Shulmani', the house of Shulman, which is Shalem. The land of Jerusalem would have been named after the temple of this main god. Since it is known that elsewhere Salem had a wife called Sulamith, she was also introduced in the Jebusite pantheon.[54]

Zedek and El

Melchizedek who cannot be placed in a historical context, as has been mentioned, and Adonizedek who was king of Jerusalem in the time of the Judges are both named after Zedek, an old deity in the Near East. His name means 'Righteousness'. A fragment of an old story preserved in Gen. 14:17–20 about the meeting between Abram and Melchizedek has generated a great wealth of religious speculation which still plays a role today. 'Melchizedek king of Salem brought bread and wine; he was a priest of God Most High. He pronounced His blessing "Blessed be Abram by God Most High for handing over your enemies to you." ' Although this chapter does not deal with the history of the city of Jerusalem after the capture by David, the symbolic nature of Jerusalem in later religious thinking has been linked with this 'prehistoric' text. For Christianity all the elements of theological reflection on the 'meaning' of the 'Son of God' are expressed in the Letter to the Hebrews in the New Testament, 7:2: 'By the interpretation of his [i.e. Melchizedek's] name, he is, first "king of righteousness" and also king of Salem, that is, "king of peace"; he has no father, no mother or ancestry, and his life has no beginning or ending; he is like the Son of God. He remains a priest for ever.' For the early Christians he was a 'foreshadowing' of the ideal priest and king who had appeared at the fulfilment of time as the Son of God. Such typological studies were conducted as late as the early Protestant times in the West and they aimed at clarifying the meaning of Christ as well as serving apologetic purposes, an activity already manifest in the chapter of the Letter to the Hebrews.

The expression 'God Most High' is interpreted in our time as referring to El-Eljon of the high-god who is best known from Ugarit. And when Salem is taken to refer to Jerusalem, or Melchizedek was King of Jerusalem, then El must have been at the head of the Jebusite pantheon. This has again given rise to much speculation about the role of this El in Israelite religion. Certainly the tiny fragments of information that refer back to Bronze Age Jebusite religious institutions are out of proportion to the religious and scholarly speculation that followed during three millennia of interpretation.

Ḥiba

Little can be said about this name. The second part of the name of the king of the Amarna Age, Abdiḫiba, is also found in other names, such as Eliḫiba (2 Sam. 23:32). The name is known from Hurrite texts as that of a goddess but whether she was a member of the Jebusite Pantheon cannot be established. The name also seems to occur in Hittite religion.

Conclusions

Two aspects can be mentioned as the outcome of this survey of the attempts to reconstruct the Jebusite religion.

1 It seems clear that this religion formed part of the world of Canaanite worship, although we cannot say, as is possible now for Ugarit, which elements played an important role in that religion.

2 The introduction of a new political organization in Israel by David involved the takeover in the new sanctuary of some Jebusite religious elements, namely those which were specifically attached to or derived from the position of a Near Eastern monarch.

THE HISTORY OF JERUSALEM IN THE BRONZE AGE[55]

The Middle Bronze Age

In the Middle Bronze Age eẓ-Ẓahūra was the location of the earliest Jerusalem. People lived on the hill, but there is no historical or archaeological information about the nature of the settlement. Although Kenyon had but scanty archaeological evidence for drawing the line of the Middle Bronze Age defence wall of the city on the map, there is no evidence to contradict her reconstruction. Subsequent excavations on Ophel by Shiloh have confirmed the line of the wall along the east slope. Kenyon gave much attention to the course of the north wall which ran uphill from the east. It is not certain, however, that the city was defended on its north side by a single wall. Stronger and larger defence measures were probably needed to secure the safety of the city against attacks from the north, which is the only direction from which enemy attacks could be expected. In the late Bronze Age there seems to have been a citadel on that side which may have had a predecessor in the Middle Bronze Age. It is still not certain whether the underground access to the water of the Gihon spring was constructed in this period. But since the defence wall along the eastern slope included the area where the ancient entrance to the water source was located it is very likely that the shaft through the rock was dug in this period.

There is no indication that this town existed for a long time. No C^{14} dates are available but analysis of the pottery shapes dates it to the 18th century BC. It is possible that the city was destroyed by the invading Hyksos about 1700 BC and not rebuilt by them. Although large areas of the eastern slope of the hill west of the Middle Bronze Age wall have been excavated during the last 25 years, no traces of habitation were found that could be attributed to the 17th–15th centuries BC.

A study of a large tomb found in 1953 on the west slope of the Mount of Olives has been published by S J Saller.[56] The pottery found in this tomb was dated to the 16th–14th centuries BC on the basis of a comparative study of pottery shapes. The majority of the objects belong to the Late Bronze Age, but few could be attributed to the 16th century. One may assume that there were more tombs dating from the same time. Of the original rock-cut tomb of Saller only the lower part remained showing that the tomb had had a bilobate shape which is also found elsewhere in this period. The tomb had not been continuously used but had remained closed for longer periods. Similar tombs may have existed in the area, but they have disappeared completely because of the erosion of the rock or subsequent digging of fresh tombs. The western slopes of the Mount of Olives and the area around Gihon are one large cemetery, and the earliest tombs found there date from the end of the 4th millennium BC.[57] But still, one tomb dating from the 16th century is not enough to conclude that there was an inhabited city and not one in ruins.

The Late Bronze Age

It is not until the 14th century BC that it is certain that the city was inhabited again. It has been suggested on the basis of literary analysis that the Jebusites only occupied the city from the 12th to the 10th century BC. But a change of population at the end of the Late Bronze Age has not been confirmed by archaeological investigations. The Jebusites may have rebuilt the site in the early 14th century and occupied it for 400 years. Kenyon suggested that the Jebusite town wall was the same or a rebuild of the Middle Bronze Age one. Where she expected to find the north section of this wall she excavated a series of terraces which, according to her, added to the building space inside the town and made the steep slope habitable. This structure is likely to have been part of the citadel on the crest of the hill and of its defences. This suggests that one should probably not look for a single wall along the northern section of the defences. Rather one would expect that the 'bastion' which was excavated on the eastern slope continued over the ridge to the west where it developed into a true citadel. This citadel was considerably higher than the present surface. This is the area of 'Site H' in Kenyon's excavations. Since the field documents of the excavation of Site H have not yet been studied we only have one remark by Kenyon about the archaeological situation.[58] 'On the present surface of the hill was a patch which "skimmed" the edge of a complicated succession of very massive walls along the southern boundary of the site. One could disentangle them structurally but stratigraphical evidence to the north was interrupted by the path, and to the south had been destroyed by the earlier excavations.' Kenyon was, however, confident that there was the northern limit of the spray of Late Bronze Age pottery sherds and therefore of the city of the Jebusites.

In our reconstruction there was a high citadel on the north side of the lower town. The town would have been defenceless once the citadel had been captured. It has often been thought that Sion was not identical with the town of the Jebusites. Sion, as distinguished from Jerusalem, referred to the 'acropolis' of the town which protected its northern and most vulnerable side.[59]

In 2 Sam. 5:6–9 we read that 'David and his men marched on Jerusalem against the Jebusites living there. These said to David: "You will never get in here. The blind and the lame will hold you off." . . . But David captured the fortress of Zion, that is, The Citadel of David. That day David said: "Whoever strikes the Jebusites and goes up to the conduit . . ." . . . David went to live in the fortress and called it The Citadel of David. David then built a wall around it, from the Millo going inward.' No one has yet been able to turn these disparate pieces of information into an intelligible and coherent story. Indeed the text may have been composed from fragments of different accounts. But it seems to be clear that the fortress of Zion was captured and that it was henceforth called the Citadel of David. There is no mention of the capture of the town of Jerusalem and this may reflect a historical reality. When the Jebusites settled on the hill, probably in the 14th century BC, they built a stronghold which they made nearly invincible. There was a town attached to it which hardly played a role in matters of political and military power or control over the surroundings. By the time the tribes of Judah and Benjamin had agreed on the border between the territories they occupied, this border ran through the Hinnom valley past the hill of Jerusalem (Josh. 15:8). In this text a location is described as 'the flank of the Jebusite, that is to say Jerusalem . . .' Jerusalem was the 'flank' or the 'shoulder' of the Jebusites and this again may indicate that the settlement as such was not an important element in Jebusite life. In the same chapter of Joshua (vs 63) we read: 'But the sons of Judah could not drive out the Jebusites who lived in Jerusalem, the Jebusites lived in Jerusalem side by side with the sons of Judah, as they still do today.' The same is said of the Benjaminites in Judges 1:21.

The town by itself was not a strongly defended place, even if, as Kenyon has suggested, the Middle Bronze Age town wall was still functioning. The fortress of Zion was the means by which the Jebusites could maintain themselves. Since archaeologists did not find a Late Bronze Age successor of the Middle Bronze Age wall it is generally assumed that the Middle Bronze Age wall continued to be in active service in the Late Bronze Age. This is not necessarily true. Scholars have speculated about the origin of the Jebusites. Maisler considered them to be of Hittite origin.[60] They may indeed originally have been an aristocratic family which owned lands and lived in a castle, next to which was a settlement. Whether this settlement was by itself protected by a defensive wall does not seem to have been of much consequence to them. At any rate much historical information about Late Bronze Age Jerusalem becomes more comprehensible if Jerusalem is thought of as being a fortress, called Zion, to which a settlement was attached, called Jerusalem. It was the possession of the fortress which appealed strongly to David and its capture was little more than a 'palace revolution'.

NOTES

List of Abbreviations

BZAW Beihefte zur Zeitschrift für die Alttestamentlische Wissenschaft
CAH Cambridge Ancient History, 2nd ed.
ICC International Critical Commentary
JBL Journal of Biblical Literature
JPOS Journal of the Palestine Oriental Society
PEQ Palestine Exploration Quarterly
PJB Palästinajahrbuch
QDAP Quarterly of the Department of Antiquities of Palestine
RB Revue Biblique
VT Vetus Testamentum
ZAW Zeitschrift für die Alttestamentlische Wissenschaft

1 J H Hayes and J Maxwell Miller, *Israelite and Judaean History*, London, 1984, ch. II–V.
2 R de Vaux, 'Les Patriarches hébreux et les découvertes modernes', *RB* 55, 1948, 327–336.
3 W F Albright, 'The Egyptian Empire in Asia in the Twenty-first Century BC', *JPOS*, vol. III, 1928, 247–248.
4 R A S Macalister and J G Duncan, 'Excavations on the Hill of Ophel, Jerusalem 1923–1925', *Palestine Exploration Fund Annual*, London, 1926.
5 K M Kenyon, *Digging up Jerusalem*, London, 1974.
6 Y Shiloh, 'Excavations at the City of David I, 1978–1982', *Qedem*, 1984.
7 H J Eggers, *Einführung in die Vorgeschichte*, Munich, 1959, ch. 3.
8 Kenyon, op. cit., 1974, ch. 4.
9 N Sethe, *Die Ächtung feindlicher Fürsten, Völker und Dingen auf altägyptischen Tongefäßscherben des Mittleren Reiches*, Berlin, 1926.
10 W C Hayes, 'Chronology, Egypt – to end of twentieth dynasty', *CAH*, vol. I, ch. VI, part 1.
11 A Mallon, 'Jérusalem et les documents égyptiens', *JPOS*, vol. VIII, 1928, 1–6.
12 G Posener, 'Syria and Palestine during the twelfth dynasty', *CAH*, vol. 1, ch. XXI, part 2.
13 Ibid.
14 J Skinner, 'Genesis', *ICC*, 1930, 267.
15 R H Smith, 'Abraham and Melchizedek', *ZAW*, LXXVII, 1965, 149ff.
16 M Peter, 'Wer sprach den Segen nach Genesis xiv 19 über Abraham aus?' *VT*, vol. XXIX, 1979, 114–120.
17 J A Knudzon, *Die El-Amarna-Tafeln*, Leipzig, 1907.
18 K Galling, *Biblisches Reallexicon*², 1977, 160.
19 J Simons, *Jerusalem in the Old Testament*, Leiden, 1952, 60.
20 Albright, op. cit., 247–248.
21 K M Kenyon, *Amorites and Canaanites*, London, 1963.
22 Th. L Thompson, 'The Historicity of the Patriarchal Narratives', *BZAW*, 133, Berlin, 1974.
23 Kenyon, op. cit., 1963.
24 J Bottero, 'Syria during the third dynasty at Ur', *CAH*, vol. I, ch. XXI, part 4.
25 J V Seters, 'The terms "Amorite" and "Hittite" ', *VT*, vol. XXII, 1972, 64–81.
26 K M Kenyon, *Archaeology in the Holy Land*, London, 1979, ch. 7.
27 M Noth, *The Old Testament World*, London, 1966, 257.
28 See note 17.
29 W F Albright, 'The Amarna Letters from Palestine', *CAH*, vol. II, ch. XX, 107.
30 Kenyon, op. cit., 1974, and Shiloh, op. cit.
31 L-H Vincent and A M Steve, *Jérusalem de l'ancien Testament*, IIIème partie, Paris, 1956.
32 Simons, op. cit.
33 'Excavations in Palestine, 1932–3', *QDAP*, III, 1933, 177.
34 I Neuville, 'Le Préhistorique de Palestine', *RB*, 1934, 301–382.
35 B Vandermeersch, *De Evolutie van de mens*, Natuur en Techniek, 1982, 301–304.
36 Vincent, op. cit., 615.
37 H Gunkel, 'Mythus und Mythologie', *Die Religion in Geschichte und Gegenwart*, IV, 2nd ed., 381–382.
38 Macalister, op. cit., 173f.
39 Shiloh, op. cit., 11.
40 Kenyon, op. cit., 1979, 72.
41 Kenyon, op. cit., 1963.

42 Kenyon, op. cit., 1974, 78.
43 Shiloh, op. cit., 12.
44 Kenyon, op. cit., 1974, 95.
45 Kenyon, op. cit., 1974, 100.
46 Kenyon, op. cit., 1974, 77.
47 Shiloh, op. cit., 21.
48 G Henton Davies, 'An approach to the problem of Old Testament Mythology', *PEQ*, 88, 1956, 83–91.
49 F Stolz, 'Strukturen und Figuren im Kult von Jerusalem', *BZAW*, 118, Berlin, 1970.
50 C Hauer, 'Who was Zadok?', *JBL*, 1963, 89–94.
51 A J Wensinck, *The ideas of the Western Semites concerning the Navel of the Earth*, Amsterdam, 1916.
52 S Terrien, 'The Omphalos Myth and Hebrew Religion', *VT*, XX, 1970, 317.
53 J A Soggin, 'The Davidic-Solomonic Kingdom', in J H Hayes and J Maxwell Miller, op. cit., ch. IV.
54 B Maisler, 'Das vordavidische Jerusalem', *JPOS*, vol. X, 1930, 189.
55 J J Schmitt, 'Pre-Israelite Jerusalem', in C D Evans, W W Hallo and J B White, *Scripture in context, essays on the comparative method*, Pittsburg, 1980, 101–122.
56 S J Saller, *The excavations at Dominus Flevit*, part II, 'The Jebusite burial place', Jerusalem, 1964.
57 K Galling, 'Die Nekropole von Jerusalem', *PJB*, 32, 1936, 90–95.
58 Kenyon, op. cit., 1974, 91.
59 Simons, op. cit., ch. IIIa.
60 Maisler, op. cit., 186.

CHAPTER II

Jerusalem from 1000–63 BC

George E Mendenhall

THE IMPERIAL PERIOD: THE REIGNS OF DAVID AND SOLOMON, 993–922 BC

The City of Jerusalem

At Hebron David had been acclaimed as king over the northern as well as the southern tribes of the ancient federation by about the year 1000. However, the persistent rivalry and even hostility between the two major regional groups of the old tribal federation made it highly inadvisable to identify himself too closely with the old royal dynastic traditions of the city of Hebron. Furthermore, the city was too far removed from the centre of the population of the old federation that lay considerably north of Jerusalem, and therefore a new seat of the kingship was needed that could transcend the old tribal rivalries by being identified with none of them. The central hill country city of Jerusalem was perfectly located at the boundary line between the tribes of Judah and Benjamin, and well up into the hill country where it would be secure from sudden incursions by the Philistines of the coastal plain or by the various hostile entities of the Transjordanian plateau or the tribal groups of the Sinai and Negev fringe areas.

The city was evidently well fortified, the remnants of the old Jebusite wall recently excavated being an excellent witness.[1] Sufficient attention has not been given by scholars to the fact that the biblical narratives tell us virtually nothing about the existing population of the city, or their fate after its capture by David and his cohorts. Not even the name of the Jebusite king is given, though he may be referred to in the old list of thirty-one kings removed at the time of the so-called 'Conquest of Palestine'.[2] Discussion of the capture of the city has centred instead, as did the old narrative itself, on the obscure 'sinnor' by which David's armies obtained access to the city, i.e. on the military tactics involved. There is no hint of a 'herem', a mass slaughter of the Jebusite population with a subsequent mass replacement of that population with Yahwists. It is specifically this feature of the old biblical narrative that forces the conclusion that David's capture of the city was much more in the nature of a foreign military coup d'état than of a violent destruction and resettlement of populations. As was usually the case in ancient history, the replacement of a ruling regime meant merely the accession to power of a new monarch together with a few of his closest associates in important positions. The rest of the Jebusite establishment remained intact.

This conclusion is rendered virtually certain by three subsequent facts also recorded in the biblical sources. The first is that the royal administration described most fully for the regime of King Solomon is nearly identical to that which had long been characteristic of Pharaonic Egypt: at the head, of course, was the king himself, then there was the official whose title was 'The One over the House' (though this office may not have been created at first, since it corresponded to the office of Grand Vizier, whose authority extended over all the government officials except the army). Then there followed the 'Secretary' who was in charge of foreign affairs, the 'Recorder' who had charge of internal matters and security, and the 'King's Friend', whose functions are obscure. In the court of King Solomon, the post of 'Secretary' was held by two brothers, Elihoreph and Ahijah, sons of one Shesha, whose name is certainly non-Semitic, possibly Hurrian (*šeš* = 'brother') so the father's name would be the semantic equivalent of the common Semitic name given to the second son *'aḥīya* (1 Kings 4:3). (It was doubtless these Jebusite scribes who introduced the unified Phoenician alphabet to the Yahwist administration and subsequently to the village tribes. It is agreed by all that the Phoenician alphabet of the tenth century was uniform throughout all Palestine, Phoenicia and Syria.) The simplest, and historically the most plausible, explanation for this identity of administration is that David merely continued to keep in office most of the existing bureaucracy, including the mercenary professional warriors who constituted the tiny standing army of the former Jebusite king. In all probability that political structure had been inherited from the city of Jerusalem which is so well attested in the Amarna archives of the Egyptian Empire period.

The second fact has been highly controversial since the late 13th century, but it seems now can no longer be denied. That the Jebusite bureaucracy included a priesthood dedicated to the cult of El-Eljon or some such old Canaanite deity can be taken for granted:[3] a kingship without a priestly class, cult, and temple of some sort is unthinkable in the ancient world. The specific function of such institutions was to legitimize and furnish an ideological foundation for the political regime that was usually established simply by superior military power. The essence of the old official theology of the ancient Near Eastern *Jāhilīyah* was that kings ruled not by the consent of the governed, but through being 'chosen' by a committee of supernatural beings whose decision had become known on a previous battlefield.

Under King David there were two 'priests', evidently neither superior in rank to the other. Abiathar had been his companion since the days when he had had to flee for his life from King Saul, and there can be no doubt whatever of his authentic Yahwist origins from the priesthood of Shiloh that served as the cultic centre for the Yahwist federation in the days immediately preceding the formation of the monarchy. The second priest, Zadok, can only have been inherited from the Jebusite establishment, and could not have been dismissed from his cultic functions without serious problems arising between David and the population of the city who were essential to his administration. That the old Jebusite priesthood became the established priesthood of the Solomonic Temple is demonstrated beyond reasonable doubt by the nature of the Temple ritual itself which was thoroughly a continuation of the old Canaanite custom, as Dussaud pointed out many decades ago.[4] That the system was not only Canaanite, but also absolutely foreign to the monotheistic Yahwist tradition is illustrated by the condemnation of the system by most of the Yahwist prophets, and by the repeated flat assertion that it was no part of the original Mosaic Yahwist tradition, e.g. Amos 5:25–27; Jeremiah 7:22.

In the Egyptian bureaucracy the king himself as a member of the assembly of gods was the head of the priesthood, but there was a chief priest who was in charge of the priestly bureaucracy. The assimilation to the pagan pattern is illustrated by Solomon's presiding over the rituals and sacrifices connected with the dedication of the temple, 1 Kings 8:5, 62. (Only a half-century earlier, the first king of the tribes, Saul, had been bitterly condemned by the prophet Samuel for presuming to offer a sacrifice himself, 1 Samuel 13:8–14).

The old Canaanite cities of the land had a political and fiscal bureaucratic and administrative system for centuries before the time of King David,[5] though it certainly would have been simple compared to the elaborate bureaucracy of the much wealthier Ugarit to the north. On the other hand is the inescapable fact that the Yahwist villagers and peasants had no such capability or tradition at all. The literacy necessary for political administration is characteristically irrelevant and not valued by village peasant populations, and the only source available to King David for such organization and administration of his far-flung kingdom had to be an existing system which was available to him in the Jerusalem population. It is again a constant in political history that the bureaucracy as well as the professional army cares little about the identity or ideology of the ruling regime, so long as they receive their salaries. *Cuius regio, eius religio* ('whose rule, his religion') was a constant all through the history of politics.

The Jebusite bureaucracy included of course a standing army that probably constituted the personal bodyguard and escort of the king. In this case they were the *kerētī* and *pelētī* 'Cretans and Philistines', mercenary professionals who owed allegiance to no one other than the king himself. Other important personages of the army also were undoubtedly military professionals who either were taken over with the capture of the city, or who were subsequently recruited in the process of the Davidic conquests of the Canaanite cities and the neighbouring kingdoms. Through this process the military technology of the early Iron Age was introduced into the political state.

One of the most important of such mercenaries was a high ranking officer identified as 'Uriah the Ḥittite' (2 Samuel 11:3), whose wife was Bath-Sheba ('daughter of the Seven Gods, probably Pleiades, *šeba*'' written in cuneiform as *sibitti*). David's adultery with the woman led to his engineering her husband's death, so that he could marry her. The identification as 'Hittite' has only accidental connection with the Hittites of the Late Bronze Age empire in Anatolia: in the early Iron Age northern Syria was known as the 'land of the Hittites' because a number of cities in that area continued the political and cultural traditions of the Hittite empire long after it had been destroyed.

The third argument for David's takeover of the existing bureaucracy is to be found in the very curious treatment of many new names that figure prominently in the narratives dealing with the period. The prophet Nathan, for example, a sort of 'court prophet' and advisor to the king, is introduced with not even a patronymic to identify him. In contrast to virtually all the other Yahwistic prophets, we are told nothing of his origins or background. The reason is very simple: he was already the court prophet prior to David's coup, and was very valuable to the king as an advisor and intermediary between David and the pagan urban Jebusite population over whom he now ruled in addition to the Yahwist, monotheistic villagers of the countryside. As pointed out above, the same is true of the second priest of David, Zadok. At some point, very likely in the time of Solomon himself, the authentic genealogy of the Aaronid priesthood was inserted into Zadok's own, also authentic, genealogy,[6] that extends back to the time of the Jebusite takeover of Jerusalem, probably a generation or two before the formation of the Yahwist.

Still a fourth argument for the continuity of the Jerusalem population may be found in the language of the prose narratives of the Hebrew Bible that all scholars agree is basically the standard educated language of the city of Jerusalem. Unfortunately, the historical study of biblical Hebrew is at such a primitive level that the contrast between this scribal dialect of Jerusalem and the dialects of the Yahwistic villages cannot yet be described. Anyone who has dealt with the old Yahwist, pre-Monarchic poetry will, however, recognize that there is quite a contrast – and this cannot be accounted for merely on the basis of a chronological distance between the two dialects. The contrast is the more important in view of the fact that the Jerusalem dialect in particular has numerous linguistic isoglosses with Ugaritic. The connection between Jerusalem of the pre-Davidic period and northern Syria can now be traced well back into the 14th century BC.[7]

The exilic prophet Ezekiel accurately summed up the situation with his famous words concerning Jerusalem (Ezekiel 16:3): 'Your origins and birth were of the Canaanites; your father was an Amorite and your mother a Hittite.' It has been only in the past half century that numerous discoveries have been made which illustrate the historical foundations of Ezekiel's statement. Translated into social history, what it says is that the city of Jerusalem was a typical Canaanite city, and its culture and population derived fundamentally from the Amorite territory of northeast Syria, and upon this basis there was superimposed a cultural and political regime that stemmed from northern Syria, for at this time northern Syria was widely known as 'the land of the Hittites'. Virtually everything we know about the city illustrates this history. Even the name, Yebus, by which the city was known in the biblical record until its seizure by King David, contains a root that is quite common in Amorite onomastics, and in various dialect forms including that with the *šin* which appears also in the Transjordanian place-name, *Yabēš-gil'ad*. The meaning of the root is as yet unknown, but it certainly has no connection with the South Canaanite homonym that means 'to be dry'. It is interesting to note that the sibilant contrast is identical to that reflected in the *šibbolet* incident (Judges 12:6).

The prophet Ezekiel was by no means alone in affirming that the city of Jerusalem was not only foreign to the monotheist tribes of Yahweh, its policies and practices were a catastrophe merely waiting to happen. Already a century and a half earlier the prophet Micah (1:5) proclaimed: 'What is the sin of the house of Judah? Is it not Jerusalem?'

The entire history of Jerusalem until its destruction at the hands of the Babylonian empire is thus the history of an on-going struggle between the traditions of the monotheistic Yahwists and the urban polytheism of Jerusalem (as well as the other Canaanite cities) that had been incorporated into the Davidic empire and by the time of his successor, Solomon, had become culturally and politically predominant. The entire political tradition of the biblical period was only a slight adaptation of the long-established Canaanite political structure and ideology, and this was inevitable since the early monotheistic Yahwism proclaimed Yahweh as king, and like the other monotheistic world religions, had no ideology for the establishment or legitimation of a monarchy.

It must be emphasized that the city which David conquered and made his capital was tiny by modern standards. It measured little more than roughly 350 x 100 meters and the total population could hardly have been more than a couple of thousand people. The resources of the old Jebusite city must hae been very limited, since the territory to the north was a part of the Yahwist tribe of Benjamin and immediately to the south the population was largely Yahwist Judah. Consequently, when it became the capital of a large population that had been unified several generations earlier under the Yahwist federation, the standing and economic status of the city and its population was enormously enhanced.

Like a number of other 'cities' of the time, it probably included not much more than the royal palace, and housing for the support personnel of the king, his staff and his military personnel. The entire complex of the city and its surrounding fields became what would later be termed 'crown property' under the old pagan doctrine that what the king seized by armed force became the personal property of the king. According to 2 Samuel 5:9 David himself renamed the city *'ir davīd*, 'the city of David'. It is significant that this name did not persist: rather, the old pre-Jebusite name attested already in the 19th century Execration Texts from Egypt as well as in the Amarna Letters of the 14th century, Uru-salim (or the like), became the only designation for the city in subsequent history.

The legal doctrine of crown property is illustrated, however, by the fact that a field in the immediate environs of Jerusalem was allocated to David's cousin and chief of staff, Joab, and a contiguous field was allocated to one of his eldest sons, Absalom, as we learn from the narrative of Absalom's return from exile in his mother's pagan native land, Geshur (2 Samuel 14:28–33). This custom of allotting what were later termed 'prebendal domains' to important personages of the royal court as sources of income is well attested at Mari in the Middle Bronze Age, and at Ugarit in the Late Bronze Age. There can be little doubt that David simply took over and continued the royal practice of the preceding Jebusite regime.

The Davidic Kingdom

The large population base consisting of the religious tribal federation extending from the proverbial Dan to Beersheba furnished the first essential to the development of political power, even though it is clear that there was by no means a uniform enthusiasm for the Davidic monarchy. This can be seen in the rebellions of Shimei and Absalom. Nevertheless, the very large scale unity operated well enough for David to establish a large territorial state within the period of a couple of decades. It is doubtless for this reason that the Jerusalem regime could succeed in such a state formation at a time when the other regions of the eastern Mediterranean were just beginning to emerge from the Early Iron 'Dark Age'.

The first stage after the capture of Jerusalem was the incorporation by armed force of most of the old Canaanite city states into the kingdom, as well as the Philistine cities and their satellite villages. Especially from the list of provincial governors that comes from the time of Solomon it can be seen that many of those old royal cities had now become the residence of royal governors. The fiscal system seems to have remarkable similarity to that of Mari in the

Middle Bronze Age. With the incorporation of the urban populations there was not only a great increase in the power base of the kingdom, but there was also an enormous expansion of the cultural inventory. As always, it was the urban peoples who had the technical and cultural tradition and expertise necessary for the formation of a prestigious political regime. Yet even the relatively impoverished Palestinian cities were not able to furnish the necessary skills and materials for the building programmes of David and Solomon. Instead, King Hiram of Tyre sent carpenters and masons together with cedar wood to build even the new palace of King David (2 Samuel 5:11). Even that was evidently not satisfactory, for in the next generation, Solomon spent thirteen years building a new palace for himself (1 Kings 7:1), nearly twice the time spent on building the Temple.

The second stage was the incorporation by conquest of considerable parts of Transjordan, namely Edom, Moab and Ammon. The interlocking alliances in northern Transjordan led to the defeat of the king of Damascus, and the incorporation of all the territory controlled by the latter into the Davidic empire. The extension of empire to the Euphrates River at Tiphsah could hardly have been much more than a legal fiction, however, since the little archaeological evidence now available strongly indicates that there must have been an extremely sparse population in the region between the oasis of Damascus and the Euphrates Valley that itself was virtually depopulated in the Early Iron Age.

The biblical traditions state flatly that David spent so much time and energy on his imperial wars that he had no time or motivation for the building activities that usually characterize empire-building. The taxation of the empire resulted in a surplus of funds stored, according to tradition, in the sacred treasury. It is not surprising that for the most part, the old Yahwist tribal elements were quite content to share the glory and prosperity that resulted from such inflow of capital funds. The only recorded prophetic protest of excesses and progressive paganization of the administration up to the very end of Solomon's reign was that of the prophet Gad who pronounced drastic punishment for the Davidic census (2 Samuel 24). This royal institution that is recorded already in the Middle Bronze period at Mari doubtless represented a centralized administration of the manpower and economic resources of the entire kingdom, and certainly must have been an instrument by which the royal administration took control of such matters from the local and tribal authorities.

The famous reproach of David by the court prophet Nathan for the adultery with Bathsheba and the consequent contrived death of her husband had nothing to do with the Yahwistic ethic, but was based instead upon a normal revulsion against such misuse of power that might endanger David's standing with the Jerusalem bureaucracy and professional warriors. As a matter of fact, virtually all of the Davidic family of whom we have information would have been subject to the death penalty under the old Mosaic covenant ethic of the federation period. The very fact that Nathan was a prime mover in the successful ploy to obtain the accession of Bathsheba's second son, Solomon (1 Kings 1), is the best indication that Nathan had little concern for that Yahwist tradition.

The ephemeral empire had little long-lasting effect in ancient Near Eastern history, but the ideological changes that accompanied the transition to kingship had fateful consequences to the present day. In the first place, it must be emphasized that the Yahwist federation was characterized by a bitter hostility to the political religions of the old urban polytheisms and their gods, termed correctly *ba'alim*, which were essentially hypostatized symbols of sovereignty of the various kings or local parochialisms where they were worshipped. The wars of the federation were essentially resistance operations either to throw off the political domination of ambitious politicians, many if not most of whom were very recent newcomers to the region, such as the Philistines; or they were wars fought to avoid the re-imposition of such foreign political and economic controls. During the period of the federation, such battles were not always successful simply because the bonding of the federation, in spite of its profoundly religious foundations, was too weak to guarantee a large enough participation on the part of those tribes that were not directly involved in a specific local conflict.

Under the circumstances, it is not surprising that the early Mosaic prophetic faith contained no specific or implicit ideology for legitimizing a political state: it was the kingdom of Yahweh that explicitly ruled out the idea that any mere earthly king could command the loyalty of the far-flung Yahwist villages. On the other hand, only the useless bramble bush in the Parable of Jotham (Judges 9) wanted to be king – a typical and timeless illustration of the attitude of village populations toward the pretensions of political ambition.

The politicizing of the old prophetic faith began with the introduction of the Ark of the Covenant into the city of Jerusalem under royal aegis (2 Samuel 6). It seems that a rather lavish temporary structure was erected, which served to declare the continuity with the Tabernacle of the old Exodus and Wanderings traditions. Many scholars believe that the description of the Tabernacle in the priestly materials of Exodus 26–27 is actually a reminiscence of the Davidic Tabernacle.

With the incorporation of the old pagan Canaanite city states into the Davidic empire, however, the situation was drastically changed. Not only were those cities accustomed to kingship, their society and economy demanded, it would seem, such centralization of power and control. It is not surprising, then, that the adaptation of the old prophetic Yahwist tradition to furnish divine support for the new monarchy was derived also from the pagan mythical tradition. Mediated through the prophet, Nathan, the proclamation of the divine 'choice' of David with the promise of dynastic succession, is the mirror image of the classic tradition already enshrined in the Code of Hammurapi. Put in modern, secular terms, it meant simply that the rule of the king and his successors was not by the consent of the governed, but was a divine charter in which the deity resigned from rule in favour of a mortal king. It cannot now be determined whether or not there were any conditions set that would make that charter provisional upon the 'obedience' of the king to predetermined rules of conduct. The high probability was that there were none, though the traditions as we now have them usually include such conditions that were doubtless the result of the Deuteronomic reform of the much later King Josiah. Certainly throughout the history of the monarchy there is little indication in the narratives we have that the king regarded his rule as dependent upon such conformity to externally imposed standards. The extremely strong reaction of Josiah to the discovery of the fact that there might be such conditions (2 Kings 22:11–13) is proof enough that such ideas had not been a part of the operating ideology of the kings. The 'Messianic theology' is thus thoroughly pagan in origin and in its operation almost until the end of the kingdom and the Davidic dynasty.

Another important aspect of the ideology of the monarchy that must have been fully developed at least by the time of Solomon is the introduction of a new 'common ancestor', Abraham, that replaced the original common ancestor of the Twelve Tribes, Jacob. There had to be such a 'genealogical' common origin in order to bridge the gap and end the conflict between the Yahwist villages and the Jebusite pagan urban establishments. For this purpose, the royal scribes reached far back into pre-Mosaic tradition, that was probably transmitted in some epic form for centuries, before it was re-written to fit the needs of the Israelite monarchy. It reflected very old traditions of the origin of some pre-Mosaic dynasty with the migration from Amorite territory in northern Syria. Probably that dynasty was at Hebron itself if only because of the tomb at the Cave of Machpelah – a tradition that has no other reference in the entire biblical corpus. The tradition of the 'patriarch' Abraham was artificially linked to that of Jacob through the Abraham-Isaac-Jacob genealogy, and the genealogies already associated with Abraham were downgraded to those of the 'concubines' in a genealogical technique that can be parallelled in many a primitive tribe: when society changes, the genealogy is changed to reflect the new status. Nevertheless, it is worth noting that the royal scribes not only preserved those genealogies linking Abraham with the proto-Arabic groups of Midian, Sheba, and others well known from much later history, they preserved also the memory that those groups were originally native to Palestine proper, for which Gen. 25:5–6 is sufficient proof: 'Abraham gave all he had to Isaac. But to the sons of his concubines Abraham gave gifts, and while he was still living he sent them away from his son Isaac, eastward to the east country.' The continuity of those tribal traditions was preserved in the desert fringe, ending up in part in far-off Yemen.[8] Similarly, the ancient language of the coastal region preserved much of its character in that remote region, while the heartland language changed drastically at the transition from the Early Bronze to Middle Bronze Ages, and even more at the end of the Late Bronze Age.[9]

A necessary part of the re-adaptation of the Abraham tradition was the requisite identification of the God of Abraham with Yahweh, which was the identical process by which the older god of Jerusalem was identified also with the dynastic deity of King David. This identification was specifically stated in the late priestly code in Exodus 6:3, to the effect that the God was the same, only the *name* differed: El-Shaddai *was* Yahweh under a different name.

The result of all these changes was that Jerusalem became an imperial city for a short time, in which there was a blending of two quite distinct social and religious traditions, though the old Canaanite political polytheism was overwhelmingly dominant in the public sphere. It was remarkably successful in the creation of a working relationship between the old urban pagan political tradition and the prophetic ethical monotheism, that functioned well enough for four centuries, though without the encumbrances and pitfalls of empire after the first two generations.

THE REIGN OF SOLOMON *c.*960–922 BC

Solomon's reign was established through a palace intrigue that ensured the triumph of the urban, Jebusite tradition. As so often was the case, King David had evidently made no provision for the orderly transfer of power to a successor. Probably his oldest surviving son Adonijah assumed that according to custom he would succeed to the throne, and organized a party of celebration when his father appeared to be incompetent and moribund (1 Kings 1). It is difficult to believe that the coronation party was not a deliberate ploy designed precisely to pre-empt a similar coup on the part of some other Davidite. He thus recruited the old loyal Yahwist followers of the king, who had been his support since the days he was fleeing for his life from King Saul. Above all, Joab, cousin of the king and his military commander, Abiathar the priest who stemmed from the old Shiloh priestly line and who had shared David's tribulations in flight from the wrath of Saul, were the main supporters of Adonijah's claim to the throne. With the military and the priestly support he probably had every reason to expect his claim to legitimacy to be successful.

He did not reckon with the intrigues of the old Jebusite bureaucracy. The prophet Nathan in concert with Bathsheba obtained from King David the designation of Solomon as his successor. Moribund as he was, his word plus the support of the standing army was sufficient to guarantee Solomon's ascent to the throne, and his opponents were either executed (Joab and Adonijah) or banished (Abiathar). There can be little question that in this event the old Jebusite bureaucracy had obtained the upper hand, and the return to the old Bronze Age pagan political tradition was complete. To be sure, the name of the dynastic deity was still Yahweh, but the deity had become, so far as the bureaucracy was concerned, merely the tutelary deity of the ruling establishment. Not until the end of Solomon's reign do we again hear of the activity of a Yahwist prophet, not as a counsellor to the king, but as a messenger from that other Yahweh of Sinai tradition who ruled over human history, and declared that Solomon's empire and rule over all the tribes of Jacob was at an end because of his complete departure from the grounds of his own rule in the divine commands.

With Solomon the normal activities of ancient empires ran their ruinous course in 40 years. The surplus accumulated in the imperial wars of David plus the tribute regularly received from the subjugated territories was rapidly dissipated in ambitious building programmes and in the massive build-up of fortifications and military armaments.

In order to find room for the new buildings, Solomon greatly enlarged the perimeter of the city, probably engaged in a massive fill to increase the level area for the building of the royal palace, the royal temple, and ancillary buildings, the purpose of which is still not definitely known. It is certain that the population of the city must have increased considerably during the 80 years of the United Monarchy, but of this we have no information. Simply the increase in the bureaucracy and the need for housing for them, the military, the elaborate priestly establishment, and the support personnel would have necessitated the enlargement of the city. The Temple Mount saw the erection of a prestigious (and expensive) building for the housing of the Ark of the Covenant that David had brought with much fanfare into his royal city years before. It is a good indication of the low level of local craftsmanship that Solomon had to import skilled workmen from Tyre for the more skilled building operations. One suspects that the architectural design of the Temple also must have been furnished by Tyrian architects, since it is virtually identical to those known in northern Syria, and, as one scholar recently has demonstrated,[10] the entire building programme was a monument to Hittite imperial architecture.

A few concessions to the older pre-Davidic traditions were made: in the first place there could be no statue of the deity in the inner sanctum. Instead, the place of honour was held by the Ark of the Covenant that became the symbol of the divine presence and the guarantor of the perpetuity of the ruling regime, whatever it might be or do. There was no escape from the fact that the name of the dynastic deity was Yahweh, and He could not be represented in statuary form. All the other pagan dynastic paraphernalia were present, however, from the cherubim and seraphim, to the symbols of fertility – all of which are now known to have long established associations and history in the ancient Near Eastern world. It is quite understandable that the king of Tyre congratulated King Solomon on his decision to conform to the normal political procedures and ideologies, especially when the Tyrian king anticipated correctly a considerable profit from his contribution of building materials and skilled labour. In fact, the economic resources of the kingdom were so depleted that Solomon had to cede territory to the Tyrian king in lieu of payment for the building materials, a deal that probably enhanced the Tyrian king's respect for Solomon's wisdom (1 Kings 9:12–13).

The enormous expenditure on military fortifications and chariotry, together with his grandiose building programme, resulted in a great depletion of the royal treasury, illustrated particularly by the ceding of territory mentioned above. Perhaps more important, however, is the fact that in spite of the military build-up of chariotry, Solomon was not able to maintain control of the far-flung kingdom he had inherited, and thus the revenues from that source ceased. It is possible that it was only toward the end of his reign that the breakaway of Edom and Moab took place – we simply do not have chronological indications of the process, only of the facts. Regardless, the impoverishment of the royal treasury must be taken seriously as the major reason for the disastrous policy of his son and successor, Rehoboam, that led to the loss even of the northern Israelite tribes. With that event the pretensions to grandeur of the Davidic empire were at an end, though some elements in the society seem always to have had a nostalgic yearning for the good old days when Jerusalem ruled in pomp and glory. It is now clear that the days of empire had nothing to do with the original foundation of the Israelite people, but were rather a thorough reversion to the ancient Near Eastern political practices and ideology of the Late Bronze Age, which also had proven itself morally and economically bankrupt by the end of that era. In fact, the ruling dynasty at Jerusalem by the time of Rehoboam's son was only slightly 'Israelite'.[11]

The practice of diplomacy through intermarriage with various royal houses and important social leaders led to the formation of the enormous harem of King Solomon. It led also to the construction, according to the biblical account, of numerous temples for the gods of those foreign states in the environs of Jerusalem. Though the present form of the traditions makes only passing reference to those pagan temples, their existence is proof enough of the polytheistic nature of Jerusalem society from this time on. Jerusalem, like any other Canaanite city of the time, was a cosmopolitan urban centre in which it was politics, not a religious ethic, that dominated the decision-making process, and from Solomon on, those political decision-makers had little more use for the prophetic religious tradition that stemmed from the mission and message of Moses than had any of the other polytheistic city kings and populations. The God of the prophets had become simply another Baal, whose function was merely to serve as the ideological support for the power of the political regime.

THE GREAT SCHISM

King Solomon had dissipated the wealth of the empire through his ambitious and megalomaniac building programmes, and through the equally expensive elaboration of the military establishment, chariotry, fortifications, and the like. It is curious that in spite of the military build-up he was unable to maintain control of his inherited empire, and by the end of his reign, most of the controlled territories had regained their independence, and even in the old tribal homeland there was trouble. The progressive alienation of the grass-roots village population by the arrogant and high-handed power elite, who were only nominally, if at all, monotheists, reached its normal (and predictable) conclusion with the folly of King Rehoboam.

The loss of income from the empire gave Rehoboam only two choices. He could reduce the load of taxation upon his subjects which meant inevitably to reduce the standard of living of the royal establishment and to give up permanently ambitions for re-establishing the old imperialism of his grandfather; it is rare in history for a ruling monarch to take such a course even when alternatives are predictably disastrous, and it is not surprising that Rehoboam rejected the advice of the older and wiser men of his entourage. Instead, he followed the recommendation of his hard-line younger advisors, who saw perfectly well that reduction of taxation meant drastically reduced financial and political opportunities for themselves as part of the political/military bureaucracy.

The result was an even more drastic reduction of income to the royal treasury, for the far more affluent and populous northern tribes seceded, leaving Rehoboam with only the south (Judah) and the environs of Jerusalem itself as his domain (1 Kings 12). In addition, according to the record, there was a constant state of warfare between him and his rival Jeroboam, who took the title King of Israel. Thus, the political ideology that had brought to an end the relatively prosperous Canaanite civilization of the Late Bronze Age had the same effect when it was resurrected by King Solomon – or rather, when it was continued in Jerusalem and only slightly adapted to the religious tradition of the monotheistic village population of Yahwists.

The urge for hegemony and power meant a continuous series of ruinous wars beyond the borders of the two pagan states, and this in turn meant an increasing impoverishment of the productive population of the countryside. Nevertheless, during the course of the 9th and 8th centuries archaeological evidence as well as inscriptions show a rise in population and prosperity all over the eastern Mediterranean and inland regions. The emergence from the Dark Ages of the 12th to 10th centuries saw also the rise of relatively prosperous states that were, as usual, constantly engaged in the attempt to expand their territorial and economic control at the expense of their neighbours. The only result was to fall into the vastly superior control of the successful empire of Assyria.

THE 8TH CENTURY

During this period of rising prosperity all over the Levant the city of Jerusalem evidently shared to some extent in that process. Archaeological evidence indicates that by the 8th century the city had expanded beyond the tiny confines of the city of David and Solomon to the western hill.[12] We know from the written record that there was at least a modest specialized productivity in the city (a *sūq* of the potters is mentioned), but it seems that by and large the city, like many others in the Mediterranean world, was essentially the royal residence and temple with the attendant support personnel attached to the political bureaucracy which, of course, included the elaborate priestly establishment.

The incessant rivalries among the petty states of the region played completely into the hands of the imperial power to the east. Though an astonishing coalition was formed in the middle of the 9th century BC that met and temporarily seems to have slowed the Assyrian advance,[13] the coalition was ephemeral, and shortly afterwards renewed warfare was the rule. Though we know relatively little about the process except from the biblical record, we have no reason to believe that the same old tired political rivalry was any different elsewhere.

A century later the Assyrian empire was relentlessly in motion. A coalition between the old rivals Israel and Aram together with another state not yet located was hastily formed in 732, and together they threatened Jerusalem to force the Judean regime to join the coalition. Reluctant to do so, and terrified at the threat, Ahaz voluntarily offered submission to the Assyrian king as the only alternative, just as the king of Israel, Jehu, had done in the previous century (2 Kings 16). Exactly as the prophet Isaiah had predicted (in the famous Immanuel prophecy, Isaiah 7) within ten years both Israel and the Aramean regime in Damascus no longer existed, destroyed at the hands of the Assyrians.

Though the biblical account is understandably reluctant to go much into detail, it is clear that the submission to Assyria entailed considerable cultural changes. It is difficult, if not impossible, to say what of the great cultural changes taking place in the late 8th century are due to the Assyrian influence, for many of those changes were taking place in many other regions as well. It is necessary to emphasize the fact that what we read and know of the states of Judah and Israel during the entire Iron Age is quite representative of similar cultural and political changes taking place everywhere else in the west Semitic-speaking region.

It is clear that there were important changes in religious ideology and cultic practice. The biblical narrative specifically cites the Assyrian-style altar that was installed in the Jerusalem temple. Further, from the prophetic indictments, it is clear that there was an enormous growth in the popularity of cults involving the sun, moon, and constellations, but this phenomenon was apparently civilization-wide, and merely illustrates the fact that the Jerusalem aristocracy was 'keeping up with the Joneses'.

The capitulation to Assyria proved to be unnecessary. As the prophet Isaiah had predicted, first Damascus then Israel fell to Assyrian wrath after the futile attempt at rebellion. It is not surprising that within a decade under the new king Hezekiah, Jerusalem became the centre of a new coalition that had ambitions for independence from the Assyrian empire. In preparation for the new revolt, Hezekiah had the famous channel dug that diverted the waters of the 'Ain Sitti Maryam to the pool of Siloam that was then inside the city wall. Again, as the prophet predicted (Isaiah 1:1–23), the result was disaster. After a wide-scale devastation of the countryside and extended siege of the city, Hezekiah had to capitulate by paying an enormous sum of gold and silver, the amount of which is stated in both the biblical and the Assyrian accounts (the Assyrian account makes the amount considerably higher).

Possibly because of this economic and political disaster, the king carried out the second of two royal attempts at religious and political reform, the first being that of Jehoshaphat after the attempt by Athaliah to convert the state to outright Baal-worship after the manner of Ahab and Jezebel, a political coup that almost succeeded in wiping out the Davidic dynasty (2 Kings 11). Hezekiah's reform is described in much more detail, but seems to have had little lasting effect other than as a fateful event that for generations dominated the religious ideology of the state.

Though there does not exist any hard evidence by which we can reconstruct the events of the last years of Hezekiah, there can be little doubt that Jerusalem experienced some sort of miraculous deliverance from an Assyrian siege.[14] Almost certainly it was brought about by an outbreak of an epidemic disease in the Assyrian army which was, of course, interpreted as a divine intervention on behalf of the now-pious King Hezekiah. It also gave rise to an assurance that Yahweh would not permit the destruction of His sacred city and temple. The result was far-reaching, for this doctrine of the 'inviolability of Zion' gave a sense of false security to subsequent politicians in Jerusalem.[15] It powerfully reinforced the idea that the deity Yahweh was merely the Baal-protector of the petty state. It is not surprising that the politicians of Jerusalem could find no policy that would be compatible with social well-being and even continued existence as a body politic.

THE 7TH CENTURY

Nearly all of the first half of the century was marked by the reign of Manasseh who, according to the only sources we have, must have been the worst king Jerusalem ever had. The deep internal divisions in the city itself are illustrated by the fact that the king evidently felt it necessary to fill the 'city with blood', though unfortunately we have no information concerning the issues that impelled the king to take such action. Subsequent events strongly indicate that a severe power struggle was in process – a very frequent concomitant of too much security. It seems that during this reign from about 682 to 642, there was little attempt to rebel against the Assyrian hegemony, and it is entirely possible that this was the issue that divided the Hebrew leaders in the city.

At the death of Manasseh, his son Amon succeeded to the throne, but was within a year or so assassinated by some of his own bureaucrats. Traditions are very confused and confusing about this period, but it seems that Amon continued the policies of his father in not venturing to challenge the overwhelming Assyrian power. The fanatical hawks in his entourage no doubt wanted to follow the example of Egypt that had become independent some twenty-five years earlier. The following two decades were one of the most important epochs in the biblical history since Moses, for they brought about developments that determined to a large extent the entire future of the biblical tradition.

THE REFORM OF JOSIAH

At the assassination of Amon (only the third in the 400-year history of the Jerusalem regime), very important developments in the balance of power internally took place. For the first time, the 'people of the land' intervened in royal affairs, and put to death those of the bureaucracy who were responsible for the death of Amon (2 Kings 21:19–26). The 'people of the land' no doubt refers to the inhabitants of the countryside over against the population of the royal city, who were largely the political establishment plus the necessary support personnel. Whether or not the 'people of the land' designated specifically wealthy, large landholders, as some have speculated, is an insoluble problem and one that is probably irrelevant to the subsequent events.

The heir to the throne, Josiah, was at this time (642 BC) a lad of eight years, so the monarchy was placed in the hands of his uncle until he came of age. By that time (about 630 BC) the civilized world as it had been known for several centuries was coming to an end. It is worth speculating that the power elites all over that civilized world felt that the end was near. From Egypt to Mesopotamia there were attempts to recapture the 'glories' of an idealized and largely fictitious past. Such nostalgic attempts to recover and reconstitute a largely phoney past are characteristic of periods of decadence throughout world history. The history of Jerusalem and its regime in this period are a reflection, again, of similar cultural developments all over the civilized world. The whole complex of what scholars have long termed 'the Ancient Near East' drew rapidly to a close in a quick succession of imperial wars during the following century that left most societies exhausted and impoverished and many regions nearly depopulated.

First and foremost was the collapse of the Assyrian empire. By about 630 when Josiah was beginning to rule in his own right, Assyrian control of the west was either gone or rapidly weakening. This meant an opportunity to re-establish the 'glorious past' which could only mean the empire of David and Solomon. The collapse of Assyrian imperial power left a power vacuum in the north of Palestine that Josiah rapidly began to take over. Thus did the accident of history furnish the opportunity to engage once more in imperial ambitions driven by a historical ideology similar to what was taking place all over the ancient pagan world.

Doubtless, little more would have been accomplished by this brief excursion into imperialism than was true of any other Syro-

Palestinian petty state of the time, were it not for another much more important accident of history. As a part of this nostalgia for past glories, Josiah began a campaign to repair and refurbish the Solomonic Temple, which, after some three centuries, must have been in rather poor shape. There was an offering box in the Temple where the visiting pious were accustomed to place their gifts for the Temple. When the money was taken out about the year 622 BC there was found in the box a Torah scroll. It was brought to the attention of the king, and read to him. The royal response was extreme: it indicates beyond doubt that the content of that Torah scroll was entirely unknown to him, and in contradiction to everything that he had believed up to that time.

Ever since the 19th century there has been a high degree of consensus among scholars that the Torah scroll found in the temple is to be identified as a prototype of the legal sections in the Book of Deuteronomy, especially chapters 12–26. The legal tradition preserved in that book is without question a later description of the old Yahwist federation religious ethic that long antedated the formation of the monarchy. Its oldest form is preserved in Exodus 21–23. There is a general consensus that this entire tradition of religious 'law' stemmed from the north. It is also beyond question that there never was a time when that religious customary ethic and morality was enforced by a politically organized state.[16] Doubtless what shocked Josiah was the discovery that the old Yahwist tradition did not support the idea that Yahweh's support of the state, king, and people was an absolute one. Rather, the continuity of people and land was absolutely dependent upon obedience to the Divine Command as described in the 'Mosaic Law'. This contrasted most sharply with the old dynastic theology that affirmed Yahweh's eternal commitment to preserve the kingdom of David forever in dynastic succession. (Later theologies combined the two traditions: the king would reign forever if he piously obeyed the 'Law of Moses'.)

The result was Josiah's famous 'reform'. By definition, a religious reformation is a return to a prior tradition – an attempt to realize and establish an earlier value system. Simultaneously it entails a rejection of some features of the existing established order. The value system determines the choices of those features to be rejected. At the same time, it must be emphasized that a re-establishment of a past order is not within the realm of possibility – it is always the contemporary *concept* of the past that is made the model for reforming acts. Usually the reforming organization is incapable, however, of realizing that there may be a considerable difference between the real past and its ideas about that past. The perennial problem of political reforms, however, is the fact that the political structures cannot really create new value systems operational among the citizenry. All that they can do is establish sanctions that tend to change *forms* of behaviour, penalizing those repugnant to the reforming regime.

The catalogue of Josiah's reforming acts indicates the value system in operation:

1 Though the chronology of the various royal acts is uncertain, it seems clear that the chain of events began with the repair of the Temple, for it was in this process that the 'book of the Law' was discovered.

2 The enactment – i.e. the process by which the book of the Law was made the law of the land – took place through a solemn covenant. The initiative stemmed from the king himself, but was entered into by the entire population or their representatives. The structure of the old Mosaic covenant was preserved in the re-written Book of Deuteronomy, but it is quite clear from the narrative texts that the old covenant structure was entirely misunderstood. The purpose of the covenant now was the hope of avoiding the divine wrath that would befall them for the sins of the past. This motif, stemming from the curse/blessing formula of the age-old covenant structure, became dominant from this time on, in spite of prophetic protests, and is elaborated upon centuries later in the similar covenant of Ezra and Nehemiah.

3 The consequent removal of all vestiges of the polytheistic cults of the past centuries is a good indication of how thoroughly assimilated to the common paganism of the Syro-Palestinian people the Jerusalem monarchy had been. It was not only the Asherah – a cult symbol of unknown nature, though certainly a stela of some sort – but also a host of pagan idols and cultic installations, including even booths of some sort serving cult prostitutes in the temple itself. The horses and chariots of the deified sun are mentioned, recalling the Greek myths concerning Helios and his daily chariot ride across the sky. The defilement of the local 'high places' as well as the Tophet, where the aristocrats of Jerusalem, like those of Carthage, sacrificed their surplus offspring to Molech (?) is described at some length.

4 Included in the destruction of cult installations were the shrines dedicated to the goddess of Sidon, the gods of Moab and Ammon, and the altars associated with the Assyrian empire – all of which certainly had political implications, either for international parity relations or for political loyalty to a foreign empire. Josiah's religious

'reform' was first and foremost a statement that the political state henceforth was to acknowledge no obligations or commitments to any other political entity, a policy that eventually resulted in the destruction of the state.

5 The most savage and brutal acts, however, were carried out against the cult personnel of the old kingdom of Israel that had been destroyed by the Assyrians a century earlier. The priests serving the various shrines were murdered and their bones burned upon their own altars. In contrast, the priests of the Judean kingdom were merely removed, their shrines destroyed, and they were evidently placed on the royal payroll in Jerusalem, though they could not function as priests in the Jerusalem Temple (no doubt the Jerusalem priestly establishment saw to that).

When this slaughter of cult personnel is added to the centralization of cult at the Jerusalem Temple, it is clear that Josiah's so-called reform was in fact a typical utilization of a religious tradition for the consolidation of his political control. The destruction of ritual centres meant the obliteration of the cultic foundations of local communities and local solidarities. Since the northern kingdom of Israel and its population had not recognized the Jerusalemite regime since the time of Solomon, any local solidarities in the north would inevitably have come into conflict with Josiah's ambitions to re-establish the Davidic empire.

This identification of political ambition and parochialism with the Mosaic and prophetic tradition furnished the pattern for innumerable such alliances between religion and politics for millennia to come. The result was described by the Deuteronomic historian in extremely laconic form: 'In his days Pharaoh Neco king of Egypt went up to the king of Assyria to the river Euphrates. King Josiah went to meet him and Pharaoh Neco slew him at Megiddo, when he saw him . . .' (2 Kings 23:28f).

THE DESTRUCTION OF JERUSALEM

The untimely end of this king who, in spite of his ambition, was probably an improvement over most of the earlier (and later) kings, evidently placed the entire reform movement in disrepute. It is clear from the ongoing prophetic protests and condemnations that the kingdom itself was beyond salvation. These prophetic predictions of destruction and doom were not long in coming true, thanks to the inability of the ruling classes to believe that there could be security in anything other than their military preparations and in their ritual labours associated with the Temple. As usual, those who did have deeper insight, such as Jeremiah, risked their lives; at best, they were merely ignored or scorned.[17] Again, it is clear that the royal house and the political establishment had little or no use for the authentic prophetic faith stemming from Moses and the Sinaitic Covenant.

The ambition to be in control led first to complete subjugation by Egypt, and then by Babylonia. A heavy tribute was imposed on the petty state which doubtless increased the resentment of foreign domination, and the consequent willingness to risk everything in their futile hope of establishing independence. Jehoahaz, son of Josiah, was placed on the throne, again by the 'people of the land', but he was deposed after three months by Pharaoh Neco and taken captive to Egypt. Jehoiakim, an older brother, was placed on the throne by Neco, and evidently docilely paid tribute to his benefactor. With the defeat of Neco by Nebuchadnezzar, Jehoiakim became tributary to the Babylonian empire, as did all the territory from the Sinai border to the Euphrates. After three years he rebelled, and was attacked by Chaldeans, Arameans, Moabites and Ammonites. Before Nebuchadnezzar could send his army to put down the rebellion, Jehoiakim died and his son Jehoiachin came to the throne for three months. The city was besieged by the Babylonian army, and he capitulated to Nebuchadnezzar. This was probably in the year 596 BC.

The sources are confused as to the number of persons taken captive and relocated in Mesopotamia by the Babylonians on this occasion. Numbers range from 10,000 (2 Kings 24:16) to 3,023 (Jeremiah 52:28). From the description it is clear, however, that the intention of the Babylonian regime was to disarm Jerusalem and Judah by removing military personnel (the 'mighty men of valour'), the smiths who could produce weapons, and the political administration including the king and his bureaucracy. Naturally, the resources for making war were removed also: the royal treasury and the temple treasures. This attempt both to punish and to remove the possibility and the temptation to rebel followed standard procedures by ancient empires. As the prophets repeatedly warned, the consequences of such foolhardy reliance on war were entirely predictable. The Babylonian regime does not seem to have been bloodthirsty, however. There is on this occasion, at least, no hint of mass executions, probably because the city had voluntarily capitulated.

Strange to say, this experience resulted in no learning. Zedekiah, a third son of Josiah and uncle of Jehoiachin, was placed on the throne, and at least by the eighth year of his reign he also rebelled. Jerusalem was besieged for a year and a half from the ninth to eleventh years of his reign, and the wall was breached in August 586 BC. The king and his army fled toward Transjordan, but the king was captured near Jericho and taken for judgment to Nebuchadnezzar who was at the time in Riblah, somewhere in western Syria. It seems strange that Zedekiah's sons were executed in his presence, but he was only blinded and sent in fetters to Babylon.

Nebuchadnezzar decided upon the total destruction of the city. A month after the city fell, a high army officer arrived to burn the palace, the temple and all the big houses in Jerusalem. The chief priests, military officers, five members of the royal cabinet and various others of rank in the bureaucracy were taken to Riblah where they were executed. The rest of the Hebrew population of Jerusalem was deported to Babylonia, leaving behind only the 'poorest of the land' as peasant farmers (2 Kings 25:12).

The Babylonians installed Gedaliah, the grandson of the royal secretary who had read the 'book of the Law' to King Josiah, as governor of the remaining population. Evidently Jerusalem was left uninhabitable, for his seat was at Mizpeh thought to be Tell en-Naṣba, near al-Jib. The remnants of the old Judean army in Judea and in Transjordan where they had fled, together with other non-Hebrew population elements, began coming back, but about four years later, a descendant of the royal family who had taken flight to Rabbath-Ammon came with a contingent of soldiers and murdered Gedaliah and many others of his entourage. Whereupon, most of the politically active people fled to Egypt to escape the Babylonian reprisal, even though these murders were the responsibility of only some nine persons.

With this, the state of affairs in Jerusalem and its surrounding territory is almost completely unknown to us. To what extent Judea was depopulated is arguable. Certainly there must have been some population in the region; some biblical references seem to support the assertion that desert populations from the Sinai or the southern Transjordan infiltrated into Judea, but there is very little hard evidence. As was the constant policy of ancient empires since at least the days of the Hittites in the Late Bronze Age, the destruction of the political state and the execution of its leadership brought an end to the Judean monarchy as a political entity. It did not bring an end to the religious tradition – quite the contrary. The two generations that followed the destruction of Jerusalem were by far the most creative and impressive in religious thought and productivity of any since the time of Moses or Samuel. Freed from the socio-political ideology of ancient paganism, the rediscovery of the Mosaic tradition and its readaptation to new circumstances were one of the most remarkable developments in the history of religion. The description of that process lies beyond the purposes of the present essay.

THE RETURN FROM EXILE

Especially after the fall of Jerusalem and the exile of most of the population, the prophets were constant in predicting a return from exile, and the rebuilding of the city and community. The opportunity came with the seizure of Babylon and its empire by the Persian king, Cyrus, in 539 BC. It is clear from various sources that the political policy of the Persians was a reversal of the previous attempt on the part of empires to maintain their control by the punitive exile of rebellious populations. Cyrus sent back home the captured images of numerous gods,[18] and in the case of the Jews he issued an edict giving them permission to return to Jerusalem and Judea (Ezra 1:2–4). At the same time, specific direction was issued to rebuild the temple at Jerusalem, and all the temple treasury that had been taken by Nebuchadnezzar was delivered to Sheshbazzar, 'prince of Judah', who was evidently appointed governor by the Persian king.

The sources that we have record some fifty thousand people of various categories who returned from exile, though it is generally conceded that the list probably includes much that stems from a later period. This is reinforced by the list of property and livestock given in Ezra 2. At any rate, if the inventory does reflect the period prior to the rebuilding of the temple, it is clear that the returnees were by no means in a state of poverty. On the other hand, it is equally clear that there was enormous economic disparity in the restored society. The old royal and priestly aristocracy evidently continued their old ways, but with the disappearance of Zerubbabel the royal house was left without institutional support, and gradually disappeared as an effective political element. The vacuum was filled by the priestly families who became the effective political power in the community.

One most interesting and important entry in the census list mentions a group who could not prove their descent, 'whether they belonged to Israel', for there is other evidence that the monotheistic prophetic faith had attracted converts in Mesopotamia and elsewhere during the exilic period.

The rebuilding of the Temple did not proceed smoothly. After the foundations were laid, the existing population of Palestine requested that they take part in the work, 'for we worship your God as you do', but they were contemptuously turned away. The petty parochialism of the leadership contrasts in the extreme to the prophetic vision of Isaiah 40–66, the prophet of exile otherwise unknown, in which he contemplated the spread of the divine salvation to the ends of the earth (Isaiah 49:6). The little book of Jonah presents also a parable that seems to ridicule those (including prophets?) who were characterized by such narrow parochialism. It is not surprising that the existing local population became hostile and succeeded in bringing the work temporarily to an end. The Temple was not finally completed until 516, after a search of the archives ordered by Darius confirmed that King Cyrus actually had ordered that the Temple be built, and its costs paid for by the Persian imperial treasury (Ezra 6:6–12). Further, even the costs of animals for the daily rituals were to be supplied by the royal revenues, in exchange for prayers 'for the life of the king and his sons'.

Meanwhile, other events took place that are not adequately described in the sources. At the death of Cambyses in 522, rebellion all over the empire arose, and it seems certain that the Jerusalem regime again thought independence possible. The prophet Haggai (2:21) proclaimed Zerubbabel the 'chosen' of Yahweh in terms that indicated monarchic if not imperial ambitions. This is especially true since the same prophecy predicted the overthrow of the 'throne of kingdoms' – which never took place. The messages of post-exilic prophets in general were the reverse of the pre-exilic ones; perhaps it is for this reason that prophecy rapidly died out until it reappeared for a short time with the rise of Christianity.

This is the last reference to Zerubbabel, who was actually a descendant of the Davidic dynasty. It is entirely unknown what happened to him, but we suspect that this belated imperial ambition led to no good end. The old monarchic tradition died hard, but was transformed over the centuries into an apocalyptic expectation of a divine intervention in human history through the sending of a Messiah – anointed one – who would establish peace and justice in the earth.

THE REFORM OF EZRA AND NEHEMIAH

The sources for this event (or events?) that took place nearly a century later are so confused and confusing that no consensus has been reached concerning the chronology. For present purposes, the dating is not of much consequence, since the main outline of what happened, and the future consequences are reasonably clear. Both Nehemiah and Ezra were sent to Jerusalem by a king Artaxerxes with royal mandates and lavish funds, according to the accounts we have.

The situation in Jerusalem was evidently depressing. Though the Temple had been rebuilt and its ritual labours re-established, the level of religious and cultural life is described as very low indeed (Malachi). The city walls were still in ruins, and according to Nehemiah 7:4 the population was very small and 'no houses had been built.' In all probability few lived in the city other than the Temple personnel and perhaps the governor's retinue. It is stated specifically in Nehemiah 11:1–2 that the bureaucrats (*śarīm*) of the people resided there, but the rest of the people 'cast lots to bring one out of ten to live in Jerusalem . . . And the people blessed all the men who willingly offered to live in Jerusalem.' There is one reference to 'men of Tyre who lived in the city' selling fish and other goods on the sabbath. Nehemiah set to work in a very hasty task of rebuilding the walls in fifty-two days, and building gates to control access to the city. Again the project roused intense hostility among their neighbours who saw perfectly well that fortification of a city meant pretensions to political control, and potential rebellion against the empire.

Again it is quite clear that there was a power struggle going on within the restored society. There are repeated references to persons even in the priestly class itself who had close ties to persons outside, even including Sanballat of Samaria who is presented as one of the most dangerous of Nehemiah's opponents. Furthermore, measures had to be taken to place under control the unscrupulous greed of the wealthy in the community, who were seizing the sons and daughters, fields and vineyards of the poor who were unable to pay off their loans with interest to wealthy Jews (Nehemiah 5). Nehemiah as governor, and no doubt with considerable public support, made the moneylenders, described as nobles and officials, take a solemn oath to stop charging interest. This was already prohibited in the oldest law collection of the Torah (Exodus 22:25), but it had been a dead letter so far as urban custom was concerned probably since the time of Solomon at least. It had never, of course, been applicable in the old pagan cities incorporated by David into his empire.

By far the most important event in this reform movement is described in Nehemiah 8–10, the covenant to observe the law of God given by Moses. This event determined the future of Judaism, in that it established a written lawcode as the standard for behaviour of the community. Characteristically, no hint is given as to the precise content of the written lawcode that was read by Ezra the scribe and interpreted by Levites to the gathered community 'from early morning until midday' (Nehemiah 8:3).

Whether it was the book of Deuteronomy, the priestly code, the entire Pentateuch, or none of the above that has survived in its present form, that was read to the populace is a question to which there will probably never be a convincing answer. The motivation for this solemn vow to obey a written lawcode derived from a remote past is stated specifically in Nehemiah 9:32–38. It stated flatly that the wrath of God had come upon them because they had not obeyed that law, and therefore they were subjects (slaves) of kings that God set over them as punishment, and their economic produce went to those kings. The identification of a religious tradition with a purely political ambition and economic interest could not have been stated more clearly. In contrast, the warning against the establishment of kingship by the prophet Samuel in the first place included the fact that their own king would (and did – note Rehoboam) seize their property and even their offspring to serve his own ends (1 Samuel 8:10–18 and 1 Kings 12:9–16).

This enactment of an old lawcode was not sufficient for the concerns of the society, however. The covenant included a number of other specific obligations that were either absent in the older law collections, or were present only as generalized warnings. Pre-eminent in the new stipulations was a prohibition against intermarriage with those outside the community. Even this was not sufficient for the parochialism of both Ezra and Nehemiah. Both required and enforced the divorce of non-Judahite wives (Yahwism was not at all involved – merely the law-centred organization centred on Jerusalem). Fortunately for the future genetic wellbeing of the society the law was often enough ignored to prevent the deleterious effects of inbreeding, and the access of non-Jews into the community was also a constant. The prohibition of marriage to non-Jews remained a dogma, however, to the present day, one that could not have been at all relevant in that form to the original community of the Mosaic faith.

From this time on there was a systemic identification of the 'orthodox' community with patterns of ritual and economic behaviour that were sanctioned by an interpretation of now age-old legal collections. The power struggle centred soon on the problem of correlating archaic formulas of quasi-legal language with the realities of everyday life. In all probability the majority of persons engaged in the daily routine of productivity and family life had little to do with the abstruse arguments and definitions of the scribes. However, the old priestly lineage of the Zadokites remained as head of the community, and like most of the common people they had little use for the Torah tradition except that part which was concerned with the Temple ritual – their base of authority and prestige.

The unconcern of this priestly aristocracy for the Yahwist ethic and law is illustrated by an event that took place very shortly after the time of Ezra. John, grandson of Eliashib, a contemporary of Ezra, became high priest, but his brother, Joshua, curried the favour of the Persian governor, Bagoas, who promised the high priesthood to Joshua. A quarrel that took place in the temple itself resulted in the murder of Joshua by the high priest.[19] According to Josephus, this resulted in penalties upon the Jerusalem regime, and temporary disfavour in the Persian empire. It does not seem to have had a lasting effect, however.

The ensuing period from Ezra to the time of the Maccabean revolt is one of the most obscure in the history of the biblical tradition, perhaps because there were no important events in the history of the society. We do know that the Jerusalem priesthood was permitted to issue coinage under the name *Yehud*, imitating the famous silver coinage of Athens. We know also that Hellenistic culture was increasingly permeating Jewish society, as it was everywhere else in the Near East. The ancient Near Eastern cultural complexes were rapidly dying out everywhere together with many of the old languages. It is highly controversial to what extent the biblical Hebrew language continued in use while its twin language, Phoenician, became extinct except in the old Tyrian colony of Carthage in North Africa. Certainly, particularly under the impact of the Persian empire, Aramaic became the *lingua franca* of the entire Near Eastern world.

Again according to Josephus,[20] the Jerusalem high priest at first refused to submit to Alexander the Great in 332 BC on the grounds that he had sworn an oath to remain obedient to the last Persian king, Darius III. Josephus gives a fanciful tale of mutual dreams that resulted in Alexander's granting permission to the community to be governed by its own laws, which was extended also to Jews living everywhere in his empire. No matter the details, there can be little doubt that this was a historical fact of great importance later. The Maccabean revolt directly stemmed from this situation.

THE MACCABEAN KINGDOM

The great empire of Alexander the Great broke up at his death in 323 BC. Palestine fell under the control of the Ptolemies of Egypt, while Syria and Mesopotamia were ruled by the Seleucids. Mesopotamia was lost to the Parthians in the mid-third century, reducing the Seleucid kingdom to a fragment of what it had been. In the year 200 Antiochus III ('the Great') succeeded in taking control of Palestine from the Ptolemies, thus enlarging his territory. It did him little good, however, for ten years later he was defeated by the advancing Roman army that annexed Greece and much of Anatolia. As a condition for keeping his throne, he was required to pay an extremely heavy indemnity and annual tribute.

Jerusalem seems to have welcomed the Seleucid governance that renewed the recognition of the administration of Jewish law and gave other favourable concessions, just as the Persian empire had done centuries before. The situation turned for the worse; partly because the perennial need for money of Antiochus IV, who came to the throne in 175, combined with the perennial ambition of elements of the priestly aristocracy to bring the period of relative peace and tranquillity to an end. The high priest was Onias III, but again a brother, Joshua who changed his name to the Greek Jason, curried favour with the Seleucid emperor to obtain the high priesthood. He offered Antiochus an enormous sum, which of course the king was only too happy to accept. Onias was deported to Antioch and shortly afterwards was murdered.

Another priest who took the Greek name Menelaos outbid Jason for the high priesthood, so Jason had to flee, probably to Transjordan. Menelaos was not of the Zadokite lineage, and therefore according to traditional Jewish custom and law, had no legitimate claim to the position at all. It is clear that he, like all the priestly line, had no use for the Torah tradition, and this was powerfully reinforced by his determination to make Jerusalem into a typical Hellenistic city state. Again, he paid a considerable sum of money to have Jerusalem constituted as a *politeuma* of Antioch: a sort of detached entity of the Seleucid capital city. He renamed Jerusalem

'Antiochia in Judea', and established the typical Hellenistic institutions of gymnasium, ephebate, and Greek-style games. Since the city was still small at this time, occupying evidently only the eastern hill and the Temple mount, it seems probable that the procedure, shocking as it was to the conservative *ḥasidīm*, those loyal to the Torah tradition, did not have a serious impact on their own way of life, and at this time there was little organized resistance.

The power struggle continued when Jason returned with an army in an attempt to regain his position. The result was a brief civil war in which Jason was defeated and had to flee. Antiochus, however, regarded the event as rebellion, and as a result in 169 BC he pillaged the temple treasures, and the next year tore down the wall of the city, and built a fortress for his occupation troops that looked down on the Temple enclosure. This was actually a citadel/Greek city, with the cult of Greek gods, with a population of Seleucid mercenaries and some Hellenized Jews. Even more important, no doubt at the suggestion of his own creature, Menelaos, he was urged to issue the infamous edict that made observance of the Torah punishable by death.

The ensuing persecution and dedication of the Temple to a form of Zeus, the sacrifice of swine on the altar and the attempt to force the pious to sacrifice to foreign gods resulted in open rebellion. The consequence of the policy was the eventual establishment of what became known as the 'Hasmonean' dynasty, descendants of Mattathias and his five sons, the most famous of whom was Judas, known as the 'Maccabee' (hammer).

Since the Seleucid regime was deeply occupied at the time in trying to keep its hold on Mesopotamia which was being seized by the Parthians, the rebellion of the Maccabees was unexpectedly successful, so that in 164 Antiochus was forced to issue an edict of amnesty that ended the persecution. Judas gained control of Jerusalem itself and rededicated the Temple, an event that became a celebration in the Jewish calendar known as Hanukkah. As time went on, internal power struggles in the Seleucid regime weakened them further, and the successors of Judas succeeded in playing off one pretender to the throne against another. The fact that in 161 Judas succeeded in making an alliance with Rome was no doubt an important factor. Finally, under Jonathan the state became independent for a time about 142 BC.[21]

The succeeding period saw the transition again from a religiously based regime to a thoroughly Hellenized kingdom, characterized by many of the features that the rebellion had objected to in the first place. Jonathan, brother of Judas, was designated high priest by the Seleucid Alexander – a sufficient indication that the possessor of power no longer had much need for observance of either Jewish law or Jewish religious ethic. Another brother, Simon, was murdered in a power struggle by his own sons.

Simon's third son John Hyrcanus came to the throne in 134 and with him the dynasty began the transition to empire again. By 124 Seleucid control of the region was so weakened by wars against the Parthians and against each other, that Hyrcanus was free to seize Samaria, and destroy the rival temple on Mt Gerizim. Curiously also, he forced the Idumeans (Edomites) to be converted to Judaism, an act that had dire consequences a century later. In spite of his incessant wars, the city of Jerusalem grew so that again it expanded onto the western hill, and saw much building including the necessary royal palace, fortifications and towers. It was, after all, a period of rapid population growth and expansion all over the Near Eastern world.

With the death of Hyrcanus there ensued a period of virtually constant power struggle with repeated civil war as well as external warfare. The deep division between the priest-kings and the religious party became ever more hostile. The remnant of the Seleucid empire was constantly trying to reassert its control over Palestine as well as Syria. Various Arabian principalities became involved as well, including the Nabateans, who, as Josephus comments, 'were not very adept in warfare.'[22] The Pharisees, who seem to have enjoyed the support of the common people at this time, on occasion appealed to the Seleucid king for protection and support against their own kings, especially Alexander Jannaeus. The latter crucified some 800 of their leaders which of course shockingly demonstrated that the kingship had simply become another Hellenistic despotism.

On his deathbed, Alexander Jannaeus recommended that his widow turn over authority to the Pharisees, which she did, but with little lasting results at the time, since the two sons of Alexander continued the power struggle with the aid of various outside powers, especially that of Antipater, ancestor of Herod the Great, who had been governor of the southern regions under Jannaeus. Repeatedly both sons appealed to Roman authorities for support in succeeding to the kingship as well as the high priesthood. The religious party also appealed to Pompey to abolish the kingship, as foreign to their religious laws and customs. Therewith began a new chapter in the history of Jerusalem, but by no means an end to the power struggle.

NOTES

1 For a description, see Kathleen M Kenyon, *Digging up Jerusalem*, London, 1974, ch. 5, 98–106.
2 Joshua 12:10. An earlier king of Jerusalem, Adonizedek, organized a coalition against Joshua in the early years of the federation and was defeated, Joshua 10. Nothing further is said of the city itself in this tradition.
3 See the discussion of F M Cross, Jr, *Canaanite Myth and Hebrew Epic*, Cambridge, 1973, who fails to see the connection between the assimilation of Canaanite ideology and the Canaanite elements in the monarchy, especially under King Solomon.
4 René Dussaud, *Les origines cananéennes du sacrifice Israélite*, Paris, 1921, 2nd ed., Paris 1941.
5 For a description of the sophisticated, and changing, bureaucratic procedures having to do merely with land tenure, see the impressive dissertation of Clayton Libolt, *Royal Land Grants from Ugarit*, University of Michigan, 1985.
6 The genealogy of Zadok is exactly five generations longer than the number of generations that had elapsed between Moses and the birth of King David. I Chronicles 6 gives the official (post-exilic) genealogical version that no doubt was the normative tradition of the pre-exilic period.
7 See the discussion of the North Syrian dialect of Jerusalem already in the Amarna letters by W Moran, 'The Syrian Scribe of the Jerusalem Amarna Letters', *Unity and Diversity*, Baltimore, 1975, 146–166.
8. For further discussion see G Mendenhall, 'The Nature and Purpose of the Abraham Narratives', *Ancient Israelite Religion: Essays in Honor of Frank Moore Cross*, Philadelphia, 1987.
9 G Mendenhall, *The Syllabic Inscriptions from Byblos*, Beirut, 1985.
10 David Ussishkin, 'King Solomon's Palaces', *The Biblical Archaeologist*, vol. 36, 1973, 78–105.
11 Both Solomon and his son Rehoboam had non-Israelite mothers.
12 N Avigad, *Discovering Jerusalem*, New York, 1983, 31.
13 The famous battle at Qarqar in *c*.863 BC involved small states from the desert Arab principalities to southern Anatolia. Curiously, there is no hint of this in the biblical stories though the petty state of Israel under King Ahab was a major participant in the confederation.
14 By far the best reconstruction of events thus far available is that of John Bright, *A History of Israel*, 3rd ed., Philadelphia, 1981, Excursus I, 298–309.
15 Note especially the bitter protest of Jeremiah, chapter 7. For this pointing out of some unpleasant facts, he nearly lost his life.
16 In general, ancient 'lawcodes' were not the basis for legal actions or judicial decisions. See the discussion of G Mendenhall, 'Ancient Oriental and Biblical Law', *The Biblical Archaeologist*, 17, 1954, 50–74.
17 The famous episode of the first book-burning in history took place when King Jehoiakim had Jeremiah's prophesies read to him, and put them in the fire part by part as they were read to him (Jeremiah 36). The narrative clearly indicates, however, that there were at least some officials who were sympathetic to the prophets and took their message seriously. They were not strong or numerous enough to determine political policy.
18 See the barrel inscription of Cyrus (*Ancient Near Eastern Texts*, 316). Restoration of deities, sanctuaries, and populations was a systematic policy of Cyrus, no doubt intended as a measure to secure loyalty on the part of subject kings and populations.
19 Josephus, *Antiquities of the Jews*, book XI, ch. VII.
20 Antiochus is usually blamed for this: however, Josephus specifically records that the initiative came from Menelaos, and the accuracy of the account is reinforced by the fact that some years later Menelaos was executed by the succeeding Seleucid king, *Ant.*, XII, ix, 7.
21 A detailed study of the history of the revolt is found in *Der Gott der Makkabäer*, Berlin, 1937.
22 *Ant.*, XIV, ii, 3.

CHAPTER III

Jerusalem under Rome and Byzantium 63 BC – 637 AD

John Wilkinson

In September 63 BC the first Roman leader captured Jerusalem, and almost exactly seven hundred years later, in 638 AD, Jerusalem was to surrender its relation with the Roman empire. Both Jerusalem and Rome had changed a great deal in seven centuries. As far as Jerusalem was concerned the arrival of Pompey in 63 BC was the beginning of a Roman effort to control the Jews, and ended two centuries later in the expulsion of the Jews from Jerusalem. The next two centuries saw Jerusalem under another name as a normal Roman colony in the eastern empire, with Judaism banned. And the last three centuries, from 324 to 638, began a period of Christian ascendancy over Jerusalem.

Rome too was changing. In 27 BC the Roman Emperor had reached the full extent of his power, and was by then ruling in one way or another over all the coastline of the Mediterranean Sea. Indeed he was also worshipped as a god, and one of the first temples built to him must have been the one erected in Sebaste by Herod the Great.[1] Emperors continued, and sometimes there was rivalry between two of them. Then in 330 AD the old city Byzantium was dedicated as the new city Constantinople. It aimed to be 'the New Rome' and it had its own senate. Hence, in 410 when Rome in Italy fell to Alaric the Visigoth, Constantinople became the capital. So the change from purely Roman power to power based on Byzantium or Constantinople was a gradual process. It started with the rebuilding and dedication of the new city, and it was completed by the taking of Rome by Alaric.

Byzantium under the Emperor Justinian made an attempt to

recapture the Roman provinces to the west of the Mediterranean, but the effort proved beyond her capacity. Seventy years after Justinian's death, when the Roman armies had fought long and bitter battles against the new Persian empire, both empires were invaded by a new power, the Islamic armies of Arabia. When his forces were defeated in 636 AD by these armies at the battle of Yarmouk, Emperor Heraclius returned towards Constantinople with the words 'Farewell, Syria!' on his lips.

In 63 BC Jerusalem was the capital of a Jewish state (see figure 1) with about two-thirds of its population Jews. The rest, according to Strabo who wrote in about 19 AD, were to the south of Jerusalem Nabateans in Idumea, and around Jerusalem and to the north 'Egyptians, Arabs, and Phoenicians'.[2] It is hard to find out about the non-Jewish part of the population, since the sources available are either Jewish or anti-Jewish. It was a Jewish state which had, to begin with, made territorial advances under the Hasmonean kings, who reigned about 100 BC, and whenever they conquered some other race or tribe they offered them the chance to obey the Jewish law, and if they did not accept they were exiled. So a large number of Jews in the conquered areas were Jews reluctantly. Herod the Great, eighty years later, judged the policy of making conquered people accept the Jewish law to be mistaken,[3] and as the coins show he did not interfere with the religion of the people who came into his care.

After the two Jewish defeats of 70 and 135 AD the Jewish population of Palestine was reduced from two-thirds to one-third, and, as will be more fully argued later, continued to decrease. Of this new Palestine which was largely pagan we have very little solid information. No doubt the number of 'Egyptians, Arabs and Phoenicians' increased. They were famous, according to Junior Philosophus,[4] who wrote about them in 350 AD, for a number of things which would seem very much at home in the Greco-Roman world. Their products were famed – linen from Scythopolis, and purple from four different cities, games were famous at Caesarea and the wrestlers and boxers of Gaza and Ascalon were well known. Ascalon was famous for its philosophers and also for its onions! Their religion was either Greco-Roman religion in full, for example the temple of Jupiter Capitolinus in Jerusalem, or a mixture of local forms of worship and the official religion, for example the worship of Zeus Marnas at Gaza. 'Marnas' is only applied to the Greek name Zeus at Gaza, and that is likely to mean that Gazans went on worshipping their own god, though they called him Zeus.

From the official favouring of the Christian faith by Constantine

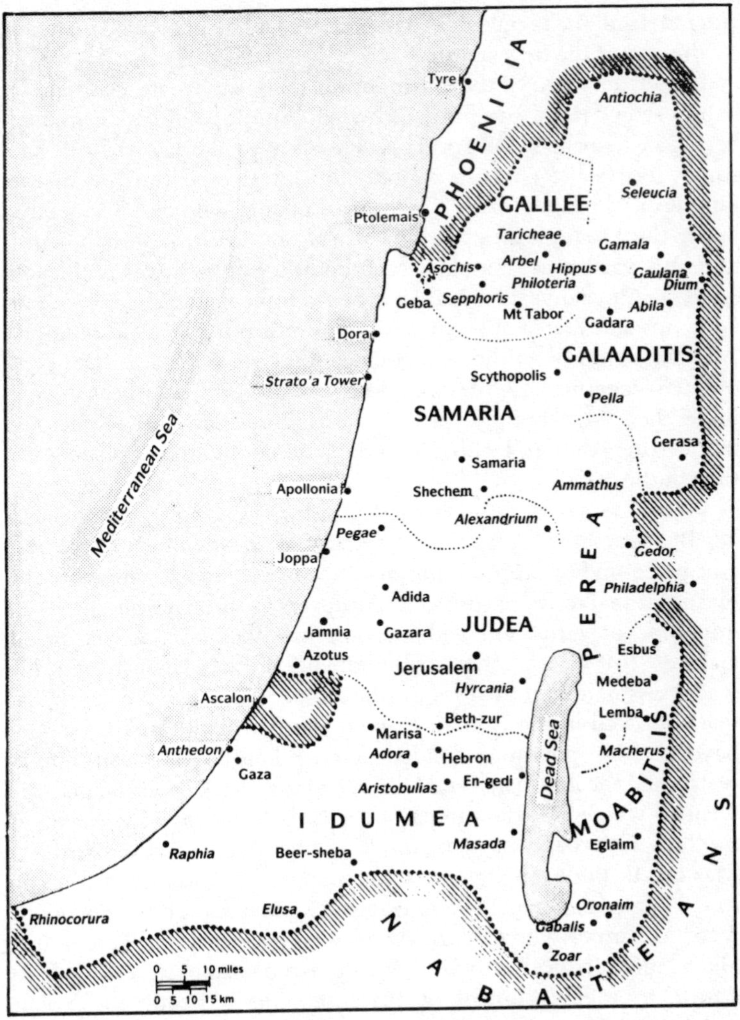

Fig. 1 Map of the Hasmonean kingdom, 76–65 BC (source: Y Aharoni and M Avi-Yonah, *The Macmillan Bible Atlas*, New York and London, 1968, map 213).

Jerusalem quickly became a Christian city. So the life of Jerusalem from about 312 to 638 is both presented in Christian sources and is the history of a city very important in the early history of the Church. In any case paganism (a name we shall use for the religion of early Greece and Rome) was on the decline in Palestine as a whole, and nearly all the people who had practised it had become Christians by the end of the fifth century.

Under the reign of the Hasmoneans the Jewish state was largely composed of Jews. But in 63 BC when Pompey came to Jerusalem he began to reverse this process. He allowed the Jews to rule the south and Galilee (figure 2), but non-Jews ruled the rest of the kingdom.[5] Pompey made the original people who had been exiles under the Hasmonean kingdom return, and there was the normal religious variety as there had been before. Pompey was politically wise, for the Samaritans had lost their temple in 129 BC on Mount Gerizim, and many of them wished to return to their old religion. And the exiles from the Syrian cities, most of whom had adopted oriental versions of Greek religions, would not have been happy under the control of the Jews. There was therefore a large population in Palestine ready to be hostile to the Jews should they ever reassert their authority.

Julius Caesar was Pompey's rival, and when Pompey was killed in 48 BC Caesar prepared new territorial arrangements. He left Antipater, an Idumean, as administrator of the Jewish state, with the Hasmonean family as princes. Antipater made Phasael, his son, governor of Jerusalem and Herod, his other son, governor of Galilee.[6] But Caesar's new arrangements did not last for long. He was assassinated on the Ides of March 44 BC, and in the confusion that followed in the Roman empire, the Parthian kingdom in and beyond Mesopotamia invaded Syria. The Hasmonean family welcomed the Parthians, and Herod had to escape. The first place he went to was Petra, the capital of the Nabatean kingdom, since his mother, Cypros, was a member of the Arabian royal family.[7] Malchus II, the Arab king, was not welcoming, and Herod went on to Cleopatra in Egypt, where he again received a rebuff. Finally he went to Rome, where Mark Antony befriended him. This young Herod might conceivably be the leader Rome had been seeking in its efforts to regain control of Palestine. So in Rome the Senate proclaimed Herod King of Judea, and then he went back to Palestine in order to fight to gain his new title. Before his flight he had governed Galilee, and in 39 BC he began by fighting there. Two years later he successfully besieged Jerusalem.[8] Mark Antony continued to befriend him, and during this time Herod took revenge on the Hasmoneans. And in 31 BC when Antony was defeated at the battle of Actium, Herod went to Rhodes to meet the victor,

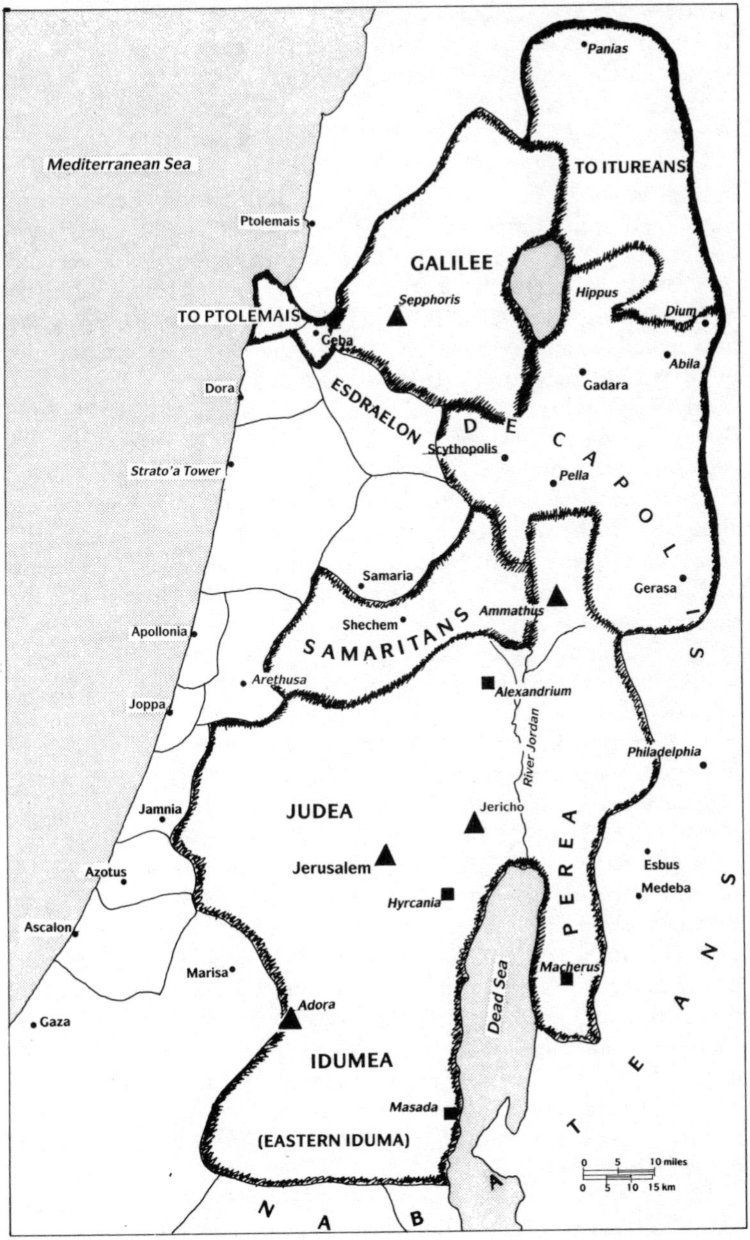

Fig. 2 Map of the new arrangement of the Hasmonean kingdom under Pompey (source: ibid, map 216).

Octavian. He managed to convince him that as he had been a friend to Antony he could also be a friend to Octavian.[9] So a friendship began which lasted throughout Herod's reign. Octavian was an extremely powerful ally, since in 27 BC he gained his title 'Augustus', and was therefore the first Roman emperor.

Herod was not particularly interested in religious questions. Indeed, in cities outside his kingdom he built temples dedicated to the Greek and Roman gods, and in Sebaste (near Nablus) one dedicated to Augustus. The last Greco-Roman honour he received was to become president of the Olympic Games.[10] Hence when he came to redesign Jerusalem his idea was that of a classical capital. His power and wealth were so enormous that some of his massive buildings and many of his streets are still in use today.

In 35 BC, when he was still friends with Mark Antony, he built the castle called 'Antonia',[11] which was in fact an adaptation of a previous fort founded by the Hasmoneans. He or they may have built the moat, which seems to have been a dry moat extending along the northern enclosure wall of the Temple area, ending in the pool called Birkat Israil. But the part immediately round the castle had water in it, and was called the 'Struthion', the Greek name for the bird 'swallow'.

The rebuilding of Jerusalem started in earnest after two years of famine in 25 and 24 BC. Herod gained great prestige by his relief of the famine, both in Jerusalem and elsewhere in his kingdom, by providing food and grain to sow.[12] But there were many people in Jerusalem who were ruined by the famine and the plague which accompanied it, and some of these people without employment Herod selected as his builders. First of all he built the palace on the west of the city (figure 3). The palace had a moat round it, at least according to the excavations which show a sharp slope at the edge of the ruins, and inside it consisted of two large buildings, of which one was called the Caesareum in honour of his friendship with Octavian, now Augustus.[13] These buildings were linked by water-gardens. At the north end of the palace he erected three towers, Phasael, Mariamme and Hippicus, which he richly ornamented, and which in time of battle became the strongest point in the palace.[14] The towers had solid bases about fifteen metres high to counteract battering rams, and the base of one of these towers, probably Hippicus, is still part of Jerusalem Citadel.

Herod also seems to have laid out the streets on the western hill of Jerusalem in a new way. The piece of street (marked by a circle in figure 3) to the east of the palace and half way across the city has been

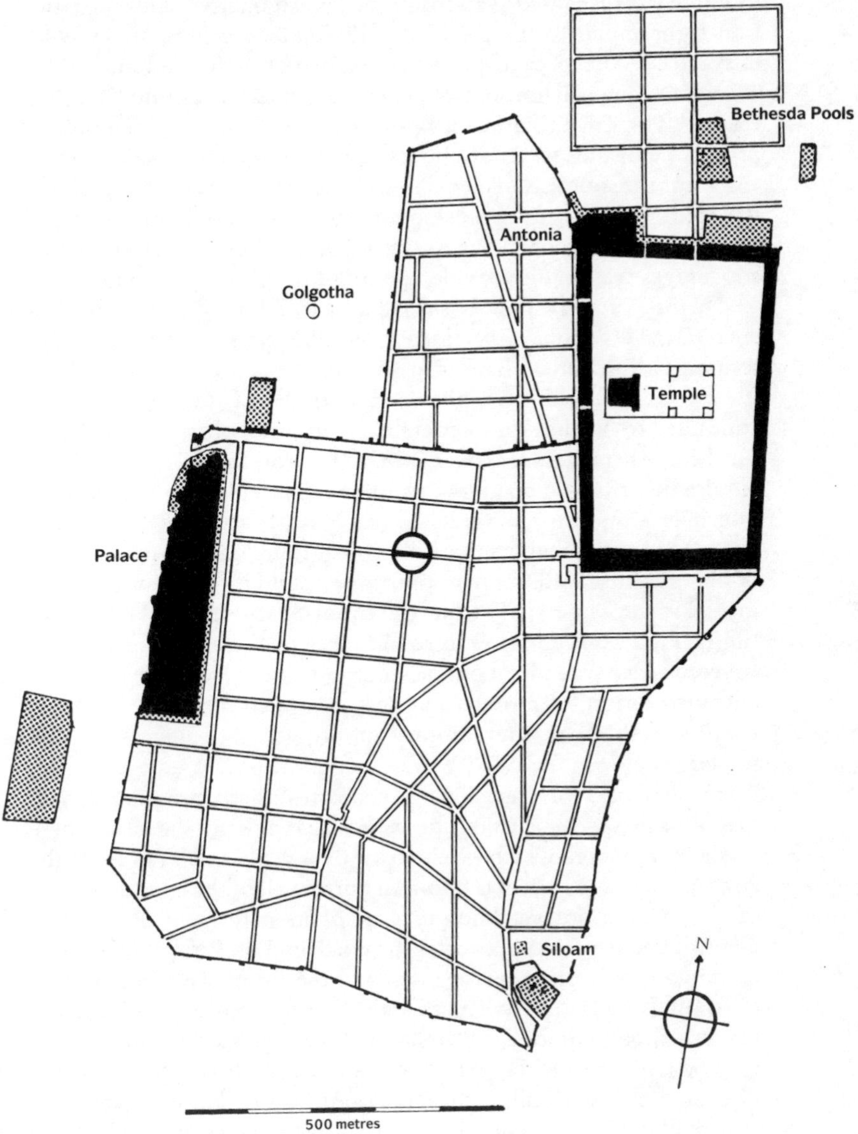

Fig. 3 Herodian Jerusalem

found in the recent excavations in the Jewish quarter, and since this is at right angles to the palace it may be that a grid of streets was introduced. The piece of street marked by the circle was built on the ruins of a Jewish house which was occupied well into Herod's reign.[15] The gridded area on figure 3 is a conjecture, based on the present lie of the streets on the western hill, and the amount of flat space. At the southeast the grid must have given way to streets along the contour line where the slope is steep. The arrangement of the grid pattern may have made traffic easier, but one of the main advantages was that it provided pieces of roughly equal value.

Then in 19 or 18 BC Herod planned to rebuild the Temple. He encountered various objections from the priests, and ended by training a thousand of them as masons and carpenters.[16] The Temple itself was finished in eighteen months, but its surroundings continued to be built for over eighty years, and when the work was finished there were over 18,000 workmen looking for employment.[17] The main task was to extend the Temple enclosure, which was built up on vaults to reach nearly to the height of the upper platform on which the Temple was founded. The foundations of the enclosure walls seem to remain all round the enclosure, which makes it the same size as the Ḥaram al-Sharīf. When Herod had finished it a high portico ran round three of its sides,[18] and a wide covered space was added on the south side, very like the basilicas of a Roman forum, to provide a place by the open court where people could get shade in the summer or protection from rain in the winter.[19]

These works of Herod were concerned with bringing a new magnificence to the city but he went on to enlarge the city. There was a market area which he enclosed by a wall which ran from the Antonia to a gate in the Hasmonean north wall of the city.[20] The line of this wall is not yet known. One of its gates, which we shall identify later, may have been at the north end of Ṭarīq al-Wād. But there is certainly a gate on the east. Near the Antonia is a Roman arch crossing Tarīq Bāb al-Asbāṭ called the 'Ecce Homo' arch. Until 1979 this was thought to be a triumphal arch. Recent research now shows it to be much more like a city gate,[21] and like the one of the city of Nicaea, which was built in the reign of Augustus. The east gate in the new wall is therefore known, and to its east is a long pool which is a continuation of the moat of the Antonia. In peace time there would have been a wooden bridge carrying the street across it, and the bridge could be taken away when there was any danger that Jerusalem would be attacked.

The water supply would have had to have additions in the time of Herod, and Josephus mentions with pride that Herod's palace – at the highest point in Jerusalem – was well supplied with water.[22] The spring of Jerusalem was the one at Siloam down in the southwest corner, and the upper part of the city had for a long time been supplied by pools to catch water in the valleys round, the contents of which were fed into the city by canals. The dates of the pools round Jerusalem are not known, but Herod may well have built the pool called Māmillā ('Breast') which is just off the map to the west, half a kilometre away, and higher than Herod's palace. Another pool which Herod may have built is the one in the 'New City', which in Herod's time had not yet been surrounded by a wall. The double pool of Bethesda in this grid of streets, still remarkably clear today, is linked with the grid by the fact that it has virgin rock as the foundation to the division between the pools, so the streets and the pool were part of a single city plan.

Herod added a theatre and a hippodrome to Jerusalem,[23] though their location is not yet known. Such entertainments were foreign to Jews, but they were very much part of a city which had any relationship with the classical tradition. But by 10 BC when the Temple was dedicated, Herod was worried more and more about quarrels in his family, and the question of who should succeed him. He was a man so determined and strong that he was apt to make decisions by himself and not delegate. Hence he had no true idea of who should be his heir, and in the end, after he had made various wills and rescinded them, he left most of the kingdom to Archelaus. He split off Galilee and Peraea (the area west of Amman between Wadi Yabnis and al-Mukhawir) for Herod Antipas, and areas to the northeast of the Sea of Galilee to Philip.[24]

Herod died in 4 BC. Immediately after his funeral all three sons went to Rome with the purpose of stating their claims, and perhaps improving on them. But Augustus wished to test all three and would not consent to their being more than princes. Herod Antipas and Philip went back and ruled their districts successfully for over thirty years, but Archelaus, once he was in power, was so cruel both to Samaritans and to Jews that they reported him to Rome, and he was banished to Vienna in Gaul. In 6 AD the governor of Syria, Quirinius, sent Romans to Judea to sell Archelaus' property, and to hold a census to find out how many people should pay taxes.[25] This is the census for which Joseph and Mary went to Bethlehem, according to the Gospel of St Luke,[26] and there Jesus was born. But the date of Jesus' birth is not certain, since he is said by St Matthew to have avoided the sentence of death passed on the Bethlehem children by Herod the Great.[27] This would imply a date in or before 4 BC when Herod died. But the census took place ten years after his death, and whether St Luke or St Matthew was correct we have no way of telling.

Direct Roman rule over Judea started with a number of short-term governors who were called procurators, but after a time prefects were appointed for a longer period: for example, Pontius Pilate, who ruled Judea for ten years. Under his rule Jesus went down from Nazareth to the Jordan and was baptised by John the Baptist. Then he started his campaign. He moved to Capernaum on the north coast of the Sea of Galilee. He chose twelve disciples, and went round with them, healing and preaching in the villages of Galilee and sometimes outside Galilee into the surrounding provinces. What kind of work did people believe that Jesus did? Jesus himself would perhaps have accepted the definition of his task as reforming the Jewish obedience to the Law. But in the Gospels, which were written by people who were his followers, he was a holy prophet, who was willing to go to any lengths in life and in death to show his devotion to God, and to share in God's own love for his neighbours. His disciples regarded him as the Messiah,[28] God's anointed leader whose coming would bring salvation. This task, whatever it was, was bound to set Jesus at odds with the conventional leaders of Judaism, but it gained him a large following among the villagers of Galilee. Eventually he went up to Jerusalem to face his fiercest opponents, and there, according to the Gospels, they arrested him and secured his crucifixion. His death was out of devotion to God, and such a death could not be the end. Three days after his burial the disciples began to see him alive again, and after he had ascended into heaven his disciples were sent out to preach the message that Jesus was the leader and the teacher by whom both Jews and non-Jews could expect blessing and salvation.

What holy places of pilgrimage in Jerusalem are in fact connected with Jesus? Christian pilgrimage seems to go back to the 2nd century, and the holy places are therefore just a century newer than the Bible itself. Four of them are genuine both in the Bible and in pilgrimage, and the fifth – Pilate's palace – is not genuine but we shall see that there is a very simple reason why not. The first two are pools, the one at Siloam, to which Jesus sent the man born blind after his sight had been restored,[29] but the pool was restored in Roman times and it is not possible to say what it looked like in the time of Jesus. The second is the Pool of Bethesda where he cured the paralysed man.[30] The third place is the Garden of Gethsemane. As a garden it has disappeared ever since the Roman siege of 70 AD, for during the siege the Romans used all the trees as props for earthworks, and at a late stage in the battle they had to send eleven miles away to get more.[31] But the general location of Gethsemane is certain. The last place connected with Jesus is Golgotha where he was crucified, and 'nearby', according to the Gospels,[32] the Holy Sepulchre where he was buried. The crucifixion of Jesus was a public event. It is therefore extremely likely that the exact spot would be remembered, and in fact no other place was ever considered until the end of the 19th century.

After Jesus had ascended into heaven some of the Christian community stayed in Jerusalem. With the Jewish authorities they were unpopular, and there were three martyrs. But some other Jewish teachers taught that Christians should be left alone: if their teaching did not come from God they would perish, but if the Christian community 'is of God, you will not be able to overthrow them!'[33]

The Jews had one more monarch who was a member of the Herodian family, Herod Agrippa, his grandson, who reigned from 41–44. Then more Roman prefects took over the government. Under Felix, governor from 52–60, there were bandits in Judea, some of them religious bandits, determined to overthrow Roman rule.[34] Trouble was caused in Caesarea between the Syrian inhabitants and the Jews. Felix was succeeded by Festus, and then the Roman administration went sharply downhill. Albinus, governor from 60-62, was said to have received bribes from the bandits, who made allies of all who wished to see the end of Roman rule. Gessius Florus, who was governor from 64–66, continued to receive the bandits' bribes, and when in June there was further trouble in Caesarea he went to Jerusalem.[35] He brought up two cohorts from Caesarea, and the disagreement with the Jews became so intense that the cohorts rushed on the crowd and fought with them. Florus went down to Caesarea. He had not pacified the Jews, and sent for military help from the governor of Syria, Cestius Gallus. Gallus prepared for war against the Jews, and marched on Jerusalem, arriving there in mid-November. He went straight from Mount Scopus, his camp, to Bethesda, which shows that the wall to the north had not yet been built. But having approached the city he then inexplicably retreated, and on his retreat down the road to Emmaus was pursued by the Jews. The Twelfth Legion and its auxiliaries were defeated, and the Jews killed over 5,000 troops.[36]

The Jews now prepared for a more serious war, and it was at this point that they completed the wall to the north of the city which had been planned, but not finished, by Herod Agrippa (figure 4). They built the wall in an emergency, between the time of Cestius Gallus' defeat and the arrival of the Roman army under Vespasian in the spring. Hence it is not surprising that they used any stones which they could find, among them several which had been made for some of the monuments of the time of Herod the Great. During this emergency the Jewish troops under different leaders quarrelled, and perhaps at this stage the Christians made their escape to Pella, beyond the Jordan.

The main Roman army under Vespasian fought in Galilee for three years, and then Vespasian was made Emperor.[37] He left the Judean campaign to his son Titus, who went back to besiege Jerusalem. He arrived in January or February (70 AD). In May he broke through the new north wall, and a week later the wall round the markets built by Herod the Great. There was then continuous fighting to gain the Temple, for Herod the Great had not only made it magnificent, but very easy to defend.[38] The Romans took the strongest point on the Temple enclosure, the Antonia, late in July, and from there attacked the Temple, where sacrifice stopped on 6 August. The Romans entered the Temple on about 28 August, and then spent a month clearing the Upper City and the palace.[39]

Titus stayed a month more in Jerusalem. He completely destroyed the Temple, and gave orders that the rest of it and the whole city should be levelled with the ground. The only thing that he spared was the wall at the west of the city, to give protection to the Tenth Legion whom he left behind as the garrison, and the three towers at the north of the palace, Phasael, Mariamme and Hippicus.[40] The results of his order to destroy the city can be seen by the remains of the north wall, of which very few stones are left. But a month was not enough to ensure the destruction of such a large city as Jerusalem. Walls were demolished, but the outline of the city was to remain, even though the demolition of the walls made the area round the temple enclosure a ruin of discarded stones. Some Jews stayed in Jerusalem, but the council moved down to Jamnia and Jerusalem was no further use as the Jewish headquarters. The Jews had been thoroughly defeated, and it would take sixty years more before they could gather strength to make their final stand against Rome.

The Levant began to look more important as an eastern defence against the rivals of Rome, at this stage still the Parthians, and in 106

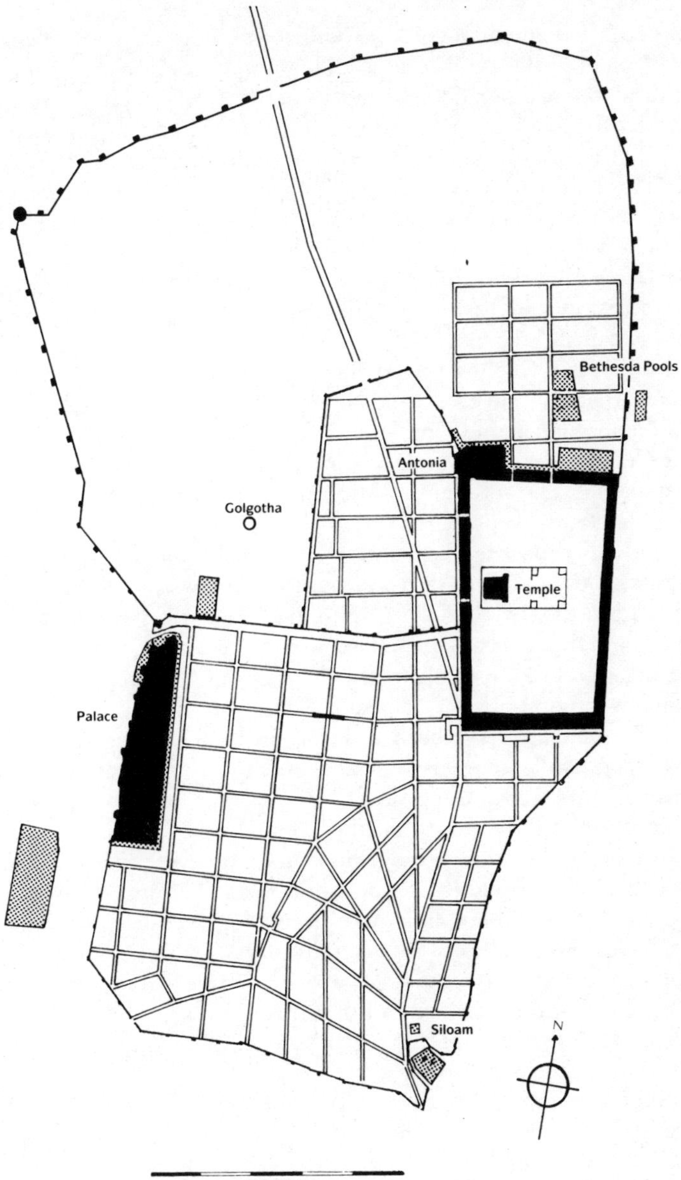

Fig. 4 Jerusalem in 68 AD

Emperor Trajan conquered the Nabatean kingdom, which became the Roman province of Arabia.[41] He set up forts along the frontier. Arabia stretched north to Bostra, its new capital, and in the south it crossed the Wadi 'Arabah and included the desert of Sinai to the south of Idumea. Later on in 357 this south part became Palaestina Tertia.[42] Hadrian, who succeeded Trajan, paid a visit to Arabia, and some of the Jews planned a further revolt against Rome. The leader of the revolt was Bar Cochba, whom some regarded as a Messiah. The occasion for the revolt was the news that Hadrian had forbidden circumcision and that he intended to make Jerusalem a Roman colony called Aelia Capitolina.

In 131 Bar Cochba forced the Romans and other non-Jews to leave Jerusalem. He proclaimed independence, and probably carried out the services in the Temple site as far as possible. But the forces of Bar Cochba were too small to survive. His men were driven from Jerusalem in 135, and Bar Cochba himself died at the siege of Bether, six miles southwest of Jerusalem.[43]

Hadrian proceeded with his plan to make Jerusalem a Roman colony, and the Roman decision was that no Jews should be allowed within the district of Aelia Capitolina. This was Jerusalem's new name, and the area contained the districts of Gophna, Herodium and the area west of Jerusalem which was called 'Oreinē', or 'Hill Country' (figure 5). The decree of Rome concerning the expulsion of Jews seems to have been couched in the following form: 'It is forbidden to all circumcised persons to enter and to stay within the territory of Aelia Capitolina. Any person contravening this prohibition shall be put to death.'[44] The decree was meant to stop Jews from living there, and Christians who were like Jews were probably also excluded. But almost all Semitic peoples are circumcised, and there must have been a lot of exceptions made to the decree. For example, the veterans of the Tenth Legion, soldiers who had served for twenty-five years, may have had the right to live in the city, and the majority of them were Syrians and Arabs. The defeat of the Jews meant that they were reduced from two-thirds to one-third of the population.

Aelia Capitolina was a new city, which was based on Herodian Jerusalem, but was divided in a different way. Stones from Herodian Jerusalem are reused in Aelia very frequently, but their presence is not enough to guarantee the fact that the monument was erected by Herod. There are two major texts describing Aelia. The first, which raises more questions than it solves, is the account of the buildings Hadrian erected which is part of the *Paschal Chronicle*. The questions

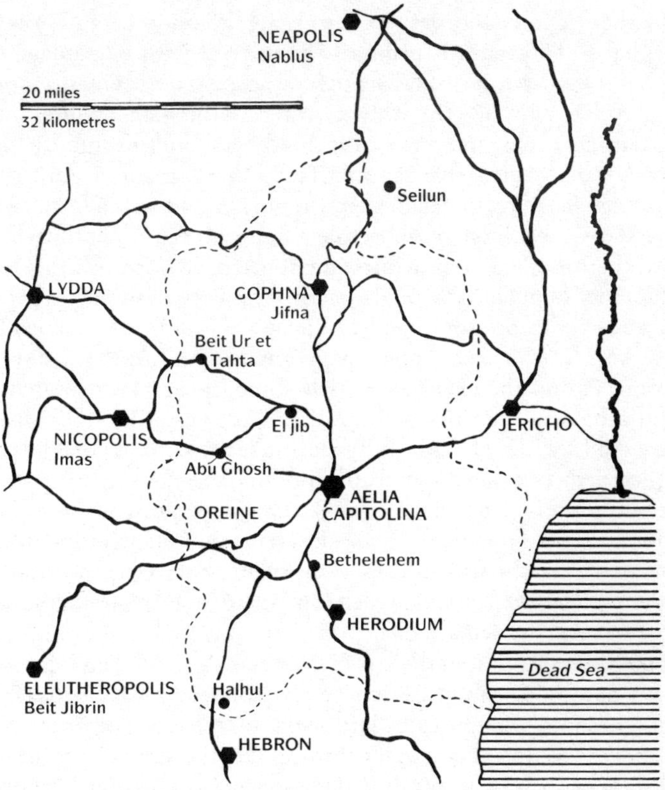

Fig. 5 District of Aelia Capitolina, where Jews were not allowed to live after 135 AD.

raised by this sentence will be dealt with in the bracketed sections.

> He founded the two *demosia* [which may mean any public building, such as halls, prisons, baths or amphitheatres], and the theatre, and the *tricamaron* ['three rooms', which might be the Temple of Jupiter Capitolinus, with three rooms dedicated to the gods Jupiter, Juno and Minerva], and the *tetranymphon* [which might be any pool dedicated to the nymphs, and may well be the square pool of Siloam], and the *dodecapylon* ['building with twelve gates'] formerly called *anabathmoi* ['flight of steps'], and the *quadra* ['square' – either *dodecapylon* or the *quadra* might be the enclosure which had held the Temple].[45]

The other text is the earliest surviving account of a Christian pilgrimage. Though it is primarily concerned with pilgrimage ten years after Constantine came to power it seems to explain a great deal about Aelia.[46] In fact the only two new Christian buildings are Constantine's two churches, which had been built during the first ten years of Roman rule favourable to the Christians. Christian pilgrimage had already taken shape in the 2nd century. We know of a cave shown to Christians in Bethlehem which the writer must have known before 130 AD, in which Christ had been born. We first hear of the Holy Sepulchre through a sermon preached in 160, where it says three times that the sepulchre is in the middle of Jerusalem.[47] Some sort of Christian pilgrimage must therefore have existed before 130, and the chances are that some of the places visited by pilgrims have as their first witness the memories of Jesus' disciples. As we shall see, not all of the holy places are the same as far as history is concerned. But one of the features of the earliest pilgrimage to be written down is that, apart from the two new churches which are mentioned, the remainder of the sites have no Christian buildings. They are the landmarks, plants, ruins of an eastern city, and except for the biblical associations which Christians attached to them, they were not specially remarkable.

The general layout of the city is shown in figure 6, and it is called by two names. The pilgrim, whose place of origin was Bordeaux in Gaul, goes into what he calls 'Jerusalem' by the east gate of the city, just north of the Temple enclosure. He is shown round the enclosure, which he is told was the remains of Solomon's Temple, and then goes out of one of the gates to the south of the enclosure. As he does this he is leaving Jerusalem. He goes west, and has the Pool of Siloam pointed out on his left, and it is to be noted that there is already a city wall running between the inner and the outer pools. Going on up to the top of the western hill he turns left through what he calls 'the wall of Sion'. He goes to the north, through what had a short time before been the camp of the Tenth Legion, and emerges by a door in the north wall by a street which leads toward the northern gate, the Gate of Neapolis. He is back in Jerusalem again. Thus the wall which bounded Jerusalem must have been at some point north of the gate where he left the Temple and since there was already a city wall meeting the west wall of the temple enclosure, it seems likely that this was the wall, but that it was made to face in the other direction. The area called 'Jerusalem' in Aelia Capitolina was thus a very small city, but since the later Roman cities were in some cases merely converted villages the size had nothing to do with its status as a city.

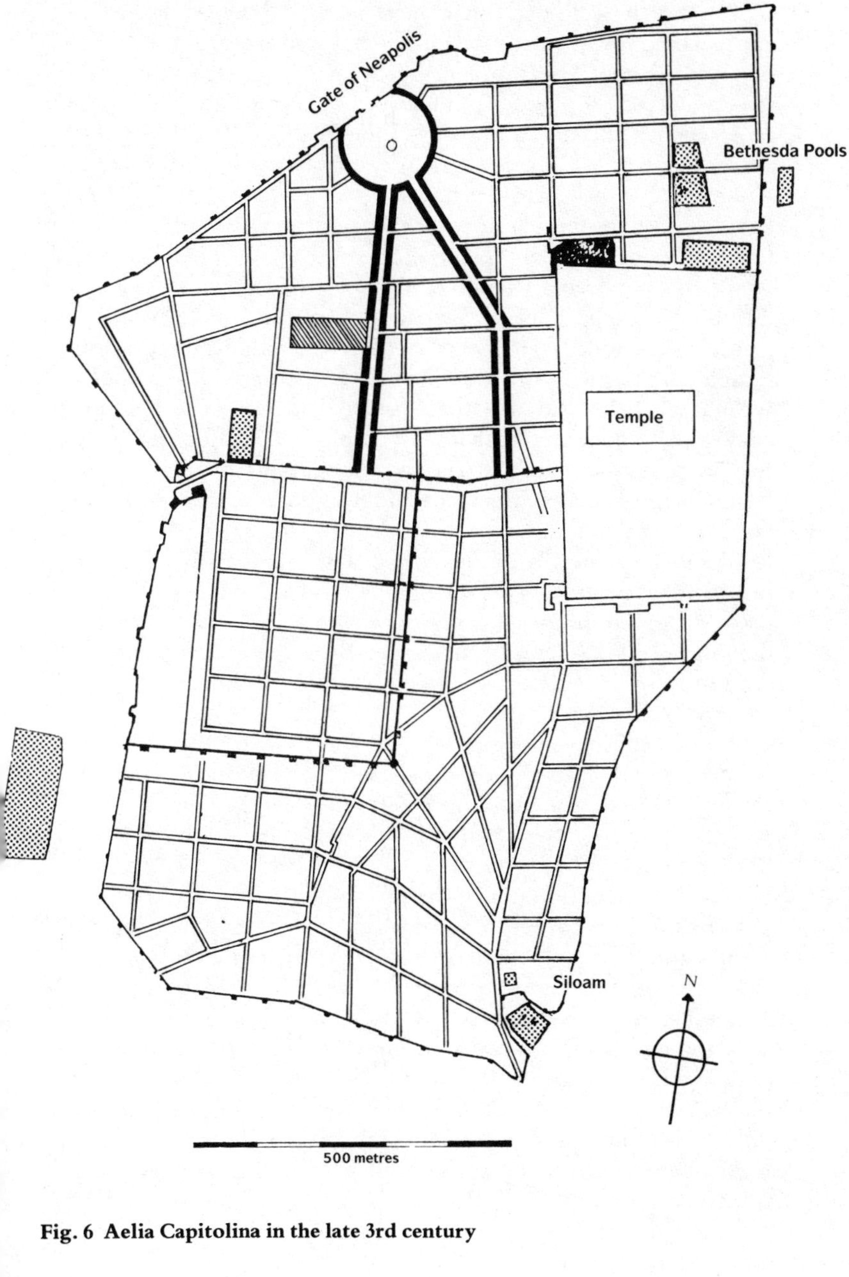

Fig. 6 Aelia Capitolina in the late 3rd century

The north wall was on a new line, and where it had hills approaching it was cut away from them by an artificial valley. Some of it was moated. The forum inside the north gate had two columned streets attached to it whose sidewalks were covered. This perhaps represents an addition to the city made in about 200 AD. Half way along the western street there was the entry to the Temple of Aphrodite, which had been built by Hadrian over the Holy Sepulchre. In the temple enclosure the pilgrim saw marble, and on it two statues of emperors, Hadrian and Antoninus Pius. The marble seems to have been a Roman addition to the ruined site where the Temple had stood. But the pilgrim, and a visitor who went to the Temple site about a century before him, say nothing about a Roman temple on the site of the Jewish one.[48] So perhaps Dio Cassius was wrong when he said that the Romans had built a temple in the enclosure,[49] and it may be that the Temple of Aphrodite, half way up the western colonnaded street, was neighbour to the Temple of Jupiter. Unfortunately the archaeological finds so far reported have not led to any clear layout for either of the Roman temples, except for the formal gateway of the temple (and later the Holy Sepulchre) in Khān al-Zait street. This is built of Herodian masonry, which was taken from the heaped-up masonry which was the result of the demolition of the temple enclosure. Both the inner moats at the Antonia and the palace were filled up, and the Antonia moat was covered by a street.

The Bordeaux pilgrim was shown four of the five places connected with Jesus in the Gospels, but the place shown him where Pilate tried Jesus is in a strange position. When the pilgrim emerges from Sion through the north wall he sees to the right the ruins of the house of Pilate.[50] In fact this may not have been the house of Pilate, but it may well be the council chamber where Christ was tried by the Jewish council before he was taken to Pilate. Early pilgrimages in Aelia Capitolina could not have visited the palace where Pilate lived, since this was in a military area. The trial of Jesus had to be remembered somewhere else. And this may have been the reason why the trial by Pilate was not linked with the citadel (the palace built by Herod), but with some other ruins.[51] Apart from these places there were some which were purely devotional, like the cave 'On the Mount of Olives', where both parts of Jesus' teaching were remembered and also his Ascension, which was a strange thing to remember in a cave.[52] There were also some places which did not correspond to places in the Bible, but were already based on the stories told by local guides.

The official religion of Aelia Capitolina was the official religion of the Roman empire, and there are signs of the worship of Serapis (the Egyptian-Greek god of healing) at Bethesda Pool. But Christians seem to have been of the same race as the other people. Two of the bishops of the 3rd century had the names Mazabanes and Zabdas,[53] names which come from Palmyra which was a strong Arab centre at that time. They started as a minority, worshipping in a house just to the south of the legionary camp which occupied the present Armenian quarter which they called Sion. This was doubtless called after the heavenly Sion mentioned in the New Testament,[54] and a sign that the church stood for heaven. But the church grew from a minority into a force seriously to be reckoned with in the 3rd century. Eusebius, who had been born in Caesarea Maritima in about 260, and later its bishop, wrote an *Ecclesiastical History* in which he describes the growth. House churches were being replaced with larger church buildings.[55] One of the greatest – and later on the most controversial – of Christian teachers took up his residence in Caesarea, Origen the Alexandrian. Christians were growing in confidence, but they were still members of an illegal community. The case of the Emperor Philip is a good example of their dilemma. Philip was an Arabian from the village of Shahba, east of Busra Eski Sham and he was a Christian. But when he reigned as Emperor from 244 to 249 he had to give up his Christianity. He favoured Christians, but the public duties of a Roman emperor prevented him worshipping in a Christian way, and meant that he had to take part in many pagan rites.[56] Fifty years later Emperor Diocletian, feeling the threat from Christians, took steps to curb their growing power. He ordered the army to be purged of Christians, and in 303 decreed that all Christian scriptures should be burned and all church buildings destroyed.[57] Christianity was not permitted, and Christian leaders were made to sacrifice to the Roman gods. Two people from Aelia were martyred, Procopius and Vales. This persecution went on at intervals for seven years, till 310.

But another person was soon to take power who was willing to regard the Christians as friends. In 312 Constantine ordered that churches should be rebuilt at the state's expense. And in 324 he came to control the east part of the empire. He was not himself a Christian, for the same reason that Philip the Arab was not. But he had had a dream of some Christian symbol with the words 'In this sign conquer!'[58] just before he defeated his rival at the Milvian Bridge outside Rome. He was determined that Christianity should prosper and be united, and when he came towards the end of his life he

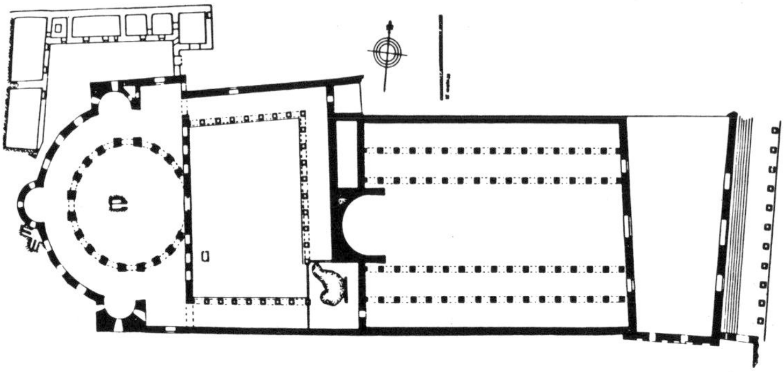

Fig. 7 The 4th century church buildings on the Holy Sepulchre site

became a Christian by being baptised.

Jerusalem was thus turned from a Roman city with very little interest to the Empire into a city of great importance. The history of the city is thus largely to be understood in terms of its Christianity, and as a centre of pilgrimage. In view of this Constantine ordered the Holy Sepulchre to be uncovered. The site was known as the 'Martyrium',[59] and the first church built by Constantine had that name. Figure 7 shows the plan of the buildings started by Constantine on the site, but they were not all completed at once. After the Jerusalem Christians had found the Holy Sepulchre a priest named Eustathius was sent from Constantinople to start building the church, and later on an architect called Zenobius (another Palmyrene name).[60] The Bishop of Jerusalem first decorated the tomb and gave it a porch, but the circular building was not yet built round it. They went on to build the court with Golgotha in the corner, and the Martyrium Church to the east of it, with the court from which people came in from the street. The Anastasis, as far as we can tell from Eusebius' *Life of Constantine*,[61] was not yet built for nine years, and the first record of its completion comes in 347, ten years after Constantine's death. It may be that Zenobius was sent in 336 to complete the church, but that on Constantine's death he became short of money. Indeed the most recent scholar to examine the Anastasis believes that the columns surrounding the tomb were originally columns cut down to half size.

Constantine's policy was the same as Hadrian's towards the Jews. They were not allowed to live in Jerusalem, but they made pilgrimage to the western wall of the Temple, and once a year on

'The Ninth of Āb' they were allowed into the Temple site to lament its destruction.[62] Christians on the other hand were triumphant.[63] After a life like Eusebius' where he had seen the churches grow, only to be destroyed in 303, and a long period of persecution beginning, the new tolerance to the church seemed one of God's special blessings. The character of Jerusalem soon changed, and seventy years after Constantine had come to power the city was full of monks and nuns. Public services in Jerusalem were conducted in Greek with an official translator standing by who said the words in Aramaic.[64] Hence the words were in both the languages of Syria. But when foreigners came, for instance Latin-speakers, there were unofficial translators into Latin. Foreign visitors came to Jerusalem in considerable numbers.[65] Some went back to spread the news of a newly-active church in Jerusalem, some of whose customs were noticed by the visitors and followed when they returned home. Some foreign visitors stayed, and many became monks and nuns. The monastic life had started in Egypt, but soon a reputation for holiness was gained by the monks and nuns in Palestine, and the desert of Judea to the east of Jerusalem became a school of monks whose nationalities were Latins, Persians, Indians, Ethiopians and Armenians. Since they were out in the desert the monks sometimes had great influence over bedouin tribes, and St Euthymius, one of the greatest Armenian monks, converted Aspebet, an Arab exiled from Persia, and had him made bishop of his tribe. The bishopric was called 'The Camp'.[66]

An interruption to the new peace of the church was caused by Julian's reign. As the Roman Emperor he decided to encourage everyone to return to their old religion. He therefore gave the Jews the right to live in Jerusalem, and the opportunity to rebuild their Temple. Some of the Jews were doubtful whether an order given by a Roman Emperor could be the right way to start rebuilding, for they expected the return of the Messiah to be the sign. The Temple was begun, but work ceased because of an earthquake, and as Julian himself died two months later, and the Emperor who succeeded him was an orthodox Christian, the building was abandoned.[67]

The Jews had been considerably reduced in numbers by the Second Jewish War, and after 135 many of them fled to Syria and Egypt. From being about two-thirds of the population, a majority in Palestine, they were now reduced to one third, according to Professor Michael Avi-Yonah. Apart from his studies, which concern the population of Jews in Palestine, what other evidence can we bring to bear on the question of who lived in Palestine in the Byzantine period?

The population cannot in fact be counted, since we do not know the total. Let us guess that it was about two million, as it was in the Palestine of 1947. In fact there are two easy (and to that extent unreliable) ways to judge the religious make-up of the people. The first is to count the number of villages in a list published in 337 AD, and see whether any are described in religious terms.[68] The second is to count the number of religious buildings of the Roman and Byzantine periods which have been excavated.

The list of villages was compiled by Eusebius of Caesarea in order to say what the location was of places mentioned in the Bible. It is incomplete, since it is only concerned with this subject. A summary of its results is given in figure 8, the left-hand diagram. 287 villages are mentioned for which no religion is named. There are eleven Jewish villages, all but two of them described as large, perhaps six Samaritan, and only three Christian. Since the Bible does not describe many sites in Galilee, where half of the Jews were living, it is unlikely to have a big enough proportion of Jews, even though Samaritans and Christians may be in the right proportions for 337 AD.

The second way of counting is to add up all the religious buildings which have been excavated from this period.[69] The right-hand diagram in figure 8 summarises these, but it is to be remembered that all the religious buildings which were erected at any time during the period are included. These number 356 buildings, 260 churches, and of synagogues 85 Jewish and 11 Samaritan. This method too has its limitations. There is nothing said about other religions. And of the synagogues more than three had probably gone out of use well before half way through the period.

In fact Avi-Yonah gives results which make a good deal of sense out of these figures. His guess about the effect on the Jews of the Second Jewish War is illustrated on the left side of the graph in figure 9. He argues that economic and political troubles in the 3rd century reduced the Jewish part of the population from one-third to one-fifth, and then there was a steady but slow decline to about 9 per cent.[70] His figures do not precisely agree with the other two methods, but they harmonize with them. The result is at least clear in showing the Jews after the end of the 3rd century were a small minority in Palestine. The majority of the villages described by Eusebius in 337 was pagan,★ but the large number of churches found

★ Many of these pagan villages were populated by Arabs. Arab tribes lived in Palestine and in the vicinity of Jerusalem centuries before the Arab conquest of the city in 637. Among those tribes were Lakhm, Judhām, ʻĀmila, Kinda, Qais and Kināna. There were also several clans belonging to the Qaḥṭānī tribe of Quḍāʻa. (Source: Yaʻqūbī, ibn Wādiḥ, *Kitāb al-Buldān*, Leiden, Brill, 1860, p. 117.)

The Editor

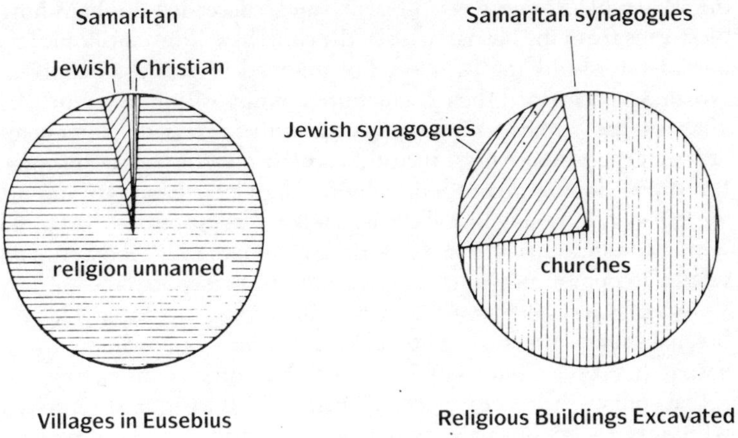

Fig. 8 Eusebius' count of religious villages, and totals of religious buildings excavated in Palestine.

show that they were mostly converted to Christianity by 638 AD, the end of the period covered in this chapter.

The last two centuries of Byzantine rule over Palestine were marked by a great disagreement which on the face of it was doctrinal. It started with the Council of Ephesus, at which the bishops of all the church except the Syrian bishops and the legates of

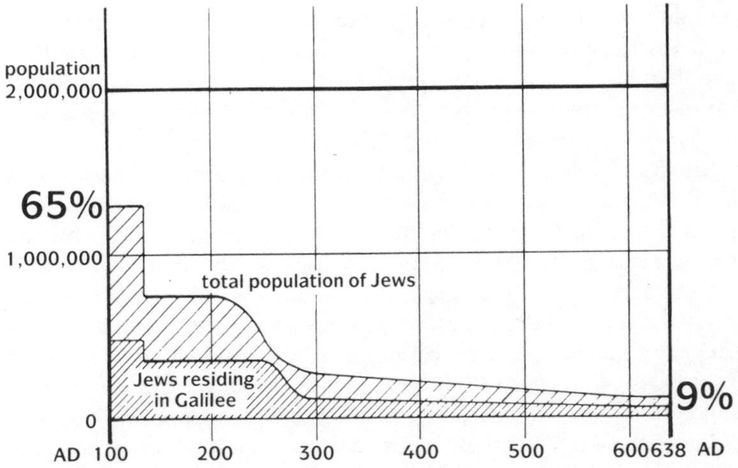

Fig. 9 Diagram of Professor Michael Avi-Yonah's estimate of the number of Jewish residents in Byzantine Palestine

the Pope of Rome were present, and succeeded in banishing Nestorius from the Patriarchate of the church of Constantinople. As one of the results the people who followed Nestorius, mainly in North Syria, formed their own church in opposition to the official view of the Empire. Two years later there was an agreement between the proponent of the official view and the Syrian bishops. But the bishops were not won over to adopt exactly and to support the view of the council. In fact this doctrinal question also had to do with the question of independence from Byzantine power, and would go on not only until 638 but until the present day.

As far as Jerusalem was concerned the bishop elected in 428 was Juvenal, who was not content to be bishop but wanted to be patriarch. At the Council of Ephesus he put forward his claims, but at that council they were rejected. Then in 438 the Empress Eudokia, who was to be Juvenal's opponent for thirteen years, came on pilgrimage to Jerusalem. Eudokia liked Jerusalem, and when in 444 AD she had a disagreement with her family, and in particular the Emperor's sister Pulcheria, Eudokia was sent into exile to Jerusalem. Due to her rank she ruled Palestine.

At first, largely through her disagreement with Pulcheria, she opposed the official Byzantine view of the disputed doctrine, and supported the independence movement, which included a great many monks throughout Syria and Palestine. She was extremely generous to Christians and built them many monasteries, hostels and churches. She is also credited by many modern scholars with building the walls of Jerusalem, but 'walls' may in fact mean the ecclesiastical buildings. It rests on a quotation, no doubt used by people who wished to get funds from Eudokia. *Eudokia* in Greek means 'good pleasure', and Psalm 51:18 says, 'In thy good pleasure (*eudokia*) build thou the walls of Jerusalem'.[71]

In 451 there was another international council of bishops, called by Pulcheria, which met in Chalcedon. A minor achievement was Juvenal's claim to be patriarch, which succeeded in 451. But the newly-elected patriarch was thought to have obtained his patriarchate through treachery. Word came back to Eudokia that the party she supported was beaten, and this party, the Monophysites as they were called, formed separate churches, of which the Copts and Ethiopians, the Syrian Jacobites and the Armenians are the modern representatives, which shows how widely the opposition spread geographically. A Monophysite bishop of Jerusalem, the monk Theodosius, was appointed, and when Juvenal returned as patriarch with a guard of soldiers he was forced to go into hiding in the desert of Ruba, just west of Qumran.[72]

When Bishop Theodosius died in 457 Eudokia looked at the confusion in the church, and, not knowing what to do, she wrote to the holiest man she knew, St Simeon Stylites who lived on his pillar near Antioch. She asked for a teacher, and St Simeon replied that she had a teacher close at hand in the monk Euthymius. She met Euthymius, and was so impressed with him that she was reconciled to the orthodox patriarch Anastasius, who had succeeded Juvenal.[73] Eudokia's last act was to build the church of St Stephen three hundred and fifty metres north of the Damascus Gate. The building was finished in 460, St Stephen's relics were laid there, and very soon afterwards Eudokia died, and was also buried in the church.[74]

Doctrinal peace was not yet restored to the church, and quarrels succeeded each other for the next ninety years. Peace was threatened by the determination of the Samaritans to declare an independent state. In 484 they rose up and nominated a king called Justus. They were cruelly defeated by Emperor Zeno, and a church built on their place of sacrifice on Mount Gerizim. In 529, under the Emperor Justinian, they again revolted, this time under a king called Julianus, and did a great deal of damage to churches. In the area of Jerusalem they destroyed the churches in Emmaus (Nikopolis, now Latrun) and Bethlehem. Emperor Justinian was the last person to build a church in Jerusalem in the Byzantine period.[75] Besides rebuilding a church at Bethlehem he continued to build a church which had been planned by the Arab patriarch Elias and St Saba and called 'New Church of the Mother of God'. The church was destroyed by an earthquake, but the foundations have been excavated. The church complex contained two hospitals with a hundred beds for sick pilgrims, and another hundred for local people.[76]

This is the latest church on the mosaic map of the Holy Land, which was found on the floor of a Byzantine church at Madaba, across the Jordan. It was made in about 575 and is shown in plate 10. The top of the map is east, and the walls are arranged in an oval of which the top left hand corner is missing: it may have contained the pools and church at Siloam. Only the west wall of the temple enclosure is shown. The lower of the two columned streets (see figure 10) goes past the Martyrium church, which is shown upside down as the central feature below the bottom street, and on to the New Church of the Mother of God. It ends at the wall of Sion, and the vertical line to the right of the New Church may perhaps

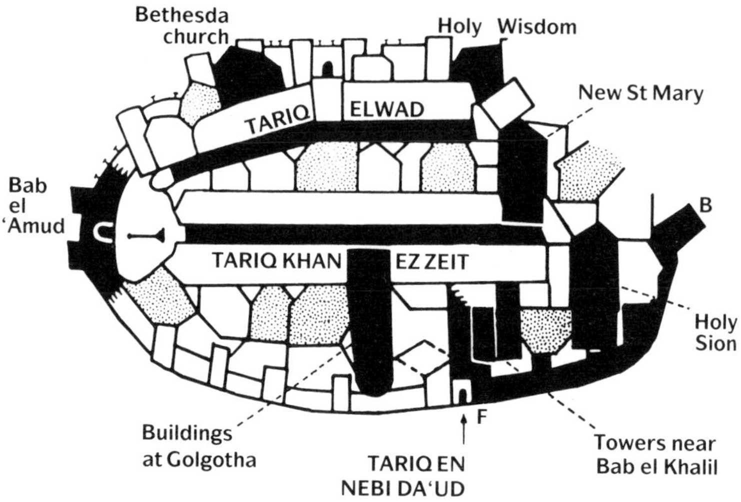

Fig. 10 Key to the Madaba mosaic map (see plate 10)

represent the continuation to the east of the wall. The end of the upper columned street has an arch near the north gate, which may perhaps be the old gate of the wall with which Herod the Great enclosed the market area. The road continues to the right, and has a fork running to the east gate, then it goes on to the bridge which carries the road over from the upper city to the temple enclosure platform. Beyond this it cannot be seen, but it was also extended, so the excavations show, to beyond the present Dung Gate. Churches which it is possible to identify are the church at Bethesda by the east gate, Holy Zion down in the bottom right corner, and a church which is up next to the crack and next to the bridge. This is the Church of Holy Wisdom, the place where Christians commemorated Christ's Trial by Pilate. The map of Jerusalem in the 6th century is shown in figure 11.

The Parthians had been attacking Rome ever since 41 BC. But in 224 AD Ardashir, the grandson of Sasan, conquered the Parthians and created a new Sasanid Persian empire.[77] He renewed the attack against Rome, and in 260 AD even the Emperor Valerian fell into Persian hands. Justinian made a fifty-year treaty of peace with Persia, and Chosroes II owed his place on the Persian throne partly to the friendship of the Byzantine Emperor Maurice. Chosroes started to reign in 591. But in 602 Maurice died, and Chosroes invaded Syria. When his general, Shahr-Barz, took Damascus in 613 he cut off

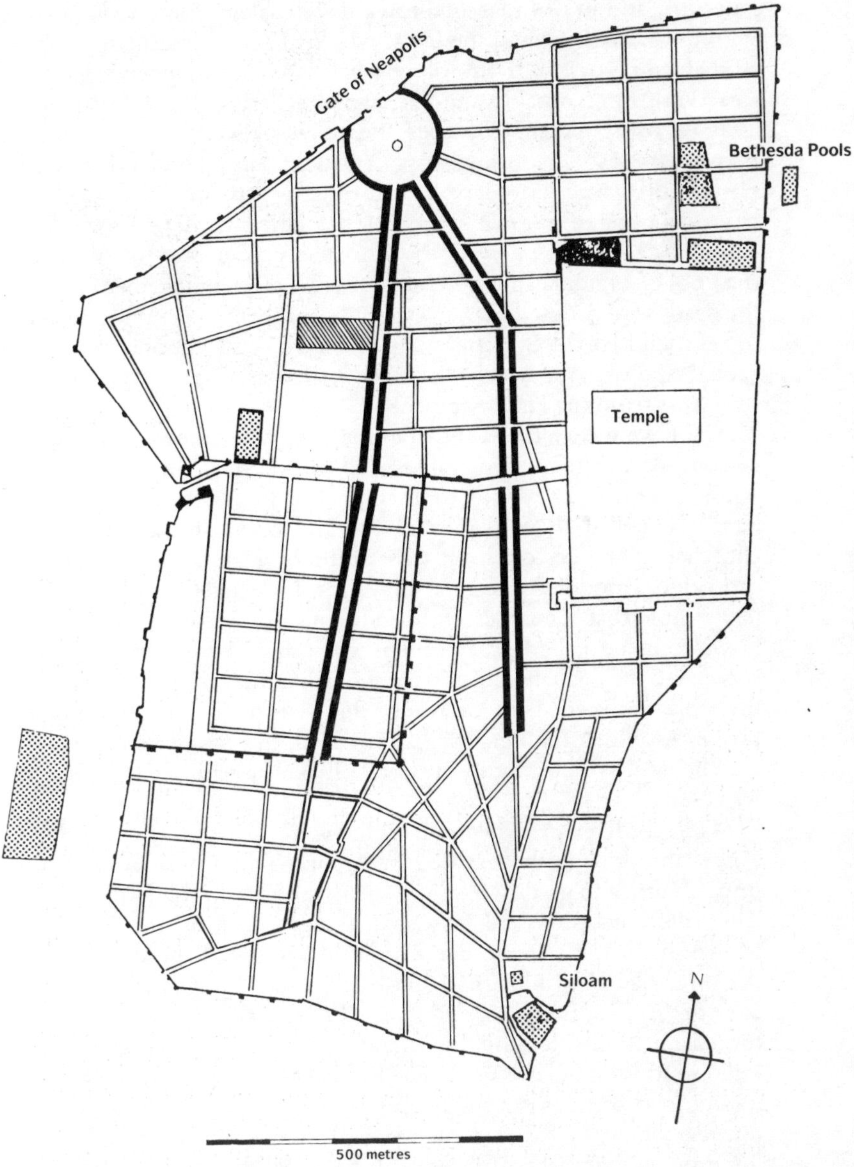

Fig. 11 Jerusalem in the late 6th century

Palestine, and in 614 marched towards Jerusalem. He was friendly with the Samaritans and the Jews, who had been persecuted by the Roman emperors, and some of the Christians in Jerusalem wished to treat with him, notably the Patriarch Zacharias. But he was not allowed to approach Chosroes. Peace was disturbed by a fight between Christian and Jewish young men. The Persians therefore started to besiege Jerusalem, and forty days later they entered the city, slaughtered a great many of the citizens, and burned the churches.[78] A great many of the Christian prisoners were taken to the Pool of Māmillā and were sold as slaves or died there, and when the dead were counted there were 33,877 of them.[79] Prisoners likely to be useful to the Persians were taken away to Ctesiphon, their capital, and with them went Patriarch Zacharias, carrying the relic of the Cross from the Holy Sepulchre.

The Jews were left in control of the city, while the Persian army continued. But they then realised the weakness of the Jews in the whole country. They thus took control of Jerusalem from Jewish hands, expelled them from the city by force, and allowed the churches to be restored. In 628 Emperor Heraclius, after long campaigns, mounted a counter-attack, and reached Ctesiphon. The news came that Chosroes was dead. The Roman army was most unwelcome near the Persian capital when those who were likely to succeed to the Persian kingship were starting their rivalry. Heraclius therefore succeeded in securing the return of the Byzantine provinces which the Persians had invaded, the release of captives, and the return of the relic of the Cross. In 629 he returned the relic to Jerusalem.

While the Roman and Persian armies were confronting each other a new threat to both appeared in Arabia. This threat caused the imperial army to go down to Mu'ta, six kilometres south of Kerak. They defeated three chiefs who had been sent by the Prophet Muḥammad. Only the leader whom the army had appointed after the three had been killed, Khālid b. al-Walīd, escaped. Five years later the Arabs came back and reached the outskirts of Gaza. They turned north and fought the imperial forces at Ajnadain, twenty miles southwest of Jerusalem. The Roman forces were defeated, and for the rest of the year the people in the cities were afraid to go outside the walls for fear of attack. It was even impossible for Sophronius, patriarch of Jerusalem, to travel the short distance to Bethlehem on Christmas day.[80] Another defeat of the Roman army took place at the Yarmouk in 636, and the army retreated finally from Syria.

Jerusalem still remained intact, and some of the citizens still hoped for a return of the Roman army. It had been besieged by the Arabs from 637, but they were hesitant to overpower it, since they were not familiar with the economy of Syria and wished its wealth to continue under the men who had managed it before. In 638 the Caliph 'Umar received the message that Aelia would surrender, but to him alone. He therefore set out from Jabia near the Sea of Galilee, soon to receive the surrender of the patriarch, and in return guarantee the security of the city.

NOTES

1 Josephus, *War*, 1, 403.
2 Strabo, *Geography*, XVI, 2, 34 (Loeb vol. VII, 281). See also *The History of Barsauma of Nisibis*, ed. F Nau, *Resumé de Monographies Syriacques*, 8(18), 1913, 274.
3 Josephus, *Antiquities of the Jews*, 15, 254, 365.
4 Junior Philosophus, ed. A Riese, *Geographi Latini Minores*, Heilbron, 1878, 110f.
5 Josephus, *War*, 1, 155–58.
6 Ibid, 203.
7 Ibid, 181.
8 Ibid, 349–53.
9 Ibid, 388–90.
10 Ibid, 426–28.
11 Josephus, *Ant.*, 15, 292.
12 Ibid, 311.
13 Ibid, 318.
14 Josephus, *War*, 2.439, 5.163–5.
15 See N Avigad, *Discovering Jerusalem*, Nashville, Tennessee, 1983, 83-95 and figure 77.
16 Josephus, *Ant.*, 15.388–90.
17 Ibid, 20.219.
18 Josephus, *War*, 5.190–2.
19 Josephus, *Ant.*, 15.412–13.
20 Josephus, *War*, 5.146.
21 See R Blomme, 'Faut-il revenir sur la datation de l'Arc de l'"Ecce Homo"?', *Revue Biblique*, 1979, 244–71.
22 Josephus, *War*, 5.181.
23 Josephus, *War*, 2.44 and *Ant.*, 15.268.
24 Josephus, *Ant.*, 17.189.
25 Josephus, *Ant.*, 17.355.
26 Luke 2:1.
27 Matthew 2:16.
28 Mark 8:29.
29 John 9:7.
30 John 5:2.
31 Mark 14:32, and Josephus, *War*, 6.5–6.
32 John 19:42.
33 Acts 5:39.
34 Josephus, *Ant.*, 20.161, 168, 171.
35 Josephus, *War*, 2.296.
36 Ibid, 540.
37 Ibid, 4.588.
38 Josephus, *Ant.*, 15.396.
39 Josephus, *War*, 6.374.
40 Ibid, 7.1.
41 Dio Cassius, *Roman History*, 78.14.5. (Loeb vol. VII, 389).
42 Libanius, *Letter*, 337.

43 Justin Martyr, *I Apol.* (tr. T B Falls in series FC = Fathers of the Church, 84), Eusebius, *Eccl. Hist.*, 4.6.
44 The late Professor Michael Avi-Yonah's reconstruction in *The Jews of Palestine*, Oxford, 1976, 19, 132–3, 222, 241.
45 *Paschal Chronicle* in *Patrologia Graeca*, 92.613.
46 *Itinerarium Burdigalense* in *Corpus Christianorum* 175, 13–21, and English translation in J Wilkinson, *Egeria's Travels*, Warminster, 1981, 153–63.
47 Melito of Sardis, *On Pascha*, ed. S G Hall, 72, 94.
48 Origen, *C. Matt.*, 24.15 (Fr. 469, iv), *GCS* XII, 193f.
49 Dio Cassius, *Roman History*, 69.12 (Loeb vol. VII, 447).
50 *Itin. Burd.*, 593.2, 17 (tr. 158).
51 Antoninus Piacentinus, *Itin*, 23 (*Corpus Christianorum* 175, 141 and translation in J Wilkinson, *Jerusalem Pilgrims before the Crusades*, Warminster, 1977, 84).
52 *Acts of John* 97:102 (tr. M R James, *The Apocryphal New Testament*, Oxford, 1924, 254), Eusebius, *Dem. Ev.* IV.18.20–23 (*GCS*[VI], 278), *Itin. Burd.*, 595.5 (18, tr. 160).
53 Eusebius, *Eccl. Hist.*, 4, 6 (tr. McGiffert in series *NPNF* = Nicene and Post-Nicene Fathers, 177) and Cyril of Jerusalem, *Cat.*, 16.4 (tr. L P McCauley in *FC* second vol., 78).
54 Hebrews 12:22.
55 Eusebius, *Eccl. Hist.*, 8.1–2 (tr. 323).
56 See F M Abel, *Histoire de la Palestine*, vol. 2, Paris, 1952, 199.
57 Eusebius, *Eccl. Hist.*, 8.1–2 (tr. 323).
58 Eusebius, *Life of Constantine*, 1.27 (tr. McGiffert, *NPNF*, 489).
59 Zephaniah 3:9, cited by Cyril of Jerusalem, *Cat.*, 14.9, *PG*, 33.832 (tr. second vol. 35).
60 Philostorgius (ed. J Bidez, fr. 13, *GCS* 208) quoted by Theophanes, *Chronographia*, ed. de Boor, 33.11.
61 Eusebius, *Life of Constantine*, 3.33–39 (tr. 529f.).
62 *Itin. Burd.*, 591.5 (16, tr. 197), Exodus R. 2.2
63 Jerome, *Comm. Soph.*, 1.15 (ed. M Adrian, *Corpus Christianorum* 76A, 673).
64 *Egeria's Travels*, tr. J Wilkinson, 47.3–4, 146.
65 Jerome, *Ep.*, 46.10, 108.33 (tr. W H Fremantle, *NPNF*, 211).
66 Cyril of Scythopolis, *Life of Euthymius*, 78 (tr. Festugière, 24.17) and 80 (26.12).
67 Gregory of Nazianzus, *Or. V. contra Julianum*, 4 (*GCS* 35, 688).
68 Eusebius, *Onomasticon*, *GCS* III, 1.
69 Synagogues are taken from F Hüttenmeister and G Reeg, *Die antiken Synagogen in Israel*, (*BTAVO* B.12.1–2), Wiesbaden, 1977, and churches from A Ovadiah and C G de Silva, *Levant* 16, 154–164.
70 M Avi-Yonah, *The Jews of Palestine*, 132–3, 241.
71 John Malalas, *Chron.*, 14, (*PG* 97.532–3).
72 Zacharias Rhetor, *Hist.*, 2, 3 (ed. E W Brooks, *CSCO Scr. Syr.* 3.5, 108–9).
73 Cyril of Scythopolis, *Life of Euthymius*, 102–3 (49.3).
74 Ibid, 107 (53.5).
75 *Codex Iustin.* I, tit. V, 12, 10 and John Malalas, *Chron.*, 18 (*PG* 97.667).
76 Procopius of Caesarea, *The Buildings of Justinian*, 5.6.22–26 (Loeb vol. VII, 347).
77 Dio Cassius, *Roman History*, 80.3 (Loeb vol. IX, 483).
78 Sebeos, *Histoire d'Heraclius*, (tr. F Macler, Paris, 1904) 24, 64–70.
79 Strategius, *Capture of Jerusalem*, 9.5–6 (ed. and tr. G Garitte, *CSCO* 203, 16).
80 Sophronius, *Orat.* 1, *On the Birthday of Christ* (ed. H Usener, *Kleine Schriften* 4, Leipzig, 1913, 173, 175).

CHAPTER IV

Jerusalem in the Early Islamic Period 7th–11th Centuries AD

Abdul Aziz Duri

The early Islamic period in the history of Jerusalem begins with the conquest of the city some five years after the death of the prophet Muḥammad, and ends with the occupation of Jerusalem by the Crusaders in 1099.

Veneration for Bait al-Maqdis started from the beginning of Islam. The verse on the *Isrā'*,[1] revealed in Mecca about a year before the *Hijra* (*c*.621),[2] refers to the *Isrā'* (nocturnal journey of the Prophet) from Mecca (al-Masjid al-Ḥarām) to al-Masjid al-Aqṣā. Many early reports explain that by al-Aqṣā is meant Bait al-Maqdis, or preferably the Ḥaram (the Noble Sanctuary), and adds that the ascension (*Mi'rāj*) was from there.[3] Many commentaries and pious stories on the ascension followed to develop later into a vast literature.

Bait al-Maqdis was further elevated when it became the first *qibla* – direction of prayer – in Medina. Zuhrī (d. 741) reports that the mosque built by the Prophet had its *qibla* towards Bait al-Maqdis.[4] Early reports agree that this was immediately after the *Hijra* to Medina, and continued for about a year and a half,[5] before the Muslims were directed to turn to Mecca in their prayers.[6]

Traditions contributed much to the sanctity of Bait al-Maqdis, especially the famous *Ḥadīth*: '. . . you shall only set out to three mosques, the Ḥarām mosque [in Mecca], my mosque [in Medina], and the Aqṣā mosque.'[7] Though reported with slight verbal variants, it gave al-Masjid al-Aqṣā an elevated position.[8]

Other *āthār* (sayings) attributed to the *Ṣaḥabā'* (Companions) and *ṭābi'ūn* (followers) circulated early, reflecting the growing veneration for Bait al-Maqdis.[9]

Accounts of the conquest of Bait al-Maqdis, its date, 'Umar's visit, and the *ṣulḥ* (pact) with it, varied. They are coloured by local, political, and religious interests, and this is indicative of the city's special position.

Reports differ about the date of the conquest of the city and its surrender. Saif b. 'Umar (180/790), in Ṭabarī, gives too early a date, 15/636,[10] while some reports make it 17/638.[11] But it is generally held that 'Umar stopped at Sargh in 17 AH[12] because of the plague. Most early reports put the date of the conquest in 16/637,[13] and this seems to be more likely.

Reports also differ whether Jerusalem surrendered to a commander (Abu 'Ubaida) or the caliph 'Umar in person. The visit of the caliph, which is definite, partly accounts for this. A critique of the sources shows that Syrian reports indicate that Jerusalem stipulated the presence of the caliph for surrender, and that the *ṣulḥ* was given by him.[14] Medinese reports[15] and Kūfī reports (usually from Kūfā and Medina)[16] make the surrender of Jerusalem to commanders of 'Umar. It seems that reports which assert the presence of the caliph in the surrender of Jerusalem, and his *ṣulḥ* with it, want to emphasise the importance of the city. Non-Muslim reports and tales follow the same line in their interest.[17]

There was no military (or strategic) importance for the city, and it could not impose special conditions on the conqueror. Its surrender and *ṣulḥ* came under the supervision of Abu 'Ubaida. 'Umar came at that time to Jābiya (the main station for the Arab forces) in order to look into the affairs of Syria and the Arab forces there. He then visited Jerusalem, the place of the *Isrā'* and the first of the two *qiblas*. His presence could be taken as a confirmation of the *ṣulḥ*, and this probably lent itself to accounts stipulating his presence.[18]

Accounts differ again about the terms of the *ṣulḥ* with Jerusalem, especially between the early and later sources. This is probably related to the city's sanctity, with its great churches, and the development of relations with the Christians. Early reports generally indicate that the *ṣulḥ* was in line with pacts given to other cities in Syria. It guaranteed the safety of the people, their property, and their churches, in return for the payment of the *jizya* (poll-tax).[19] Ya'qūbī (284/897) was the first to give the text: 'You are given safety of your persons, properties and churches which will not be encroached upon [lit. inhabited] or destroyed unless you cause some public harm.'[20] A similar text is given by Eutychius.[21] This is in line with the general trend of pacts of the conquest.

But whereas the *ṣulḥ* with other cities or conquered provinces is only referred to in the annals of the conquest, the text of the *ṣulḥ* with Bait al-Maqdis seems to develop in context, and to assume wider dimensions (to cover all Christians in Syria).[22] Already, Saif b. 'Umar gives some significant additions. Their churches are not to be 'inhabited' or destroyed, and not to be encroached upon or partly seized. The people are not to be compelled (*yukrahūna*) in religion and not to be maltreated (*yuḍārrūna*), then 'no Jew is to live with them [i.e. Christians] in Ilya [i.e. Aelia Capitolina].'[23] Such details are out of step with the trend of the types of *ṣulḥ* at the time, and could only reflect later trends. The reference to the Jews finds no support in Arab sources, and only Michael the Syrian mentions it.[24] It is probably of Christian provenance, and a late source, Ḥimyarī, states that 'the Christians made it a condition that Jews are not to be allowed to live with them.'[25] Ibn al-Jawzī, who seems to give the same account of the *ṣulḥ* produced by Saif, does not mention the Jews.[26]

Al-Muṭahhar al-Maqdisī refers to the *ṣulḥ* which stipulated that churches would not be destroyed and monks would not be driven away.[27] In the 5th/11th century, however, we receive the much enlarged text, and it is now called 'the covenant of 'Umar' (*al-'Uhda al-'Umariyya*). It is first given by al-Musharraf b. al-Murajjā (5th/11th century) as the *'Ahd* of 'Umar to Bait al-Maqdis (and other cities in Syria), and it is what the people of Jerusalem pledged to observe.[28] The text of the covenant in Ibn 'Asākir[29] (571/1176), Mujīr al-Dīn al-Ḥanbalī[30] and Ibn Qayyim al-Jawziyya[31] follow closely the lines of al-Musharraf, with little variation. Besides, the first reference to a text of the *'Ahd* kept by the people of Bait al-Maqdis comes from Ibn A'tham (314/926) who says: '. . . and 'Umar wrote them a writ [*kitāb*] which they inherit until our time, and God knows best.'[32]

Such development in the terms of the *ṣulḥ* could be linked to some important factors: the sanctity of Bait al-Maqdis for Christians, its having the first patriarch and the most venerated churches, and its being the centre for pilgrimage. But the development of relations with the Christians, starting with the caliph, 'Umar b. 'Abd al-'Azīz, to Hārūn al-Rashīd, to al-Mutawakkil, and to the Fāṭimids, has a direct bearing on the question.[33] The fact that the *'Ahd* of 'Umar developed from a *ṣulḥ* by the Muslims, to pledges undertaken by the people of Bait al-Maqdis, leads to the conclusion that the text of the *'Ahd* was developed to include conditions which have no relevance to the period of the conquest, and that it received juridical formulation capable of meeting new developments.[34]

'Umar came to Bait al-Maqdis on a Monday and stayed for a few days.[35] This visit is coloured by Christian and Jewish anecdotes, attributing some activity to the caliph which serves their interests.[36] 'Umar's visit to Kanīsat al-Qiyāma (the Church of the Resurrection) and his refusal to pray there,[37] Ka'b al-Aḥbār's presence (an involved figure) and its occasion, and 'Umar's guide(s) to the Ḥaram are examples.[38] However, the visit is related to the special place of Jerusalem, and the historical reports emphasized that 'Umar went to the area of the Ḥaram, which the Christians neglected and left unused for scriptural reasons, cleared the ground by the Rock and prayed nearby south of it. Clearly, he meant to have the place of prayer there. Azdī reports that ' 'Umar set [*khaṭṭa*] the *miḥrāb* [prayer niche] there to the east, which is the place of his mosque.'[39] Muqātil b. Sulaimān (150 AH) gives the earliest reference and states clearly that the Muslims built the mosque in the time of 'Umar.[40] Al-Muhallabī (4th/10th century) states that 'Umar cleared the site of the Ḥaram, and the Muslims built a mosque there.[41] Al-Muṭahhar al-Maqdisī reports that 'Umar built a mosque in Bait al-Maqdis.[42] Some later sources also make reference to this mosque.[43]

Theophanes states that 'Umar started building the mosque in 643 AD (22 AH).[44] Michael the Syrian,[45] and Eutychius,[46] both refer to the building of the mosque by 'Umar. Thus it is clear that 'Umar, during his short visit, indicated the place of prayer in the Ḥaram and marked the *miḥrāb*, and that the first mosque was erected in his lifetime.[47] The first external account of this mosque comes from Bishop Arculf who visited Bait al-Maqdis *c.*680 AD, during the caliphate of Mu'āwiya.

'Umar appointed 'Ubāda b. al-Ṣāmit as judge and teacher in Bait al-Maqdis, an act reserved for Arab centres of provinces.[48] There is reference to many of the Companions (*ṣaḥabā'*) who visited the city, as an act of piety, and some died there.[49] Abu 'Ubaida, the commander-in-chief, headed for the city to pray there and died on the way.[50] The third caliph, 'Uthmān, donated the Silwān spring, by the city, as *waqf* – a pious endowment – for the benefit of its people.[51] It was the beginning of rich Muslim endowments for Bait al-Maqdis through the ages.

With the Umayyads Bait al-Maqdis received special attention, for political as well as religious reasons. The city's sanctity meant great Islamic prestige for the Umayyads. It was no coincidence that more than one Umayyad caliph received the *bay'a* [oath of allegiance] in Jerusalem.

Mu'āwiya was quite conscious of the significance of Bait al-

Maqdis. During his conflict with ʿAlī, he made a pact with ʿAmr b. al-ʿĀṣ in Bait al-Maqdis.[52] Then, while still in conflict with al-Ḥasan b. ʿAlī, he received the *bayʿa* of the Syrians in Bait al-Maqdis in 40/660 in the mosque.[53]

He stressed the sanctity of Bait al-Maqdis, for he is reported to have said from the pulpit of its mosque: 'The area between the two walls of this mosque is dearer to God than the rest of the earth.'[54] He even extended this sanctity to Syria, and called it 'the Land of Resurrection.'[55] Khālid b. Mi'dān (103/721) reports that Muʿāwiya related a Tradition, saying: 'Go to al-Shām, for it is God's choice of His countries, He elects there the best of His creatures.'[56] On another occasion he spoke of God's glory in the sacred land which God made the place of the prophets and the virtuous (*ṣāliḥīn*) of His servants, and had it inhabited by the Syrians.[57]

Pilgrimage continued to Bait al-Maqdis, and life was fairly lively. Bishop Arculf, who was there during the reign of Muʿāwiya, states that people from different countries and nationalities came to Jerusalem and held an annual fair (on 12 September) with many trading activities. Besides, he talks of the mosque, a simple oblong building in the Ḥaram area,[58] mostly in wood, which could accommodate (as reported) 3,000 people. This meant that the Arabs there numbered two or three times this figure. This is understandable if it is remembered that (Christian) Arab tribes, especially Lakhm and Judhām, lived in Palestine before the conquest,[59] and there are references to (Christian) Arabs in Jerusalem during the conquest.[60] Arabs certainly increased later, since ʿUmar sent ʿUbāda b. al-Ṣāmit as judge and teacher. It would now be generally accepted that the greater part of the indigenous population of Palestine was arabized in the early centuries of Arab rule, and most of the Arab population of Palestine today is descended from races inhabiting the country through the past.

Muʿāwiya's attitude and policy towards the city were actively followed by his successors. The special position of the sacred lands is seen in the fact that the governors of Palestine were chosen from Umayyad princes like ʿAbd al-Malik[61] and Sulaimān b. ʿAbd al-Malik, or especially chosen from trusted dignitaries like ʿAmr b. Saʿīd (al-Anṣārī), appointed by Muʿāwiya,[62] and Ibn Baḥdal al-Kalbī, father-in-law of Yazīd I and appointed by him.[63]

Two of the Marwānid (Umayyad) caliphs received the *bayʿa* in Jerusalem. ʿAbd al-Malik became caliph when Ibn al-Zubair was already proclaimed caliph in Medina. Thus he went to Jerusalem to receive the *bayʿa* there, to give the occasion a special significance.[64]

Sulaimān b. 'Abd al-Malik received the news of his succession while near Balqā', but he went to Bait al-Maqdis to receive the *bay'a* from the delegation that came there for this purpose, and celebrated the occasion in the courtyard of the Aqṣā mosque, by the Ṣakhra (Rock).[65] When 'Umar b. 'Abd al-'Azīz wanted to call some governors of Sulaimān to account, he had them brought to Bait al-Maqdis to take the oath by the Rock.[66] Moreover, the Umayyad caliphs, Mu'āwiya, 'Abd al-Malik, al-Walīd, Sulaimān, 'Umar b. 'Abd al-'Azīz, and Yazīd b. 'Abd al-Malik, frequently visited the city.[67]

Bait al-Maqdis was not one of the administrative centres; since these centres were to be bases for the Arab *muqātila* (troops), to meet their needs in pastures and climate, and to be directly linked to the Arabian Peninsula, Bait al-Maqdis with its Ḥaram was hardly suitable. Sulaimān thought of making it his capital, but understandably abandoned the idea. But Bait al-Maqdis had its governor, and its judge, due to its special position.

The great monuments of the city were erected by the Umayyads, basically to emphasize the sanctity of the Ḥaram and to gain respect and renown among Muslims. 'Abd al-Malik (65–86/685–705), the second founder of the Umayyad dynasty, is renowned for building the Qubbat al-Ṣakhra (the Dome of the Rock) in 69–72/691–92.[68] He conceived the project soon after his accession, although he was facing major troubles. It is not irrelevant to note that he was Medinese by education and a traditionalist.

Writers differ as to the motives of 'Abd al-Malik, as the reports are involved. Ya'qūbī (284/897), a Shī'ite, reports that the caliph wanted to divert pilgrimage to the Dome of the Rock to keep people away from the call (*da'wa*) of his rival, Ibn Zubair. When people protested, he invoked the authority of Zuhrī (124/741) for a tradition limiting (religious) visits to three mosques.[69]

Eutychius (324/940) and some later historians reiterated this report.[70] Al-Muhallabī (4th/11th), a geographer with Shī'ite leanings, attributed the measure to al-Walīd, to prevent Syrians learning about the superiority of the Prophet's family over the Umayyads.[71] Both Ya'qūbī and Muhallabī state that pilgrimage to Mecca stopped throughout the Umayyad period. Such reports reflect politico-religious conflicts.

Goldziher accepted Ya'qūbī's report, to be followed by Creswell.[72] But Goitein and Grabar rejected this report on the ground that pilgrimage to Mecca is reported to have continued under 'Abd al-Malik, that other early sources do not mention such a measure, that such action was too dangerous to take, and finally the plan and location of the Dome do not fit such an idea.[73] We may add that Zuhrī was then too young and unknown to be quoted. Basawi indicates that Zuhrī's first visit to Damascus was in 82/701, and his audience with the caliph was casual.[74]

'Abd al-Malik probably meant to express the splendour of Islam in architectural terms in a city of magnificent churches, as Maqdisī indicated.[75] It is more important, however, that he wanted to show the sanctity of the Ḥaram, and to acquire great prestige among Muslims. All this is implied by the inscriptions in the Dome which reflect some Islamic-Christian dialogue of the time, state basic Islamic concepts, and give a vindication of Islam and its universality as the final revelation.[76]

The choice of the Rock had its significance. Some early reports link it with the *Isrā'* and *Mi'rāj.*[77] Other reports indicate that 'Abd al-Malik himself linked the sanctity of the Rock with the *Mi'rāj.*[78] Besides, it is reported that 'Umar looked especially for the Rock.[79]

It is likely that stories were circulated by Muslims[80] and non-Muslims about the Rock, but they are hardly relevant here.[81] Thus the Dome, in a way, commemorates the *Isrā'* and *Mi'rāj.*[82]

The Umayyads were proud of the Dome as a great Islamic monument.[83] Even the 'Abbāsid, al-Mahdī, noted, with some envy, that the Dome was an achievement of the Umayyads to which the 'Abbāsids could offer no parallel.[84] 'Abd al-Malik also ordered the construction of two new doors in the walls of the city.[85]

Other great monuments were built by the Umayyads. The Aqṣā mosque was built at this time. Sources differ as to the builder, between 'Abd al-Malik and his son, al-Walīd.[86] Creswell tended to the latter on the evidence of some Aphrodito papyri.[87] It is likely that 'Abd al-Malik ordered the building of the Aqṣā mosque, and that al-Walīd participated in some part of the construction.[88]

An impressive Umayyad building complex has been excavated to the south and southwest of the Aqṣā mosque. It is likely that one of its two units, which had direct access to the Ḥaram, was for the city's governor. Other buildings could be for distinguished guests and for the Umayyads who were frequent visitors.[89] All this is indicative of the special status of Bait al-Maqdis and could add to the prestige of the Umayyads.

Milestones discovered around Jerusalem in the late Ottoman period indicate that 'Abd al-Malik ordered the construction of a highway from Damascus to Jerusalem.[90] It is also known that the Umayyads established a mint in Jerusalem. Coins struck there carried the Roman name 'Ilya'.[91]

The process of the arabization of Jerusalem accelerated, especially after the measures taken by 'Abd al-Malik regarding the arabization of the *dīwāns* and the coinage. Around the end of the 7th century AD Arabic replaced Greek as the dominant language in the city. It seems that the Arab population of Bait al-Maqdis was now fairly large, as they took a stand against the last Umayyad caliph, Marwān. This led to their punishment and the partial destruction of the city wall in 128/745.[92]

The Umayyads (and Syrians) propagated traditions and sayings extolling Bait al-Maqdis for political reasons. Yet the sanctity of Bait al-Maqdis was general. 'Abbāsids and 'Alids referred to Bait al-Maqdis in support of their causes. Thus the Mahdī (Saviour) is connected with Bait al-Maqdis. The black banners ('Abbāsid) will continue 'their victorious march from Khurāsān until they are implanted in Bait al-Maqdis.'[93] Thus veneration for the city was universal.

With the advent of the 'Abbāsids, the Islamic significance of Jerusalem grew. In their emphasis on the Islamic line, the new dynasty showed great respect for the Holy City. Al-Manṣūr (the second caliph) paid a visit to it on his way back from the pilgrimage (in 140/758).[94] In fact, this visit was in fulfilment of a vow.[95] Manṣūr visited
Bait al-Maqdis a second time in 154/771.[96] His son (and successor), al-Mahdī, journeyed to Bait al-Maqdis in 163/780 to visit and pray in the Aqṣā.[97]

Jerusalem was shaken by two earthquakes at this period, and the Aqṣā mosque suffered. Manṣūr undertook great reconstruction work after the eastern and western parts were ruined.[98] However, a second earthquake (probably in 154)[99] did much damage to the Aqṣā and al-Mahdī (in 163) ordered wide reconstructions, increasing the width of the mosque and reducing its length.[100] Maqdisī (387/997) speaks highly of Mahdī's work which he saw.[101]

Under al-Ma'mūn (198-218/813-833) the construction of the eastern and northern gates of the Ḥaram took place. This was completed in Rabī' II 216/May 831.[102] Though his name replaced that of 'Abd al-Malik (but not the date) on the Dome there is no reference to any construction by him there.[103]

Walls were also repaired or rebuilt when they suffered from man or earthquake, and constant attention was focused on the Ḥaram. All buildings inside the Ḥaram had some clear Islamic connotation. Al-Sayyida, mother of the caliph al-Muqtadir, ordered (*c*.301/913) the repair of the cupola of the Dome of the Rock and provided each gate with a magnificent wooden porch.[104]

Theophanes alone reports that al-Manṣūr, on his visit, ordered Jews and Christians to tattoo their names on their hands for the *jizya*.[105] This is hardly likely, for it was al-Rashīd who ordered that non-Muslims in frontier areas should show themselves by their garb to guard against foreign spies.

The story of the embassies between Charlemagne and Hārūn al-Rashīd (by Eginhard 820) and the presentation of the keys of the city to the former has no historical basis.[106] But it is clear that some hostels and a library were established in Bait al-Maqdis by the emperor. Credit is given to Muslims for their fine treatment of the pilgrims, and a commercial fair was held annually on 15 May.[107] In the reign of Ma'mūn, the patriarch carried out some repairs in the buildings of the Holy Sepulchre.[108]

Bait al-Maqdis was by now a city fully arabized and islamized. Its sanctity and openness to scholars, pilgrims and traders, and the green country around, provided an existence fairly secure from trouble and want. The saying that God ensured good sustenance to the people of the city is significant.[109] Yet it was not totally free from hardships. Earthquakes hit it.[110] A famine is reported by Eutychius in the days of al-Ma'mūn.[111] The peasant rebellion led by al-Mubarqa' al-Yamānī (227/841) in the caliphate of Mu'taṣim shook Bait al-Maqdis. He entered the city, and its population, Muslims and others, fled and places of worship were pillaged.[112]

Referring to the growth of sanctity of Bait al-Maqdis, the *Ḥadīth* (Traditions)[113] literature forms the core of information. Traditions were reported about the merit of visiting al-Masjid al-Aqṣā and praying there.[114] Such traditions were actively and widely circulated during the Umayyad period. The fact that the tradition limiting (religious) visits to three mosques was evoked by some historians in connection with the building of the Dome of the Rock is significant.

There are traditions which simply stress the *faḍā'il* of Bait al-Maqdis or the merit of visiting it, or of praying in the Aqṣā mosque.[115] Yet there are traditions which limit travel to the mosques of Mecca, and Medina, or give prayers in the Aqṣā less merit than the mosque of Medina or even advise against travel to Bait al-Maqdis.[116] The authorities reporting these traditions come from the period between the last third of the 1st/7th century and the first quarter of the 2nd/8th (Jābir b. 'Abdallāh, 78/697; 'Aṭā 115/733; Qatāda 117–8/735–6). It was a period of bitter political conflict between the Umayyads and opposition movements (Zubairī, 'Alid, 'Abbāsid), and all tried to find in the *Ḥadīth* moral or religious support.

The position of the Ḥarām in Mecca or the mosque in Medina is not involved in these traditions, it is rather the stance of the Umayyads and the opposition parties.[117] This situation finds an echo in some statements.[118] The poet Farazdaq speaks of two houses that are looked after (*wulātuhu*), 'the House of God and the Noble House in Ilya'. In praising Sulaimān b. 'Abd al-Malik, Farazdaq refers to him as the righteous *imām* in the Aqṣā mosque.[119]

Qur'ānic exegetists and *quṣṣāṣ* (popular preachers) as well as pious men contributed to the *faḍā'il* of Bait al-Maqdis. Muqātil b. Sulaimān (80–150 AH) related in his *tafsīr* [exegesis] a considerable number of verses concerning the Holy Land and Jerusalem.[120] For example, he relates Sūra II, 142, on the change of the *qibla* and the comment of Quraish that Muḥammad became confused and longed for his birthplace, and was returning to the religion of Mecca.[121] He drew from the Isrā'iliyyāt, for which he is criticized. Yet he is widely quoted by later writers on Bait al-Maqdis.[122] He seems to have delivered lectures in the Aqṣā to a lively audience.[123]

In fact the Isrā'iliyyāt produced a flood of literature on Bait al-Maqdis. These were tales and anecdotes related by new converts, and were mainly of Jewish origin. They were attributed mostly to Ka'b al-Aḥbar (32/652) and Wahb b. Munabbih (124/728).[124] Abu Raiḥāna (86/705), a converted Jew, used to recount tales (*qaṣaṣ*) in the mosque of Bait al-Maqdis.[125] The Isrā'iliyyāt had a great impact on popular ideas about Bait al-Maqdis, but have no historical or religious value. Obviously they are not Traditions, and should not be confused with them. They were in wide circulation in the latter decades of the 1st/7th century.[126] Strong doubts were cast on the credibility of the Isrā'iliyyāt and their sources, but they were tolerated when they did not contradict Islamic beliefs.

Thus anecdotes from the Isrā'iliyyāt are related on the authority of some followers (*ṭābi'ūn*) or even Companions (like 'Abdullāh b. 'Amr, 65/683–4, Rajā' b. Ḥaywa, 'Abdullāh b. 'Umar, Makḥūl, 113/731).[127] Al-Zuhrī (124/742), while on a visit to Bait al-Maqdis, was shown a shaikh who used to speak of the *faḍā'il* of Bait al-Maqdis from books.[128] Sometimes Isrā'iliyyāt are even attributed to the Prophet to give them some credence.[129]

However, sayings about the *faḍā'il* (with no indication of sources) are widely circulated on the authority of some followers or people who died in the early decades of the 2nd/8th century. Reference could be made to figures like 'Aṭā' b. Ibn Abī Rabāḥ (114–5/732–3), Makḥūl (113–4/731–2), Qatāda (118/736), and later Thawr b. Yazīd

(153/770) and Muqātil (150/767).[130]

Thus by the 2nd/8th century the lines of the sanctity of Bait al-Maqdis in Traditions, *tafsīr*, and anecdotes were well established. Between the 2nd/8th and the 5th/11th centuries literature on the *faḍā'il* of Bait al-Maqdis reached its outer limits in scope and emphasis,[131] as seen in Ḥadīth collections, literature, *tafsīr* and works on the *faḍā'il* of Jerusalem.

The first works on the *faḍā'il* that reach us come from the 5th/11th century. Histories of some cities, usually administrative centres like Medina, Wāsit and Baghdad, were written in the 3rd–4th/9th–10th centuries.[132] In these works, attention centres on political and administrative history, or on biographies. Here, a work on the conquest (*futūḥ*) of Jerusalem is attributed to Isḥāq b. Bishr (206/821).[133] Another work by al-Ramlī (261/875) was written on the Companions who settled in Palestine.[134] Then works on *faḍā'il* followed. The first on the *faḍā'il* of Damascus by Rab'ī came from the 5th/11th century.[135]

Some geographical works of the 4th/10th century significantly talk of Bait al-Maqdis,[136] indicating interest in the city. But the 5th/11th century saw much activity in writing on the *faḍā'il* of Bait al-Maqdis. Wāsitī wrote *Faḍā'il al-Bait al-Muqaddas*[137] before 411/1019 and Abu 'l-Ma'ālī al-Musharraf b. al-Murajja b. Ibrāhīm al-Maqdisī wrote his *Faḍā'il al-Quds wa-'l-Shām*[138] about the middle of the 5th/11th century. It is reported that Shaikh Abu 'l-Qāsim al-Rumailī 'started writing a history of Bait al-Maqdis and its *faḍā'il*, in which he gathered many things,' but the work was lost as the author was killed by the Crusaders in 492/1099.[139] These works dealt mainly with the *faḍā'il* of Jerusalem and the sanctity of places there. They were so comprehensive on the *faḍā'il* that later works (6th/12th century on) could only add a section on biographies of scholars and pious people who lived in Jerusalem or who came there.[140]

This expanded *faḍā'il* literature drew mainly on the Ḥadīth and on *āthār* (sayings attributed to Companions and Followers) on the one hand, and on anecdotes and stories from the People of the Book (i.e. Christians and Jews), including *qaṣaṣ al-anbiyā'* (stories about the prophets). Space precludes a full discussion, but a few references would be apposite. Al-Musharraf b. al-Murajjā summarizes points of emphasis in his book, saying 'someone asked me to present all that reached me on the *faḍā'il* of the sacred mosque, which God the Almighty elevated, ennobled, and made the place of resurrection (*maḥsharan wa-mansharan*), the *qibla* of all prophets, and the bastion of the elite of the faithful (*awliyā'*), and what [God] bestowed on it of all good merits and great virtues.'[141]

Thus much is said about the merits of visits to Bait al-Maqdis[142] and the blessings of living or staying there.[143] It is the place of the second and final *hijra* (the first being to Medina), and all the virtuous will go there.[144] It is the place of resurrection, and on the eve of the Day of Judgement, God will send his best creatures to Jerusalem and to the Holy Land.[145]

The virtues of the Aqṣā mosque and prayers there are much expanded.[146] The Rock in Bait al-Maqdis will be the bastion of Muslims against al-Dajjāl (Anti-Christ).[148] It is the place where – to all Islamic groups – the *Mahdī* comes, or triumphs, to restore justice and plenty to the earth.[149]

In brief, Bait al-Maqdis combines all virtues; it is the holy of holies.[150]

Such notions had a great impact on people's minds. Thus Maqdisī (387/997), a native of the city, says 'it combines (the merits of) this life and the hereafter, that it has all virtues, for it is the place of resurrection; and if Mecca and Medina were elevated by the Ka'ba and the Prophet, they will be brought – on the Day of Judgement – to Bait al-Maqdis.'[151] He indicates that the plain of al-Sāhira is the place of resurrection,[152] and this is repeated by Nāṣir-i Khusrau in the next century (104/438). Khusrau reports: 'It is said that al-Sāhira will be the place of *qiyāma* [resurrection]; therefore multitudes from all corners of the earth come to it and live there until they die.'[153] Such ideas probably account for the advent of some pious people to spend their last years in Bait al-Maqdis.[154] In fact some governors and rulers stipulated that they be buried there.[155] The city was now called al-Quds, as he states, and people went there for its veneration as shown in the *ta'rīf.* Nāṣir reports that those who were unable to go on pilgrimage to Mecca came to al-Quds and stood [*mawqif*] in the Ḥaram and sacrificed for the Aḍḥā festival,[156] as is usual in Mecca. He further noted that as many as 20,000 came in some years.[157] Late in the 5th/11th century Ṭarṭūshī noted and criticized this innovation (*bid'a*). Being in Bait al-Maqdis on the day of 'Arafa (near Mecca), he saw throngs of country people and inhabitants of the city assemble in the Aqṣā mosque facing the *qibla* and praying in loud voices as if they were in 'Arafa.

He further heard that some people believed that if they repeated the ceremony every four years, that would count as a pilgrimage to Mecca.[158] He also noted some innovations relevant to praying (mid-Sha'bān and Rajab).

It is not definite when this *ta'rīf* started in Bait al-Maqdis.

Qalqashandī implies an earlier date than the 5th century AH as he states that people used to come to the Dome of the Rock on the day of 'Arafa and stand there. He then adds: 'That is the origin of the *ta'rīf* in Bait al-Maqdis and the mosques of provincial centres.'[159] Ibn Kathīr (quoting Sibṭ Ibn al-Jawzī, 7th/13th century) assigns that to the time of 'Abd al-Malik when people used to stand by the Rock, circulate round it, make their sacrifice and cut their hair (as they do on the Ḥajj). Ibn al-Zubair used that to attack 'Abd al-Malik vehemently.[160] This odd report seems to be an elaboration of the report of Ya'qūbī (3rd/9th century) based on later practice. Basawi (d. 277/890) gives a report attributed to Zuhrī, that when 'Umar entered Jerusalem he said: *Labbayka Allāhumma Labbayk* (usually said by pilgrims when they approach Mecca).[161] This is a later report in support of the *ta'rīf*. So probably the *ta'rīf* practised widely in Bait al-Maqdis appeared late in the 4th/10th century or early 5th/11th century.

The biographical sections in later works[162] list practically the same names for our period. They carefully list Companions and Followers and those after them (i.e. until the middle of the 2nd century AH), who came to the city to visit or stay. This is connected basically with the city's sanctity. After that great scholars (like Sufyān al-Thawrī, al-Awzā'ī, Wakī' b. al-Jarrāḥ, al-Shāfi'ī) and famous mystics (like Sarī al-Saqatī, Dhu 'l-Nūn al-Miṣrī and Bishr al-Ḥāfī) are noted. While sufis – mystics – came for spiritual reasons, all scholars participated in the cultural life of the city. The number of visitors understandably declined after the Fāṭimid occupation (358/969), as is evident from works written on the city. The Fāṭimids seem to have established a cultural centre (*dār al-'ilm*) there, mainly to propagate Ismā'īlī ideas.[163] Thus Maqdisī (387/997), who wrote at this period, states that Bait al-Maqdis had only a small number of *'ulamā'*. He also notes that the Aqṣā mosque was devoid of groups (circles) and séances of learning.[164] Maqdisī presumably voiced his uneasiness about Fāṭimid controls, and the decline in the number of scholars who came to Bait al-Maqdis and hence missed the free discussions and scholarly debates.[165] Thus he complains that the jurist (*faqīh*) is neglected; yet there were jurists, who were generally conservative. Besides, the *fuqahā'* used to sit (for teaching) in the mosques – afternoons and evenings – and the *qurrā'* (Qur'ān readers) had their circles (*majālis*) in the city.

He also notes that the Ḥanafites had a circle in the Aqṣā mosque, in which they read from a book (*daftar*), while the religious group, al-Karrāmiyya, had circles in their *khānaqāhs* (sufi hostels). Preachers were usually from the *quṣṣāṣ*.[166] Was that conservatism and absence of *bid'a* (innovation) a reaction to Fāṭimid propaganda?

Yet applied sciences fared well, for Maqdisī states that the city has every expert and doctor.[167] The Fāṭimids encouraged such studies, and some families had some tradition in those fields.[168] Most doctors and secretaries (*kuttāb*) were Christians, while most bankers, dyers and tanners were Jews.[169]

The Fāṭimids, sometimes, depended on Christians and Jews in government chanceries and finance, and this probably explains Maqdisī's remark about the Christians and Jews having the upper hand (*ghalaba*) in the city.[170] Socially Jerusalem was open to large numbers of pilgrims 'and on no day was the city free of strangers.'[171] In addition to Muslims coming to visit, to teach or to study, some of the pious would start their *iḥrām** for the Ḥajj from Jerusalem, and this is specially true of Maghribīs.[172] With visitors and pilgrims goes much activity in crafts and trade. Maqdisī spoke highly of its clean market, rich in goods, and allotted by crafts, and of the mosque, the largest.

Social relations between Muslims and others were usually good. Maqdisī says that Muslims participated in Christian feasts, usually agricultural.[173] Fāṭimid policy towards Christians and Jews was more than friendly, but they suffered persecution for a time by the unpredictable caliph, al-Ḥakīm (386–411/996–1021). This culminated in the destruction of the Holy Sepulchre (400/28 September 1009). However, al-Ḥakīm changed his mind before he died and let Christians rebuild their churches. The Holy Sepulchre was rebuilt under al-Ẓāhir (418/1027).[174] In this period an earthquake in 407/1016 damaged the mosque; the Dome partly collapsed, and was rebuilt by al-Ẓāhir in 413/1022.[175] The mosque and walls of the city, affected by the earthquake in 425/1033, were also rebuilt in 425.[176] Al-Mustanṣir renovated the northern front of the mosque in 458/1065.[177] The excellent work carried out[178] indicates that the Fāṭimids were not less keen than previous dynasties in asserting the sanctity and Islamic significance of Bait al-Maqdis.

Nāṣir-i Khusrau (who visited the city between 14 March and 20 April 1047 AD) noted that things were plentiful and cheap.[179] Jerusalem had beautiful markets and high buildings. It had a great number of craftsmen, and each craft had its market (*sūq*).[180] This reflects the business side of the city. It was a big town, and it was second to Ramla in the 4th century AH.[181] It was on its way to

* Inaugurating the pilgrimage to Mecca in which pilgrims use two pieces of unsewn cloth to cover the body, abstain from shaving and sexual intercourse.

becoming the first in the second part of the 5th/11th century.[182] Nāṣir-i Khusrau gives the number of 'its men' as 20,000.[183] The reference to men usually means families, and this would put the figure around a hundred thousand.

On the cultural side Nāṣir-i Khusrau refers to a great hospital with rich *waqfs* dedicated to it, from which medicines for its numerous patients are dispensed and salaries for doctors are paid.[184] Medicine was taught there.[185] He also refers to two sufi hostels by the mosque where they live and pray, thus illustrating the sufi tradition.

After 463/1071 Bait al-Maqdis was generally in the Saljuq sphere, and more open to scholars.[186] In 465/1072 the 'Abbāsid *da'wa* returned to it.[187] Clearly Bait al-Maqdis, not Ramla, was now the first city in Palestine.[188]

In the 5th/11th century, the first *madhhab* – one of the four schools of jurisprudence – was Shāfi'ite, to be followed by a Ḥanafī, and late in the century each of these two had a *madrasa* (school, college). The Ḥanbalī *madhhab* had a small following, for it was only introduced by Abu 'l-Faraj al-Shīrāzī (486/1093).

Maqdisī missed the spirit of intellectual disputations and of inquiry, of which he was a fine representative, in the last quarter of the 4th/10th century. He was a great traveller and a critical observer. Muṭahhar b. Ṭāhir al-Maqdisī (fl. 355/966) was a fine historian and a great student of religions. Muḥammad b. Sa'īd al-Tamīmī was a Maqdisī doctor and a botanist who made a study of medical plants in Palestine. Both Maqdisī and Tamīmī had scholarly traditions in their families, for Maqdisī's grandfather was a noted engineer, and Tamīmī's grandfather was a doctor.[189]

The 5th/11th century witnessed a wide variety of cultural activities, which centred on Islamic studies, especially Ḥadīth and *fiqh*. Great scholars from Muslim countries, east and west, came to visit Bait al-Maqdis or to settle there. Its own scholars, as well as visitors, participated in a rich cultural life.

Its leading scholar was the Shāfi'ite, Naṣr b. Ibrāhīm al-Maqdisī (490/1096). He was active in *ifta'* (giving legal opinions) and teaching. He taught at the Naṣriyya school, and many scholars were his students.[190] 'Aṭā' al-Maqdisī (Abu 'l-Faḍl) was shaikh of the Shāf'ī scholars in the Aqṣā, with a lively circle. Abu 'l-Qāsim Makkī b. 'Abd al-Salām al-Rumailī (d. 492/1099) was a great Ḥadīth scholar and a very active teacher. He is reported to have written a history of Jerusalem but did not finish it because he was killed by the Crusaders.[191]

Abu 'l-Faḍl Muḥammad b. Ṭāhir al-Qayṣarānī (507/1112-3)

represents broadly the interest of the age. He was active in studies on Ḥadīth, Arabic language and mysticism. He travelled extensively and had a wide impact.[192]

Among more important visitors was Abu 'l-Faraj al-Shīrāzī (486/1093), who settled in the city and introduced the Ḥanbalī *madhhab*. He participated actively in cultural life.[193] The great Ghazālī came to Bait al-Maqdis *c.*488/1095 for contemplation, worship and to visit the holy places. He stayed at the Naṣriyya *zāwiya* (or school), and delivered lectures in the Ḥaram. Here he wrote *al-Risāla al-Qudsiyya* (at the request of some of his audience), not *Iḥyā' 'Ulūm al-Dīn.*[194] The Andalusian *faqīh*, Abu Bakr al-Ṭarṭūshī, came to Bait al-Maqdis about 484/1091, stayed for more than three years, and taught in the Aqṣā mosque. Abu Bakr Ibn al-'Arabī, who left al-Andalus in 484/1091 on his journey to the east, attended his lectures.

Ibn al-'Arabī gives a vivid picture of the active cultural life. It was a meeting place of scholars from Muslim lands between Khurāsān and al-Andalus. He notes the schools in the city, and specifies one Shāfi'ī school by Bāb al-Asbāṭ, and one Ḥanafī school by the Holy Sepulchre. He was impressed by the circles of study and the *majālis* of disputation between the Sunnī *madhhabs* and other Muslim groups, or between people of the three religions. Among Muslim groups there were the Mu'tazila, the Karrāmiyya and the Mushabbiha. He noted the three main fields of Islamic studies: *kalām, uṣūl al-fiqh* and *masā'il al-khilāf.* Ibn al-'Arabī was so taken by the lively and varied cultural activities that he stayed in the city for over three years.[195]

The last decade of the 11th century AD was a time of great turbulence, in the Arab East as well as in Europe. Dissensions between the rulers of Egypt and Syria reached a climax. It was the right time for the Crusaders to attack the East. In 491/1098, the Fāṭimids, led by al-Afḍal al-Jamālī, recovered Jerusalem from the Saljuqs of Syria. But it was a brief interval, for in the very next year the Muslims lamented the loss of Bait al-Maqdis to the Crusaders. It was the great sanctity of the city, however, that made it the symbol for the *jihād* against the invaders.

NOTES

1 Sūra XVII, 1.
2 Ibn Sa'd in a collective *isnād*, I, 213, Balādhūrī, *Anṣāb*, I, 255. He adds another report which makes it 18 months before the *Hijra*. Ibn Kathīr, on the authority of 'Urwa and Zuhrī, makes it a year before the *Hijra*, in Rabī' I. See also Ibn Sa'd, vol. IV, pt. 1, 153.
3 Ibn Hishām, *Sīra*, II, 36–7, 39, 41, 43; Ibn Isḥāq, *Sīra* (ed. M Hamidullah), 275; Balādhūrī, *Anṣāb*, I, 255, says it is the mosque of Bait al-Maqdis. See also p. 256, Ibn Sa'd, IV, 153, and for further details I, 213 ff. Ṭabarī refers to differing reports about the meaning of al-Masjid al-Aqṣā and indicates that the most trustworthy is that it is masjid Bait al-Maqdis (the mosque of Bait al-Maqdis), *Tafsīr*, Bulaq, 1328, XV, 5; see also pp. 7, 12, 13–14.
4 Ibn Sa'd, I, 239–40.
5 Sūra II, 144.
6 Reports differ between 16 and 17 months. See Ibn Sa'd, I, 241, 243, 619.
7 See Wensink, *Concordance et indices de la Tradition Musulmane*, vol. II, 439.
8 See for example: Ṣan'ānī, *Musannaf*, V, nos. 9158, 9160, 9162; Ibn Ḥanbal, *Musnad*, II, 238, III, 51–53, 64; Muslim, III, 1014–15; *Kanz al-'Ummāl*, XIII, 233.
9 Like 'Abdullāh b. 'Amr, 'Aṭā' (d. 114), Qatāda (118), and Makḥūl (113). See Wāṣitī, 15–16, 26, Ibn Sa'd, IV, 231.
10 Quoting Khālid and 'Ubāda, from Salim b. 'Abdullāh in Ṭabarī, I, 2403; see also I, 2406. Khalīfa gives the same report from Salim I, 125.
11 Two reports in Balādhurī, *Futūḥ*, 138–39, one of which is from Awzā'ī; see Ibn Isḥāq in Ṭabarī I, 2511, Saif from Hishām b. 'Urwa and others, Ṭabarī I, 2521–22.
12 Abu Zurā'a virtually rejects this date, *Tārīkh*, I, 178; see also Ibn 'Asākir, II/553, 4.
13 Wāqidī, in Balādhurī, *Anṣāb* (ms) pt. 2, 594; Ibn al-Kalbī in Khalīfa's history, I, 124; Ibn Sa'd, I, 283; Saif b. 'Umar in Ṭabarī, I, 2408; al-Walīd b. Muslim in Abu Zurā'a, I, 176–7; Ya'qūbī, 2/146–7, Ibn 'Asākir, *Tārīkh*, I, 553–4. See Donner, *Conquests*, 151–2.
14 Balādhurī, (from Abu Ḥafs al-Dimashqī), *Futūḥ*, 138–9; another report of Hishām b. 'Ammār al-Dimashqī from al-Awzā'ī, 139; Abu Zurā'a, from Sa'īd b. 'Abd al-'Azīz, *Tārīkh*, I, 77; see also report of Yazīd b. 'Ubaida, ibid, I, 176; Ibn 'Asākir, *Tārīkh*, I, 553–4; al-'Azdī (from Ḥasan b. Ziyād al-Ramlī), *Futūḥ*, 242–5, 247–52. See Ibn A'tham, *Futūḥ*, 289, 291, 292, 296–301, who gives a similar report without indicating his source. Khalīfa (from Ibn al-Kalbī), I, 124–5, like al-Awzā'ī in Balādhurī; Maqdisī, *al-Bad'*, V, 185.
15 Salim b. 'Abdullāh, in Ṭabarī, I, 2413, and Khalīfa, II, 125; Yazīd b. Abi Ḥabīb in 'Ubaid, *Amwāl*, 224–5; Balādhurī, *Futūḥ*, 139; Ibn Sa'd states the 'Umar came to Jabiya and attended the conquest of Jerusalem, III, pt. 1, 203.
16 Abu 'Ubaid quotes Hishām b. 'Ammār al-Dimashqī to the effect that 'Umar sent a commander from Jābiya to Jerusalem, and it surrendered to him, *Amwāl*, 225-6. The same report is in Ibn 'Asākir, *Dimashq*, I, 553. Saif b. 'Umar in Ṭabarī, I, 2397–2402. See Ya'qūbī, II, 160–1. In a weaker report (he states: *wa-yuqālu*), he refers to the presence of 'Umar, 2/167.
17 Eutychius (Sa'īd b. al-Batrīq), *History*, II, 16–17 and 17–18, see Ṭabarī, I, 2397–2402.
18 Ibn Sa'd states: ''Umar had left for Jābiya in Ṣafar 16 AH and stayed there for 20 nights. He then attended the conquest of Bait al-Maqdis and distributed the booty at Jābiya.' I, 283.
19 See 'Azdī, *Futūḥ*, 250; Balādhurī, 139; Ibn A'tham, *Futūḥ*, I, 291; Ṭabarī, I, 2404.
20 Ya'qūbī, II, 167. It begins: 'This is a *kitāb* [writ] given by 'Umar to the people of Bait al-Maqdis.'
21 Eutychius, *History*, II, 16: 'This is a writ from 'Umar b. al-Khattāb to the people of Ilya', they are given safety of persons, sons, properties and churches which will not be destroyed or inhabited.'
22 See Ibn 'Asākir, *Dimashq*, 1.563 ff.
23 See Ṭabarī, I, 2405–6.
24 Michael le Syrien, *Chronique*, II, 45. Jewish pretensions were not lacking, for in addition to the presumed role of Ka'b al-Aḥbar, a Jewish report claims that the Jews asked 'Umar to allow two hundred Jewish families from Egypt to reside in Bait al-Maqdis, but the patriarch's objections made the caliph agree to seventy families. See *E. Judaica*, art. 'Jerusalem'. Egypt was invaded about four years later.
25 Ḥimyarī, *Al-Rawḍ al-Mi'tār*, 69.
26 It is quite common to find in later sources early accounts or reports. See Ibn al-Jawzī, *Faḍā'il al-Quds*, 123-4: ''Umar wrote to the inhabitants of Bait al-Maqdis: I guarantee for you the safety of your persons [blood], properties, families, your crosses [*ṣulbān* not *ṣalāt*] and your churches. You will not be taxed beyond your means, . . . and you pay the *kharāj* [i.e. *jizya*] like the other cities of Palestine.'

27 *K. al-Bad' wa-'l-Tārīkh*, V, 185.
28 Al-Shaikh al-Musharraf b. al-Murajjā, *Faḍā'il Bait al-Maqdis wa-'l-Khalīl* (ms), 57. The *isnād* given is rather weak.
29 Ibn 'Asākir, *Dimashq*, I, 563–68.
30 *Al-Uns al-Jalīl*, I, 253–4.
31 *Aḥkām Ahl al-Dhimma*, II, 657 ff.
32 Ibn A'tham, *Futūḥ*, I, 196.
33 See Tritton, *The Caliphs and their Non-Muslim Subjects*, especially pp. 5 ff., 21 ff., 52–2, 47–55, 115–118, 119, 120, 124. 'Umar b. 'Abd al-'Azīz ordered that non-Muslims should not wear turbans or dress like Muslims. Kindī, *Wulāt*, 60; Ibn 'Abd al-Ḥakam, *Sīrat 'Umar*, 167. Rashīd ordered (in 191 AH) that non-Muslims, in areas near the Byzantine frontiers should have dresses and mounts different from those of Muslims for reasons of security. Ibn al-Athīr, VI, 206. Al-Mutawakkil was the first to issue restrictive measures (in 239/853) on non-Muslims in matters of dress, mounts and education. Ṭabarī, III, 1384, 1419.
34 It is to be expected that the Mamlūk and Ottoman periods left their traces. See the final text of the *'Ahd* issued by the orthodox patriarchate on 1/1/1952, in 'Ārif al-Ārif, *Al-Mufaṣṣal fi Tārīkh al-Quds*, 91–92.
35 'Azdī, 259, says that he stayed until Friday. Al-Muṭahhar al-Maqdisī simply states that he stayed there for days (V, 155).
36 See Ibn A'tham, I, 299–300.
37 Eutychius, II, 17–18, gives a Christian account.
38 It is not clear when Ka'b was converted, or whether he was there, or how he came. See 'Azdī, 259 ff. Ibn A'tham, I, 296, says he became Muslim after the conquest of Jerusalem. Others say he was converted and went to Jerusalem before, and that 'Umar asked for him (!) See Ṭabarī, I, 2408–9, Abu 'Ubaid, *Amwāl*, 225–6, Ibn 'Asākir, *Dimashq*, I, 557.
39 'Azdī, *Futūḥ*, 259. The same statement is given in pseudo-Wāqidī, *Futūḥ al-Shām*, I, 151.
40 Muqātil b. Sulaimān, *Tafsīr*, I, 62–3.
41 *Majallat Ma'had al-Makhṭūṭāt*, 1958, 54.
42 Al-Muṭahhar al-Maqdisī, *al-Bad'*, V, 185; see also IV, 87.
43 Al-Musharraf, 53; Ḥimyarī, *Al-Rawḍ al-Mi'tār*, 69, says that 'Umar built the *qibla* in the forefront of the mosque. Qalqashandī (quoting *al-Rawḍ*) states that 'Umar built the first mosque, IV, 101. See Suyūṭī, *Ithaf al-Akhiṣṣa*, I, 238–40. See also Ibn Khaldūn (Bulaq), I, 279.
44 *Chronicle*, tr. H Turtledove, Philadelphia, 1982, 42.
45 *Chronique*, II, 423.
46 Eutychius, II, 18, says: ''Umar built the mosque and left the Rock at the back of the mosque.'
47 Al-Muṭahhar al-Maqdisī alone says, IV, 87: 'Bait al-Maqdis remained in ruins until it was built [*'ammarahā*] by 'Umar, then Mu'āwiya b. Abi Sufyān.' Does this imply that Mu'āwiya later contributed to the building? El'ad refers to an apocalyptic Jewish *mirdash* which states that Mu'āwiya built the walls of the Temple Mount (A El'ad, *Muslim Holy Places in Jerusalem, visitation and ritual in the Umayyad period* [mimeograph copy], 18).
48 Ibn Ḥajar, *al-Iṣāba* , II, 260, and Ibn 'Abd al-Barr, *al-Iṣāba* (in the margin of Ibn Ḥajar), 441–42.
49 See M b. Hibban al-Bustī, *Mashāhir 'Ulamā' al-Amṣār*, 50–51; Ibn Sa'd, VII, 401, 408, 417; Abu Zurā'a, 226. The subject was recently studied in detail in Asali, *Ajdādunā fi Tharā Bait al-Maqdis*, see pp. 33, 106, 199, 200, 219.
50 Ibn Ḥajar, *al-Iṣāba* , II, 245; Abu Zurā'a, 593, 690; Ibn 'Asākir, *Tārīkh*, I, 316–7.
51 Maqdisī, *Aḥsan al-Taqāsīm*, 171; Harawī, *Ziyārāt*, 21.
52 Ibn Sa'd gives the text of this pact, IV, 254; see also Ibn 'Asākir, *Tārīkh*, 316–7.
53 Ṭabarī, II, 15; al-Maqdisī, *al-Bad'*, IV, 87; Wellhausen (from a Syrian source), 96–97; *Tārīkh al-Khulafā'* (anonymous), 121.
54 Al-Musharraf b. al-Murajjā, *Faḍā'il*, 149.
55 Balādhurī, *Ansāb*, IV, pt. 1, 32.
56 Ibn 'Asākir, *Dimashq*, I, 60.
57 Naṣr b. Muzāḥim (d. 212 AH), *Siffīn* (ed. A S Harun, 2nd ed. 1382 AH), 31.
58 *Palestine Pilgrims' Texts Society*, vol. III, New York, 1971, 4–5; J Wilkinson, *Jerusalem Pilgrims before the Crusades*, 1977, pp. 7–8, 95.
59 See Duri, 'The Arabs and the Land in Syria' (Arabic) in *First International Conference on Bilād al-Shām (1974)*, 25–26.
60 'Azdī, *Futūḥ*, 259; Ibn A'tham, I, 296.
61 Balādhurī, (ed. Ahlwart), 164–65.

62 Balādhurī, *Ansāb*, IV, pt. 1, 359.
63 Ibid, 259.
64 Khalīfa b. Khayyāṭ, *Tārīkh*, I, 329. It was in Ramaḍān 65/685.
65 S Munajjid, *Mu'jam Bani Umayya*, 67; al-Musharraf b. al-Murajjā, 31–32; Muthīr al-Gharām, 45.
66 Wāṣitī, 87.
67 See for example Ibn 'Abd Rabbihi, *Al-'Iqd al-Farīd*, II, 474; Basawi, II, 370.
68 See K Creswell, *Early Muslim Architecture*, I, 65; Jahshiyārī, *Wuzarā'*, 8; Eutychius, II, 29; Wāṣitī, 87; van Berchem, *CIA*, IIème, 'Jerusalem "Ḥaram" ', 234 ff.
69 Ya'qūbī, *Tārīkh*, II, 311.
70 *History*, II, 39. Eutychius says that Walīd ordered the *ṭawāf* around the Dome. See also Taghribardī, *Nujūm*, I, 217, Ibn Kathīr, *Bidāya*, VIII, 280, *al-Uns al-Jalīl*, I, 240–41.
71 *Majallat Ma'had al-Makhṭūṭāt*, 1958, 54.
72 Goldziher, *Muslim Studies*, II, 44 ff., Creswell, op. cit., 65–67.
73 See Grabar, *The Umayyad Dome of the Rock*, 15–16; Goitein, *Studies in Islamic Civilisation*, 115 ff.
74 Basawi, *Al-Ma'rfia wa-'l-Tārīkh*, 626–9; Duri, *The Rise of Historical Writing among the Arabs*, tr. by L I Conrad, 117–18.
75 Maqdisī, *Aḥsan al-Taqāsīm*, 159, 168.
76 See Grabar, op. cit., 53 ff.
77 See Wāṣitī, 70–74, 114–17; Ibn 'Abd Rabbihi, *Al-'Iqd al-Farīd*, VI, 265.
78 See Ya'qūbī, I, 311; Mahallabī, op. cit., 54. Though the reports are coloured politically, yet the reference is significant.
79 See Abu 'Ubaid, *Amwāl*, 225, for a Syrian tradition from Hishām b. 'Ammār al-Dimashqī.
80 It is attributed to Zuhrī that all prophets prayed towards the Rock, and that it was sanctified three times, and that it is meant by Sūra VII,1.
81 See Grabar, op. cit., 38 off; see Wāṣitī, 51.
82 See Nāṣir-i Khusrau, *Riḥla*, 30–31; *EI*[2], art. 'Al-Ḳuds'.
83 See the statement of Sulaimān b. 'Abd al-Malik in Jahshiyārī, 148.
84 Al-Mahdī confided this view to his minister, see Musharraf b. al-Murajjā, 186.
85 Ibn Kathīr, XI, 261.
86 Wāṣitī, 83, says that 'Abd al-Malik built it. The report is from al-Walīd b. Ḥammād al-Ramlī and goes back to Rajā' b. Haywa (112 AH) and Yazīd b. Sallām, who supervised the building. See also *al-Uns al-Jalīl*, I, Amman, 1973, 269–70. Eutychius, II, 42, mentions al-Walīd, also Ibn al-Athīr, V, 10. Al-Walīd is usually credited with the mosque of Damascus and that of Medina.
87 Creswell, op. cit., I, 373; Wāṣitī, 81–83; al-Musharraf, 58–59; Ibn Kathīr, *Bidāya*, VIII, 280.
88 *al-Uns al-Jalīl*, II, 270 and *EI*[2], art. 'Al-Ḳuds', V, 341, El'ad, op. cit., 21 ff.
89 *Jerusalem Revealed, Archaeology in the Holy City, 1968–1971*, The Israel Exploration Society, Jerusalem, 1973; Benjamin Mazar, *The Mountain of the Lord*, New York, 1975, 262–67.
90 Abdullah Mukhlis, *Majallat al-Kashshāf*, vol. 2, no. 1, 1925, 25.
91 Samir Shamma, *Majallat al-Quds al-Sharīf*, no. 10, Jan. 1986, 45–46.
92 Wellhausen, *The Arab Kingdom*, (Arabic tr. by Abu Rida), 368; Theophanes, 112.
93 See Wāṣitī, 54; Ibn 'Abd Rabbihi, *'Iqd*, IV, 386.
94 Ṭabarī, III, 129; 'Azdī, *Tārīkh*, II, 218; Kindī, *Wulāt*, 106.
95 Mas'ūdī, *Murūj*, VI, 212.
96 Ṭabarī, III, 372; Kindī, *Wulāt*, 218; Ibn Taghribardī, *Nujūm*, I, 29.
97 Ṭabarī, III, 501; 'Azdī, *Tārīkh*, II, 243; Basawi, *al-Ma'rfia wa-'l-Tārīkh*, I, 150.
98 Ibn Taghribardī speaks of the first earthquake in 131/748, which was severe and 'ruined' Bait al-Maqdis, *Nujūm*, I, 311.
99 See Ibn al-Athīr, V, 612.
100 See Wāṣitī, 83–84.
101 Maqdisī, *Aḥsan*, 168. See Yāqūt, IV, 597.
102 Van Berchem, op. cit., 248–49, 250.
103 Ibid, 250 ff.
104 Ibid, 260, and 7 ff.
105 Theophanes, 138, while Michael the Syrian, II, 522, speaks of an increase in taxes.
106 See Duri, *The First 'Abbāsid Period* (in Arabic), Baghdad, 1945, 149–56.
107 Bernard the Wise reported, *c.*870, that he stayed in the hospice of the glorious Emperor Charles, and mentions a great library and 12 mansions. See J Wilkinson, *Jerusalem Pilgrims before the Crusades*, 1977, 142.

108 Eutychius, II, 55 ff.
109 See Wāsiṭī, 39.
110 Probably the last in our period was in 460 AH. Ibn Qalānisī, *Dhail Tārīkh Dimashq*, 94; Ibn al-Athīr, X, 57.
111 Eutychius, loc. cit. Other sources do not refer to it.
112 Michael the Syrian, III, 103; see Ibn al-Athīr, VI, 371–72.
113 *Ḥadīth* is here the sayings attributed to the Prophet.
114 See Kister, 'You shall only set out for three mosques', *Le Muséon*, LXXXII, 1–2, 1979, 173 ff.
115 Ibn Māja, *Sunan*, Cairo, 1349, I, 429; *Kanz al-'Ummāl*, XIII, nos. 1330, also 1368, 1379, 1380.
116 See Ṣan'ānī, *Muṣannaf*, V, nos. 9131, 9163, 9173; Mundhirī, *Targhīb*, Beirut, 1968, II, 212. See also *Muṣannaf*, V, nos. 9164, 9166.
117 *Kanz al-'Ummāl*, XIII, nos. 1368, 1379, 1380.
118 See *Aghānī*, Bulaq, XIX, 59.
119 See the *Dīwān*, II, 32, 73.
120 See Muqātil b. Sulaimān, *Tafsīr*, I, ed. M Shiḥata, Cairo, 1969, 41 ff., 62–63, 75, 104–105, 135, 184, 279, 305–6, 350–51.
121 Muqātil, *Tafsīr*, I, 74. He explains that *Sufaha'* here refers to the Quraish, while Basāwī (II, 628) indicates that the word refers to the Jews.
122 Ibn al-Faqīh, *Buldān*, 93; al-Musharraf b. al-Murajjā, *Faḍā'il*, 216–17, and 254 ff.
123 Al-Musharraf, 235, *al-Uns al-Jalīl*, I, 292.
124 R Na'nā'a, *Isrā'iliyyāt*, 169 ff., 187.
125 Muthīr al-Gharām, 27–28.
126 Wāsiṭī, *Faḍā'il*, 23.
127 See Wāsiṭī, 15–16, 19–20, 22–23.
128 I.e. the books of the Christians and Jews. See Wāsiṭī, 165; Suyūṭī, *Itḥaf*, I, 95 ff.
129 See, for example, Wāsiṭī, 19–20.
130 Thus, see Wāsiṭī, 22–23, 28, 41; al-Musharraf, 259 ff.
131 See al-Musharraf for a large number of reports and accounts from the 4th/10th century, as 222, 257, 269–70, 284.
132 *History of Medina* by Ibn Shabba; *History of Wāsiṭ* by Baḥshal; *History of Baghdad* by Taifūr. Note should be taken of the *History of Mecca*, the cradle of the Islamic movement, by Azraqī.
133 Khāṭib, *Tārīkh Baghdād*, VI, 326.
134 Mūsā b. Sahl b. al-Qādim al-Ramlī (d. 261 AH) wrote: *Kitāb man nazala Filasṭīn min al-Ṣaḥabā'*, Ibn Ḥajar, *Iṣāba*, II, 365.
135 Al-Rabā'ī, *Faḍā'il al-Dimashq*, ed. al-Munajjid, Damascus, 1950.
136 Al-Muhallabī, *al-Masālik wa-'l-Mamālik al-'Azīzī*, has a chapter on Bait al-Maqdis. See *Majallat Ma'had al-Makhṭūṭāt*, I, 1958, 49–55, where a fragment was edited by S Munajjid. Incidentally the work was presented to the Fāṭimid al-'Azīz. Maqdisī, *Aḥsan al-Taqāsīm*, ed. de Goeje, *BGA*, is another example.
137 Ed. by Hassoun, Jerusalem, 1979.
138 Still in manuscript.
139 *Al-Uns al-Jalīl*, I, 289. See also Sivan, 'The Beginnings of Faḍā'il al-Quds Literature', *Israel Oriental Studies*, I, 1971, 263 ff. K al-'Asalī, *Makhṭūṭāt Faḍā'il Bait al-Maqdis*, 1981, 24 ff., 39–40.
140 Muthīr al-Gharām, Suyūṭī, *Itḥāf al-Akhiṣṣa* and *al-Uns al-Jalīl*.
141 Al-Musharraf, 3.
142 See *Kanz al-'Ummāl*, XIII, nos. 1379, 1368, 1380; al-Musharraf, 92–93, Wāsiṭī, 40.
144 Ibn al-Faqīh, *Buldān*, 94.
145 Wāsiṭī, 22, 28, 121–22; al-Musharraf, 87–88, 245 ff.
146 Ibn al-Faqīh, 94–95; al-Musharraf, 86–87; Wāsiṭī, 23, 24–25.
147 Wāsiṭī (from Zuhrī), 51.
148 Nu'aim b. Ḥammād, *Kitāb al-Fitan*, 45^{a}–148^{a}.
149 Ibid, 49^{a} ff., 52^{a-b}, 56^{a}, 57^{a}, 59^{a-b}; Wāthima, *Bad' al-Khalq wa-Qiṣaṣ al-Anbiyā'*, 297–98; al-Musharraf, 228, 230–31, 233; Wāsiṭī, 54.
150 Wāsiṭī, 39, 41; see al-Musharraf, 55, 259 ff.
151 Maqdisī, *Aḥsan al-Taqāsīm*, 166–67.
152 Ibid, 172.
153 Nāṣir-i Khusrau, *Riḥla*, 2.
154 Ibid, 29.

155 See Kindī, *Wulāt*, 296, for some Ikhshīdids; Ibn al-Qalānisī, 79. Takin b. 'Abdullāh, governor of Egypt (d. 321 AH), Ikhshīd (d. 324 AH) and his two sons were buried there. Ibn Taghribardī, *Nujūm*, III, 211, 256, 326–27; Kindī, 281; see also Ibn al-Qalānisī, 79, and K al-'Asalī, *Ajdādunā fī Tharā Bait al-Maqdis*, 24, 221.
156 The feast at the end of the Ḥajj.
157 *Riḥla*, 19–20.
158 Ṭarṭūshī, *Kitāb al-Ḥawādith wa- 'l-Bida'*, ed. M Talibi, Tunis, 1959, 116–17. He refers to other *bida's* (innovations) like *Ṣalāt Raghā'ib* (begun in 448 AH) and *Ṣalāt al-Rajab* (begun after 480), 121–22.
159 Qalqashandī, *Ma'ālim al-Ināfa*, I, 129.
160 Ibn Kathīr, *al-Bidāya*, VIII, 280–81. He adds that people (in Syria) were so enchanted by the beauty of the Dome that they came to it from everywhere and neglected the Ḥajj. They even made signs and indications relevant to the hereafter (*Ākhira*) like al-Ṣirāt, Bāb al-Jinna and Wādī Jahannam. See El'ad, 54 ff.
161 Al-Basawi, *Kitāb al-Ma'rifa wa-'l-Tārīkh*, I, 365.
162 *Muthīr al-Gharām of al-Maqdisī al-Shāfi'ī (765/1364)*, ed. A S Khalidi, Jaffa, 10 ff. Al-Suyūṭī (874/1469), *Itḥāf al-Akhiṣṣa*, I, 20 ff. Mujīr al-Dīn al-Ḥanbalī, *Al-Uns al-Jalīl*, 285 ff.
163 See A J 'Abd al-Mahdī, *Al-Ḥaraka al-Fikriyya*, Amman, 1980, I, 15–16.
164 Maqdisī, *Aḥsan al-Taqāsim*, 163.
165 He says there is no *Majlis nazar wa-lā-tadrīs*, 167.
166 Maqdisī, 167, 182.
167 Ibid, 166.
168 See Iḥsān 'Abbās, *Al-Ḥayāt al-'Umrāniyya . . . fī Filasṭīn*, Third Bilād al-Shām Conference, II, Amman, 1983, 357.
169 Maqdisī, 183.
170 Ibid, 167; see Tritton, op. cit., 26, 131; *EI*², art. 'Fāṭimids'.
171 Ibid, 166.
172 Ibid, 243.
173 Maqdisī, 182–83.
174 Tritton, op. cit., 54–55; Ibn al-Qalānisī, *Dhail Tārīkh Dimashq*, 66–68; Ibn al-Athīr, IX, 209; Eutychius, II, 125. See also Duri, 'The Jews in Muslim Society', in *Al-Qaḍiya al-Filisṭīniyya*, I (issued by Ittiḥād al-Jami'āt al-'Arabiyya), 1983, 102 ff.
175 Ibn al-Athīr, IX, 295; *al-Uns al-Jalīl*, I, 261. Van Berchem, op. cit., 263–66; Harawī says he read in the ceiling of the Dome the date Dhu 'l-Qa'da, 426 AH, *Kitāb al-Ziyārāt*, 26, 290–91.
176 Van Berchem, IIème, Cairo, 1925, 15.
177 See Ḥamad Yūsuf, *Bait al-Maqdis*, Jerusalem, 1982, 132.
178 See *Riḥla*, 58–59.
179 He was in al-Quds on 5 Ramaḍān till 1 Dhu 'l-Qa'da 438/14 March–20 April 1047.
180 Ibid, 56.
181 Ibn Ḥawqal, *BGA*, 2nd ed., Kramers, 171.
182 See *EI*², art. 'al-Ḳuds'.
183 *Riḥla*, 56. Ibn al-Athīr gives this figure to the Karrāmiyya in Bait al-Maqdis, X, 20.
184 *Riḥla*, 59.
185 See Ibn Abi 'Usaibiyya, *'Uyūn al-Anbā' fī Ṭabaqāt al-Aṭibbā'*, ed. N Riza, Beirut, 1965, biography of M S Tamimi, 546–48.
186 Ibn al-Athīr, X, 68.
187 Ibid, X, 88.
188 See ibid, X, 103, 147; Ibn Taghribardī, *Nujūm*, V, 87, 115; Dhahabī, *'Ibār*, III, 252; Ḥamad Yūsuf, *Bait al-Maqdis*, 136 ff.
189 Maqdisī, 163; Ibn Abi 'Usaibiyya, *'Uyūn al-Anbā'*, 547; see I 'Abbās, op. cit., 356–57.
190 'Abd al-Jalīl 'Abd al-Mahdī, *al-Ḥaraka al-Fikriyya*, 16–18.
191 Ibid, 24–25; I 'Abbās, op. cit., 359.
192 'Abd al-Mahdī, op. cit., 26–27.
193 Ibid, 28–29.
194 Ibid, 19–21; Ṭibāwī, *Jerusalem*, 14; *al-Uns al-Jalīl*, I, 210–02; see Ibn al-Athīr, X, 252.
195 I 'Abbās, *Riḥlat Ibn al-'Arabī*, al-Abḥath, AUB, 1968, 81 ff.; also I 'Abbās, *Al-Ḥayat al-'Umrāniyya*, Third International Conference on Bilād al-Shām, II, 1983, 359–61; 'Abd al-Mahdī, op. cit., 2, 21–22, 29–33.

JERUSALEM 16 AH/637 AD – 492 AH/1099 AD A CHRONOLOGY

16/637	Arabs conquer Jerusalem. Caliph 'Umar enters the city, and issues covenant to its people.
34/654–55	'Ubāda b. al-Ṣāmit, companion of the Prophet, dies in Jerusalem.
38/658–59	Mu'āwiya b. Abi Sufyān, later caliph, and 'Amr b. al-'Ās, conclude a pact of mutual support at the Dome of the Rock.
40/660–61	Mu'āwiya receives the *bay'a* in Jerusalem.
50/670	Bishop Arculf of Gaul visits Jerusalem.
53/672–673	Fairūz al-Dailamī, companion of the Prophet, dies in Jerusalem.
58/677–78	Shaddād b. Aws, companion of the Prophet, dies in Jerusalem.
Ramaḍān 65/ March–April 685	'Abd al-Malik b. Marwān, the Umayyad caliph, receives the *bay'a* in Jerusalem.
68/687–88	Construction of the Dome of the Rock is started.
72/691–92	Construction of the Dome of the Rock is concluded.
85 or 86/704–705	Companion of the Prophet Wāthila b. al-Aqsa' dies in Jerusalem.
*c.*90/708–09	Construction of al-Aqṣā Mosque is concluded.
96/715	Caliph Sulaimān b. 'Abd al-Malik receives his *bay'a* in Jerusalem.
130/747–48	Earthquake in Palestine. Al-Aqṣā Mosque and the Church of the Holy Sepulchre are severely damaged.
135 (or 185)/ 752–53	Rābi'a al-'Adawiyya, illustrated woman mystic, dies and is buried on the Mount of Olives. 'Aṭā' b. Muslim al-Khurāsānī, scholar and mufassir, dies in Jerusalem.
140/757–58	Al-Manṣūr, Abbāsid caliph, visits Jerusalem.
141/758–59	Al-Aqṣā Mosque is repaired and renovated.
154/771	Earthquake hits Jerusalem; al-Aqṣā Mosque is damaged. Al-Manṣūr visits Jerusalem and orders repair of al-Aqṣā.
158/775	Another earthquake hits Jerusalem; al-Aqṣā is damaged again.
163/779–80	The 'Abbāsid caliph, al-Mahdī, visits Jerusalem and orders restoration of the mosque.
205–207/ 820–822	'Abdullāh b. Ṭāhir (governor of Syria 820–822 AD) builds a portico in al-Aqṣā.

216/831–832	The 'Abbāsid caliph, al-Ma'mūn, orders restoration of the Dome of the Rock.
217/832–833	The word *al-Quds* appears on coin issued by al-Ma'mūn.
253/868	Monk Bernard the Wise visits Jerusalem.
255/868–69	Muḥammad b. Karrām, leader of the Karrāmiyya sect, dies and is buried in Jerusalem.
264/877–78	Aḥmad b. Ṭūlūn, governor of Egypt, occupies Palestine.
292/904–05	Rule of the Ṭūlūnids in Palestine ends.
296/908–09	'Īsā b. Mūsā al-Nawsharī, first 'Abbāsid governor in Egypt after the fall of the Ṭūlūnids, is buried in Jerusalem.
301/914	Umm al-Muqtadir, the mother of the 'Abbāsid caliph, orders construction of the gates of the Ṣakhra.
326/938	Fire damages the Holy Sepulchre.
328/940	Muḥammad al-Ikhshīd, founder of the Ikhshīdid state in Egypt, occupies Palestine.
331/942–43	Takīn b. 'Abdullāh, 'Abbāsid governor of Egypt, is buried in Jerusalem.
334/945–46	Muḥammad al-Ikhshīd is buried in Jerusalem.
335/946–47	Muḥammad b. Aḥmad al-Maqdisī al-Bishārī, famous geographer, is born in Jerusalem.
342/953–54	Al-Ḥasan b. Ṭugj, brother of al-Ikhshīd, is buried in Jerusalem.
349/960–61	Anujur, al-Ikhshīd ruler of Egypt, is buried in Jerusalem.
350/961–62	Kāphūr, minister of the Ikhshīdids, orders restorations in al-Ḥaram al-Sharīf.
355/965–66	'Alī b. al-Ikhshīd, ruler of Egypt, is buried in Jerusalem.
	Muḥammad al-Sanhājī, Maghribī governor of Jerusalem, attacks the Holy Sepulchre and kills John, the Patriarch of Jerusalem.
358/969	End of Ikhshīdid state.
359/969–70	The Fāṭimids occupy Jerusalem.
380/990–91	Geographer al-Maqdisī dies.
400/1009	The Fāṭimid caliph, al-Ḥākim, orders destruction of the Church of the Holy Sepulchre.
405/1014–1015	Al-Ḥākim revokes measures against Christians.
407/1016	Earthquake damages Dome of the Rock and some walls of al-Aqṣā.
408/1017–18	Dome of the Rock is repaired by al-Ḥākim.
410/1019–20	Church of the Holy Sepulchre is rebuilt by order of al-Ḥākim.

411/1020–21	Al-Ḥākim pledges security for Christians.
413/1022–23	Dome of the Rock is rebuilt by the Fāṭimid caliph, al-Ẓāhir.
418/1027	Dome of the Rock is restored.
	The Fāṭimids conclude an agreement with the Byzantines concerning the restoration of the Church of Resurrection (Holy Sepulchre).
424/1033	The Fāṭimids strengthen the wall of Jerusalem.
425/1033	Earthquake in Palestine; Mosque of Jerusalem and its walls are severely damaged.
	The Fāṭimid al-Ẓāhir repairs the walls of the Ḥaram and the fortifications of the city walls.
426/1035	Al-Aqṣā Mosque is rebuilt, and the Dome of the Rock repaired under al-Ẓāhir.
437/1045–46	Moroccan traveller Khālid al-Balawī visits Jerusalem.
438/1047	Persian traveller Nāṣir-i Khusrau visits Jerusalem.
439–40/1048	Italian merchants establish in Jerusalem a hospital served by the brothers of St John.
445/1053–54	Aḥmad b. Marwān, prince of Diyār Bakr, endows two buildings in Jerusalem as a waqf for the benefit of visitors from Diyār Bakr.
445–46/1054	Relations of the Patriarchs of Jerusalem with Rome severed after schism in the Christian Church.
	Arab patriarchs govern Jerusalem Church until 1534 AD.
*c.*450/1058–59	Shaikh Naṣr al-Dīn al-Maqdisī establishes a school/madrasa in Jerusalem.
456/1063-64	The Fāṭimid caliph, al-Mustanṣir, restores walls and fortifications of Jerusalem.
457/1065	12,000 German and Dutch pilgrims make a collective pilgrimage to the holy places.
458/1066	The Fāṭimid caliph, al-Mustanṣir, builds the facade of al-Aqṣā Mosque.
460/1068	Earthquake splits the Dome of the Rock.
465/1072–73	Turkomen under Atsiz storm Jerusalem and expel the Fāṭimid garrison.
	Nūr al-Dīn Zangī orders the manufacture of a *minbar* for the Aqṣā Mosque in Aleppo.
469/1076-77	Inhabitants of Jerusalem revolt against their Turkomen rulers. Atsiz enters the city and kills about 3,000 people.
470/1078	Soldiers of Tutush, Saljuq governor of Damascus, storm Jerusalem, and kill Atsiz.
479/1086–87	Tutush gives Jerusalem to Artuq b. Aksab.
484/1091–92	Artuq hands Jerusalem over to his sons Suqman and Il-Ghāzī.
489/1095	Abu Ḥamīd al-Ghazālī visits Jerusalem and gives himself up to worship and meditation at al-Aqṣā Mosque.

490/1096	Famous scholar Naṣr al-Maqdisī dies in Damascus.
491/1098	Fāṭimids led by al-Afḍal al-Jamālī recover Jerusalem from the Saljuqs.
Rajab 492/ June 1099	Crusaders put Jerusalem under siege.
29 Sha'bān 492/ 15 July 1099	Crusaders enter Jerusalem, storm al-Aqṣā Mosque and kill some 70,000 persons.

The Editor

CHAPTER V

Crusader Jerusalem 1099–1187 AD

Mustafa A Hiyari

JERUSALEM UNDER THE SALJUQ TURKS

In 486/1093, only half a century after Nāṣir-i Khusrau visited Jerusalem and six years before its capture by the Crusaders, a young Andalusian student, the future famous scholar Abu Bakr b. al-ʻArabī, visited the Holy City on his way to Mecca to perform the Ḥajj (pilgrimage) in the company of his father. At that time the cultural and intellectual activity in the city was so diverse and interesting that he decided to stay there to continue his studies. Many Shāfiʻī and Ḥanafī scholars were teaching in their schools, but what interested him most were the new methods of discussion and teaching unfamiliar in his home country.[1]

Ibn al-ʻArabī's stay in Jerusalem continued for more than three years. Later he wrote an itinerary, *Riḥla*, about his trip to the east, extracts of which are still preserved in his other works. The sections relating to Jerusalem give a vivid, though incomplete, picture of some aspects of life in the Holy City during the ninth decade of the 5th century AH (tenth decade of the 11th century AD).[2]

Jerusalem and most of Palestine were at the time of Ibn al-ʻArabī ruled by Saljuq Turks, since Atsiz b. Awaq al-Khwārazmī had occupied it twenty years earlier (Shaʻbān 466/April 1074). During that period, the city witnessed a cultural revival, particularly in religious and *fiqh* studies, that it had never seen during the 110 years of Fāṭimid domination (358–466/869–1074). Mujīr al-Dīn, the well-known compiler of the history of Jerusalem in the second half of the 9th century AH, attested to this fact. No eminent scholar in any branch of learning is mentioned in his work during that period,[3] but for the short Turkish rule he listed a number of prominent scholars who resided in the city or visited it for short periods.[4] Abu al-Fatḥ Naṣr, al-Tartushī, al-Ghazālī, and Ibn al-'Arabī were among them.[5]

The extant extracts of the *Riḥla* and other extracts preserved in the works of Ibn al-'Arabī stress certain distinctive features of the educational and social life in the Holy City: first, the existence of two Sunnī schools for the Shāfi'ites and the Ḥanafites which were founded during the Turkish period. Prominent professors held regular lectures and seminars for their students; second, the inter-religious dialogues held in the city in which Muslim, Christian and Jewish scholars participated and discussed diverse topics.[6] A third feature, which is more significant, is the attitude of the inhabitants towards the internal feuds of the ruling class in the city. He says that he witnessed in the city an incident the like of which could never happen in his home town or any other town in al-Andalus. His narrative, telling in more than one respect of the Jerusalemites' past experiences, is worth quoting in detail:

> In the Tower of David I witnessed a very strange incident. Someone revolted against the governor of the city and entrenched himself in the Tower. The governor attempted to assault him by using his archers for some time. Meanwhile, the city, although small,[7] continued its normal life as usual. No market was closed because of these disturbances (*fitna*), no one of the commoners (*'awāmm*) participated in it by making violence, no ascetic (*mu'takif*) left his place in al-Aqṣā Mosque and no discussion (*munāẓara*) was suspended. The soldiers alone were divided into two groups fighting each other, and no one else cared or moved from his place. If such an incident happened in our country (al-Andalus) fighting would spread near and far, work and life would stop, shops would close . . .[8]

That studied indifference of the inhabitants of Jerusalem was the result of their recurring past sufferings as a consequence of similar civil disturbances. A sketch of the history of the city during the 11th century AD would give a clear picture of such experiences. The Holy City suffered greatly from disasters that were inflicted by man and nature.

The 11th century opened, as far as Jerusalem is concerned, with the destruction of the Church of the Holy Sepulchre and the persecution of the Christians there on the orders of the Fāṭimid caliph al-Ḥākim, and was concluded with the blood baths of the Frankish occupation which nearly exterminated all of its inhabitants by the sword. Between the beginning of the century and its end, Jerusalem witnessed a series of developments that had their impact on its future. A short survey of these developments would help us to understand the Crusader period in Jerusalem.

In 399/1009, al-Ḥākim wrote to the governor of Palestine ordering him to destroy the Church of the Holy Sepulchre. On Thursday 5 Ṣafar 400/28 September 1099, the church was levelled to the ground.[9] In addition, a policy of harassing the Christian inhabitants of the city began which led to their departure en masse to Byzantine lands. Thereafter, the Church of the Holy Sepulchre became a central issue in the diplomatic relations between the Fāṭimid caliphate and Byzantium. In 405/1014–15 and after, when al-Ḥākim abolished some of the measures taken against the Christians, a Byzantine ambassador was sent to Cairo where he was received by al-Ḥākim himself. The outcome of the embassy is not known, but Jerusalem and Palestine were dominated by the Jarrāḥids of Tayyi' for a short time[10] during which their amīr, as self appointed ruler of the country, appointed a patriarch for the city, helped the Christians to rebuild the Church of the Holy Sepulchre and shared, as Yaḥyā b. Sa'īd informs us, in the expenses as far as his limited means could allow.[11]

After the death of al-Ḥākim cordial relations between the Fāṭimids and the Byzantine empire were resumed and negotiations between the two sides started to be resolved in 418/1027 in the signing of an agreement. The treaty stipulated, among other things, 'the opening of the Church of the Holy Sepulchre'. The Byzantine emperor and the kings of Christendom, says al-Maqrīzī, 'sent money and other materials to the church and it returned as it was'.[12] Yaḥyā b. Sa'īd, however, says that during the negotiations, which dragged on for a long time, the 'king' of Byzantium asked permission to rebuild the Church of the Holy Sepulchre at his own expense, as well as all other ruined churches in the land of al-Ẓāhir of Egypt, and to appoint the patriarch of Jerusalem. In return, the emperor promised to release all Muslim prisoners captured during his reign and that of his predecessor.[13] No final agreement was reached and negotiations continued.[14] Late in 424/1033, al-Ẓāhir ordered the rebuilding of the walls of Jerusalem, but a strong earthquake that took place on Thursday 10 Ṣafar 425/4 January 1034 stopped the work and destroyed half of the city of Ramla and sections of its wall, most of Jericho, Nablus and neighbouring villages and a part of al-Aqṣā Mosque.[15]

Negotiations between the Fāṭimids and Byzantium went on, and in 427/1035 a treaty was concluded between the two sides for a period of ten years.[16] The Caliph al-Ẓāhir died that same year but the new caliph, al-Mustanṣir, confirmed the treaty. The main article of the treaty stipulated that the Byzantine emperor should release five thousand Muslim prisoners before he could rebuild the Church of the Holy Sepulchre. Following this agreement, the emperor spent large sums of money on the reconstruction.[17] In 433/1037 the treaty was abrogated by the Byzantines when they attacked northern Syria, but no Fāṭimid retaliation was recorded against the Church of the Holy Sepulchre or the Christians of Jerusalem. Four years later good relations between the two powers were resumed and they exchanged ambassadors and presents.[18] Less than a year later (Ramaḍān 438/ March 1047),[19] Nāṣir-i Khusrau visited Jerusalem and described the 'large' and prosperous city. His visit took place nine years after the conclusion of the treaty and his description of the state of the walls and the Church of the Holy Sepulchre confirms the execution of the terms of the agreement. According to Nāṣir, the walls were in excellent shape and the church was completed and finely decorated.[20] Nine years later, however, relations between the two powers deteriorated. This was caused by the rise of the Saljuq power in the east and the permission given by the Byzantine emperor to the Turks to proclaim the *khuṭba* in the mosque of Constantinople in the name of the 'Abbāsid caliph and the Saljuq amīr.[21] As expected, al-Mustanṣir retaliated and ordered the closure of the Church of the Holy Sepulchre and the confiscation of its contents. He dismissed the patriarch and detained him in a separate house, closed all the churches in Egypt and Syria, increased the *jizya* tax on Christians and ordered all monks to pay the *jizya* for four years in advance.[22]

It was during this period that we find the first indication of granting an endowment (*waqf*) for people coming from outside Syria. In an inscription dated 445/1053–54, the Marwānid prince of Diyār Bakr donated two adjoining houses just outside the walls of al-Aqṣā Mosque for all those coming from Diyār Bakr to visit Jerusalem.[23] It is interesting to note that this happened at a time when the Fāṭimid caliphate was seeking the support and active participation of the Marwānids in al-Basāsīrī's movement to topple the 'Abbāsid caliphate. Other Mashāriqa groups might have had *waqfs* in the city, but no extant documentation is available.

The rise of the Saljuq sultanate in the east and the advance of their forces and Turkomen tribes towards Syria (Bilād al-Shām) initiated a new era in the history of Palestine. In Jerusalem new internal and external developments, caused to a large extent by the Turkish challenge and the inability of the Fāṭimids to meet it, began. During the second half of the eleventh century 'the Quarter of the Patriarch' was created, the original house of the hospital was founded, the Turkomen occupied the city and ruled it as deputies of the Saljuq sultans for more than twenty years, al-Afḍal b. Badr al-Jamālī regained Jerusalem for the Fāṭimids (491/1098), and a year later it was stormed by the Franks. Let us now briefly consider each of those developments.

Until only a decade or so before the Turkomen occupation the inhabitants of Jerusalem, Muslims and Christians alike, 'dwelt together indifferently',[24] but when the Quarter of the Patriarch came into being, the living quarters for both changed. The Muslims were forced by the order of the Fāṭimid caliph 'to move to other parts of Jerusalem, leaving that quarter . . .' to the Christians alone.[25] The reason given by our only authority on this matter, William of Tyre, was that the walls of the city were in a bad condition and the Fāṭimids ordered the Christian inhabitants to fortify a part of it. Unable to do so by their own means, the Christians asked for permission to contact the Byzantine emperor to support them. An agreement was reached between the caliph and the Byzantine emperor Constantine, which stipulated that the latter should finance the fortification of the Christian section (which was completed in 1063) provided that the Christian inhabitants would be the sole inhabitants of their quarter.[26]

The boundaries of the Christian quarter, as specified by William of Tyre,[27] were as follows:

> The outer boundary is formed by the wall which extends from the west gate, or the gate of David, past the corner tower which is known [in William's time] as the tower of Tancred as far as the north gate which is called by the name of the first martyr, Stephen. The inner boundary is formed by the public street which runs from the gate of Stephen straight to the tables of the money changers [St Stephen's Street of the Crusaders], and thence again back to the west gate.[28]

The whole quarter, as also was stipulated by the treaty, was put under the jurisdiction of the patriarch, and it was known, during the Crusader period, as the Quarter of the Patriarch.[29]

Another gift was given during that period by Caliph al-Mustanṣir, just before the Turkish occupation, to European merchants. This gift was a piece of land in the Christian quarter[30] given to the Amalfitan merchants for their accommodation in

Jerusalem. They built a monastery which was later known as St Mary of the Latins, the convent of St Mary Magdalene to provide shelter for female pilgrims, and a hospice and a church of St John which became the hospital of St John.[31]

Immediately after these developments, Jerusalem was taken by the Turkomen.

THE TURKOMEN OCCUPATION

In a letter sent by Atsiz b. Awāq al-Khwārazmī, the leader of the Turkomen groups that invaded southern Syria, to the 'Abbāsid caliph and the Saljuq sultan,[32] the Turkomen amīr described how he and his men took Jerusalem in Shawwāl 465/June 1073. Atsiz advanced and besieged the city but he refused to assault it or capture it by force saying, '[It is] God's sanctuary. I will not fight it.' The Fāṭimid governor of the city was a Turk and at the beginning he refused to surrender. But the long siege and the scarcity of food within the city forced him to negotiate. He sent messengers to Atsiz saying, 'I am with you. I refused to surrender before out of loyalty to the one in whose service I am. I have done my duty and now if you give me safe conduct *(amān)* for myself and my property I will surrender the city and join you.'[33] Atsiz gave him a written *amān* and swore to abide by its terms. In addition he granted him an *iqṭā'* of a number of estates (*ḍiyā'*) which the governor had enumerated. The governor then opened the gate of the city, Atsiz and his men entered and he gave an *amān* for all the inhabitants. Moreover, he ordered his men not to touch anything of the great wealth in the city and he appointed guards to protect it, 'something that the inhabitants did not expect'.[34]

The Fāṭimid garrison – composed of Turks, Sudanese infantry and Masāmida Berbers – remained in the city and so did, it seems, the administrative officials of Jerusalem such as the *qāḍī*, the *muḥtasib* and *ṣāhib al-shurṭa*. The Turks joined Atsiz, the others stayed on as private citizens.

Four years after the capture of Jerusalem, Atsiz was in Egypt fighting to establish the authority of the 'Abbāsid Caliphate and the Saljuq Sultanate in that country. He was defeated (Rajab 469/January–February 1077) and fled with some of his troops to Damascus which he entered on 10 Sha'bān/9 March of the same year.[35] In Jerusalem the pro-Fāṭimid inhabitants revolted against the Turks, took all their properties, captured the women and enslaved the children. The walls of the strong citadel protected those who were stationed or lived there.[36]

Atsiz, upon learning of these developments, regrouped what had remained of his Turkomen forces, hurried towards Jerusalem and besieged it. He did not assault it, hoping to quell the revolt peacefully. He sent a messenger to the city demanding surrender and promising safe conduct for all. The inhabitants refused the offer and threatened to fight him. Again, he himself advanced to the wall and addressed them in the hope of reaching a compromise but they refused and cursed him. Atsiz then assaulted the city for a day and a night but in vain. Atsiz's women, who were confined within the citadel's walls, found their way out through a postern (*ratq*) in the outer wall. They joined him and showed him the way. Thus he entered with some of his troops, opened the gate for the rest of the army, and immediately attacked the rebellious inhabitants. The *qāḍī* and the witnesses, who seem to have been leaders, were killed together with some three thousand others. Only those who took refuge in the precinct of the Noble Sanctuary (al-Ḥaram al-Sharīf) were saved, but they were ordered to pay ransom money.[37]

Atsiz's main headquarters were in Damascus. He left Jerusalem and appointed as his deputy there a certain Turmush who resided with Atsiz's women and baggage in the Tower of David. When Tutush b. Alp Arslān came to Syria to reinforce the Turkomen against the Fāṭimid threat, he killed Atsiz (Rabī' 472/September 1079) and dominated all his lands. He then commissioned Artuq b. Aksab as governor and *muqṭa'* (vassal) of Jerusalem and its district. Turmush surrendered the city without resistance and Tutush compensated him with an *iqṭā'* equal to that he gave up. It included the citadel of Ṣalkhad in the Hawrān and its territories. Atsiz's cousin, wife and daughter, who were living at the time in the citadel in Jerusalem, were afraid of Tutush for their life and left Syria for Baghdad.[38]

The Artuqids ruled Jerusalem for a period of almost twenty years which were peaceful and prosperous. In 482/1089 a new mosque was built,[39] the ruined church of St Anne was transformed and built as a Shāfi'ī school, and a Ḥanafī school was established.[40]

After the death of Artuq the city was given to his two sons, Suqman and Il-Ghāzī. The two brothers ruled there peacefully until Sha'bān 491/July 1098 when al-Afḍal b. Badr al-Jamālī led a large expedition to Jerusalem and besieged it. He attempted first to take it without using force, but the Artuqids refused to surrender. Al-Afḍal then bombarded it with mangonels and other machines.[41] Ibn

Muyassar says that a section of the wall fell and the Artuqids realized the impossibility of further resistance and surrendered.[42] Sibṭ b. al-Jawzī, relying on more contemporary evidence, says that fighting continued for forty days, after which the inhabitants sent messengers to al-Afḍal promising to open the gate if he gave them safe conduct. Al-Afḍal accepted the offer, the inhabitants opened the gate and the Fāṭimid troops entered the city. Meanwhile, Suqman and his brother left the city from another gate, one for Edessa and the other for Baghdad.[43]

THE LATINS IN JERUSALEM

In July 1098 al-Afḍal took possession of Jerusalem for the Fāṭimids, organized its affairs, left a a governor (*iftikhār al-dawla*) with a suitable garrison and returned with his forces to Cairo. Meanwhile, the Crusaders in northern Syria had occupied Antioch (3 June). Two or three months before that date, al-Afḍal's ambassadors were in the Frankish camp before Antioch negotiating with the Franks and proposing a division of the Saljuq lands in Syria between them: the Franks were to take northern Syria and the Fāṭimids Palestine. But the Frankish leaders, knowing the main aim of their expedition, 'did not commit themselves to any specific arrangement.'[44] The Fāṭimid embassy returned home.[45] Early in June 1099 the Frankish forces appeared before the walls of Jerusalem.

At the beginning of the siege, the city was crowded with tens of thousands of people who fled before the advancing Frankish forces and sought the protection of its fortifications, thereby increasing its fighting force. The Christian inhabitants were mostly forced to leave the city for the Muslims feared their co-operation with the Franks. The inhabitants of Bethlehem had already done so by sending a delegation to al-Ramla and inviting Frankish leaders to take their town.[46]

The Frankish forces besieged Jerusalem at two main sections of the wall, the southern where Raymond St Agilier and his men were stationed on Mount Zion and the northern section extending from the Damascus Gate to the northwestern corner of the wall opposite the plain of al-Sāhira where Godfrey and his men were encamped. The defence of the first section was mostly the responsibility of the garrison in the Tower of David, while the other section was defended mostly by the experienced inhabitants supported by the garrison and the soldiers who took refuge in the city.

For almost forty days the Crusader forces continued assaulting the walls of the city using all siege machines which they had or could build. What won the day in the end was the famous tower (al-Burj) which was constructed with materials and help provided by the skilled Genoese sailors who joined the forces of Godfrey. Raymond's men used first scaling ladders, but to no avail, so they decided, in their turn, to build a tower.

The men of Jerusalem, and the women, defended the northern wall bravely. One Crusader source says:

> The attackers often had to defend against relief forces [coming from other sections], while pounding and undermining the walls at the same time, in most cases hoping that despair and starvation would force the defenders to give up. Though the Muslims might protect their walls with sacks of straw and chaff, ropes and tapestries, huge wooden beams and mattresses stuffed with silk, still the Crusaders hammered away.[47]

Thus the experienced fighters within the city succeeded in repelling the Frankish attacks. But when the latter used the 'famous' tower[48] to which the defenders were not accustomed, the Crusaders won the day and stormed the city.

At noon of Friday 15 July 1099, after a month of continuous assault, and 'amid the sound of trumpets and with everything in an uproar . . . shouting "God help us"', the Franks forced their way into the city. The defenders fled through the narrow streets, the Franks following them.[49] An atrocious massacre followed. Almost all the inhabitants of the city, men, women and children, were massacred in the streets, alleys, houses, and wherever they were found. Those who took refuge in al-Ḥaram al-Sharīf hoping to be spared, as was the custom on previous occasions, were mostly massacred. Their number was estimated at some ten thousand persons.[50] Of the sixty or seventy thousand estimated to have been within the city's wall, only a small portion escaped massacre. The garrison within the strongly fortified David's Tower and those who managed to reach it were spared by an agreement concluded between Raymond St Agilier and Iftikhār al-Dawla and were given safe conduct to Ascalon and Egypt.[51] Some dignitaries and learned men were spared in the hope of selling them for large ransoms. One case mentioned by Mujīr al-Dīn is very informative. Shaikh 'Abd al-Salām al-Anṣārī was captured by the Franks. When they knew that he was a learned man, they took him to different parts of Palestine to

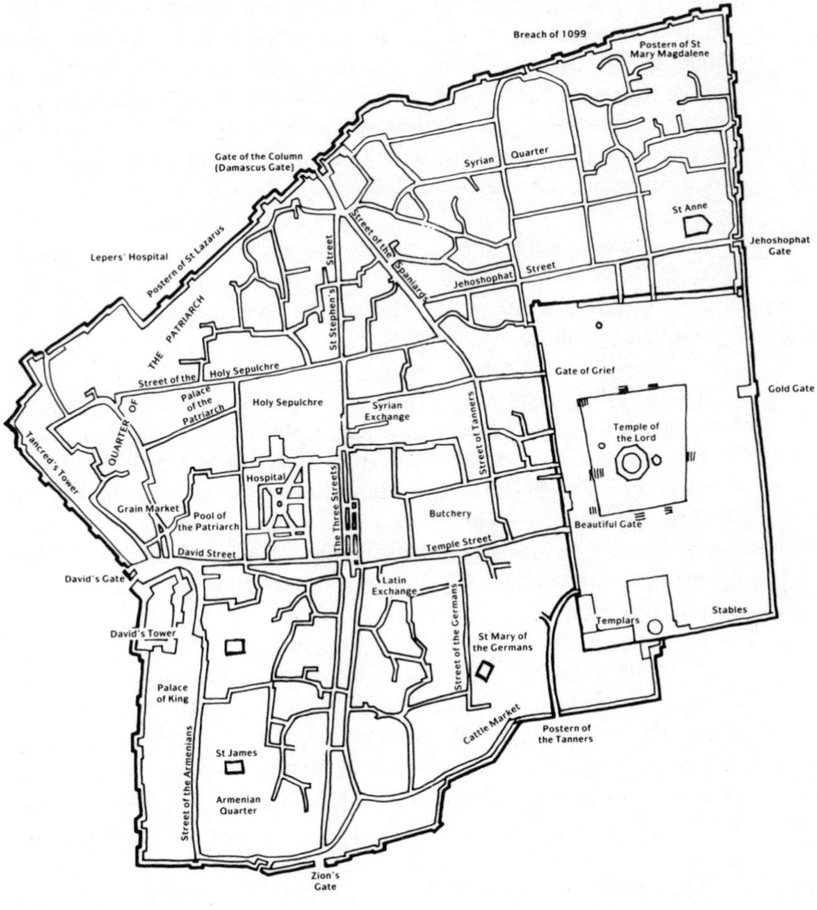

Fig. 12 Jerusalem in the Crusader period

be ransomed for a thousand dinars. When nobody paid the specified amount, he was killed. ʻAbd al-Jabbār b. Aḥmad of Isbahān was also killed. Both were Shāfiʻī scholars who came to Jerusalem during the Turkish domination.[52] Some groups of the spared captives were forced to clear the streets, the houses and the court of the Ḥaram of tens of thousands of human corpses, which were either collected in heaps and burnt or were thrown over the walls. When Fulcher of Chartres came to Jerusalem with Baldwin I some months later, the smell of rotting corpses was still infesting the air. He says:

> Oh, what a stench there was around the walls of the city, both within and without, from the rotting bodies of Saracens slain by our comrades at the time of the capture of Jerusalem, lying where they were hunted down.[53]

The Frankish expedition realized its main aim. The capture of Jerusalem for Christianity was accomplished. 15 July became a 'national' day and was celebrated each year by a pompous ceremony.[54] The first day after they entered the city and massacred the inhabitants, 'the clergy and laity, . . . going to the Lord's Sepulchre and his most glorious Temple, singing . . . and making offerings . . . visited the holy place . . .', weeping for what God had delivered to them.[55]

Jerusalem was emptied of all its inhabitants. Muslims and Jews were either killed or expelled. The native Christians and Greek clergy were forced, as mentioned above, to leave the city before the siege. The victorious Franks took possession of the houses and their contents. This was done according to the well-known 'law' of conquest. Fulcher of Chartres gives a true picture of how this was achieved:

> They entered the houses of the citizens, seizing whatever they found in them. This was done in such a way that whoever first entered a house . . . [and left an article of his arms at the door or anything else] was not challenged by any other Frank. He was to occupy and own the house or palace and whatever he found in it as if it were entirely his own. Thus they mutually agreed upon this right of possession. In this way many poor people became wealthy.[56]

A new episode began in the annals of the Holy City which extended over eighty-eight years. It was a short one compared to the long and rich history of the city. Nevertheless many changes took place within its walls, of which two will be considered in this chapter: the topographical and the socio-political.

The topographical changes that the Franks introduced in Jerusalem can be grouped into two categories: a change of function for some existing buildings to enable them to serve new purposes and the construction of new ones to serve the needs of the new inhabitants. Those changes, however, did not distort the general view of the city, which remained mostly as it was, but they added new decorations and refinements to suit the tastes of the new citizens.

The walls of the city were generally still intact since little serious damage was caused by the siege. The damage was repaired and two new additions were made: Tancred's Tower in the southwestern corner and St Mary Magdalene's postern in the northeast corner. The Shāfi'ī school was transformed into a church (St Anne) as it was in olden times.[57] Al-Aqṣā Mosque became the residence of the Latin king until it was granted to the Templars, who made it their central headquarters, adding new buildings to it, and al-Ṣakhra mosque became the Templum Domini. A new palace was built for the Latin king east of David's Tower. The Amalfitan complex continued its services and became the headquarters of the order of the Hospitallers. Hospices for European and oriental pilgrims of different nationalities were built in different sections of the city. New churches, monasteries and convents were also erected. Gate names, street names and place names were changed, especially if the old ones could not be accommodated to Latin. New markets, it seems, were also built.[58]

The socio-political changes in Jerusalem were radical. A new population of Latins, native Syrian Christians and other oriental Christian minorities replaced the old Muslim, native Christian and Jewish communities. A new political and administrative system was established. The social organization of the city, its institutions, daily life, celebrations and general festivities were also changed. The main features of these developments are summarized below.

REPOPULATING THE CITY

In July 1099 Jerusalem was emptied of all its previous inhabitants. They were replaced by the Franks who occupied its houses and appropriated everything they found therein. But not all those who entered the city stayed and settled in it. Most of those who participated in the capture of the Holy City left it for home or for other territories occupied by the Franks. According to William of Tyre, those who ultimately stayed in Jerusalem were small in number. They were scattered all over the city and, during the early period after the occupation, lived in a state of constant fear and insecurity.

> . . .Even within the city walls [Ramla, Jerusalem and Jaffa were the only ones occupied by the Franks], in the very houses, there was scarcely a place where one could rest in security. For the inhabitants were few and scattered . . . They broke into deserted cities whose few inhabitants were scattered far apart, and overpowered many in their own very houses. The result was that some stealthily, and many quite openly, abandoned the holdings which they had won and began to return to their own land.[59]

It was not only the lack of security that led the Franks to leave Jerusalem, but also the economic conditions in the city. For the unskilled Franks, mostly of peasant background, to gain a livelihood in the Holy City was very difficult. Jerusalem was a city that depended on the crafts and services needed by the tens of thousands of pilgrims who came each year to visit the holy places, and the majority of the new settlers were not trained or experienced in either. Therefore, some of them left for home, others for the newly captured commercial towns on the coast and some went to the countryside in the company of their lords.

This state of gradual depopulation led the Latin king to issue an edict by which an annual population count was made, and any house found unoccupied for a year and a day was taken back by the authorities.[60]

Those measures were not sufficient to populate the city and provide its inhabitants with necessary services needed by them and also by the continuous flow of pilgrims who visited the holy places. King Baldwin I (1110–1118) realized with great concern, William of Tyre reports, 'that the Holy City was almost destitute of inhabitants. There were not enough people to carry on necessary undertakings of the realm. Indeed there were scarcely enough to protect the entrances to the city and to defend the walls and towers against sudden hostile attacks . . .'[61]

To correct this situation King Baldwin I realized that he had to depend on the local Syrian Christian population. But most of the previous Christian inhabitants of Jerusalem were scattered either in the countryside or had moved to the commercial centres on the coast. A source was found. His expeditions and excursions east of the River Jordan acquainted him with the Christians living there whom he considered suitable for his purpose. 'He sent after these people and promised them improved conditions. In a short time he had the satisfaction of receiving them with their wives and children, flocks and herds, and all their household . . .' Many others came without invitation.[62] The king granted the new inhabitants a large section of the city 'which seemed to need this assistance most and fitted the houses with them.'[63] This section was known at that time as the Syrian Christian Quarter.

By the end of the third decade of the establishment of the Latin capital in the east, two main quarters of Jerusalem were populated, the Patriarch's Quarter where the Latins finally settled and the 'native' Christian Quarter. The boundaries of the first had been established since the sixth decade of the 11th century and the second occupied, most probably, the area within the old city limited by the following boundaries: Jehoshophat street which extended from the gate in the eastern wall called by that name to where it meets the street of the Spaniards in the west. The latter street formed the western boundary from its meeting with Jehoshophat street to St Stephen's gate [Damascus Gate or Bāb al-'Amūd]. The northern boundary was the northern wall of the city and the postern of St Mary Magdalene which occupied the northeastern corner of the city. The church of St Anne was not included in the quarter and the church of St Mary Magdalene was built to serve the new community.[64]

The establishment of Latin authority in Palestine, the maintenance of security in the nearby towns and on the roads leading to Jerusalem led to a gradual increase in the population of the city until it reached, towards the end of the first Latin kingdom, some ten thousand persons permanently settled there.[65] But this increase created, it seems, a problem of providing the city with the necessary foodstuffs. All food that was brought to the city was taxed. In 1120 the patriarch requested the king to remit that tax so that the city could be provided with its needs. The king issued the following edict:

> I, Baldwin II . . . yielding to the prayers of our father, Patriarch Guarmund, to the clergy and chapter of the Holy City of Jerusalem, do, with the approval of the nobles, now and in the

future remit the customs duties which have previously been demanded and given at the city gate by those bringing grain and vegetables into the city . . . Those dues seemed indeed burdensome and damaging not only to those coming to visit the Church of the Sepulchre of the Lord as well as to the residents of the Holy City. I therefore free of all exaction all those who wish to bring in grain or vegetables, beans, lentils, or peas through the gates of Jerusalem. Let them have free licence to go in and go out and sell without molestation where and to whom they wish, whether they are Christians or Muslims.[66]

In addition to the two main quarters mentioned above, other sections in Jerusalem were inhabited during the course of the 12th century. The number of Armenian clergy and laity grew steadily and they were settled in the southwestern section of the city around St James' Church. Other groups were settled in other empty parts of the city. The Germans were the last to come. John of Würzburg, a German who visited the Holy City in the sixties of the 12th century, was dismayed to find that no place was ascribed to or given the name of Germany or the Germans, although they were prominent participants in the first expedition.[67] A few years later, a German street, a hospice and a St Mary of the Germans were established to the east of the street of Mount Zion.[68]

Two generations after the establishment of the Latin Kingdom, John of Würzburg also mentions other national and religious groups which were settled in the city and maintained small chapels and churches:

For there are Greeks, Bulgarians, Latins, Germans, Hungarians, Scots, Navarres, Bretons, English, Franks, Ruthenians, Bohemians, Georgians, Armenians, Jacobites, Syrians, Nestorians, Indians, Egyptians, Copts, Capheturici, Maronites, and very many others . . .[69]

Those different groups of the inhabitants of Jerusalem could be distinguished, according to the anonymous pilgrim who visited the city just before Saladin recaptured it in 1187, by some of their traits, their style of dress and the way they grew their beards. His observations would enable a stroller in the streets of the city at that time to differentiate between the 'nationalities' and religious groups living there. The following are the major groups and their distinguishing features: the Latins (or Franks) were warlike men,

1 Macalister's so-called 'Tower of David', in reality Maccabean

2 Steps, cisterns and entrance of the 'Tomb of the Kings'

3 Herod's Gate

4 'Solomon's Stables', the vaulting beneath the southeast corner of the Ḥaram

5 The 'Tomb of Absalom' and the southeast corner of the Ḥaram wall

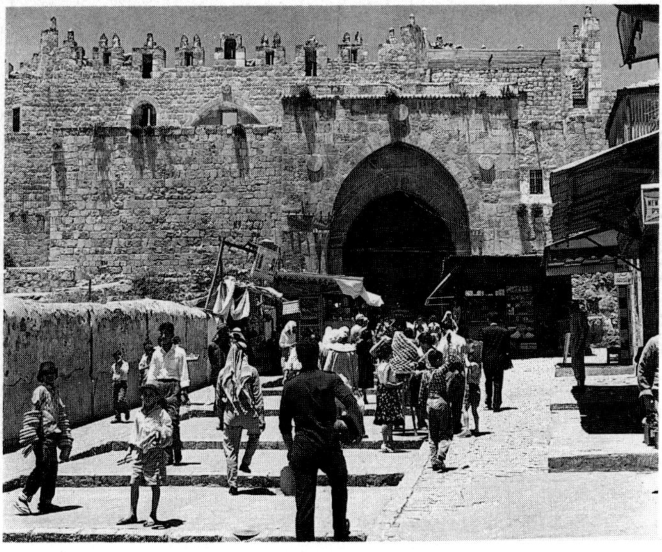

6 The inside of the Damascus Gate and the beginning of the Cardo Maximus

7 **Inscribed column of the X Legio Fretensis, near the Greek Orthodox Patriarchates**

8 The Hadrianic gate beneath the Damascus Gate

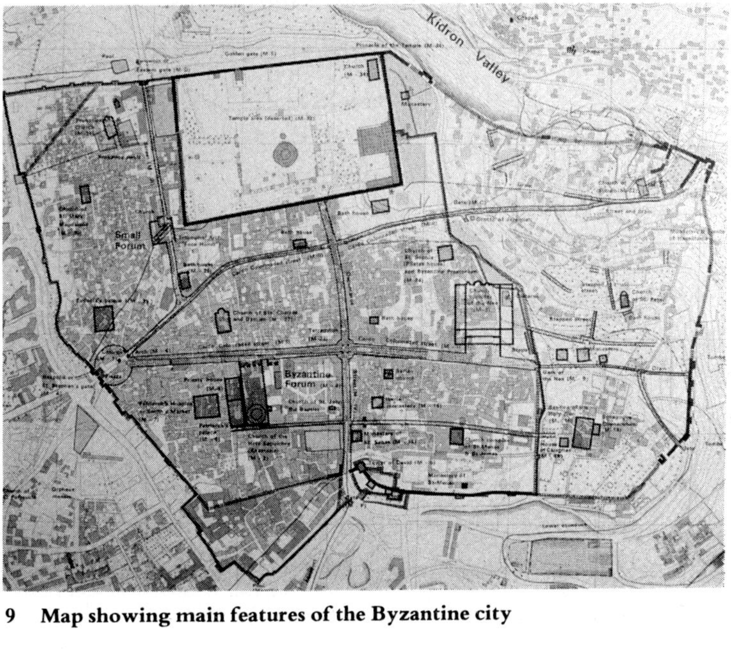

9 Map showing main features of the Byzantine city

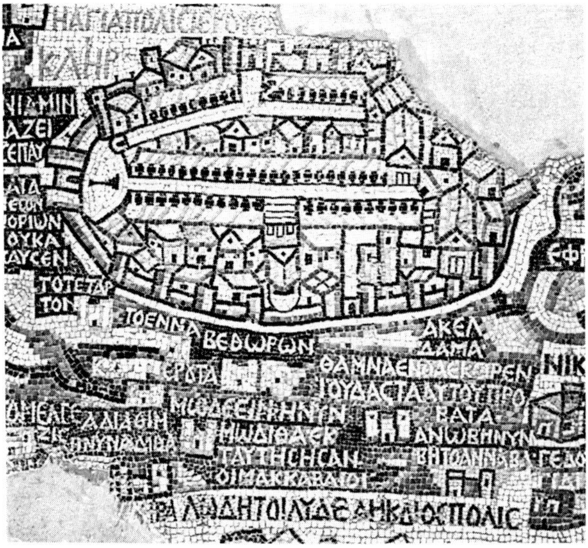

10 The Madaba mosaic map of Jerusalem

11 The straight joint at the southeast corner of the Ḥaram

12 The Triple Gate in the south wall of the Ḥaram before excavation

13 The East Qanāṭir on the Ḥaram platform

14 The south wall of the Ḥaram and the Golden Gate

15 Ṭarīq al-Saray and the Chapel of St Veronica

16 The Chapel of the Ascension

17 The upper part of the Holy Sepulchre with scaffolding in position

18 The Tomb of the Virgin

19 The Qubbat Sulaiman in the Ḥaram

20 The east wall of the Old City (Sheep Market)

21 The Damascus Gate

22 St Stephen's Gate

23 David Street

24 A market off Ṭarīq Khān al-Zait

25 Government House

26 The Rockefeller Museum

27 **Schneller Orphanage**

28 **Windmill maintained by public funds**

bareheaded and the only ones who shaved their beards. The Greeks were cunning, grew their beards long and in a certain style, but they were not much practised in arms. The Syrian Christians were different from all other groups. They were 'useless in war' and 'for the most part they do not let their beards grow like the Greeks, but trim them somewhat . . . They are everywhere tributary to other nations . . . They use the Saracenic [Arabic] alphabet.' They were, however, similar to the Greeks in other ways. The Armenians, who were numerous in the city at that time,[70] differ in many respects from the Latins and the Greeks. They had some slight skill in arms and a language of their own. The Georgians also had a language of their own, a way of growing their beard and a special type of hat. 'They let their hair and beards grow long and wear hats a cubit long. All of them, both churchmen and laymen, wear the tonsure, round and square respectively . . . and imitate the Greeks in almost all respects.'[71]

SOCIETY AND SOCIAL LIFE IN JERUSALEM

Before the Frankish occupation, the city of Jerusalem had its own social structure and administration like any other Islamic city in the area: a ruling class of soldiery of either Fāṭimid troops or Turks and the general population of *'ulamā'* and merchants (forming the leadership), craftsmen and traders (of all levels), as reflected in the specialized streets mentioned by Nāṣir-i Khuṣrau, and other commoners who provided the different services the city needed.

The administration of the city and its inhabitants was centred around the military governor and the representatives of the different departments of government (*dawāwīn*). The *qāḍī* was the most important among them in any urban community, and he had his witnesses and scribes. He ruled according to the *Sharī'a* whether of the Shi'ī (Fāṭimid) or Sunnī (Turks) schools. His jurisdiction included all Muslims in the city and its administrative district except in *maẓālim* (grievances) cases which were brought before the governor with the judge at his side. Christians and Jews were governed by their own 'laws' except in cases which involved Muslims. In addition, there were the two institutions of the *ḥisba* and the *shurṭa*. Each had its own head, assistants (*a'wān*) and men in numbers suitable for the administration of the city's affairs.[72]

After the capture of Jerusalem by the Franks in 1099, all this was changed and a new society gradually emerged with a new administration. At the beginning, the new inhabitants were all Latins who participated in the First Crusade. They were composed, in addition to the clergy, of two main social groups. The upper class was formed of high nobility, the baronage and the knights who were predominantly settled in cities.[73] They formed the ruling class and the core of the fighting force of the kingdom. The second class was composed of the peasantry of Latin Europe. According to J Prawer, 'it is among the thousands of pedites [men who became free by joining the crusade] of the First Crusade that we have to look for the elements which would later form the class of burgesses.'[74] It is clear that the majority of those who were settled in Jerusalem were of rural background, and as such were not trained in the trades, crafts and services which formed the economy the city needed. The course of the siege of Jerusalem in June–July 1099 is indicative in this regard. The Frankish army was 'unable to build siege towers and other machinery until the arrival at Jaffa of Genoese ships bearing materials and craftsmen experienced in more complicated skills of construction.'[75]

Gradually, there appeared in Jerusalem a new but distinct class of non-nobles as an integral part of the city's life. J Prawer attributes the beginning of this organization to the privilege granted by Baldwin I to the canons of the Holy Sepulchre when he granted his optimates, milites and burgesses the right to concede freely their revenues to the Holy Sepulchre.[76] Their position in the city was determined by their living within the city, their large numbers and their occupations.[77] J Richard states that 'It is probable . . . that the burgesses of Jerusalem had an exceptional role to fill, and that the greater among them were separated by only very little from the lesser knights.'[78] Their role formed the backbone of the city's economy and provided some five hundred sergeants for the army.[79] Their life in the city was governed by the 'burgesses courts'. Its jurisdiction was limited to the Franks alone, 'since the burgesses of Jerusalem never included the local Christian population.'[80]

The two military orders (Templars and Hospitallers) formed, during the 12th century, two distinct groups of Europeans living in Jerusalem. Like the high nobility, the knights, the burgesses and the clergy, they were not integrated in the city's society. Both were governed by their own rules of conduct.[81] So also were the other classes which had their own courts.

The native Christians and the other oriental Christians lived in their respective quarters and were to a certain extent governed by their own 'courts'. The 'court of the *ra'īs*', according to J Richard, 'judged minor matters according to the custom of each community.'[82]

Jerusalem was the capital of the Latin kingdom. The king was the head of its government. The king's secular representative in administering the city was the viscount.[83] He was the chief tax agent and police officer. He was supported, it seems, by the methessep (Arabic *muḥtasib*).[84] The function and duties of this office were clearly specified by law:

> The duty of the methessep is to go every morning to the public places, that is to say, to the butcher shops and the places where bread and wine and other things are sold. There he should take care that no fraud takes place among the sellers and that there be no shortage of bread, as the court has ordered, and that the published prices should be observed, particularly for bread, wine, cartage, and fish . . . Thus he should go around the city supervising these affairs . . . To that end he should have inspectors to report to him the malpractices that he cannot detect on his own . . . He in turn should report to the viscount whatever he has discovered. And if he discovers anyone acting improperly or charged with such, he should have him taken into custody by one or two sergeants whom he should have with him as often as possible and have the accused brought before the viscount and explain the crime or the accusation. If the viscount cannot for any reason hear the charge, the methessep can and should remand the person to prison and bring the case to the attention of the viscount on the earliest possible occasion. Thus he can arrest anyone and put him in prison, but he cannot and should not release anyone from prison without an order from the viscount or the court . . . He is also responsible for conducting, in the company of sergeants, the convicted to the place of their punishment, likewise those condemned to be broken or to lose their life or limb . . .[85]

The jurisdiction of the viscount or methessep included all those inhabitants of the city who were involved in trade or crafts. Most of them worked in the market, and the people of the same profession gathered in one market or place as was the case before the Frankish occupation. Thus there were special places and markets in Jerusalem for cooks, money changers, smiths, skinners, tanners and others.[86] In other aspects of their life they were ruled by their 'special courts' and the higher courts of the realm.

Church religious festivities and some other religio-secular ones were an important aspect in the life of Jerusalem. A large number of its inhabitants and crowds of pilgrims participated in these occasions. During the 12th century, there was a large number of such festivities and celebrations in the church calendar of which the Easter celebrations were the most important. Others, like the celebration each year of the capture of the city on 15 July, the anniversary of Duke Godfrey three days later, and the coronation ceremony upon the selection of a new king, were introduced after the conquest in 1099.[87]

Easter festivities in Jerusalem were very old. Al-Maqrīzī mentions that it was customary each year for large numbers of Christians to leave Egypt, in great pomp, as Muslims do in their pilgrimage (*ḥajj*), to perform Easter celebrations in the Church of the Holy Sepulchre.[88] Yaḥya b. Sa'īd informs us that 'it was the custom of the Christians of Jerusalem each year to carry, on Palm Sunday, an olive tree in a procession from the church in al-'Azarīyya [Bethany] to the Church of the Holy Sepulchre. They proceeded through the streets of the city, carrying the Cross high above their heads, chanting and praying. The governor of the city, with all his men, rode with them to prevent people from molesting them.'[89]

During the 12th century, the celebrations on Palm Sunday proceeded as follows. Before sunrise, all the clergy of the churches of Jerusalem, priors of Mount Zion and the Mount of Olives, the abbots of St Mary in the valley of Jehoshophat, and the patriarch went to Bethany. The Holy Cross was brought by the treasurer of the Holy Sepulchre. At the same time, the inhabitants of Jerusalem and pilgrims, carrying palm and olive branches, with some clergy, gathered in the precinct of the Templum Domini (Qubbat al-Ṣakhra). One of the prelates there would bless the olive and palm branches then lead the procession from the precinct and through the gate of Jehoshophat to the valley of the same name. There they met the clergy's procession from Bethany and all followed the patriarch bearing the Holy Cross and ascended the slope towards the Golden Gate (Bāb al-Raḥmah) which was opened each year especially for this occasion, and all gathered again in the holy precinct. After circling the Cross in the Templum Solomonis (al-Aqṣā Mosque), the procession ended with prayers in the precinct of the Templum Domini.[90]

Another famous Easter ceremony was that of the descent of the 'Holy Fire' which is described vividly by Daniel,[91] the Russian pilgrim, and need not be repeated here.

On 15 July each year the Franks celebrated the capture of

Jerusalem. Early in the morning of that day, the patriarch led a procession from the Church of the Holy Sepulchre to the Templum Domini. There the procession halted to perform prayers at the southern entrance of the temple in the area facing al-Aqṣā Mosque. Prayers completed, the procession then advanced to the burial place beyond the walls, where the Franks who fell during the capture of the city were buried. This performed, all participants then crossed Jehoshophat street outside the northern wall of the Holy Precinct and proceeded to that section of the northern wall of the city (Tower of the Stork) where the Franks entered the city.[92] Here the patriarch delivered a sermon to the assembled crowd and thanksgiving prayers were performed.

Three days later (18 June) the anniversary of Duke Godfrey was celebrated. This celebration, John of Würzburg records, 'is solemnly observed by the city with plenteous giving of alms in the great church, according as he [Godfrey] himself arranged while yet alive.'[93]

The coronation of a new king of the Latin Kingdom was yet another opportunity for celebration. Beginning with Baldwin II, the coronation of the kings took place at the Church of the Holy Sepulchre. After the completion of the religious ceremonies, a procession would proceed from the church to the king's residence beside the Tower of David where a grand feast for all the nobility of the kingdom and the knights would be laid down. It was the duty of the burgesses of the city of Jerusalem to provide for the serving of this banquet.[94]

JERUSALEM AND THE LATER CRUSADES

Bertrand of Blanquefort, master of the Order of the Templars (1156–1169), once said that his greatest fear was that a single Muslim 'prince' would 'reunite the two most powerful realms, Cairo and Damascus, and abolish the very name of Christian'.[95] His contemporary, William of Tyre, expressed similar views more than once in his famous work.[96] That 'prince' was to emerge in the person of Ṣalāḥ al-Dīn Yūsuf b. Ayyūb (Saladin) who, in a little more than fifteen years after he controlled Egypt, united not only the two realms but also some parts of al-Jazīra (a district on the Euphrates). On 4 July 1187 he defeated the Franks in the decisive battle of Ḥaṭṭīn (Ḥiṭṭīn), almost annihilated their fighting force, and captured Jerusalem three months later.

Even when Saladin was still a commander in the service of Nūr al-Dīn, he was frequently reminded by poets and learned men (especially ʻImād al-Dīn al-Iṣfahānī) of his duty to liberate Jerusalem and al-Ḥaram al-Sharīf from the Franks. Historical records, and some historians and preachers who were in his company even on the battlefield, kept the reminiscences of the atrocities and massacres of July 1099 alive. Thus, when on 20 September Saladin encamped before the northern wall of Jerusalem and began siege operations, he was determined to take the city by force. For a week his troops continued pressing the defenders of the wall not far from the point where the Franks forced their way into the city eighty-eight years before. Different sections of the wall were undermined by tunnelling, and a part of it fell. The yellow banner of Saladin was hoisted on the top, but the defenders rallied and forced the attackers to retreat. Finally Balian of Ibelin, a survivor of Ḥiṭṭīn and now leader of the defenders of Jerusalem, contacted Saladin and negotiations began. The Ayyūbid sultan was still determined to capture the city by the sword, but the threats of Balian to destroy the Muslim holy places and kill the five thousand Muslim prisoners in the city, and also the pressure of his commanders (amīrs) made him accept surrender on certain conditions.[97] Wisdom won the day and Jerusalem was spared the atrocities of war and destruction.

Once again, and after three generations, Jerusalem witnessed drastic changes in some of its topography, structure of population, administration and social life. A general outline of these changes is necessary.

The general physical feature, topographical or otherwise, of Jerusalem remained unchanged. Medieval methods of construction and destruction were not so developed to achieve that purpose. Many changes, as we have seen above, were made during the Latin period to serve the spiritual, social, intellectual and daily life of the completely new population. This happened again after 1187. After entering Jerusalem, Saladin kept his camp outside the city. He was aware, during his short stay, of the need to fortify and strengthen the city wall so as to withstand future sieges and assaults. However, for the present there was no immediate threat. The walls could wait since there were other urgent religious and administrative measures to take. The first priority, of course, was the Noble Sanctuary (al-Ḥaram al-Sharīf). All structural additions and decorations made by the Templars and the Augustinian canons during their habitation in the area, the refectory, the church and the dividing partition within al-Aqṣā Mosque, were destroyed or removed. The same was done to additions and constructions introduced inside and outside the Dome of the Rock. All was cleared away and the whole precinct was cleaned properly, the Dome area was washed with rose water brought by Saladin's nephew and trusted lieutenant, Taqī al-Dīn 'Umar, especially for that purpose.[98] The *miḥrāb* of al-Aqṣā Mosque was renewed and plated with marble. The *minbar* (pulpit) of Nūr al-Dīn, completed and stored safely for the purpose, was brought from Damascus and installed in its proper place. Other mosques, long neglected, were rebuilt or renewed. *Imāms*, *khāṭibs* (Friday preachers) and other qualified personnel needed for the necessary duties and upkeep of al-Ḥaram were appointed. Saladin also took care of the citadel which became, as of old, the residence of the governor and the garrison. Here also he appointed an *imām*, a *mu'adhdhin* and other officials. The sultan also changed the function and use of some of the Crusader buildings. The church of St Anne was transformed to a Shāfi'ī school and was called thereafter al-Ṣalāḥiyya. Ibn Shaddād, the famous biographer of Saladin and *qāḍī*, was appointed as its first president (*shaikh*).[99] In the 13th century, Ibn Waṣīl's father was another of its scholars.[100]

The Quarter of the Patriarch, the living centre of the Franks, clergy and laity, was empty. Here Saladin, after consulting with the learned men (*'ulamā'*) and the *ṣūfiyya*, dedicated the patriarch's palace as a *ribāṭ* for the latter group and made a large endowment (*waqf*) to meet its expenses as is testified by its extant deed.[101] A part of the large Hospitallers' compound, a church, was transformed into a hospital. Grants were specified for its expenses and rare drugs were brought to it.[102]

The walls of Jerusalem, as mentioned above, needed rebuilding and strengthening. Saladin was aware that Jerusalem was vulnerable to serious attacks, and the possibility of a Latin recapture of the city was ever present in his mind. When he captured Ascalon (5 September 1187), the northern gate to Egypt, his main aim was not fulfilled since Jerusalem was still in the Latins' hands. When Jerusalem was captured Ascalon had to be destroyed. One of the two cities had to be sacrificed, since he could not protect both. Ascalon was sacrificed, its walls and houses were systematically dismantled and demolished (1191).[103] Thus relieved, the sultan returned to Jerusalem (587/1191) and established his headquarters inside the city in the previous canons' house in the Patriarch's Quarter near the Church of the Holy Sepulchre.[104] Immediately reconstruction began. Complete sections of the wall were rebuilt and fortified with towers. A deep ditch was hewn in the rock, the stones extracted were used as building material. Saladin himself supervised the work and even helped by carrying stones.[105] Sections of the wall, towers and other works were distributed among the participants. His sons, relatives and amīrs with their men shared in the work.[106] Al-Malik al-ʻĀdil, the sultan's brother, fortified the southwestern section on Mount Zion. The church there and its compound, that extended for a distance twice an arrow's shot from the old wall, were enclosed by a new wall.[107] The early Ayyūbids also introduced a major development within the city walls. Al-Malik al-Afḍāl Nūr al-Dīn ʻAlī, the 'king' of Damascus (ruled 582–592/1186–1196), dedicated a whole area in the city (as *waqf*) for the benefit of Maghāribah staying or coming to visit Jerusalem and he later built a school for the Mālikīs in the quarter.[108] According to Mujīr al-Dīn, the original *waqf* document seems to have been lost, but the *waqf* was recorded and officially registered and deposited in the Sharīʻa court's archives.[109] The document carefully defined the boundaries of the quarter.

During the period between 1193 and 1219 the city of Jerusalem was gradually repopulated, more schools and sufi *zawāya* were dedicated and more *awqāf* were made for the upkeep of religious institutions.

In spite of the continuous struggle and intrigues among the 'kings' of the Ayyūbid house, life in the city was peaceful, but the arrival of the Fifth Crusade, the siege and occupation by the Crusaders of Damietta (spring 1218) spread terror in Ayyūbid domains. In Syria, rumours were widespread that the Franks were intending to advance to Palestine and take Jerusalem. Al-Muʻaẓẓam ʻĪsā, who was at that time in Egypt to support his brother al-Kāmil, gathered his amīrs for consultation. They said 'there were no troops in al-Shām [Syria] and if the Franks took Jerusalem, they would dominate all Syria.' Thereupon al-Muʻaẓẓam decided to destroy the city wall and wrote to his brother, al-ʻAzīz, and his Ustādhdār, ʻIzz al-Dīn Aybak, who were, it appears, in Jerusalem, ordering them to carry out his plan. However, ʻUthmān and Aybak refused to obey and replied that they could defend the place properly. Al-Muʻaẓẓam was infuriated and wrote again: 'If they [the Franks] took it [Jerusalem] they would kill everyone there [remembering and reminding them of the massacre of July] and dominate Syria and the world of Islam.' In addition al-Muʻaẓẓam dispatched masons, miners and engineers to execute the work. In Muḥarram 616/1219 the systematic dismantling of the walls began and only the Tower of David was spared. This action caused a great commotion in the city. 'Women, girls and old men gathered in large numbers within the Ḥaram precinct, tore their hair and clothes and then left the city without taking any of their belongings or even seeing their families. They scattered in all directions; some went to Egypt, others to al-Karak and some went to Damascus . . .'[110] Thus, insecure and unprotected, the inhabitants of Jerusalem deserted their city which became henceforth only a place for passing visitors, pilgrims, devoted ascetics, pious men, state officials and the garrison.[111] For a century after 1219 Jerusalem became no more than a village. Even that, as Ibn Faḍl Allāh al-'Umarī asserts, was not true, 'it was not until recently [first half of the 14th century] counted as a village. The citadel, which was destroyed [1242] remained in ruins until 717 [1317] when it was rebuilt by Bukhtamur the Jūkindār, the *kāfil* [protector] of the [Mamlūk] provinces.' Moreover, al-'Umarī comments, 'its existence or non-existence were the same, since it had no fortifications . . .'[112]

After 1187 the population of Jerusalem underwent a change. This time the change was not as radical and complete as it was in 1099. Between 4 July 1187 and late September when Saladin besieged it, Jerusalem became the gathering centre of all the Latins in Palestine who moved towards it seeking the protection of its walls. Al-Qāḍī al-Faḍīl asserts that only Jersualem remained to be taken by the sultan, in which every fugitive and displaced Latin gathered from near and far.[113] When Ascalon surrendered to Saladin, the Latins there were escorted to Jerusalem.[114] Others came in large numbers from Darum, Gaza, Ramla and the numerous villages around the city. The city was so crowded that even the churches and the streets were full and no one could walk easily.[115]

However, in less than two weeks of the forty days stipulated in the surrender agreement, all the Latin inhabitants of Jerusalem left the city, except those who were unable to pay the ransom and who were therefore enslaved.[116] Their quarters, markets, shops and other institutions became empty. Only the native inhabitants of the Christian quarter, some Greek clergy and other oriental Christian groups remained.

Native Christians, who were included in the surrender agreement, paid the ransom and asked Saladin to allow them to remain in their homes. They were willing to pay the poll tax (*jizya*) and continue their usual life in the Holy City.[117]

Thousands of Muslims visited Jerusalem immediately after October 1187, but most of them left the city after a short stay; they either returned home or continued their way to perform the pilgrimage to Mecca.[118] Saladin remained encamped on the Mount of Olives and stayed long enough to arrange the basic affairs of the city before departing (30–31 October) to Damascus. Ḍiyā' al-Dīn 'Īsā al-Ḥakkārī (a trusted Kurd) was appointed governor of the city, and he deputized his brother al-Ḍāhir. Siyārūkh was given the post of *nāẓir* (in charge of the affairs) of al-Ḥaram. Later he became the governor.[119] A suitable garrison manned the citadel.

The first Muslims who settled in Jerusalem after 1187 were the soldiers and the civil officials, with their families; the *'ulamā'*, the *fuqahā'* and the sufis who staffed the newly established *madrasas* (schools) and *ribāṭs* (hospices); the *nāẓirs*, *khāṭibs*, *mu'adhdhins*, teachers and preachers of the Ḥaram and other mosques. All were settled within and around the Holy precinct and in different sections of the Patriarch's Quarter. When Saladin returned to Jerusalem in Dhū al-Qa'dah 587/1191, life in the city was gradually returning to normal. The sultan rebuilt the walls, established and equipped a hospital and increased the endowments of previous charitable foundations.

Two new, although small, quarters were created within the walls of the city: the Maghāriba Quarter and the Jewish Quarter. The latter quarter, it seems, was situated to the west of the first with the Sharaf residential area in between. During the Latin period only a few Jews lived in Jerusalem[120] near the citadel. The Sultan's tolerant policy allowed the Jews to return to the Holy City. Thus they gradually began to constitute a community. Three groups, according to J Prawer, settled this time in Jerusalem: the Ascalonites who moved to it after Saladin dismantled its walls in 1191, the Jews from the Maghrib who fled to the east around 1198–99, and the Jews from France – some three hundred families – who migrated in two groups in 1210.[121] The developments of the first half of the 13th century led to their migration to the coast. The dismantling of the walls of Jerusalem (1219) made the city vulnerable and insecure. When Jerusalem was handed over to Frederick II (1229) anti-Jewish legislation of the Latin period was re-established and all Jews were prohibited again from living in the city. 'Following some negotiations, however, a Jewish family was allowed to live in Jerusalem, and so to assure a halting place for Jewish pilgrims, who were allowed to visit the city.'[122]

The sixty years of Jerusalem's history since 1187 could be divided into two distinct periods. The dividing date was the year of the dismantling of the newly fortified walls. Only the Tower of David was left intact by the miners and masons of al-Mu'aẓẓam.

Security and safety, basic requirements in medieval cities and towns, could be maintained only through fortifications, garrisoning and suitable defence machines and arms. In 616/1219, Jerusalem was suddenly deprived of all. The walls were levelled to the ground, most of the fighting force was taken away to other places and stored arms and machines[123] were transported to Damascus.[124] Yet, the inhabitants could have endured such a situation if the political conditions in the area were stable and the Ayyūbid dynasty united. Saladin was dead (1193) and so was the master diplomat of the Ayyūbid family, al-Malik al-ʿĀdil (1218), Damietta was taken by the Latins and Syria was threatened. All this led to the decision of al-Muʿaẓẓam which had a far-reaching effect on the future of Jerusalem for more than a century. The Crusader kingdom was still dominating parts of the Palestinian coast and some strongholds in the interior with Acre as its capital as a result of the Third Crusade and the treaty of Ramla (1191). The rivalries among the many 'kings' of the Ayyūbid family reached a climax. In such a state, most of the newly settled Muslim inhabitants and some of the old 'native' Christians left the city for new places where they could find security and gain their livelihood.

Some of the inhabitants of Jerusalem may have returned after the end of the Fifth Crusade. The basic institutions established by Saladin were somehow still functioning.

But in 1229/626 there was a serious turn in events. Due to dissension among the Ayyūbid kings in Cairo and Damascus, which resulted in a great weakening of the Islamic front, the Sultan Malik al-Kāmil made a grave decision; to the consternation of all Muslims he started negotiations with the German emperor Frederick II and soon thereafter Jerusalem, with the exception of the Ḥaram area, was handed over to him. The main pretext was al-Kāmil's inability to defend the city. The normal life of Jerusalem was again disrupted.

Ten years of Latin domination (1229–1239) did not re-establish Frankish authority in Jerusalem. The Ayyūbid king of Kerak reoccupied the city in 1239, and the Tower of David, the last refuge for security, was destroyed. Four years later the Franks returned to the city (1243), but before they could settle, the Khwārazmians occupied it (1244) and dealt the final blow. Jerusalem was finally restored to Islam. These developments and the continuous threat, real or imaginary, posed by the Latin kingdom, left Jerusalem, as al-ʿUmarī records, in ruins for a long time. It was only after 1291 that it began slowly and gradually to revive.

Nothing is more telling, in describing the fortunes of Jerusalem during the three centuries outlined above, than the conclusion reached by William of Tyre in the eighties of the 12th century:

> Thus the Holy City, . . . with the frequent shifting of events, it often changed masters, and, according to the character of each prince, it experienced both bright and cloudy intervals. Its condition, like that of a sick man, grew better or worse in accordance with the exigencies of the times, yet full recovery was impossible.[125]

NOTES

1 Ibn al-'Arabī was impressed by the methods of teaching and discussion. See Iḥsān 'Abbās, 'Riḥlat Ibn al-'Arabī ilā Mashriq kamā ṣawwaraha' Qānūn al-Ta'wīl', *al-Abḥath*, vol. 21, pt. 1, March 1968, 59 ff, 65 the study) and 81 of the text.

2 Ibn al-'Arabī remained in Palestine for more than three years. He left Jerusalem in 489/1096 just two years before its capture by the Franks. Ibid, 84–86.

3 In Mujīr al-Dīn's history, *Al-Uns al-Jalīl bi-Tārīkh al-Quds wa-'l-Khalīl*, Amman, 1973, there is no mention of any prominent scholar or dignitary who lived in or visited Jerusalem between the years 341 and 480 AH. *Uns*, I, 297.

4 *Uns*, I, 297–302.

5 Naṣr was the shaikh of the Shāfi'īs of Syria (al-Shām) in his time. He visited Jerusalem and stayed there for a while in al-Naṣriyya *zāwiya* at Bāb al-Raḥma (inside the Golden Gate of the Crusaders). Al-Ghazālī also visited Jerusalem and stayed at the same place as Naṣr and the *zāwiya* was called al-Ghazāliyya after him. Al-Ṭarṭūshī visited the holy city and was there when Ibn al-'Arabī arrived. *Uns*, I, 297–98, 299 and 301.

6 *Riḥla*, 81–82.

–Ibn al-'Arabī considered Jerusalem as a small city. It is possible that he was comparing it to the large cities he had visited such as Cairo. Nāṣir-i Khusrau who visited it fifty years earlier considered it a large city. Nāṣir came from the East. See *Diary of a journey through Syria and Palestine*, tr. Guy Le Strange, *PPTS*, vol. 4, London, 1893 (reprint, New York, 1971), 21.

8 *Riḥla*, 66–67.

9 For a contemporary Christian account see Yaḥyā b. Sa'id, *Tārīkh*, Beirut, 1909, 195–96. See also al-Maqrīzī, *Itti'āẓ al-Ḥunafā' bi-akhbār al-a'immah al-Fāṭimiyyīn al-Khulafā'*, vol. II, ed. Muhammad H M Ahmad, Cairo, 1971, 81.

10 *Itti'āẓ*, II, 107–08. For the Jarrāḥid domination, see Mustafa A Hiyari, *al-Imāra al-Ta'iyyah*, Amman, 1977, 47 ff; M Canard, 'Djarrāḥids', *EI*².

11 Yaḥyā , *Tārīkh*, 201.

12 *Itti'āẓ*, II, 167.

13 According to Yaḥyā, the exchange of messengers began after the death of al-Ḥakīm. *Tārīkh*, 243–44, 266, 269. For the terms, see ibid, 271. Yaḥyā also says that negotiations continued for three and a half years. Ibid, 271.

14 Ibid, 271.

15 Ibid, 272.

16 *Itti'āẓ*, II, 182.

17 Ibid, 187.

18 *Itti'āẓ*, II, 194.

19 Nāṣir-i Khusrau, *Safarnāma*, Arabic tr. Yaḥyā al-Khashshāb, 3rd ed., Beirut, 1983, 55.

20 Ibid, 74–75.

21 Since 418/1027, the mosque of Constantinople was opened for prayer. The *khuṭba* in the Friday prayer was proclaimed in the name of the Fāṭimid caliph, al-Ẓāhir, alone. The Fāṭimid caliph sent lamps and mattresses to it and appointed a *mu'adhdhin*. *Itti'āẓ*, II, 176. This practice continued until 446/1052–53, when negotiation for the renewal of the treaty failed. Empress Theodora also allowed the ambassador of the Saljuqs to pray in the mosque of Constantinople and proclaim the *khuṭba* in the name of the 'Abbāsid caliph. *Itti'āẓ*, II, 230; Ibn Muyassar, *al-Munṭaqa min akhbār Miṣr*, ed. Ayman F al-Sayyid, Cairo, 1981, 14.

22 *Itti'āẓ*, II, 230.
23 M H Burgoyne, 'A recently discovered Marwānid inscription in Jerusalem', *Levant*, vol. XIV, 1982, 118–21.
24 William of Tyre, *A History of Deeds Done Beyond the Seas*, 2 vols., tr. Emily A Babcock and A C Krey, New York, 1976, reprint of 1941 ed., I, 407.
25 Ibid.
26 Ibid; J Prawer, 'The Patriarch's Lordship in Jerusalem', *Crusader Institutions*, Oxford, 1980, 298.
27 No Arabic source I consulted mentions the foundation of the quarter or its boundaries. It seems that William had access to the archives of the Church of the Holy Sepulchre. The reason given by William is not mentioned by other sources. Nāṣir, as stated above, says that the walls were in good condition. No strong earthquake is recorded between 1047 and 1063. It is possible that this part of the wall was neglected since Jerusalem was not seriously threatened for long. However, the serious economic conditions of Egypt and the civil war were aggravated by the Turkomen threat. This might have led to demanding the inhabitants fortify their towns and cities.
28 *WT*, I, 407–408.
29 Ibid. For details of the legal position of the quarter and the patriarch before and after the Crusader occupation, see Prawer, ibid.
30 The gift was granted after the creation of the quarter. The land must have been empty or in ruins. J Riley-Smith is of the opinion that the monastery and the convent were built on earlier foundations. *The Knights of St John in Jerusalem and Cyprus, c. 1050–1310*, London, 1967, 34–36.
31 Ibid, pt. 1, ch. 2.
32 The text of the letter is not extant, but the content is preserved in a manuscript of *Mir'āt al-Zamān* of Sibṭ Ibn al-Jawzi. Sibṭ, for this period, was copying or summarising the contemporary historian, Muḥammad b. Hilāl al-Sābi' who had access to the chancery in Baghdad.
33 *Mir'āt al-Zamān*, Bibliothèque Nationale Ms., fol. 148a. See also *Akhbār al-Dawla al-Saljūqiyya min Mir'āt al-Zamān*, ed. A Savim, Ankara, 1968, 169.
34 Ibid.
35 Ibid, fol. 167a–169a; Ibn Muyassar, *Munṭaqa*, 44.
36 *Mir'āt*, fol. 169a.
37 Ibid. So much money was taken that Fāṭimid silver dirhams were exchanged in Damascus fifty for one dinar which was originally thirteen to a dinar.
38 Ibid, fol. 176a and b.
39 M H Burgoyne and Amal Abul Hajj, 'Twenty-four Medieval Arabic Inscriptions from Jerusalem', *Levant*, vol. XI, 1979, 117.
40 Ibn al-'Arabī, *Riḥla*, 80–81.
41 *Mir'āt*, fol. 228; Ibn Muyassar, *Munṭaqa*, 65–66.
42 Ibid, 66. He also mentions that al-Afḍal was very generous with the two brothers and permitted them to leave after giving them robes of honour (*khil'a*).
43 *Mir'āt*, fol. 228b.
44 S Runciman, *A History of the Crusades, vol. 1: The First Crusade and the Foundation of the Kingdom of Jerusalem*, New York, 1964, 229, and n. 1, 230, for his contemporary Frankish sources.
45 It seems that al-Afḍal decided to advance to Jerusalem after the return of his ambassadors. The troops of the atabeg of Damascus were still engaged in the operations in northern Syria.
46 See Fulcher of Chartres, *A History of the Expedition to Jerusalem*, 1095–1127, tr. S Fink, New York, 1969, 115–16; William of Tyre, *History*, I, 335 f; Runciman, op. cit., 280–81; Hans E Mayer, *The Crusades*, tr. John Gillingham, Oxford, 1972, 59–60; *A History of the Crusades*, ed. K Setton, vol. 1: *The First Hundred Years*, ed. Harry W Hazard, 332.
47 Roland Finucane, *Soldiers of the Faith*, London and Melbourne, 1983, 96–97, based on William of Tyre's narrative, *History*, I, 362.
48 An expression used by Ibn al-Qalānisī for the moveable 'castle' used by the Franks during the siege of Tyre.

It is significant to note that in most successful Crusader sieges the 'tower' was used. Muslims were not accustomed to this kind of machine but later they developed warfare tactics to counter it.
49 Fulcher, *Expedition*, 121; William of Tyre, *A History of Deeds*, I, 370 ff.

50 Fulcher, ibid, 121–22. Arabic sources say that some seventy thousands perished by the sword in al-Aqṣā mosque alone. Ibn al-Athīr, *al-Kāmil fī 'l-Tārīkh*, X, Beirut, 1979, 283; al-Maqrīzī, *Itti'āẓ*, III, ed. M H Ahmad, Cairo, 1973, 23; Ibn al-Qalānisī does not mention any figure, but says that large numbers were killed. *Tārīkh Dimashq*, ed. S Zakkār, Damascus, 1983, 222.
51 Fulcher, ibid, 124. See also Runciman, *History*, I, 286.
52 Mujīr, *Uns*, I, 298–99.
53 Fulcher, *Expedition*, 132.
54 See below the section on festivities and celebrations in Jerusalem.
55 Fulcher, ibid, 123.
56 Ibid.
57 According to the Ayyūbid historian, Abu 'l-Fidā, St Anne was a church before Islam and became a school during the Islamic period before 1099. *Al-Mukhtaṣar fī Akhbār al-Bashar*, III, Beirut, n.d., 83.
58 Michael H Burgoyne mentions that the Crusaders built a large market off the present Ṭarīq al-Wād (the section of the Ṭarīq that was called during the Crusader period Street of the Furriers), the Sūq al-Qaṭṭānīn of Mamlūk and later times. *Mamlūk Jerusalem*, London, 1987, 80, col. 2.
59 William of Tyre, *A History of Deeds*, I, 409.
60 Ibid, 409.
61 Ibid, 507. This means that during the first two decades of the establishment of the Latin Kingdom, security was not established in the areas captured. Jerusalem was still underpopulated and far from its normal population of 10,000. See Josiah C Russel, 'The Population of the Crusader States', *A History of the Crusades, vol. 5: The Impact of the Crusades on the Near East*, ed. Norman P Zacour and Harry W Hazard, Madison, 1985, table 2, 306.
62 William of Tyre, *History*, I, 507–08.
63 Ibid.
64 See Michel Join-Lambert's excellent map, p. 193, in his *Jerusalem*, tr. Charlotte Haldane, London, 1966.
65 See source in n. 18.
66 See *Cartulaire Sepulchre*, 1849, 83–85, as tr. in Peters, *Jerusalem, the Holy City in the Eyes of Chroniclers . . .*, Princeton, 1985, 306.
67 *Description of the Holy Land*, tr. Aubrey Stewart, *PPTS*, V, New York, 1971, 40.
68 Ibid, p. 69.
69 Ibid, p. 41.
70 When Saladin captured Jerusalem some fifteen hundred Armenians were exempted from paying ransom money since they were granted to two of his *amīrs* who considered them as *ra'iyya*, since the *amīrs* ruled Edessa and Harran.
71 *Anonymous Pilgrims* in *PPTS*, IV, New York, 1971 (reprint of 1894 ed.), 27D29.
72 These were generally the basic Islamic institutions one finds in a medium-sized capital of an administrative centre, and Jerusalem was such a centre during the 11th century AD. Some of those offices in Jerusalem were mentioned in the sources, others could be deduced from later evidence such as the *methessep* of the Frankish administration of the city which was an adaptation of the Islamic office of *muḥtasib*.
73 J Prawer, 'Social Classes in the Latin Kingdom: the Franks', *A History of the Crusades*, V, 130.
74 Ibid, 145.
75 William of Tyre, *History*, I, 355 f.
76 J Prawer, ibid.
77 Ibid, 150.
78 J Richard, *The Latin Kingdom of Jerusalem*, tr. Janet Shirley, Amsterdam, 1979, vol. A, 122.
79 Ibid, 126 and taken from John Ibilin's list.
80 J Prawer, op. cit., idem, 'The Origin of the Court of Burgesses', *Crusader Institutions*, 263–95.
81 For the rule of the Templars, see Stephen Howarth, *The Knights Templar*, London, 1982, ch. 2; for the Hospitallers, see J Riley-Smith, *The Knights of St John*, pt. 2.
82 J Richard, op. cit., 223. See also John La Monte, *Feudal Monarchy in the Latin Kingdom of Jerusalem*, New York, 1970 (reprint of 1932 ed.), 108.
83 The viscounts, J Richards says, 'appear to always have been knights, but with some exceptions', op. cit., 222. To Prawer, 'The city's ruler would appoint a viscount without the formal assent of the burgesses, and was supposed to take their advice in proclaiming city ordinances.''Social Classes . . . , *History of the Crusades*, V, 158.
84 Peters, *Jerusalem*, 301.

85 Peters' translation (*Jerusalem*, 301–302) of *Recueil Lois*, II, 243–44.
86 This evidence is gathered from pilgrims and travellers' descriptions of the city during the 12th century AD.
87 For a relatively detailed description, see J Prawer, *The Latin Kingdom of Jerusalem*, London, 1972, 176 ff. and the note for his sources.
88 Maqrīzī, *Itti'āẓ*, II, 74–75.
89 Yaḥyā, *Tārīkh*, 194.
90 J Prawer, ibid, 178.
91 *The Pilgrimage of the Russian Abbot Daniel in the Holy Land, 1106–1107 AD*, tr. C W Wilson, New York, 1971 (reprint of 1895 ed.), in *PPTS*, IV, 74 ff.
92 John of Würzburg, *Description*, 39–40.
93 Ibid, 40.
94 J Richard, *The Latin Kingdom*, vol. A, 129.
95 Howarth, op. cit., 125 (quotation).
96 See *A History of Deeds*, II, 225, (for Nūr al-Dīn), 406–408, 490–91. He says: 'Thus . . . all kingdoms round about us obey one ruler, they do the will of one man, and at his command alone, however reluctantly, they are ready, as a *unit*, to take up arms for our injury . . . This Saladin . . . now holds under his control all these kingdoms.'408.
97 The conditions of surrender stipulated that the Latins in the city should be allowed to leave with their personal belongings but leave behind their horses, machines and all military equipment, that every man should pay ten dinars, every woman five dinars and every child (male or female) one dinar. Al-Iṣfahanī, *al-Fatḥ al-Quṣṣī fi 'l-Fatḥ al-Qudsī*, ed. M M Subuh, Cairo, (n.d.) 127; Ibn al-Athīr, *al-Kāmil*, II, 549; *Uns*, I, 348; Runciman, *History*, II, 466–67.
98 See *Fatḥ*, 140–44.
99 Ibid, 145, 611–12; *Uns*, I, 340, 391; Ibn Shaddād, *al-Nawādir al-Sulṭāniyya wa-'l-Maḥāsin al-Yūsufiyya*, ed. M J al-Shayyāl, Cairo, 1964, 239.
100 Ibn Wāṣil, *Mufarrij al-Kurūb fī Akhbār Banī Ayyūb*, IV, ed. Hasanien Rabi', Cairo 1972, 141–42, 208. The extent of its *waqf* is specified in a document published in *Awqāf wa-amlāk al-Muslimīn fī Filasṭīn*, ed. M Ipşirli and M D Tamimi, Istanbul, 1982, 35.
101 Published by Kamil al-'Asali in *Wathā'iq Maqdisiyya Tārīkhiyya*, I, Amman, 1983, 91 ff.
102 *Fatḥ*, 612; *Uns*, I, 391.
103 Sibṭ Ibn al-Jawzī, *Mir'āt al-Zamān*, VIII, Hyderabad, 1370 AH, 410, 413; *al-Kāmil*, XII, Beirut, 1979, 69 ff.
104 The church was closed for a few days then it was reopened. Some advisors of Saladin suggested to him to destroy it but he refused. *Fatḥ*, 145–46.
105 See *Fatḥ*, 562, 565, 582, 610. 'Abd al-Laṭīf al-Baghdādī, who visited Jerusalem at that time, describes the daily programme of Saladin during the rebuilding and fortification of the wall. *Al-Ifāda wa-'l-I'tibār*, ed. Ahmad Gh Sabana, Damascus, 1983, 151.
106 Ibid, 578; *al-Kāmil*, XII, 74.
107 *al-Kāmil*, XII, 86–87.
108 *Uns*, II, 49.
109 Ibid. The extant document supports *al-Uns*' evidence. See A L Tibawi, *The Islamic Pious Foundations in Jerusalem*, London, 1987, 14, and Arabic text Appendix II.
110 Ibn Taghribardī, *Al-Nujūm al-Ẓāhira fī Mulūk Miṣr wa-'l-Qāhira*, VI (reprint), 244–45.
111 The fate of the native Christians after 1219 is not recorded by the sources I was able to consult, but it seems that they too left the city. Ibn Wāṣil, whose father was appointed president of al-Ṣalāḥiyya soon after (622/1225) says that 'most of the residents left . . . only a few stayed.' *Mufarrij*, IV, 32.
112 Al-'Umarī, *Masālik al-Abṣār fī Mamālik al-Amṣār*, section ed. Ayman F Sayyid, Cairo, I, 138.
113 *Uns*, I, 345.
114 *al-Kāmil*, II, 546.
115 Ibid, 549–50. There are different estimates in the sources about the number of those who were in the city during Saladin's siege. 'Imād al-Dīn states that there were more than a hundred thousand (ten times its normal population as stated above); sixty thousand were fighting men. *Fatḥ*, 128. Ibn al-Athīr is more certain of the number, which suggests that he was relying on some kind of documents available to him. He says, 'there were exactly sixty thousand men, cavalry and footmen, in addition to women and children . . .' To him this number was not strange since the city was large. *al-Kāmil*, II, 549. More accurate numbers could be calculated from the number of those who paid the *qaṭī'a* (stipulated in the agreement). Some 20,000 Latins paid the specified sum. 18,000 of the poor and needy were

released by Balian. 15,000 were enslaved (7,000 men and 8,000 women). 1,500 Armenians were released without payment. 5,000 were Muslim prisoners. There were in all some 60,000 excluding native Christians whose numbers are not specified. These numbers are not compatible with the two knights and 60 sons of burgesses who were raised by Balian to the rank of knights. Yet, the city was very crowded. The situation was similar to that of 1099.

116 Native Christians and merchants of Saladin's army bought most of what the Frankish inhabitants had to sell very cheaply. What was worth ten dinars was bought for only one. *Fatḥ*, 135; *al-Kāmil*, II, 251–52.

117 *Fatḥ*, 136; *al-Kāmil*, II, 552–553.

118 *Fatḥ*, 134.

119 Ibid, 579 and gives the text of Siyārūkh's diploma pp. 580–81. Al-Ḍāhir died 585 AH and 'Īsā died towards the end of the same year. Saladin left 'Īsā's deputy for a while then appointed Siyārūkh. 'Izz al-Dīn Jurdik was appointed governor in 588. *Nawādir*, 240.

120 Benjamin of Tuleda, *Travels*.

121 J Prawer, '"Minorities" in the Crusader States', *A History of the Crusades*, V, 97.

122 Ibid, 100.

123 In addition to the arms and war machines left by the Franks in the city as was stipulated by the agreement, al-'Azīz 'Uthmān b. Ṣalāḥ al-Dīn left all his magazine of war equipment and arms of all kinds in Jerusalem. *Fatḥ*, 144.

124 *Mufarraj*, IV, 32.

125 William of Tyre, *History*, I, 63–64.

CHAPTER VI

Jerusalem under the Ayyūbids and Mamlūks 1187–1516 AD

Donald P Little

Ṣalāḥ al-Dīn's triumphant restoration of Jerusalem to Islam was the subject of the first Friday sermon delivered at al-Masjid al-Aqṣā after its deliverance from some eighty years' captivity by the Franks. Since this was obviously an important public occasion, to be attended by Ṣalāḥ al-Dīn himself and the leading figures of his army and state, there was considerable rivalry among the religious scholars in his retinue for the honour of delivering the sermon. From those *'ulamā'* who prepared sermons in hope of being selected, the sultan chose al-Qāḍī Muḥyī al-Dīn b. al-Zakī, chief Shāfi'ī judge of Aleppo. Given the importance and solemnity of the occasion, Ibn al-Zakī must have chosen the words with care; in any case the sermon does provide an eloquent resumé of the status of Jerusalem in the eyes of Ṣalāḥ al-Dīn and his spiritual advisors of the image of the city they wished to propagate among Muslims. As such the sermon deserves scrutiny.

It begins conventionally with citations from the Qur'ān of passages lauding God and with the *qāḍī*'s own special praise for His aid in 'cleansing His Holy House from the filth of polytheism and its pollutions.'[1] This single phrase contains the core of the sermon's message, namely that God and His agents are to be thanked for restoring the Holy House (Bait al-Maqdis: Jerusalem) to Muslims. Much of the rest of the *khuṭba* consists of an enumeration of the reasons why Jerusalem is a holy place to Muslims, praise for its deliverers, and an exhortation for continued prosecution of Holy War against the Franks. Of these parts the most interesting one is the list of merits – *faḍā'il* – of Jerusalem. As is well known, the *faḍā'il* of cities formed the basis of a whole genre of Arabic literature which gained special prominence as far as Jerusalem is concerned around this point in time, in conjunction, that is, with the military campaigns of Zengī, Nūr al-Dīn, and Ṣalāḥ al-Dīn, culminating in the capture of Jerusalem in 1187.[2] The listing of the *faḍā'il* in Ibn Zakī al-Dīn's *khuṭba* serves to remind Muslims of what they had been fighting for in the battle for Jerusalem and why they should continue to struggle on its behalf. The Islamic merits of al-Quds as Ibn Zakī al-Dīn articulated them before Ṣalāḥ al-Dīn and his notables are the following:

> It was the dwelling-place of your father Abraham; the spot from which your blessed Prophet Muhammad mounted to heaven; the *qibla* toward which you turned to pray at the commencement of Islamism, the abode of the prophets; and the place visited by the saints; the cemetery of the apostles; the spot where the divine revelation descended, and to which the orders to command and prohibitions were sent down: it is the country where mankind will be assembled for judgement, the ground where resurrection will take place; the holy land whereof God hath spoken in his perspicuous book; it is the mosque wherein the Apostle of God offered up his prayer and saluted the angels admitted nearest to God's presence; it is the town to which God sent his servant and apostle, and the Word which he caused to descend on Mary and his spirit Jesus, whom he honoured with that mission and ennobled with the gift of prophesy without removing him from the rank he held as one of his creatures . . . This temple is the first of the two *qiblas*, the second of the two sacred Mosques, the third after the two holy cities (Mekka and Medīna) . . .[3]

Because of the sanctity of Jerusalem thus depicted, Ṣalāḥ al-Dīn's conquest of it deserves to be likened with the holiest battles fought in Islamic history: Badr, Qādisiyya, Yarmouk, and Khaybar, in which the Prophet himself achieved stunning victories against his enemies and the Arab Muslim armies defeated the mighty Sasanian and Byzantine empires. Lest, however, the victors assembled in al-Aqṣā lapse into complacency at this commendation of their splendid feat, Ibn al-Zakī reminds them of their duty to stay on the path of righteous obedience to God in order to remain assured of His favour. More specifically, he recalls their duty to persevere in *jihād*. Finally, the sermon ends with praise of the conqueror as 'purifier of the Holy House', and with pious hope that his empire will expand and be preserved by his sons and brothers.[4] As we shall see, this turned out to be a vain hope indeed.

But there can be little doubt that Ṣalāḥ al-Dīn and his followers regarded the capture of Jerusalem as the crowning achievement of a *jihād* long waged against the enemies of Islam, to be continued by his successors. Some seventy letters proclaiming the victory were sent to leaders of the Muslim world, including the 'Abbāsid caliph in Baghdad.[5] Within the city, Ṣalāḥ al-Dīn took measures to sanctify the Dome of the Rock and al-Aqṣā Mosque. The *minbar* that Nūr al-Dīn had had constructed for Jerusalem Ṣalāḥ al-Dīn transported to the city and installed in al-Aqṣā.[6] New pious institutions were established under his patronage, including a Shāfi'ī *madrasa*, a sufi monastery, and a hospital, all of which bore his name. The Church of the Holy Sepulchre was restored to the orthodox church and Jews were permitted to remain or settle in the city.[7] In order to reconstitute the Muslim presence, the sultan is said to have installed various Arab tribes in and around the city.[8] When he departed for Acre less than a month after the fall of al-Quds, he entrusted its administration to the amir Ḥusām al-Dīn Sārūj al-Turkī.[9]

Details of the protracted negotiations over Jerusalem between Ṣalāḥ al-Dīn and Richard the Lion Hearted during the Third Crusade need not detain us. Suffice it to say that Richard's demands that the city be surrendered to him, divided between Christians and Muslims, and ruled jointly by the sultan's brother al-'Ādil and the king's sister, Queen Joanna of Sicily, were rejected. To Richard's vow that he would not abandon Jerusalem, Ṣalāḥ al-Dīn replied:

> Al-Quds is to us as it is to you. It is even more important for us, for it is the site of our Prophet's nocturnal departure and the place where people will assemble on Judgement Day. Therefore do not imagine that we can waver in this regard.[10]

To ensure its defence in 587/1191, Ṣalāḥ al-Dīn used Frankish prisoners to dig a deep fosse and to rebuild walls and towers around vulnerable parts of the city.[11] Nevertheless, although the anticipated attack never materialized, Ṣalāḥ al-Dīn concluded a truce before Richard's departure from the Holy Land. The only clause of this accord directly affecting Jerusalem gave Richard the right to authorize pilgrims to visit the Holy City. But the status of the city was also affected by the agreement to recognize the Franks' right to free passage to the coast of Palestine, from Tyre to Jaffa.[12]

Ṣalāḥ al-Dīn had succeeded in regaining Jerusalem for Islam, in restoring Muslim shrines and establishing new religious institutions and in making the city accessible to Christians and Jews. In line with the re-sanctification of the Ḥaram mosques, his new religious institutions were housed in buildings previously occupied and used by Christians rather than in new edifices. The most famous and important of these foundations, al-Madrasa al-Ṣalāḥiyya, a college for teaching Shāfiʿī *fiqh*, was installed in the Church of St Anne in 588/1192.[13] From Mujīr al-Dīn al-ʿUlaimī's biographies of the heads of this *madrasa* it is evident that it had great prestige as the seat of the dominant school of law in Jerusalem under both the Ayyūbids and the Mamlūks.[14] Al-Khānqāh al-Ṣalāḥiyya, a monastery for sufis, was placed in the former residence of the Patriarch of Jerusalem, adjacent to the Church of the Holy Sepulchre. Thanks to a copy of the endowment deed for the khānqāh, dated 585/1189 and preserved in the Ottoman archives of Jerusalem, we know that Ṣalāḥ al-Dīn intended this building as a residence for indigent sufis, both Arab and non-Arab. In return for their lodgings, the sufis were expected to participate in recitations of the Qur'ān and in *dhikr* ceremonies as well as in prayers for the benefit of their patron sultan.[15] A hospital, al-Bīmāristān al-Ṣalāḥī, was established in a church in the Tanners' Quarter (Ḥayy al-Dabbāgha), close to the Church of the Holy Sepulchre.[16] Richly endowed, it dispensed the usual services of hospital and apparently functioned also as a teaching centre for medicine.[17] There is ample evidence that several of Ṣalāḥ al-Dīn's successors shared his sentiments toward the Muslim sanctuaries and contributed to Muslim pious activities in the city, mainly through erecting religious edifices. Ṣalāḥ al-Dīn's oldest son, al-Malik al-Afḍal (d. 622/1225) endowed and built al-Madrasa al-Afdaliyya around 590/1194 for the use of Mālikī *fuqahā'*.[18] The location of this school in the Maghribī Quarter was appropriate, since most of the Mālikīs traced their origins from North Africa. One of the most famous of the Ayyūbids, al-Malik al-ʿĀdil (d. 615/1217), was responsible for building ablution and drinking fountains within the Ḥaram. Moreover, during his reign there are no less than ten inscriptions in Jerusalem bearing the name of his son, al-Malik al-Muʿaẓẓam ʿĪsā (d. 624/1226), that attest to his sponsorship of building activities ranging from restoration of the arcades of the Ḥaram to construction of a tower in the citadel. In addition al-Muʿaẓẓam, who apparently 'considered himself an independent ruler' in Palestine[19] undertook to build two *madrasas*, one for the Ḥanafīs called after him al-Madrasa al-Muʿaẓẓamiyya, endowed in

606/1209 and completed in 614/1217–18, and another for the teaching of Arabic, called al-Madrasa al-Naḥwiyya in 604/1207.[20]

But, competing with the Ayyūbids' veneration for the city and their efforts to embellish it and enrich its spiritual life were other, more practical, considerations. After Ṣalāḥ al-Dīn died in 589/1193, the simple fact soon emerged that al-Quds was not essential to the security of an empire based in Egypt or Syria. Accordingly, in times of political or military crisis, the city proved to be expendable. Given the internal frictions within the Ayyūbid family and the recurrent Frankish desire to recapture the Holy City for Christendom, such crises were frequent.

As is well known, whatever unity and loyalty Ṣalāḥ al-Dīn had been able to nourish in the Ayyūbids diminished with his death as his heirs began to quarrel among themselves over his territory and sovereignty. In the rivalry between his sons al-Afḍal and al-'Azīz, their uncle al-'Ādil, played a decisive role, first supporting the former and then the latter; eventually, in 592/1196 al-'Ādil gained the viceroyship of Damascus for himself under al-'Azīz. However, when al-'Azīz died in 595/1198, the struggle with al-Afḍal was renewed.[21] It ended in his defeat and al-'Ādil's assumption of the sultanate of Egypt and Syria. Although Jerusalem remained on the periphery of this power struggle, it was, of course, affected. Significantly, in spite of – or perhaps because of – the sanctity of al-Quds, no member of the Ayyūbid family lived or ruled there until around 601/1204, when al-Mu'aẓẓam 'Īsā made it his chief residence.[22] Before that time, in accordance with Ṣalāḥ al-Dīn's own precedent, it was granted in fief to high-ranking military officers either of slave (*mamlūk*) or Kurdish origin. Not unnaturally, as the contest for control of the empire shifted back and forth among the contenders, the governors of Jerusalem were changed frequently. 'Izz al-Dīn Jurdik al-Nūrī, a *mamlūk* of Nūr al-Dīn's, was appointed by Ṣalāḥ al-Dīn in 588/1192 after conclusion of the truce with Richard. He remained in office until 591/1195 when al-'Ādil replaced him with the Kurdish commander Ḥusām al-Dīn Abū al-Hayjā' al-Hadhbānī al-Samīn. In the meantime al-Afḍal had offered but later refused to cede his authority over Jerusalem to al-'Azīz. In 592/1196, when al-'Azīz succeeded in capturing Damascus, he dismissed Abū al-Hajā' and appointed Ṣalāḥ al-Dīn's *mamlūk*, Ṣārim al-Din Khuṭlukh al-'Izzī, to the post. He was kept on when al-'Ādil became sultan of Egypt and Syria in 596/1200. Khuṭlukh was succeeded by al-Mu'aẓẓam 'Īsā, who ruled the city in his own name with aid of a *mamlūk* amīr.[23]

Although little is known about the economic history of the city under the Ayyūbids, there are indications that its economic base was not as sound as it might be in the absence of a steady flow of European pilgrims, then, as now, a major source of income for the city. In order to supplement its revenues, a third of those of Nablus were diverted to al-Quds. An indication of the economic strength of the *iqṭāʿ* of Nablus relative to Jerusalem's is the fact that the administrator of Nablus offered to assume all the expenses of Jerusalem and those of troops assigned there.[24]

Nevertheless, despite political disorder and economic uncertainties, the status of Jerusalem remained stable until 1219 and the siege and ultimate capture of Damietta in Egypt by the army of the Fifth Crusade. Before that date a series of truces had been concluded with the Latin Kingdom of Jerusalem whereby al-Malik al-ʿĀdil was able to ensure the security of his base in Egypt and his commercial agreements with Italian city states in exchange for territorial and other concessions, such as the delivery of Jaffa, Lydda, Ramla, and Nazareth to the Franks in 1204. During al-ʿĀdil's reign, the only hint of a threat to Jerusalem occurred in 1203 but failed to materialize when the Frankish troops poised to attack were reduced by epidemic. In 607/1210–11 aggressive Crusader activity in Syria, around Homs, led al-ʿĀdil to build a strong fortress on Mt Tabor in order to defend the approaches to Jerusalem. In 1219, however, with the successful landing of Crusaders in Egypt, the situation changed drastically as al-ʿĀdil's successor, his son al-Kāmil, summoned the Ayyūbids of Palestine and Syria to his aid in Egypt.[25] As we have seen, al-Muʿaẓẓam ʿĪsā, Prince of Damascus, had chosen Jerusalem as his principal residence, and sponsored much construction in the city. It is ironic, then, that he became the instrument for destroying its fortifications. This decision al-Muʿaẓẓam reached in Egypt when he realized that the absence of his own and other Ayyūbid troops from Syria left Palestine vulnerable to Christian attack. After all, the ostensible purpose of the Fifth Crusade was to facilitate the capture of the Holy City by attacking the seat of Muslim power in Egypt. In fact, al-Muʿaẓẓam had learned that a body of Franks had designs on al-Quds. Accordingly, he ordered that the fortifications of Jerusalem as well as those of Mt Tabor, Safad, Kerak, Tibnin and elsewhere be razed lest they fall into Frankish hands and serve as bases for further expansion.[26] In view of Jerusalem's religious significance, this step was not regarded lightly by the Ayyūbids themselves, the inhabitants of the city or the Muslim chroniclers. When al-Muʿaẓẓam's brother and another officer hesitated to carry out the command and offered to guard the city themselves, al-Mu'aẓẓam informed them by letter, 'If the Franks conquer it [Jerusalem] they will kill all whom they find there and will have the fate of Damascus and lands of Islam in their hands. Necessity requires its destruction.'[27] Al-Mu'aẓẓam himself arrived to oversee the work in the spring of 616/1219. According to the contemporary historian Sibṭ Ibn al-Jawzī (d. 654/1256), after the walls had been razed, women, children, the old, and infirm fled the city for Damascus, Cairo and Kerak, leaving their families and possessions behind.[28] A later historian, al-Maqrīzī (d. 845/1441) states that al-Mu'aẓẓam 'caused all the inhabitants to leave, only a few remaining; and he removed all the weapons and engines of war in the city.'[29] All this caused great alarm 'like that of the Day of Resurrection . . . it was a misfortune, the like of which had never befallen Islam.'[30] As calamitous as this outrage inflicted on Jerusalem and Islam seemed to historians and poets, political and military considerations prevailed. Indeed, we know that the sultan al-Kāmil and his brother, al-Mu'aẓẓam 'Īsā, offered to surrender the entire kingdom of Jerusalem with the exception only of Kerak and Shawbak if the Franks would leave Egypt. Led by the papal legate Pelagius, the Franks refused to accept these terms at this time.[31] But similar ones served as the basis of the agreement between al-Kāmil and Frederick II some ten years later whereby Jerusalem was again lost temporarily to Islam. The reasons behind al-Kāmil's decision to surrender Jerusalem were the same as those that had led to dismantling its walls. The seat of al-Kāmil's kingdom was in Egypt. An unfortified Jerusalem in Frankish hands would pose no threat to Egypt and would fulfil the Crusaders' ostensible purposes. Frederick was characteristically frank, even cynical, in pointing out these factors to al-Kāmil:

> You have corresponded with me about my coming, and the Pope and the other kings of the West are acquainted with my zeal and my goals. But Jerusalem is the root of their belief and the goal of their pilgrimage. The Muslims have destroyed it; therefore for them it has no economic significance. If the Sultan, may God strengthen him, could decide to confer on me the capital of the land with the right to visit the other Holy Places, this would show his wisdom and I could raise my head among the other kings.[32]

And in a letter to an Ayyūbid envoy:

> If I did not fear losing my respect among the Franks I would not have burdened the Sultan with such. For myself personally,

> neither Jerusalem nor anything else in Palestine is a goal worth struggling for . . . However, I must preserve my standing among them.[33]

Nevertheless, amidst these practical considerations, al-Kāmil did not lose sight of the religious significance for Muslims, so that the agreement specified that the Ḥaram al-Sharīf with its sanctuaries remain in Muslim hands, administered by Muslim officials with the insignias of Islam displayed there as customary. 'All the practices of Islam, with the call to prayers and the prayers themselves, should continue to be observed within the sacred area.'[34] In extenuation of his retrocession of the city to Frederick, al-Kāmil declared, 'I conceded to the Franks only ruined churches and houses. The Mosque (in the Ḥaram) remains as it was, and the practices of Islam continue there . . .'[35] Furthermore, he argued, to strengthen his case, that the city could easily be reconquered at a later date. An important factor left unmentioned, however, is the renewed strife within the Ayyūbid family. Without a united front in Syria and Egypt al-Kāmil was not prepared to cope with a Crusader army within his territories, and Jerusalem became a pawn in family struggles. The key factor in this respect was the brothers' war between al-Kāmil and al-Mu'aẓẓam, reflecting the difficulty in controlling an empire consisting of Egypt and Syria. The depth of al-Kāmil's fear of al-Mu'aẓẓam's power in Syria and Palestine was his offer to Frederick in 623/1226 to cede cities in Palestine, including Jerusalem according to the historian al-'Ainī (d. 855/1451), in return for the emperor's aid against his brother.[36] Although al-Mu'aẓẓam had earlier co-operated with his brother in a negotiated peace with the Franks, he rejected Frederick's overtures of 624/1227. From Damascus he refused to be a party to the surrender of Ṣalāḥ al-Dīn's conquests and, though mortally ill, moved to Jerusalem in order to ensure the destruction of whatever defences remained. Al-Mu'aẓẓam died soon after, but the damage had already been done, and al-Kāmil failed to rally the Ayyūbids against an invasion already in progress.[37]

As might be expected, news of the surrender of the city was received with dismay by Muslims. *Imāms* and *mu'adhdhins* from Jerusalem harassed al-Kāmil in his camp at Tell-al-'Ajūl and had to be driven away. Ibn al-Jawzī was required by al-Kāmil's enemy in Damascus, al-Malik al-Nāṣir Dā'ūd, to preach against the fate of Bait al-Maqdis in the Mosque of the Umayyads.[38] According to al-Maqrīzī, the loss 'was a great misfortune for the Muslims, and much reproach was put upon al-Kāmil, and many were the revilings of him in all lands.'[39] Frederick apparently acted with extraordinary sensitivity for the Muslim holy places when he visited the Ḥaram on the occasion of his coronation at the Church of the Holy Sepulchre. There are reports that he knocked to the ground a Christian priest carrying a Bible into al-Aqṣā without authorization, and he requested that the call to prayer be restored at the Ḥaram when he learned it had been suspended during his stay.[40]

The truce of ten years and a half held during al-Kāmil's lifetime (he died in March 1238). Although the city was raided by Muslims from Hebron and Nablus shortly after Frederick's departure in 1229, and Christian pilgrims were harassed along the road leading from the coast, the Ayyūbids made no effort to regain the city. On their side, the Franks kept their word not to refortify the city, until, that is, the truce expired in 1239. Nevertheless, their efforts were not enough, so that al-Nāṣir Dā'ūd, at that time ruler of Kerak, was able to force the Franks to abandon the city after a short siege toward the end of the year. Again, however, internecine strife among the Ayyūbids caused Dā'ūd and his allies to give the city back to the Franks in return for their pledge of assistance against al-Malik al-Ṣāliḥ Ayyūb, sultan of Egypt.[41] At this point the status of Jerusalem reached its nadir under the Ayyūbids. The Christians were given possession of the Dome of the Rock. According to al-Maqrīzī they 'set wine bottles on the Rock' (for purposes of Communion?) and 'hung bells in the al-Aqṣā Mosque.'[42] But this outrage was soon drastically remedied with the invasion of Khwārazmian troops summoned by al-Ṣāliḥ Ayyūb to eliminate his enemies in Syria. In the course of their progress through Palestine the Khwārazmians marched into Jerusalem in the summer of 1244, massacred the Christian inhabitants and ravaged their shrines, including the Church of the Resurrection.[43] Thus Jerusalem was restored to the Ayyūbids and so remained until the death by assassination of the last Ayyūbid sultan of Egypt, Tūrānshāh. It is interesting to note that Tūrānshāh's father, al-Ṣāliḥ Ayyūb, shared the mixed sentiments of his forebears toward the city. For, even though al-Ṣāliḥ Ayyūb paid tribute to the sanctity of al-Quds by erecting Qubbat al-Mūsā in the Ḥaram,[44] he, too, was willing to sacrifice the city for strategic considerations, if, that is, the security of Egypt was at stake. This emerges clearly from the testament he left to guide his son and successor, Tūrānshāh, as ruler of Egypt. Realizing that the immediate issue facing Tūrānshāh was the presence of the Seventh Crusader army at Damietta, al-Ṣāliḥ Ayyūb offered the following counsel:

> If you are unable to contain the God-forsaken enemy and they march out from Damietta against you [in Cairo] and, if you lack power to cope with them and help fails to reach you in time, and they demand from you the coast [of Palestine] and Bait al-Maqdis, give these places to them without delay on condition that they have no foothold in Egypt.[45]

Tūrānshāh did not have to act on this advice. He was murdered in 648/1250 by disaffected Mamlūks. Thereby a new state was established in Egypt which lasted more than 250 years, until 1517. Some thirteen years were required to bring the Ayyūbids' Syrian possessions into the Mamlūk orbit, as the various Ayyūbid and Mamlūk factions contested the authority of the regime in Cairo. During this time the status of Jerusalem was unstable. In 1251 al-Nāṣir Yūsuf of Aleppo offered to cede Jerusalem to the Crusaders led by Louis IX in exchange for an alliance against the Mamlūks, but Louis refused. Two years later, in 651/1253, Yūsuf gave Palestine west of the Jordan, including Jerusalem, to the Mamlūk sultan Aibek in return for peace. But Palestine and Jerusalem were restored to the Ayyūbids in 1256 as a result of the defection of dissident Mamlūks to various Ayyūbid courts in Syria.[46] The decisive event in the history of Jerusalem of this period was the Mamlūks' defeat of the Mongol army in 1260 at 'Ain Jālūt, close to Nazareth, for it was this battle and the expulsion of the Mongols beyond the Euphrates that enabled the Mamlūks to establish their sovereignty in Palestine. Beginning with the following year, a steady stream of governors appointed by the Mamlūks served in the city until the end of the dynasty. Under the Mamlūks, as we shall see, the city retained its importance as a Muslim sacred place; the significant change in its fortunes was political. Henceforth, for the first time since the reign of Ṣalāḥ al-Dīn, it was to remain firmly in the hands of Muslims, no longer to be offered as a prize in political, military, and diplomatic contests. The reason for this change lay in the Mamlūks' success in driving the Crusaders from the Holy Land. Although this was not achieved until 690/1291 with the fall of Acre to al-Malik al-Ashraf Khalīl and involved earlier truces with various Frankish principalities, the status of Jerusalem never figured in the negotiations, probably because the Crusaders were not strong enough to pose a major threat to Mamlūk interests in Palestine.

The very fact that Jerusalem was no longer the target of European aggression, or any other for that matter, brought an element of stability. In this respect it is significant that the Mamlūks saw no reason to rebuild the city's walls throughout the two and a half centuries of their rule. In none of the campaigns with the Crusaders and the Mongols was Jerusalem ever threatened, even though battles with both enemies were fought in Palestine. Moreover, the Mamlūk state, in comparison with the Ayyūbid, was stronger, better controlled, and more centralized, despite internal rivalry and strife manifested in repeated attempts by amīrs stationed in major cities of Syria to assert their independence.

The reduced political significance of Jerusalem can be seen also in its administrative status within the Mamlūk empire. In his chancery manual *Zubdat Kashf al-Mamālik*, Khalīl b. Shāhīn al-Ẓāhirī (d. 873/1468) does not even mention the city among the eight administrative sectors (*mamālik*) into which Syria was divided. Instead, these were based on major cities such as Damascus, Aleppo, Tripoli, and Hama and much smaller, but strategically important, towns like Alexandretta, Kerak, Safed, and Gaza.[47] According to al-Qalqashandī (d. 821/1418), Jerusalem was first a *wilāya* (governorate) and later a *niyāba* (viceroyship) under the jurisdiction of the viceroy of Damascus. The viceroys of Jerusalem were chosen from amīrs of middle rank (*amīr arba'īn*); the governors had been soldiers (*jundīs*), not, that is, officers.[48] These officials were appointed by the viceroy of Damascus until around 800/1398; thereafter, except in times of strife between Egypt and Syria, they were appointed by the sultan in Cairo.[49] The names and dates of many of these officials have been recorded by the great historian of Jerusalem, Mujīr al-Dīn al-'Ulaimī, who lived during the last years of the Mamlūk period. We know very little about them as individuals. With few exceptions they were amīrs: forty-nine of a total of fifty-six recorded. Most of the others were judges.[50] The presence of a few *qāḍīs* in the company of Mamlūk officers points to the religious dimension of the highest administrative post in Jerusalem. This aspect is underscored by the various titles the holder of the office bore. Some of the rulers of Jerusalem were known simply as Nā'ib al-Salṭana (Viceroy); others as Nāẓir al-Ḥaramain al-Sharīfain (Supervisor of the Two Sacred Enclaves (Jerusalem and Hebron)). In the reign of Sultan al-Nāṣir Muḥammad, the two titles were combined in the same person. This practice was often followed thereafter but by no means consistently since a member of the learned, religious bureaucracy was sometimes charged with supervision of the two *ḥarams*, while 'secular' affairs were left to the Mamlūk viceroy.[51] Here it is noteworthy that the shrines of Abraham and his family at Hebron (al-Khalīl) were linked with those of Jerusalem. The sanctity of Hebron in Muslim consciousness and its association with that of al-Quds have not yet received the attention they deserve. Research in the Ḥaram documents discovered recently in the Islamic Museum in Jerusalem indicates that the Shāfiʿī chief judge was also an extremely important official who operated independently of and in concert with the Mamlūk *nā'ib* and *nāẓir*. In the case of al-Qāḍī Sharaf al-Dīn ʿĪsā b. Ghānim al-Anṣārī al-Khazrajī (d. 797/1395), for example, it is clear from his additional title, Nāẓir al-Awqāf al-Mubrūra bi-'l-Quds al-Sharīf (Supervisor of Pious Endowments in Jerusalem), that responsibility for the religious endowments and shrines of Jerusalem was divided, in as much as other officials, mainly Mamlūk amīrs, as we have seen, were entrusted with supervision of the Ḥaram.[52] This division of responsibility may have been due in part to the enormous growth in the construction, restoration, and maintenance of religious monuments in Jerusalem under Mamlūk patronage. During the period sultans and amīrs, scholars and merchants, pious men and women in retirement lavished their wealth to adorn the city and to ensure the perpetuation of their names in the aura of its sanctity. The sultans are well known for their architectural achievements in Cairo, Damascus, Tripoli and other major cities in their empire. Although Jerusalem did not play a major role in their political and military considerations, its importance to them as a Muslim sacred place is well documented. The most prominent sultans of the Baḥrī period (1260–1389) – Baybars, Qalāwūn, and al-Nāṣir Muḥammad – are known to have visited al-Quds. These same sultans were joined by three others – Kitbughā, Lājīn, and Shaʿbān – in undertaking restorations of the shrines of Jerusalem and Hebron as well as construction of new buildings.[53] Typically, al-Nāṣir Muḥammad, famed for his construction activities in Cairo, extended his patronage to Jerusalem. The Ḥaram received his special attention. Both the Dome of the Rock and dome of al-Aqṣā were restored, and the western *riwāq*, arcades, and terraces around the Rock were completed.[54] Burjī sultans also visited the city: Barqūq, Faraj, and Qā'itbāy.[55] In this period (1382–1517) Sultan Qā'itbāy stands out for repairs to al-Aqṣā and construction of his great *madrasa*, al-Ashrafiyya, as well as the *sabīl* bearing his name, also in the Ḥaram.[56] Mamlūk amīrs shared the sultans' enthusiasm for erecting religious structures in the Ḥaram. The Amīr Tankiz, long-time viceroy of Damascus (712–40/1312–40), was responsible for a magnificent complex in the western precincts; other amīrs built *madrasas* at the northern borders.[57] Such projects transformed the character and appearance of the sacred enclave during this period:

> For instead of being simply an area surrounded by a portico and reached through a number of more or less monumental gates, the northern and western sides of the Ḥaram became a show place of facades to buildings whose function was no longer connected to the Ḥaram but received a certain value or grace from it . . .[58]

In addition to monuments surviving in the Ḥaram, there is increasing documentary evidence of the Mamlūk sultans' concern for the Ḥaram. *Waqfiyyas* for some of these works have been recently published or summarized by Dr K J Asali.[59] In the Ḥaram documents we find seven decrees issued by sultans Baybars, al-Nāṣir Muḥammad, Sha'bān, Jaqmaq, Īnāl, and Khushqadam, all of which related to supplying adequate revenues for the maintenance and staff of buildings in the Ḥaram.[60]

Outside the Ḥaram, Jerusalem also benefited from the architectural patronage of Mamlūks, particularly from amīrs. Besides those who served in administrative capacities in the city, many, we know, chose to retire there because of the quiet atmosphere and mild climate. Jerusalem became a veritable 'centre of exiles' during the Mamlūk period: 'the most important place of banishment in the region, nay in the whole Mamlūk Sultanate, was undoubtedly Jerusalem.'[61] Its closeness to Egypt and the absence of strong fortifications and of a large number of troops that might serve the interests of disaffected amīrs recommended it to sultans as a place of exile. In any event, many amīrs undertook to build religious edifices in the vicinity of the Ḥaram, in clusters mainly along the streets leading from its gates. Thus, to mention only one gate, we find outside Bāb al-Ḥadīd a hospice, Ribāṭ al-Kurd, built in 695/1296 by a *mamlūk* of Sultan Qalāwūn, Saif al-Dīn Kurd; across the street, al-Madrasa al-Arghūniyya, endowed and built by al-Amīr Arghūn al-Kāmilī in 758/1358; further along the street leading from Bāb al-Ḥādid, al-Madrasa al-Ḥanbaliyya, built for members of the Ḥanbalī school of law by al-Amīr Baydamur al-Khwārazmī, Viceroy of Syria, in 781/1379.[62]

But it was not just sultans and amīrs who provided religious buildings for Jerusalem during the Mamlūk period. Along the same street, next door and above the Ribāṭ al-Kurd, a eunuch in charge of Sultan Khushqadam's harem, Jawhar al-Qunuqbāy, erected in 844/1440 a *madrasa* called al-Jawhariyya;[63] across the street a chancery official in Mamlūk service during the reign of Qā'itbāy caused al-

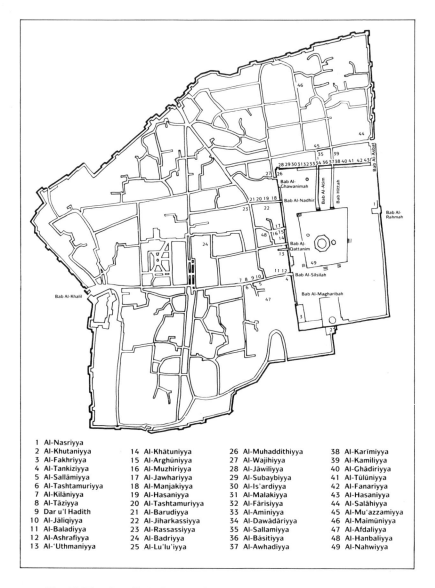

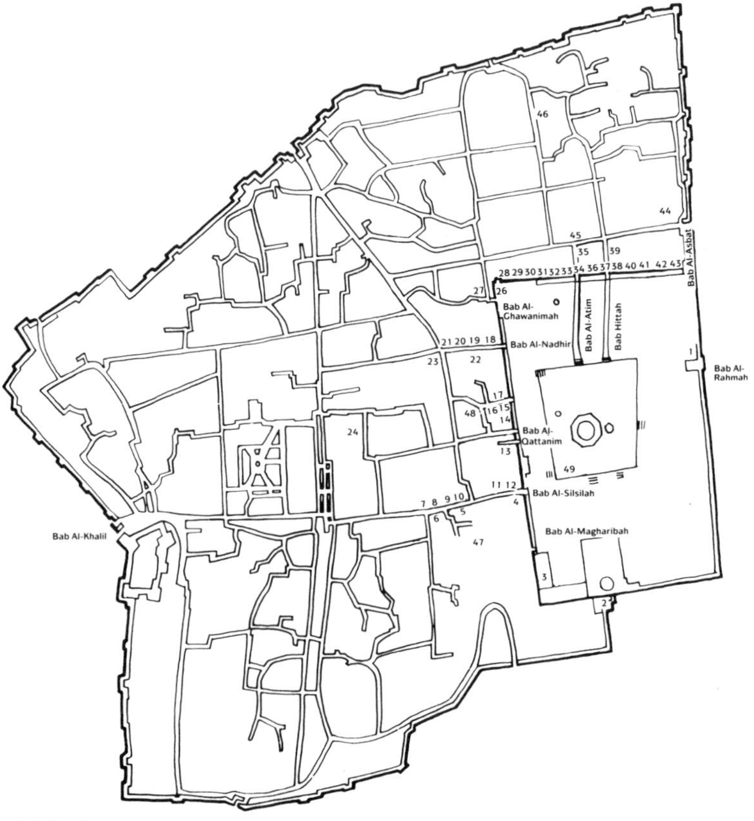

1 Al-Nasriyya
2 Al-Khutaniyya
3 Al-Fakhriyya
4 Al-Tankiziyya
5 Al-Sallāmiyya
6 Al-Tashtamuriyya
7 Al-Kilāniyya
8 Al-Tāziyya
9 Dar u'l Hadith
10 Al-Jāliqiyya
11 Al-Baladiyya
12 Al-Ashrafiyya
13 Al-'Uthmaniyya
14 Al-Khātuniyya
15 Al-Arghūniyya
16 Al-Muzhiriyya
17 Al-Jawhariyya
18 Al-Manjakiyya
19 Al-Hasaniyya
20 Al-Tashtamuriyya
21 Al-Barudiyya
22 Al-Jiharkassiyya
23 Al-Rassassiyya
24 Al-Badriyya
25 Al-Lu'lu'iyya
26 Al-Muhaddithiyya
27 Al-Wajihiyya
28 Al-Jāwiliyya
29 Al-Subaybiyya
30 Al-Is'ardiyya
31 Al-Malakiyya
32 Al-Fārisiyya
33 Al-Amīniyya
34 Al-Dawādāriyya
35 Al-Sallamiyya
36 Al-Bāsitiyya
37 Al-Awhadiyya
38 Al-Karīmiyya
39 Al-Kamiliyya
40 Al-Ghādiriyya
41 Al-Tūlūniyya
42 Al-Fanariyya
43 Al-Hasaniyya
44 Al-Salāhiyya
45 Al-Mu'azzamiyya
46 Al-Maimūniyya
47 Al-Afdaliyya
48 Al-Hanbaliyya
49 Al-Nahwiyya

Fig. 13 Islamic colleges in Jerusalem

Madrasa al-Muzhiriyya to be built.[64] Elsewhere in the city private citizens financed the construction of buildings for religious purposes. Al-Madrasa al-Sallāmiyya, for example, was built outside Bāb al-'Atm sometime after 700/1300 by the famous merchant and diplomatic agent of the Mamlūks, al-Khawājā Majd al-Dīn Abū al-Fidā' Ismā'īl al-Sallāmī.[65] Wealthy women of foreign origin who took up residence in Jerusalem were also patrons. For example, al-Madrasa al-Bārūdiyya was endowed in 768/1367 by al-Sitt al-Ḥājja Sufrā Khātūn, presumably the wife and daughter of merchants; a lady of eastern origins, Ughul Khātūn al-Qāzānīyya al-Baghdādiyya, was responsible for building al-Madrasa al-Khātūniyya in 782/1380; adjacent to the Ḥaram a woman of prominent Anatolian origin, Isfahān Shāh Khātūn, built al-Madrasa al-'Uthmāniyya in 840/1437 (in the Burjī period), south of the Khātūniyya, outside Bāb al-Maṭhara.[66]

Just these few examples demonstrate that Muslim Jerusalem enjoyed a period of major and sustained growth under the Mamlūks, in contrast to the sporadic progress made under the Ayyūbids. But aside from transforming the appearance of the city, what effect did all this construction have on its life? It is obvious that the buildings both reflected and contributed to the re-Islamization of the city after the Mamlūks had eliminated the Christians as rivals for dominance. Although there are no reliable demographic studies for the period, the Muslim population must have grown and the new buildings must have been erected to accommodate the increased Muslim presence. In the same vein, the restoration and adornment of the two major shrines of the Ḥaram, as well as the addition of subsidiary structures, certainly helped to re-establish the city as a pilgrimage centre for Muslims. A flurry in the construction of hospices (*ribāṭs*) to house visitors to the city served the same purpose. Of the seven hospices known to exist in Jerusalem, five can be identified as Mamlūk structures, including the Ribāṭ al-Manṣūrī, endowed by Sultan Qalāwūn in 681/1282.[67] Other Mamlūk buildings which reflect the needs of a growing population, both permanent and transient, were the several markets, bathhouses, fountains, and canals constructed during the period.[68]

But besides the construction focused on the Ḥaram, there were many new buildings which served other religious purposes, mainly two: (1) instruction in jurisprudence (*fiqh*) and related Islamic disciplines and (2) cultivation of the mystical (sufi) life. Although the two were often fulfilled in one and the same building, *madrasas* were intended primarily for the former; *khānqāhs* and *zāwiyas* for the latter. We have already seen that one of Ṣalāḥ al-Dīn's early acts after conquering al-Quds was to establish a *madrasa* for jurisprudents and a monastery for sufis. Both types of institutions flourished under the Mamlūks. No less than twenty-seven *madrasas* are known to have been established, eighteen during the Baḥrī period, nine during the Burjī.[69] It is not surprising, then, with these facilities, that Jerusalem became a centre for the study of *fiqh* and *ḥadīth*. The pages of Mujīr al-Dīn al-'Ulaimī's history teems with biographies of scholars who studied and taught in the city. Although the Shāfi'īs maintained the dominance given them by Ṣalāḥ al-Dīn, the three other schools of law were not neglected. We have already mentioned a *madrasa* specializing in Ḥanbalī *fiqh*; the Ḥanafīs and Mālikīs also had institutions of their own.[70] This diversification in *fiqh* studies reflects both the variegated character of the population and the policy of the Mamlūks inaugurated by Sultan Baybars to institutionalize the four schools of *fiqh* in the judicial system. Thus, in 784/1382–83 Sultan Barqūq installed a Ḥanafī judge in Jerusalem to join the Shāfi'ī, and in 802/1399–1400 and 804/1401–2 they were joined by a Mālikī and a Ḥanbalī respectively.[71]

Confusion in the use of such terms as *khānqāh*, *ribāṭ*, and *zāwiya* makes it difficult to estimate precisely how many sufi institutions were founded at this time. Furthermore, many *madrasas*, which we characterized as *fiqh* schools, are known to have contained facilities for sufi residents. The Tankiziyya Madrasa, for example, contained a *khānqāh* for fifteen sufis; according to the *waqfiyyas* for al-Madrasa al-Ashrafiyya dated 881/1476 and 895/1490, sixty sufis were assigned stipends from its revenues; the Madrasa/Khānqāh al-Dawādāriyya, endowed in 695/1296 by a Mamlūk amīr, accommodated thirty sufis – twenty bachelors and ten married.[72] In addition to *madrasa-khānqāhs*, many of the *zāwiyas* established during the Mamlūk period also provided facilities for sufis, though usually on a smaller scale. *Zāwiyas* associated with specific sufi orders and which are known to have flourished at this time include al-Bisṭāmiyya (*c*.770/1369); al-Wafā'iyya (782/1380); and al-Naqshabandiyya (8th/15th century).[73] It is evident both from sufi buildings and from biographical data in literary and documentary sources that sufism flourished in Jerusalem in this era. As was the case elsewhere in the Islamic world, sufis had been so well integrated with the scholarly class that jurists holding important positions in the legal bureaucracy were often prominent sufis. Al-Qāḍī Sharaf al-Dīn 'Īsā b. Ghānim al-Anṣārī al-Shāfi'ī is a case in point. In addition to his posts as Shāfi'ī judge of Jerusalem and supervisor of pious foundations, he was also Shaikh of al-Khānqāh al-Ṣalāḥiyya, probably the most prestigious sufi institution in Mamlūk Jerusalem.[74] Thanks to the Ḥaram documents we now have considerable information about a Jerusalemite scholar-sufi, Burhān al-Dīn Ibrāhīm al-Nāṣirī (d. 789/1387), who was apparently not prominent enough to be listed in Mujīr al-Dīn's biographies. Identified in several documents as 'a sufi in al-Khānqāh al-Ṣalāḥiyya', Burhān al-Dīn appears in others as a reciter of the Qur'ān, *ḥadīth*, *fiqh*, and *tafsīr* at al-Aqṣā and the Dome of the Rock, al-Turba al-Ṭāziyya, al-Turba al-Awḥadiyya, and elsewhere in Jerusalem.[75] From Mujīr al-Dīn and other sources we know that as a group the *fuqahā'* sufis of Mamlūk Jerusalem tended to be mobile, studying and working not only in al-Quds but in Cairo and Damascus as well, and thus were able to lend an element of cosmopolitanism to the cultural life of the city.[76] In this respect an obituary of the Jerusalem Qāḍī Shams al-Dīn al-Dairī (d. 1424) mentions his association 'with many Egyptian and Syrian *'ulamā'* who found Jerusalem to be their haven . . .'[77]

At the same time as Jerusalem was becoming a thriving religious centre under the protection and patronage of the Mamlūks, literary works praising its merits abounded. No less than thirty *faḍā'il* can be attributed to this era.[78] However, in certain quarters, zeal for the city was felt to be excessive. The famous 14th century Ḥanbalī reformer, Ibn Taimiyya, while acknowledging the holy character bestowed on it by the Prophet Muḥammad's nocturnal visit, attacked the popular veneration of the city contained, for instance, in contemporary pilgrimage manuals such as *Kitāb Bā'ith al-Nufūs ilā Ziyārat al-Quds al-Maḥrūs: Inducement to Visit Jerusalem the Well Protected.* Traditions and popular beliefs extolling the Rock and other sites Ibn Taimiyya dismissed as spurious, as well as raising visits to the city to the status of *ḥajj* to Mecca and Medina.[79] Nevertheless, despite the great influence and celebrity Ibn Taimiyya gained among many contemporaries for denouncing abuses and distortions of traditional Islam, his views were too extreme to be tolerated by the Mamlūk establishment and he died in prison for propagating them. There is no evidence that his attempt to curb Muslim enthusiasm for visiting Jerusalem had any practical effect.

Nor did Muslim possession of the city curb the enthusiasm of Christians for visiting their holy city. There is abundant evidence of a Christian presence throughout the Mamlūk period in the form both of European pilgrims and of local residents. Records of Christian pilgrimages are particularly rich for the 15th century, before, that is, the rise of Protestantism in northern Europe and geo-political considerations reduced the traffic. Although the travel books written by pilgrims contain stereotyped information for the most part, they do reveal that the pilgrimage to Jerusalem was supervised and controlled by the Mamlūk authorities and their bureaucracy. In exchange for fees paid for safe passage and other taxes, the Mamlūks provided dragomans and escorts to guide and protect the pilgrims. It is true that they were often subject to harassment and extortion from their hosts but not any worse than that inflicted upon them by the Venetian sea captains who provided transport to and from the Holy Land. The relevant point to make is that the Mamlūks made the Christian shrines accessible to pilgrims.[80] As far as the Christians resident in Jerusalem are concerned, we know most about the Franciscans, thanks to records of their dealings with the Mamlūk authorities and to remarks in pilgrims' narratives. The presence of monks in a monastery on Mount Zion, built around 1330, offered a source of support to the pilgrims, especially at times when there were no foreign consuls in the city. The first evidence of a foreign consul – Venetian – dates from 818/1415. In 835/1431 Genoa also secured permission to establish a consulate there.[81] However, by 1480 there was no official European representation in the city, and the Franciscan Father Guardian acted in an official capacity as protector of European pilgrims.[82] That the Franciscans enjoyed the favour of the Mamlūk authorities for the most part is amply attested by the many surviving documents granting sultans' protection along with permission to keep their buildings in good repair.[83] These records also reflect the struggle the monks had to wage against Muslim attempts, sometimes successful, to convert the property on Mount Zion into a mosque.[84]

Recent research indicates that other Christian communities were subject to similar vicissitudes in their relations with the Mamlūks and the Muslim dignitaries of Jerusalem. The Georgians, for example, had their Monastery of the Cross restored to them by Sultan al-Nāṣir Muḥammad in 705/1305, and subsequent decrees by Mamlūk sultans instruct the authorities in Jerusalem to treat the Georgians as protected peoples.[85] Be that as it may, the Mamlūks did not hesitate to act against Christians when circumstances warranted. Thus, in 1365 the Church of the Holy Sepulchre was closed in retaliation for Frankish attacks on Alexandria, and in 1476 Franciscans in Jerusalem and Bethlehem were sent to Cairo as hostages after acts of Christian piracy in the same port.[86]

The small Jewish community in Jerusalem also seems to have enjoyed the status of *dhimmīs* granted to them in Islamic law. While as in the case of the Christians there are certainly examples of strife with Muslims, mainly over holy places, the Jews 'posed no threat to the Muslim character of the town and lived peacefully with their neighbours, except for a few episodes when the wrath of the faithful Muslims was aroused against the Jews.'[87] From the Ḥaram documents we learn that Jews were able to own property in the city and to conduct business; on at least one occasion, moreover, the Shaikh of the Maghribī community intervened on their behalf against governmental abuse.[88]

If, as has been shown, the Mamlūks succeeded in re-Islamizing Jerusalem, providing for the rights and privileges of religious minorities, and establishing its political stability, how did they manage its economy? Hints have already been given. Catering to pilgrims of all three creeds was undoubtedly a major business in Mamlūk Jerusalem. Income was generated by the influx of visitors who required food and lodging, guides, transport, and souvenirs and who paid fees and taxes during their stay. Also related to the religious status of the city was the patronage provided to shrines. Most important in this respect, of course, were the endowments established by the sultans, amīrs, and wealthy Muslim civilians for the benefit of Islamic edifices, ranging from the magnificent Dome of the Rock and al-Aqṣā to the humblest *zāwiya*. These buildings provided employment not only to janitors and caretakers but also to scholars, preachers, Qur'ān and *ḥadīth* reciters, and sufis. To provide water for the Ḥaram various sultans and amīrs sponsored the construction and repairs of canals. Mamlūk officers in exile must also have acted as a stimulus to the economy as can be seen by the buildings they erected.[89] These factors were all important for the prosperity of a city which did not lie astride a major trade route or produce a substantial number of commodities for export. On the other hand, the Ḥaram documents give evidence of the presence of foreign traders from the east in Jerusalem, especially textile merchants. References to silk and cotton merchants appear.[90] The latter are certainly not surprising in view of the presence of the great cotton market, Sūq al-Qaṭṭānīn, adjacent to the Ḥaram. Soap is known to have been manufactured in Jerusalem during the period, and this industry was related, of course, to the cultivation of olives in the vicinity of the city.[91] Other manufactured goods included cotton and linen products characterized as 'al-Qudsī', such as linings for mattresses, kerchiefs, coats, prayer rugs and chemises.[92] From the descriptions of household items and garments left in the estates of late 14th century Jerusalemites, it is clear that the city was dependent on exports from as far away as Anatolia (rugs), Nishapur (caps, tunics, and chemises), Yemen (blankets), the Maghrib (coats and robes), Venice (chemises), and Portugal (leather).[93] As intriguing as these references to the economy of al-Quds may be, nothing is known of the volume of trade or the size of the native industries.

As already indicated, the revenues produced by Jerusalem under the Ayyūbids were small in relation to those of other towns in Palestine. The same is true of the Ottoman period, when its taxes were approximately a quarter of those paid by other districts.[94] Although comparable figures are not available for the interim, the Ḥaram documents demonstrate the lengths to which the Jerusalem Mamlūk Bureau of Escheat Estates (Dīwān al-Mawārīth al-Ḥashriyya) went, in conjunction with the Shāfi'ī court, to expropriate the residue of estates lacking accessible heirs in order to increase the state's revenues.[95]

Toward the end of the 15th century the political, economic, and religious situation of Jerusalem deteriorated, as was the case with other cities in the Mamlūk empire. For ten years in the early 16th century Muslim pilgrims to Mecca from Egypt and the Maghrib were unable to visit Jerusalem because of 'bedouin anarchy' south of the city.[96] This reflects the difficulty experienced by the Mamlūks in controlling the Arab bedouin in the best of times and the total impossibility once the central government collapsed as a result of insurmountable economic problems, plague, Ottoman incursions, and degeneration of the Mamlūk system itself. Jerusalem was lost to the Ottomans sometime between the Battle of Marj Dābiq in northern Syria in 1516 and the fall of Cairo in the following year.

NOTES

1 W M de Slane, *Ibn Khallikan's Biographical Dictionary Translated from the Arabic*, Paris, 1843, II, 635.

2 See E Sivan, 'Le caractère sacré de Jérusalem dans l'Islam aux XIIè–XIIIè siècles', *Studia Islamica*, XVII, 1967, 142–182, and 'The Beginnings of the *Faḍā'il al-Quds* Literature', *Israel Oriental Series*, 1971, 263–71; Issac Hasson, 'Muslim Literature in Praise of Jerusalem: Faḍā'il Bayt al-Maqdis', *The Jerusalem Cathedre*, Jerusalem, 1981, 168–84; K J Asali, *Makhṭūṭāt Faḍā'il Bait al-Maqdis: Dirāsa wa-Bīblīyughrāfiyā*, Amman, 1984.

3 De Slane, *Ibn Khallikan*, II, 636–37.

4 Ibid, 637–61.

5 Stanley Lane-Poole, *Saladin and the Fall of the Kingdom of Jerusalem*, reprint Beirut, 1964, 235.

6 Mujīr al-Dīn al-'Ulaimī, *Al-Uns al-Jalīl bi-Tārīkh al-Quds wa-'l-Khalīl*, Amman, 1973, I, 339.

7 Steven Runciman, *A History of the Crusades*, London, 1965, I, 467.

8 'Ārif al-'Ārif, *Al-Mufaṣṣal fī Tārīkh al-Quds*, Jerusalem, 1961, 176. Unfortunately, 'Ārif cites no source for this claim.

9 Ibid, 177.
10 Ibn Shaddād, *Al-Nawādir al-Sulṭāniyya wa-'l-Maḥāsin al-Yūsufiyya, Recueil des historiens des Croisades: Historiens orientaux*, Paris, 1884, III, 265.
11 Mujīr al-Dīn, *Al-Uns*, I, 383.
12 Sidney Painter, 'The Third Crusade: Richard the Lionhearted and Philip Augustus', *A History of the Crusades*, ed. Kenneth Setton, 2nd ed., Madison, 1969, II, 85.
13 K J Asali, *Ma'āhid al-'Ilm fī Bayt al-Maqdis*, Amman, 1981, 61–63, believes that Ṣalāḥ al-Dīn decided to establish the *madrasa* in 583/1187–8 but that it was not opened until 588/1192.
14 *Al-Uns*, II, 101–118.
15 K J Asali, *Wathā'iq Maqdisiyya Tārīkhiyya*, Amman, 1983, I, 83–100.
16 Al-'Ārif, *Al-Mufaṣṣal*, 178.
17 Asali, *Ma'āhid*, 294–96.
18 Ibid, 116–17.
19 R Stephen Humphreys, *From Saladin to the Mongols: The Ayyubids of Damascus, 1193–1260*, Albany, 1977, 150–53.
20 Asali, *Ma'āhid*, 104–06, 272–75.
21 It is difficult to establish which Ayyūbid held command over Jerusalem at any given time after Ṣalāḥ al-Dīn's death in 589/1193. The clearest statement is found in Max van Berchem's *Matériaux pour un corpus inscriptionum arabicarum*, pt. II, vol. I, *Jérusalem 'Ville'*, Cairo, 1922, 98–99.
22 Humphreys, *Saladin*, 145.
23 Ibid, 93,101, 108, 144.
24 Ibid, 79, 94.
25 Hans L Gottschalk, *Al-Malik al-Kāmil von Ägypten und seine Zeit*, Wiesbaden, 1958, 48–50; H A R Gibb, 'The Aiyūbids', *A History of the Crusades*, ed. Setton, II, 694–97.
26 Gottschalk, *Al-Kāmil*, 88.
27 Ibid, 88.
28 Ibid.
29 *A History of the Ayyūbid Sultans of Egypt Translated from the Arabic of al-Maqrīzī*, by R J C Broadhurst, Boston, 1980, 181.
30 Gottschalk, *Al-Kāmil*, 88, quoting Ibn al-Jawzī.
31 Thomas C van Cleve, 'The Fifth Crusade', *A History of the Crusades*, ed. Setton, II, 409–10.
32 Gottschalk, *Al-Kāmil*, 154.
33 Ibid.
34 Al-Maqrīzī, *History*, 26.
35 Ibid.
36 Thomas C van Cleve, 'The Crusade of Frederick II', *A History of the Crusades*, ed. Setton, II, 449.
37 Gottschalk, *Al-Kāmil*, 144.
38 Ibid, 158.
39 *History*, 207.
40 Gottschalk, *Al-Kāmil*, 159; 'Ārif, *Al-Mufaṣṣal*, 188.
41 Humphreys, *Saladin*, 261; Gibb, 'The Aiyūbids', 703.
42 *History*, 272.
43 'Ārif, *Al-Mufaṣṣal*, 189–90; Humphreys, *Saladin*, 275.
44 Van Berchem's *Matériaux* pt. II, II, 'Jérusalem, Ḥaram', 105–107.
45 Claude Cahen and Ibrahim Chabbouh, 'Le testament d'al-Malik aṣ-Ṣāliḥ Ayyūb', *Bulletin d'Etudes Orientales*, XXIX, 1977, 100.
46 Gibb, 'The Aiyūbids', 713; Mustafa M Ziada, 'The Mamluk Sultans to 1293', *A History of the Crusades*, ed. Setton, II, 743.
47 Paris, 131–35.
48 *Ṣubḥ al-A'shā fī Ṣinā'at al-Inshā'*, Cairo, 1913–19, IV, 197, 199; XII, 104–05.
49 Donald P Little, 'Jerusalem and Egypt during the Mamluk Period', *Egypt and Palestine*, ed. Ammon Cohen and Gabriel Baer, New York, 1984, 75–76; Boaz Shoshan, 'On the Relations between Egypt and Palestine: 1382–517 AD', *Egypt and Palestine*, 97.
50 'Ārif, *Al-Mufaṣṣal*, 221–232.

51 Huda A Lutfi, *A Study of al-Quds during the Late Fourteenth Century Based Primarily on the Haram Estate Inventories*, unpublished McGill University dissertation, 1983, 245–49. (This dissertation was published in 1985 in Berlin.)
52 Ibid, 286–303; Donald P Little, *A Catalogue of the Islamic Documents from al-Ḥaram aš-Šarīf in Jerusalem*, Wiesbaden, 1984, 9–14.
53 Little, 'Jerusalem and Egypt', 74.
54 Rashād al-Imām, *Madīnat al-Quds fi 'l-'Aṣr al-Wasīṭ (1253–1516 m.)*, Tunis, 1976, 67–70.
55 Little, 'Jerusalem and Egypt', 74.
56 Asali, *Ma'āhi*, 158–81; Christel M Kessler and Michael H Burgoyne, 'The Fountain of Sultan Qāytbāy in the Sacred Precinct of Jerusalem', *Archaeology in the Levant, Essays for Kathleen Kenyon*, Warminster, 251–268.
57 Asali, *Ma'āhid*, 118–33.
58 Oleg Grabar, 'al-Ḳuds: Monuments', *EI*², V, 343.
59 *Ma'āhid*, 159–62, 168–69, 319.
60 Little, *Catalogue*, 24–35. Some of these have been transcribed in Asali, *Wathā'iq Maqdisiyya*, I, 177–86; 189–91.
61 David Ayalon, 'Discharges from Service, Banishments and Imprisonments in Mamluk Society', *Israel Oriental Studies*, 1972, II, 1972, 34.
62 Asali, *Ma'āhid*, 320, 188, 200–201.
63 Ibid, 196–99; 193–94.
64 *Al-Uns*, II, 42; van Berchem, *Matériaux*, II, 222–223.
65 *Al-Uns*, II, 43.
66 Asali, *Ma'āhid*, 182–86, 176–81.
67 Ibid, 315–20.
68 Al-Imām, *Madīnat al-Quds*, 148–53; Lutfi, *A Study*, II, 413; *Al-Uns*, II, 35, 90, 94, 99, 284, 304; Asali, *Ma'āhid*, 126.
69 *Al-Uns*, II, 34–48; cf. Asali, *Ma'āhid*.
70 Asali, *Ma'āhid*, 116, 127, 179.
71 Little, 'Jerusalem and Egypt', 76.
72 Asali, *Ma'āhid*, 128, 162, 168, 338.
73 Ibid, 345–46, 351, 355, 358, 361, 362.
74 Little, *Catalogue*, 9–10. However, there is also evidence of ambivalent relations between sufis and jurists in Mamlūk Jerusalem. See S D Goitein, 'al-Ḳuds', *EI*², V, 333.
75 Little, *Catalogue*, 26, 27, 28, 208, 220, 232, 247. Some of the documents relating to Burhān al-Dīn's appointment have been published in Asali, *Wathā'iq*, I, 197–214.
76 Goitein, 'al-Ḳuds', 332. Little, 'Jerusalem and Egypt', 76.
77 Shosan, 'Egypt and Palestine', 100.
78 Goitein, 'al-Ḳuds', 332; Sivan, 'Le caractère sacré', 181.
79 Muhammad Umar-Memon, *Ibn Taimiya's Struggle against Popular Religion*, The Hague, 1976, 72–78; Charles D Matthews, 'A Muslim Iconoclast (Ibn Taimiya and the "Merits" of Jerusalem and Palestine)', *Journal of the American Oriental Society*, LVIC, 1936, 1–21.
80 For Christian pilgrims in Jerusalem see H F M Prescott, *Jerusalem Journey: Pilgrimage to the Holy Land in the Fifteenth Century*, London, 1954, and R J Mitchell, *The Spring Voyage: The Jerusalem Pilgrimage in 1458*, London, 1964.
81 Al-Imām, *Madīnat al-Quds*, 282.
82 Prescott, *Jerusalem Journey*, 102.
83 See Ahmad Darrāj, *Wathā'iq Dayr Sayhūn bi'l-Quds al-Sharīf*, Cairo, 1968, and Noderto Risciani, *Documenti e Firmani*, Jerusalem, 1931.
84 Joseph Drory, 'Jerusalem during the Mamluk Period (1250–1517)', *The Jerusalem Cathedre*, Jerusalem, 1981, 212.
85 Butrus Abu-Manneh, 'The Georgians in Jerusalem in the Mamluk Period', *Egypt and Palestine*, ed. Cohen and Baer, 102–112.
86 Drory, 'Jerusalem', 210.
87 Ibid, 213.
88 See Little, 'Ḥaram Documents Related to the Jews of Late Fourteenth Century Jerusalem', in *Journal of Semitic Studies* vol. 30, no. 2, 1985, 227–264.

89 Drory, 'Jerusalem', 196–97.
90 Lutfi, *A Study*, 423–24.
91 Goitein, 'al-Ḳuds', 333.
92 Lutfi, *A Study*, 441.
93 Ibid, 433–37.
94 Drory, 'Jerusalem', 197.
95 See Lutfi, *A Study*, 21–54.
96 Goitein, 'al-Ḳuds', 333.

CHAPTER VII

Jerusalem under the Ottomans 1516–1831 AD

K J Asali

THE REIGNS OF SELIM AND SULAIMĀN

The year 1516 was a memorable year for Jerusalem. About four months after the decisive victory of Sultan Selim I at Marj Dābiq (northern Syria) on 23 August 1516, the Ottomans entered Jerusalem. The day of their entry was fixed as 28 December 1516 (4 Dhu 'l-Ḥijja 922 AH).[1] Two days later the sultan himself made a special visit to the Holy City, apparently making a detour while he was on his way to Egypt.[2]

> All the ulema and pious men went out to meet Selim shāh . . . They handed him the keys to the Aqsa Mosque and Dome of the Rock. He then made presents to all the notable people, exempted them from onerous taxes and confirmed them.[3]

Selim's visit lasted for two days. On 1 January 1517 (8 Dhu 'l-Ḥijja 922) he resumed his journey to Egypt.[4]

Jerusalem, as the third holiest city in Islam, was held in special reverence by the Ottoman sultans, especially by Selim's son and more famous successor Sulaimān, designated al-Qānūnī (the Lawgiver).

During Sulaimān's long reign (1520–1566), Jerusalem enjoyed its finest days under the Ottomans. The major reconstruction works undertaken in Jerusalem in those years were reminiscent of the glorious days of the Umayyads and the heyday of the Mamlūks. Reconstruction began with an extensive restoration of the Dome of the Rock, at Sulaimān's order.[5] The mosaic surrounding the upper part of the exterior walls was replaced by faïence, while the lower part was encased with fine marble. The window and three of the four gates of the Dome were renovated.[6] The adjacent Dome of the Chain also received a beautiful faïence coating.

Jerusalemites now remember Sulaimān chiefly because he gave their city its present magnificent wall. Jerusalem had practically no wall for more than 300 years, since the Ayyūbid al-Mu'aẓẓam 'Īsā destroyed it in 1219.[7] Sulaimān's wall had the double purpose of protecting the city from foreign invaders and also from the raids of the bedouins. It is about two miles long and has an average height of forty feet. The wall has at present thirty-four towers and seven open gates, six of them bearing inscriptions recording the date of their construction.[8] The Damascus Gate (Bāb al-'Amūd), opening to the north, is a masterpiece of architectural beauty. The other old gates are the Jaffa Gate (Bāb al-Khalīl), Zion Gate (Bāb al-Nabi Dāwūd), the Dung Gate (Bāb al-Maghāriba), St Stephen's Gate (Bāb Sittnā Mariam or Bāb al-Asbāṭ), and Herod's Gate (Bāb al-Sāhira). There is also a number of closed gates: the Golden Gate (Bāb al-Raḥma), the Single Gate, the Double Gate and the Triple Gate.

The construction of the wall continued for five years (1536–1540) and entailed huge expenditure. The registers of the *sharī'a* court of Jerusalem reveal that campaigns for financing the operation were organized in various parts of Palestine[9] (supplementing allocations made by the central government). An inscription near the main entrance of the Jerusalem citadel (*al-qal'a*) indicates that a few years before the construction of the wall the citadel was also restored.

Jerusalem's chronic water problem also received the attention of the sultan. Large sums of money were allocated for the building, repair and maintenance of water installations: canals, pools, fountains and baths. The canal supplying Jerusalem with water from the pools and springs (*qanāt al-sabīl*) between Bethlehem and Hebron was repaired.[10] Also the pools themselves were repaired and later renamed after the sultan.[11] In Jerusalem itself, outside the Jaffa Gate, the so-called Birkat al-Sulṭān[12] was restored[13] and a water fountain (*sabīl*) was built near it. This was one of six beautiful *sabīls* built during Sulaimān's reign. The other five are within the wall. They are sabīl Bāb al-Silsilah, sabīl al-Wād, sabīl Bāb al-Nāẓir, sabīl Sittnā Mariam and sabīl Sulaimān. All these fountains bear inscriptions recording the year of construction: 943/1536.

Around the middle of the 16th century an important institution was established in Jerusalem: the *takiyya* or *'imara* (hospice and kitchen) of Khāṣṣekī Sulṭān. It was founded in 1551 by Khāṣṣekī Sulṭān (or Khurrem), or Roxelana, the Russian wife of Sulaimān, and it soon became the most important charitable institution in Palestine. The *takiyya* was a large complex which comprised a mosque, a *khān* (inn), a *ribāṭ* (hospice), a *madrasa* (religious school) and a kitchen *'imāra*. The kitchen (still functioning but dying out) distributed hundreds of meals daily to the guests of the hospice, to the sufis, the students and the poor in general.[14] Khāṣṣekī Sulṭān established a very large pious endowment (*waqf*) for the upkeep of her *takiyya*. The endowment included several villages and farms in four districts in Palestine and Syria, especially in the vicinity of Ramla.[15] Thus the institution was guaranteed a long life. After the death of his wife, Sultan Sulaimān endowed the *takiyya* with an additional four villages and farms in the neighbourhood of Ṣaida (Sidon).[16]

As is known, revenues from the *awqāf* (sing: *waqf*) were the normal and chief form of expenditure on social, educational and religious institutions. as well as on public utilities in general. The main function of the government was seen in the defence of the country, the maintenance of public order, and the collection of taxes.

Jerusalem inherited form Ayyūbid and Mamlūk times a large number of *awqāf* for the upkeep of the numerous mosques, schools, *zāwiyas*, hospitals and other public utilities. These endowments were cared for and increased in the Ottoman period. The Ottoman land registers (*tapu tahrir defteri*)[17] and the registers of the Jerusalem sharī'a court provide us with abundant information about the *awqāf*. In tapu tehrir defter no. 522 alone there are, in the first 30 years after the Ottoman conquest, 13 entries of various *waqfs*, public and private, for the benefit of institutions (elementary schools *maktab* pl. *makātib*, hospices, mosques, mausolea, etc.) or of persons (the descendants of the founder of the *waqf*, Qur'ān readers, members of sufi orders or the poor in general).

In the second half of the 16th century several important endowments were made, beside those of Khāṣṣekī Sulṭān and Sultan Sulaimān, referred to above. These include another *waqf* by the sultan for the maintenance of *qanāt al-sabīl*, which comprised several villages in the Hebron area.[18]

Needless to say the *waqf* played an important role in the economic life of Jerusalem. It created jobs for hundreds of people and provided hundreds of beneficiaries with steady income. It also stimulated all branches of the economy. The large construction projects that were undertaken in Jerusalem in the first century of Ottoman rule could not have been possible without an efficient administration.

From the beginning of the Ottoman conquest, Jerusalem

belonged to the province (*iyālet*, later *wilāyet*) of Damascus, one of the three provinces that constituted Syria at that time. Each province was divided into a number of districts (*sanājiq*, sing. *sanjaq*). Jerusalem had its own *sanjaq* which comprised Hebron and the surrounding villages.[19]

At the head of the administration was the district governor (*sanjaq bey* [*beg*] or *mīr liwā'*). He was almost exclusively an Ottoman Turk. The governor was a military man whose chief duties were to lead the armed forces of the *sanjaq* in time of war, to preserve public order and to control the feudal fiefs. Next to the sultan, he had the largest fief in the district (*khaṣṣī mīr liwā'*) and held office usually for one year, but the term was renewable.[20]

The governor had a deputy (*kēkhyā*), a secretary (*yāziji*), and a number of dragomans (*terjumān*).[21] The feudal cavalry in the district, the *sipāhīs*, were under the command of the *mīr alay*. The police force was headed by the *su-bāshi* – police superintendent. The citadel had a separate commander: the *duzdār*[22] who was directly attached to the central government. It was manned by *sipāhīs* and other soldiers, but chiefly by Janissaries[23] led by their *āghā*.

The civil branch of the administration was headed by the *qāḍī* (judge) who was usually a Turk appointed from Istanbul for one year. The *qāḍī* was exclusively a Ḥanafī[24] (the Ḥanafī rite was the official rite of the Ottoman Empire). The *qāḍī* of Jerusalem was one of the senior *qāḍīs* of the Empire.[25] His jurisdiction extended beyond Jerusalem to include several towns in Palestine, where he appointed a deputy (*nā'ib al-shar'*) to administer justice.[26] In addition to purely juridical and legal duties, the *qāḍī* had wide administrative functions, covering almost all fields of administration.

Another important figure in the administration was *al-muḥtasib* – the market superintendent. The *muḥtasib* was concerned exclusively with the affairs of the guilds (*ṭā'ifa*, pl. *ṭawā'if*) and with the collection of dues on commodities and transactions. His salary was paid by the shopkeepers, and he had authority to punish the shopkeepers summarily.[27]

Beside the *qāḍī* there were three prominent religious and social figures in Jerusalem. These were the *muftī*, the *naqīb al-ashrāf* and the *shaikh al-Ḥaram*. All three were Jerusalemites appointed by the sultan. The *muftī* (juris-consult) gave legal opinion regarding the interpretation of the *sharī'a*. In the 16th century he was often a member of the families of Banu Jama'a and Banu Abi 'l-Luṭf.[28] *Naqīb al-ashrāf* was responsible for protecting the rights of the descendants of the Prophet, while *shaikh al-Ḥaram* was charged with the administration of al-Ḥaram al-Sharīf. Apart from the employees of the *waqf*, the number of government officials in the Jerusalem administration was small, for the city itself was small.

The population of Jerusalem throughout the 16th century did not exceed 14,000. The following table, based on the studies of B Lewis and A Cohen in the tapu registers, shows the development of the population in the 16th century, in approximate figures:

Year	Total	Muslims	Christians	Jews
1525	4,700	3,100	600	1,000
1538	7,900	6,000	750	1,150
1553	13,384	10,100	1,650	1,634
1562	12,650	9,900	1,550	1,200
1596	7,610	7,300	210	100[29]

It is clear from this table that the population of Jerusalem reached its peak in the middle of the century, and then started to diminish. The large drop observed in 1596 may be due to the incompleteness of tapu register no. 515. The population of Palestine according to this register was 206,290, and of the Jerusalem district 42,100.

The great majority of the population were Muslim natives of Jerusalem, i.e. Arabs, but there was a small percentage of Muslims who chose to move to the Holy City from various Islamic and Arab countries, such as North Africa, Syria, Egypt, Iraq, Turkey, Bosnia, India, Persia and several countries of Central Asia.[30]

The Christians were not, and were not regarded by the state, as one single community. They were divided into a number of denominations and nationalities: Latins, Greek Orthodox, Armenians, Copts, Abyssinians, Serbs, Syrians, Georgians, etc. The majority of the Christians, however, were Greek Orthodox Arabs.

The appreciable increase of Jews in the 16th century was due to the attitude of the Ottoman authorities which allowed Spanish Jews, after their expulsion in 1492, to live in Palestine. However, the number of Jews given in the tapu tahrir registers may have been exaggerated, for in 1572 the Jews of Jerusalem complained to the authorities that their number in the tahrir registers was over-estimated. Many Jewish guests who were residing temporarily in Jerusalem, they said, were unjustly included in the registers. A census of the Jews was thereupon ordered. The census showed that the number of male Jews in Jerusalem was 115,[31] putting the total number of Jews at about 500–600.

As far as economic life in 16th century Jerusalem is concerned, Ottoman documents provide us with useful material. A recent study based on the sijill has shown that there were five main branches of industry in Jerusalem. These were: 1. food industries (oil-processing, grain-grinding, fruit-processing, manufacture of sesame, etc.) 2. textile and dyeing industry 3. leather industry 4. soap manufacture (there were 9 soap factories) 5. metal (iron and copper) workshops.[32]

Workers in industry and trade, and indeed in all walks of life, were organized in guilds (*ṭā'ifa*, pl. *ṭawā'if*) as in all other parts of the empire. Each *ṭā'ifa* laid down its own regulations for its trade and its members. The *ṭā'ifa* was headed by a shaikh, who was assisted by a deputy. Workers were classified in three grades: *mu'allim* (master), *ṣāni'* (manufacturer) and *ajīr* (wage-earner).[33]

There were about forty guilds in 16th century Jerusalem, ranging from physicians, surgeons, and architects to corn measurers, millers, pastry cooks, brokers, money changers, soap makers and spice dealers. Even singers and dancers had their own *ṭā'ifa*. No worker could work outside the guild.

As far as export-import trade is concerned, there was an active export of soap to Egypt through the port of Gaza,[34] and also of grain to Egypt, Rhodes and Yugoslavia (Dubrovnik).[35] The chief imports were rice and textiles from Egypt, clothes and coffee from Damascus, textiles and rugs from Istanbul, China, Hijaz and Iraq.[36]

Economic activities were subject to an all-embracing code of taxation. The various categories of taxes included taxes on agricultural land (this was the *'ushr* or the *kharāj*); taxes on stock-raising and livestock; market taxes imposed on the sale of various commodities (the most important of these were paid to the market inspectorate (*iḥtisāb*)); taxes on industries (oil presses, flour mills, textile and dyeing); export duties (mainly the export of soap); taxes on shop and other real property (*khāns* and bathhouses).

In view of the holiness of Jerusalem and Hebron, their people were occasionally exempted from certain kinds of taxes.[37]

In addition to the above taxes were the various taxes levied on Christians and Jews (*ahl al-dhimma* – protected people). These were the poll-tax (*jizya*) (on male adults of sound health only), pilgrims' fees, tolls on check-points on high roads (*khafar, khafāra*), fees for visits of the Holy Sepulchre, and port fees, mainly the port of Jaffa.[38]

In a holy city like Jerusalem it was natural that a large part of the revenues was drawn from fees paid by pilgrims to the Holy Sepulchre (tripled from 40,000 *akçes*[39] in 1525 to 120,000 in 1553[40]).

Revenues from the poll-tax amounted to one half of the income derived from visitors of the Holy Sepulchre.[41] The poll-tax collected from Christians and Jews in Jerusalem was restricted to the lowest of the three rates provided by the *sharī'a* (one gold piece from each household, not from individuals).[42]

As long as they paid taxes, the minorities, Christians and Jews, were left to administer their own internal affairs within the framework of Islamic law which gave them the status of *ahl al-dhimma*. Their religious affairs were regulated by their respective heads of communities.

Throughout the Ottoman period, but especially in the 17th century and after, relations between the Christian communities were fraught with antagonism and dissension. Around the middle of the 16th century dissension erupted between the Latins, represented by the Franciscan Fathers, and the Greek Orthodox over their respective rights in Christian holy places, especially the Holy Sepulchre. In 1541 a national Latin community was established in Jerusalem.[43] About the same time Patriarch Germanus (1534–1579) instituted the Hellenic Confederacy of the Holy Sepulchre whose members became the guardians of the holy places on behalf of Orthodox Christendom.[44]

To the Greek Orthodox Church belonged the great majority of Christians in the empire and their patriarch had his seat in Istanbul where he made his voice heard. The Latins, on the other hand, were a very small minority in Jerusalem (and in the empire). But they had the support of the Catholic powers of Europe, especially France, Austria and Spain. Indeed, Jerusalem figured prominently in the relations of those states with the Ottoman empire as from the 16th century. As early as 1518 Spain requested freedom of visits for Christians to Jerusalem.[45] In 1528 France requested that al-Ṣalāḥiyya madrasa be turned into a church as it formerly was, but the sultan refused.[46]

The greatest event in Ottoman-French relations in this period was the conclusion of the Capitulations in 1535, which secured for French merchants a privileged position in the empire, guaranteed French subjects the right to religious freedom and gave the Latin clergy the custody of the holy places in Jerusalem.[47] The Capitulations were granted by Sulaimān I to Francis I as a gesture of good will, as a condescension from the Ottoman empire, then at the height of its power, to a weaker partner. However, Sulaimān miscalculated, for these Capitulations, and their subsequent versions, became an instrument for unmasked intervention in the internal affairs of the Ottoman Empire.

However, Sulaimān felt no challenge from Francis. In 1524 the Franciscans on Mount Zion were evicted from the Cenacle, the place of the Last Supper, beneath which lay the tomb venerated by the Muslims as the tomb of the prophet David. When Francis intervened in 1528 his representations were of no avail. However, Francis was assured that all Christian holy places in Jerusalem would remain safe and secure.[48]

The Jews had no European power behind them at this time. The small number of the Jewish community was augmented by immigrants who fled the Spanish Inquisition, and were given refuge in Jerusalem and Safed. David dei Rossi, a Jewish Italian who visited Jerusalem in the 16th century, commented on Jewish life in Jerusalem as follows: 'Here we are not in exile as in our own country (Italy). Here . . . those appointed over the customs and tolls are Jews. There are no special Jewish taxes . . .'[49]

Prof. A Cohen, in a fine study of Jewish life in 16th century Jerusalem based on the registers of the sharī'a court, stresses the positive attitude of the Ottoman authorities towards the Jews. He emphasizes that fiscal restrictions imposed by the *sharī'a* were not applied in accordance with the letter of the law, and that not all Jews of Jerusalem who owed the *jizya* tax paid it. Those who did were expected to pay the lowest official rate.[50] He adds that the entire supervisory mechanism governing the implementation of the religious law was often slanted in favour of the Jews[51] and that the law courts protected the Jews and accepted the testimony of Jewish litigants and witnesses in contradiction of the accepted notion that their testimonies were inadmissible.[52] In conclusion Cohen says that an autonomous Jewish life in Jerusalem was encouraged and protected by Muslim rulers.[53]

LATE 16TH CENTURY AND 17TH CENTURY

In the last third of the 16th century serious cracks began to appear in the structure of the Ottoman empire. The empire embarked on a retrogressive movement which was to continue for more than two centuries. The decline gained momentum towards the end of the 17th century, and deepened in the 18th and early 19th centuries. The feudal system, with the *sipāhīs* – the feudal landlords – as its prop was gradually deteriorating. As the wars of expansion came to an end and spoils diminished, the landlords turned with increasing interest to the land, and tried to recoup the loss of spoils by merciless exploitation of the peasants. This naturally led to a sharp drop in agricultural production and ushered in the whole crisis of the empire. Many other factors combined to deepen the crisis: the discovery of the sea route to India and the consequent diversion of commercial routes from Western Asia, the large increase of silver on the markets of the Mediterranean countries after the discovery of America and the resulting depreciation of the silver coinage, the growing dissatisfaction of the Janissaries after the cessation of the spoils, and the risings of peasants and townspeople in Turkey itself and in the provinces.

The defeat of the Ottomans at the sea battle of Lepanto, 1571, by members of the Holy Alliance was a first warning. In the last years of the 16th century and the beginning of the 17th the empire was at war with both Austria and Persia. At the same time there was a peasant rising in Anatolia (1598–1605). In the first half of the 17th century the central government began to lose its control over the Janissaries. They mutinied in 1624 and in 1648 they even murdered a sultan.

The final years of the 17th century were ominous for the empire. There were heavy losses in wars with Austria, and the Ottoman army suffered a degrading retreat from the walls of Vienna (1683). In the last decade of the century Russia joined Austria in its war against the Ottomans. After military defeats the peace of Karlowitz was concluded in 1699 and entailed large losses of territory in the Balkans and south Russia. France utilized the difficulties of the empire to impose a new version of the Capitulations in 1673.

These developments had naturally adverse effects on the provinces and also on Jerusalem. In Jerusalem and its neighbourhood there was a marked deterioration in public security in the last quarter of the 16th century, particularly on the roads leading to the city. This was to last until the second half of the 19th century. The bedouins mounted their attacks on pilgrims' caravans to the holy shrines in Hebron and Nabī Mūsā.[54] They prevented preachers from delivering their sermons in mosques and imposed tolls on the pilgrims.[55] In 1587 some fief-holders assisted by about 3,000 brigands took up permanent positions for some time near the shrine of Nabī Mūsā, until they were attacked and defeated by the *sanjaq* governor, Khudaverdi.[56]

To keep the bedouins in check, the government resorted to different measures including the taking of hostages, the appointment of bedouin shaikhs as *sanjaq beys* or fief-holders and the entrusting of village or bedouin shaikhs with the protection of caravans.[57] There were even attempts to populate the country by establishing rural settlements for the nomads.[58] In 1614 forty *timar* and *ziamat* holders were exempted from participation in military campaigns outside the *sanjaq*, to enable them to defend the pilgrims' caravan to Mecca.[59] For the purpose of maintaining public security several fortresses were built and provided with men and weapons.[60] About 1630 Sultan Murad IV (1622–1639), in order to protect the springs and pools supplying Jerusalem with water from brigands, built a large fortress at Sulaimān's Pools. In the second half of the 17th century this fortress had a *duzdār* and forty soldiers equipped with cannons and other weapons. Within its precincts it had a mosque and fifty apartments for soldiers.[61] The fortress is still standing today.

However, all the measures taken by the authorities did not succeed. The main reason was that the central government, involved as it was in wars on the eastern and western fronts, was unable to allocate sufficient forces or funds for the maintenance of public order.[62]

Another source of apprehension for the people of Jerusalem in Ottoman times was their concern over European ambitions in the city. This concern was reflected in a petition addressed to Sultan Mustafa I in 1621. A royal decree issued by the sultan in that year confirmed the appointment of M d'Aramon as resident French consul in Jerusalem. The decree was received in Jerusalem with indignation. At a gathering held by representatives of the city at al-Aqṣā Mosque, a petition was drawn up which emphasized that the appointment of M d'Aramon was a dangerous novelty, being contrary to the established practice in Jerusalem, and must therefore be cancelled. The petitioners added by saying: 'Our city is a place at which the infidels look with covetous eyes . . . their schemes and plots against it never cease. The port [*askala*, i.e. Jaffa port] is only eight hours far from it . . . we fear that his [the consul-designate's] intrigues will cause others to be brought in, in addition to these we already have. We fear lest they occupy us . . ., as it happened several times before . . .'[63] The royal decree was rescinded.

In 1597 and 1598, during the Ottoman-Austrian war, the authorities in Jerusalem had suspicions that the monasteries were used as depots for weapons. So orders were issued to search them.[64] Indeed the history of the Christian communities in Jerusalem is closely bound up with the vicissitudes of relations between the Ottomans and the European powers, the rivalries of these powers among themselves, and their keenness to increase their influence in the Holy Land. As relations between the empire and France were at a low ebb during the reign of Murad IV (who expelled the Jesuits from Istanbul at the instigation of the British and Dutch ambassadors in 1628) Murad issued three firmans (1634) which gave the Greeks precedence over the Latins in religious festivals in the Holy Sepulchre. As happened several times before and afterwards such firmans were often rescinded through the intervention or pressure of one of the contesting parties. This time the three firmans of Murad were annulled after the intervention of Louis XIII. In 1673 France succeeded in renewing the Capitulations and asserting its role as 'protector of the Catholics'. Austria and Poland also intervened on their behalf. In 1642 Austria won special privileges for the Latins. Poland, in a treaty with the Porte in 1676, compelled the Ottoman government to restore the Franciscans to the Holy Sepulchre. More importantly Austria won by the treaty of Karlowitz in 1699 the right to speak on behalf of Christian interests concerning the holy places of Jerusalem. All this clearly indicates that international developments had a direct bearing on Jerusalem.

In the Holy City itself things were sometimes complicated by the direct interference of foreign diplomats in disputes over the holy places. In 1673 the French ambassador in Istanbul, Count Noitell, who was on a visit to Jerusalem, openly incited the Latins in their clash with the Greeks.[65]

The Ottomans had a hard job trying to solve contradictory claims over precedence in the holy places. Sometimes the quarrels between the Christian communities, chiefly Latins, Greeks and Armenians, were so intense that they developed into bloody clashes. This happened several times in the 17th century (e.g. in 1666, 1669 and 1674)[66] and in later centuries. European travellers were shocked at the intensity of these quarrels. Henry Maundrell, the English chaplain of Aleppo who visited Jerusalem in 1697, wrote in this regard: 'That which has always been the great prize contended for by several sects is the command and appropriation of the Holy Sepulchre, a privilege contested with much unchristian fury and animosity especially between the Greeks and the Latins, that in disputing which party should go in to celebrate their mass, they sometimes proceed to blows and wounds even at the very door of the Holy Sepulchre . . .'[67]

As we shall see later the situation deteriorated further in the 18th and 19th centuries as the empire became weaker and European intervention intensified.

The 17th century was for the Ottoman empire a century of

transition between the prosperity of the 16th century and the decline of the 18th. So it was also for Jerusalem. The old institutions such as the *madāris*, the *bīmāristān*, the *ribāṭs*, the *zāwiyas*, etc. were still functioning, although they lost some of their vitality. Evliya Celebi who visited Jerusalem in 1672[68] described the *sanjaq* of Jerusalem as prosperous. The Turkish traveller was fascinated by the Holy City, its Ḥaram, its citadel and its various institutions. He was even impressed by its economy and the abundance of its products.

In his *Siyāhatnāme* he gives us a detailed description of the city:

> Jerusalem had plenty of buildings. Its air is fresh and its water is sweet . . . [the governor] Zade Mehmet Pasha counted the inhabitants of the city. They numbered 46,000. The pasha distributed the *sūrra* ['bundle' – the annual donation to the poor] to no less than one thousand men, mostly friends and sufis.[69]

Çelebi then describes its bread, grapes, perfume and incense, and its mountains covered with olive trees. He adds:

> Jerusalem has 43,000 vineyards, and every Jerusalemite lives in these vineyards two or three months a year.
>
> Although the city appears to be small it has 240 *miḥrābs* [i.e. prayer niches], 7 schools for the teaching of *ḥadīth* [traditions of the Prophet Muḥammad], 10 for teaching the Qur'ān, 40 *madrasas*, and *zāwiyas* for 70 sufi orders, the largest of which is that of 'Abd al-Qādir al-Gilānī, Aḥmad al-Badawī, Rifā'ī and Mevlevī. There are 6 *khāns*, 6 baths and 16 *sabīls* [fountains].
>
> According to the records of the *muḥtasib* there are 2,045 shops and several markets in Jerusalem. There are also two churches for the Armenians, three for the Greeks and two synagogues.[70]

Çelebi adds further:

> There are no buildings whatever around the fortress of Jerusalem, except for the suburb of David which consists of 40 houses. Except the gardens, the vineyards and flower gardens all buildings are within the fortress. All quarters are Muslim.[71] There are altogether one thousand fortress-like lofty palaces.[72]

From various sources we know that, for security reasons, the gates of Jerusalem were closed from sunset to sunrise. All travellers and visitors had to get permission before entering the city. Henry

Maundrell got such permission 'without which no Frank dares to come within the walls.'[73] But not only Franks had to get permission. This applied equally to Muslims, as we are told by several Muslim travellers.[74]

After the dynamic changes of the 16th century Jerusalem seemed to be static in the following century. Almost all the major monuments existing in the 17th century were inherited from the past. There were a few additions and repairs: the Mamlūk fountain inside the Ḥaram known as sabīl Sha'lān was renovated in 1627.[75] Another *sabīl* was built by Ḥājj 'Abd al-Karīm Churbajī in 1685.[76] Qanāt al-Sabīl was repaired in 1656[77] and 1666.[78] Within the precincts of the Ḥaram the mosque known as Jāmi' al-Ḥanābilah was restored in 1611.[79] The largest single structure built in the 17th century in the Jerusalem area was perhaps the fortress built by Sultan Murad IV near Bethlehem.

The most important renovations were those carried out in the Ḥaram. As before, the sultans considered it a religious duty to extend their care and patronage to Islamic shrines and places of worship, primarily in Jerusalem, Hebron and Nabī Mūsā, the three principal Islamic places of pilgrimage in this period. At all times works of construction and restoration continued in the Ḥaram. In this period the Dome of the Rock was renovated by Sultan Mehmet III (1597), Sultan Ahmad I (1603) and Sultan Mustafa I (1617).

The Ottoman *Muhimme defterleri* contain many firmans and orders which show the attention given by the authorities to the sanctuaries. It was a paramount duty to maintain order at the sanctuaries and to keep them clean. Their wardens and other employees had to be pious and reliable. It was urgent to maintain and repair without delay the holy places and the shrines of the prophets, and the revenues from the *awqāf* of such places should be used primarily for their maintenance. On the other hand the government was always ready to pay expenses incurred for such restorations.[80]

As far as the administration of Jerusalem in the 17th century is concerned there is some useful information in Çelebi's *Travels*. In 1672 the pasha of Jerusalem had 500 soldiers at his command and was the commandant of the pilgrims' caravan of Damascus.[81] The fief-holders were not ordered to serve in the field, but only to accompany with their banners the pilgrims . . . and to conduct them . . . they numbered 600 men.[82] The garrison of the fortress of Jerusalem had two hundred men.[83] The majority of the villages around Jerusalem belonged to the fief-holders.[84]

As for the civil administration, the judge of Jerusalem received as much as the pasha (40,000 piastres per annum), because its district counted altogether 1600 villages.[85] In addition to Jerusalem his jurisdiction covered Hebron, Nablus, Ramla, Kerak, Lejjūn and Jenin,[86] i.e. much larger than that of the governor of the Jerusalem district. Under the judge of Jerusalem were 20 officers (*āghā*) appointed by imperial rescript. They included inter alia the night guardian of the gates, the police inspector, the chief cashier, the treasurer and the market inspector.[87]

From a tentative list of the governors of Jerusalem in the 17th century, it appears that the governors of Nablus or Gaza were given occasionally the government of Jerusalem also. Muḥammad b. Farrukh, the Circassian governor of Nablus, governed Jerusalem in 1625–26.[88] Ḥusain b. Ḥasan al-Ghazzawī, the Arab governor of Gaza, was also given the government of Jerusalem in 1660, but delegated his powers to his son Ibrāhīm.[89] The appointment of local Arab governors was a practice to be followed frequently in the 18th century.

With the exception of the judge who usually came from Istanbul (in one case he was reported to be a Tunisian[90]) the religious dignitaries were mostly from Jerusalem. Among *muftīs* known to us, four were from the Abu 'l-Luṭf family and one from the Dajānī.[91] The old families usually provided personnel for religious posts and especially for teaching (*tadrīs*). The fact that these posts were in practice hereditary contributed to the deterioration of educational standards. The majority of the incumbents of religious and teaching posts in the 17th century were in fact poorly educated. In 1670 the traveller al-Khiyārī sought in vain an accomplished scholar in al-Aqṣā Mosque.[92] Even the Friday preacher (*khāṭib*) at al-Aqṣā spoke poor Arabic.[93] According to 'Ayyāshī, the judge of Jerusalem, al-Nafātī, was appointed for ceremonial reasons, not for his scholarly ability.[94] Occasionally eminent scholars still frequented al-Aqṣā to teach there. The famous Maghribī author, Aḥmad al-Maqqarī, taught about one month in Jerusalem in 1627.[95]

The important thing, however, was that the *madāris*, though diminishing in quality and number, continued to exist. Out of approximately 56 schools during the Mamlūk period there were about 40 in 1672.[96] There were about 200 rooms for the *madāris* surrounding the Ḥaram.[97] The state paid salaries to a large number of teachers and other religious officials. In the Aqṣā Mosque alone there were 800 salaried servants who were paid from the 'private' purse of the sultan.[98]

The main burden of expenditure of the employees of the Haram and other institutions was carried now, as before, by the *waqf*. Many *waqf* institutions were overstaffed to provide job opportunities for thousands of employees in the Ḥaram as well as in the *madāris*, the *ribāṭs*, the *zāwiyas* and the *khanqāhs*, etc. In the *madāris* the number of employees sometimes exceeded that of students. Already in the 16th century (1574), the Ṭāziyya madrasa had 36 employees and Qur'ān readers, but only 26 students.[99] In 1552 the salaries of the employees of Qanāt al-Sabīl consumed two thirds of the revenue of the *waqf*, so the surplus number of employees had to be dismissed.[100] Similarly the *waqf* of the Aqṣā Mosque was supporting an excessive number of employees of various sorts, although the mosque itself was in bad need of repair.[101] Moreover, the *waqf* and its institutions had to maintain hundreds of dervishes 'from India, Sind, Balkh, Persians and Kurds, Tartars, Moghuls and Turks'[102] who lived in the porticos of the Ḥaram.

The expenses of the *waqf* increased at a time when *waqf* property was deteriorating due to neglect, or the dishonesty of some administrators. Sometimes funds allocated for *waqf* projects were embezzled by rapacious governors.[103]

THE 18TH AND EARLY 19TH CENTURIES

The inauspicious treaty of Karlowitz (1669) was followed by a series of wars and successive political and military setbacks for the empire throughout the 18th century. In the second decade of this century the empire was involved in wars with Russia, Venice and Austria. In the third and fourth decades with Persia, then again with the Austrians and the Russians. In the second half of the century Russia was the main enemy. Under the treaty of Kütchük Kainerji in 1774 the empire had to concede large losses of territory to her in the Black Sea region. Two other humiliating treaties were concluded with Austria (1791) and Russia (1791). The Ottoman empire was steadily and quickly on a descending course.

While the wars were continuing the state machinery was becoming dilapidated. One important reason for the decline was the decay of the ruling dynasty itself. The system of succession brought weak sultans to the throne. Late sultans spent huge sums of money on personal luxury and gave themselves up to the pleasure of the harem. Their continuous need for money led to the sale of public offices, and the acknowledgement of bribery as an institution. The highest offices, including those of governors of provinces, were sold. As the term of the governor's office expired usually after one year, ending often with the confiscation of the governor's property, or even his execution, the governor saw fit to gather as much money as quickly as he could and as quickly to consume what he gathered.

The expenses of war, the luxuries of the palace and the plunders of governors naturally led to an increase in taxation and unlawful exactions and consequently to the general impoverishment of the people. Taxes on peasants in particular killed all their enthusiasm for work, and many of them left their villages, and either dispersed or organized armed uprisings.

A Syrian scholar who lived in this period, Aḥmad b. ʿAlī al-Manīnī (1678–1758), spoke in general and bitter terms of the tribulations, calamities and afflictions that befell Syria in those days, of the feuds and disorders that infested her, 'due to the excessive tyranny of her rulers in past days, and because the Ottoman state looked at her with hostile and revengeful eyes . . .'[104]

The French traveller L d'Arvieux noticed in 1660 that the Bethlehem area seemed to have been deserted, for the peasants ran away from the land and concealed themselves from the rapacious governors of Jerusalem. The peasant was completely insecure with regard to his person or his property.[105]

In 1703 in Jerusalem itself the 18th century was ushered in with an uprising. It was led by *naqīb al-ashrāf* Muḥammad b. Muṣṭafā al-Ḥusainī and lasted for two years. The uprising was caused by the high-handed policy of the governor of Jerusalem, Jurjī Muḥammad Pāshā,[106] who imposed heavy taxes on townspeople and peasants alike, and resorted to cruel measures in collecting them. The people of Jerusalem rose up in arms, attacked the fortress and released the prisoners. The governor fled from the city and Muḥammad, the *naqīb* al-ashrāf, was appointed as a temporary governor. In the meantime Jurjī, the ousted governor, was appointed *wālī* of Damascus. In 1705 he sent an ultimatum to the people of Jerusalem, and ordered them to surrender their arms. Shortly thereafter, the *wālī* sent about 2,000 Janissaries and other soldiers to Jerusalem. The city was occupied, after a stiff resistance, in November 1705. The *naqīb* escaped and hid himself for some time in the fortress of Tarsus. Then he was arrested and sent to Istanbul where he was executed in 1707.[107]

The fact that the governors of Damascus were unable to put down the uprising for a long time was a clear indication of their impotence. The weakness of the central government was clearly manifested in two developments in 18th century Jerusalem. The first was the appointment of several influential Palestinian notables as governors of Jerusalem (and other Palestinian cities). The second was the rise in prestige and authority of the families of Jerusalem notables.

The days of the strong governor relying on the strong hand of Istanbul were gone, and the central government had now to enlist the support of local leaders by appointing them as governors. In 1717 a member of the well-known Ṭūqān family of Nablus, Ṣāliḥ Pāshā Ṭūqān, was the governor of Jerusalem.[108] Another Ṭūqān, As'ad Bey, was governor for three years (1788–1790).[109] Several members of the Nimr family, which ruled Nablus for many decades in the 18th century were governors of Jerusalem: 'Umar (*c.*1717–1731), Muṣṭafā (1731–1733), 'Umar, second time, 1733, Ismā'īl āghā, 1760, and Ibrāhīm āghā, 1771.[110] The historian Iḥsan al-Nimr says that the Nimr family co-operated with Jerusalemite families, the 'Alamīs, their maternal uncles, and the 'Asalīs who were the *duzdārs* of the *qal'a* (citadel).[111] He lauds the rule of 'Umar al-Nimr who was successful in 'solving problems between the Christian communities, suppressing brigands and securing the pilgrims' road'. 'Umar also repaired the wall of Jerusalem near Bāb al-Asbāṭ (St Stephen's Gate) and the shrine of Shaikh Muḥammad al-'Alamī on the Mount of Olives.[112]

In the middle of the century it seems that Jerusalem was raised for a short time to the status of *eyālet* (province), ruled by a pāshā *(mutaṣarrif)* who was independent of Damascus. In 1757 Ḥusain b. Makkī, a native of Gaza, held this post for about one year.[113]

In spite of the appointment of local personalities as governors of Jerusalem in the 18th century, it seems that the new governors, like their predecessors, were unable to solve the problem of security on the roads and check the raids of the bedouins. From itineraries and biographies of travellers and scholars we know that many of these were robbed, wounded, or even killed in attacks on pilgrims' caravans.[114]

Another indication of the impotence of the governor of Jerusalem was his inability to collect taxes from villagers and townspeople. The *wālī* of Damascus himself, accompanied by his soldiers, had to make the annual round (*dawra*) in order to collect the taxes. The people of the district were required to provide sufficient provisions (*dhakhā'ir*) for the *wālī* and his soldiers. Disobedience was severely punished.[115] Tax-collecting was the criterion of the governor's efficiency. No excuse was accepted for failure or neglect in this respect.[116]

The second development which reflected the increasing dependence of the central government on local elements to support the established order could be seen in the rise in authority and standing of leading Jerusalem families such as the Ḥusainīs, the Khālidīs, the Abu 'l-Luṭfs, etc. The weakness of the governors was a suitable occasion for them to increase their prestige and to acquire an increasing share in the administration. Having taken the lesson of the *naqīb* uprising to heart they now tried to maintain good relations with influential people in both Istanbul and Damascus.[117] But at the same time, the notable families were the sole available representatives of the people vis-à-vis the ruling circles, and so they acted as mediators between the people and these circles. In these attempts of the notable families to strengthen their position one can perhaps discern the seeds of aspiration for local autonomy. For the time being, however, the notables were contented with comfortable privileges: they held in their hands lucrative religious offices, the administration of the *waqf* and tax-farming. By acting as 'protectors' of villages they succeeded in acquiring large holdings of land.[118] In the 18th century members of the Abu 'l-Luṭf family were several times *muftīs* of Jerusalem.[119] The Ḥusainīs built up their power significantly at this time: 'Abd al-Laṭīf al-Ḥusainī was *naqīb al-ashrāf*, a post inherited from his ancestors. His son, 'Abdullāh, succeeded him in this post. His second son, Ḥasan, combined in his person the offices of *naqīb*, *muftī* and *shaikh al-Ḥaram*.[120] In addition to these religious posts the notables were sometimes entrusted with administrative duties. In 1776 the assistant *wālī* of Damascus (*kekhyā*) asked the help of 'Abdullāh b. 'Abd al-Laṭīf in the collection of the *jizya* tax. In 1798 the same 'Abdullāh was requested to help in the collection of taxes from the Banu Ḥasan tribe.[121] Some time later (in 1810) the grandson of 'Abd al-Laṭīf, 'Umar, who inherited the post of *naqīb* and *shaikh al-Ḥaram*, received a large sum of money from the *wālī* of Damascus for the repair of Qanāt al-Sabīl.[122]

The principal rivals of the Ḥusainīs in the 18th and 19th century were the Khālidīs. The Khālidī family retained for successive generations the post of *nā'ib al-shar'* (deputy judge) in Jerusalem and that of *bāsh-kātib* (chief clerk) of the *sharī'a* court.[123] An important figure was Mūsā al-Khālidī (1767–1832) who later in his life occupied the important position of *qāḍī 'askar* of Anatolia,[124] one of the three highest judicial posts in the empire.

Mūsā al-Khālidī was an eminent scholar and author who wrote several treatises on *fiqh* (Islamic jurisprudence). He was highly respected by Sultan Maḥmūd II and in the learned circles in Istanbul.[125] Beside al-Khālidī there were a number of prominent scholars in 18th century Jerusalem, such as Muḥammad al-Khalīlī (d.

1734) and Muḥammad b. Budair (1747–1805). Both were famous sufis. It appears from available material that the number of the Jerusalem *'ulamā'* in the 18th century exceeded their number in the 17th. Ḥasan b. 'Abd al-Laṭīf al-Ḥusainī mentions in his *Tarājim* – biographies of the 18th century *'ulamā'* – the names of 74 *'ālim*. Jerusalem was still attracting a number of *'ulamā'* from other countries; among those who visited it or stayed in it were 'Abd al-Ghānī al-Nabulsī and Muṣṭafā al-Bakrī from Damascus, Muṣṭafā As'ad al-Luqaimī from Damietta, and 'Alī al-Khalafāwī from Cairo.[126] Recent studies have shown that the majority of the Palestinian and Jerusalem *'ulamā'* in the 18th century received their higher education in Egypt, especially at al-Azhar Mosque.[127] There were others who went to Damascus or Istanbul.

Modern research has also revealed a bright aspect of the cultural life of 18th century Jerusalem. It was the existence of a large number of private libraries belonging to the *'ulamā'* of the city, a fact which warrants certain amendments to the dark picture usually drawn of scientific conditions in this period.[128]

If there was a certain increase in the number of *'ulamā'* in the 18th century this had little to do with the *madāris* of Jerusalem. The *madāris* were in decay, and students who sought higher education had to go abroad. It is estimated that out of 56 *madāris* in the Mamlūk period, only 35 were existing in the middle of the 18th century. At the close of the century the number was much less. The *madāris* seen by Çelebi around the precincts of the Ḥaram in the 17th century had almost disappeared. A European traveller who visited Jerusalem in the first years of the 19th century said he saw no trace of the *madāris* which had lined the Ḥaram. They had disappeared.[129]

The reason for the decay of the *madāris* was to be sought in the extinction of their *awqāf*. Although the *awqāf* were theoretically 'everlasting', their extinction through the agents of decay and the lapse of time was inevitable. In an age of social and economic crisis the process of extinction was accelerated, either through lack of maintenance or by resorting to various legal methods ending in their dismemberment or the transfer of their ownership. Even in the 15th century Mujīr al-Dīn complained that many villages which constituted the *waqf* of the Mu'aẓẓamiyya madrasa were taken away and transformed either into *iqṭā'* (fiefs) or *mulk* (private property).[130]

The extinction of the *awqāf* reached its climax towards the end of the 18th and the beginning of the 19th centuries. In the early years of the 19th century many *awqāf* had already been dismembered and their assets alienated, either through the long-term lease of the *waqf* property or the exchange of this property, sometimes for cash, i.e. its sale.[131] The most common device to establish private rights on *waqf* property was an arrangement called *khulū*, whereby a tenant is allowed to repair the *waqf*, his expenditure to become a claim in his favour on the *waqf* property.[132] Between 1805 and 1820 seventy new *khulūs* were established in Jerusalem.[133]

In fact the long-term leasing of *waqf* property led to its usurpation or its transfer to non-Muslims. Shaikh Muḥammad al-Khalīlī, in his *waqfiyya* dated 1726, lamented the transfer of *waqf* property to foreigners and stressed the danger such transfer boded for Jerusalem.[134]

The *waqfiyya* of Shaikh al-Khalīlī is a lengthy document which is full of valuable information. Among other things we know from it that Jerusalem had many vineyards, full of fruit trees, such as fig, olive, apple, pomegranate, mulberry, apricot, almond, etc. both within the city and outside it.[135] This contradicts statements made by casual European visitors who tended to stress negative aspects. L d'Arvieux for example spoke of desolation, ruin, neglected lands and roaming brigands, of 'Judaea, mountainous and sterile . . .'[136] Likewise Volney, the French traveller who visited Jerusalem in 1784, dwelt on and exaggerated the same aspects: ' . . . its [Jerusalem's] walls levelled,[137] *its ditches filled up and all its buildings*[138] embarrassed with ruins.'[139] For Volney the inhabitants of Jerusalem were 'well-deserving the reputation of the vilest people in Syria'.[140] Chateaubriand, who visited the city for only four days in 1806, surpassed both d'Arvieux and Volney and had many disparaging words about the city and its people.[141]

It was natural that there were some neglected areas in Jerusalem in those days, but there were also several beautiful villas and palaces. The sources mention the palaces of Jārallāh b. Abu al-Luṭf,[142] Nūr al-Dīn al Jamā'ī (al-Khaṭīb)[143] and Ṣāliḥ al-'Asalī.[144] There were also two palaces built by al-Shaikh al-Khalīlī, outside the city wall.[145] Al-Khalīlī noted with regret that over one hundred 'impregnable' palaces had already passed into the hands of the enemy or were demolished, and stressed the importance of building and populating Jerusalem so as to check the ambitions of the enemy who looked at Jerusalem with covetous eyes.[146]

It seems that the warnings of al-Khalīlī regarding building and populating Jerusalem went unheeded by the Ottoman authorities. There are no records of major public works in Jerusalem during this period, with the exception, of course, of the standing restorations in the Ḥaram area. During the reigns of sultans Ahmad III, Maḥmūd I and 'Abd al-Ḥamīd I, works of restoration were undertaken in the Dome of the Rock in 1705, 1735, 1752 and 1780.[147] The early years of the 19th century witnessed major restorations of the Dome. These restorations were carried out by Sulaimān Pāshā, the *wālī* of Ṣaida, in 1817 and 1818 at the order of Sultan Maḥmūd II. They continued for 21 months and cost 4,000 bags.[148]

The number of the population at the end of the 18th century, according to available information, did not appear to exceed the peak reached in the middle of the 16th century, i.e. 14,000. Volney in 1784 estimates the city's population at 12,000 or 14,000.[149] Seetzen, the German traveller and scholar who visited Jerusalem some twenty years later (1806), gives two figures that were told to him, one is 12,000 and the other is even less, 8,774. The latter figure, which he believed to be an underestimation, was broken down as follows: Muslims 4,000, Christians 2,774, and Jews 2,000.[150] A contemporary economic historian, A Bonne, estimates Jerusalem's population in the early 19th century at 12,000.[151] This figure, although approximate, being based on estimation, is perhaps not far from the truth. The figure of 26,000, based on the estimation of W Turner who visited Jerusalem in the early 19th century, is most likely exaggerated.[152]

In the absence of official statistics it is impossible to give exact figures of the population of Jerusalem at the time. The preponderance of Muslims, however, is clear. In 1821 the *qāḍī* of Jerusalem said: 'There is scarcely one Christian to a hundred Muslims.'[153] This is, of course, an exaggeration, but it is significant. In the early years of the 19th century the number of Jews was increased by 20 Ashkenazi families who arrived from Vilna in 1809.[154]

By reason of Jerusalem's holiness its population depended largely in their subsistence, now as before, on revenues generated by religious motives. In addition to the *awqāf* and pious foundations of all kinds, several cash payments were made to the people of Jerusalem. The Ottoman and Egyptian government sent an annual grant called *ṣurra* (bundle, pouch) to be distributed, according to lists, to a large number of needy people and others.[155] Jewish communities in Europe and Egypt, etc. provided their co-religionists in Jerusalem with alms known as *Halukka*. The kings of Europe, especially the king of Spain, sent considerable sums of money to the Franciscans in Jerusalem.[156]

Another 'religious' source of revenue consisted of the manufacture and export of articles of piety, such as beads, crosses, relics, etc. of which 300 chests were sent off annually to Turkey, Italy, Portugal and especially to Spain.[157] This constituted a major source of income for Christians and Muslims alike. Seetzen in 1806 mentions a big leather factory near the Church of the Holy Sepulchre, and also a number of workshops, including five mills and twenty–five baking ovens. From his description of local occupations it appears that Jerusalem had a minimum of 700 artisans and merchants.[158]

A third and major source of income was revenues from pilgrims. It was customary for Christian pilgrims to stay in Jerusalem for five or six months every year and they must have spent considerable sums. Although the number of European pilgrims diminished greatly in the 18th century, the case was different with oriental Christians, whose number in 1784 amounted to 2,000.[159]

The decrease in the number of European pilgrims in the 18th century was partly due to the spirit of secularism that was gaining ground in Europe. Paradoxically enough, at the same time there was an upsurge of 'religious' enthusiasm about the Holy City in the foreign offices of the European powers. France and Austria posed as 'protectors' of the Latins, while Russia, especially from the reign of Peter the Great (1682–1727), claimed to defend the interests of the Greek Orthodox. The attitude of the powers was reflected in almost all major international treaties. In 1740 France succeeded in forcing on the empire a new version of the Capitulations in which she asserted her role as 'protector' of the Catholics and ensured the rights of the Franciscans in the Holy Sepulchre and other religious places. This time the Capitulation privileges were given in perpetuity. In the treaty of Kütchük Kainerji (1774), Russia asserted her rights to the protection of the Greek Orthodox, and the right of Russian clerics and pilgrims to visit Jerusalem without payment of taxes or tolls.

One result of the attitude of the European powers was an unprecedented increase in dissensions between the Christian communities. Several times these dissensions developed into bloody clashes. The most violent of these clashes broke out in 1757 between the Latins and the Greeks inside the Holy Sepulchre.[160] Following these clashes Sultan Osman III issued a famous edict re-establishing the right of the Greek Orthodox to all places that were taken from them in 1690. The arrangement reached in 1757 forms the basis of the *status quo* regulating relations between the Christians today.

Relations between Christians and Muslims remained peaceful. Because of the differences between the Christian communities, the heads of these communities, in order to strengthen their position and influence in the country, tried to cultivate their relations with the governors, the dignitaries of Jerusalem, and with the common people. The heads of convents, whether Latins, Greeks or Armenians, were in the habit of giving presents to influential people and charities to the poor. These developed into fixed hereditary salaries which could be sold and transferred at will. There are many examples of such sales and transfers in the sijill.[161] The convents also paid fixed sums to the governor's treasury.[162]

LATER DEVELOPMENTS

Towards the end of the 18th century and early in the 19th the empire faced two major threats, one in Egypt and the other in the Balkans. In 1798 Napoleon invaded Egypt, and in the following year he marched into Syria. His Syrian campaign ended in fiasco before the walls of Acre. The news of the French expedition was received in Jerusalem with suspense. Sijills 280 and 281 give us some information in this regard.[163] Already in July 1798, the first month of the French invasion of Egypt, the *wālī* of Damascus acceded to the request of the notables of Jerusalem to supply them with arms to defend the city.[164] Two weeks later the *wālī* informed them that Aḥmad Pāshā al-Jazzār, the *wālī* of Ṣaida, was appointed commander in chief, and all questions relating to defence must be referred to him.[165] In September the *wālī* of Damascus ordered all able-bodied men from the *sanjaq* of Jerusalem to join the sultan's army.[166] The news of the landing of the French army in Alexandria aroused panic and indignation in Jerusalem and led to attacks on the monasteries and the taking of monks as hostages. But the *wālī* advised caution and ordered that the monasteries were to be protected 'as long as they pay the *jizya* and do not show signs of treason'.[167] Having heard reports that some communications were sent by the French to the people of Jerusalem, the *wālī* ordered that all such communications be immediately handed over to the authorities.[168]

The people of Jerusalem and all Palestine rallied behind the Ottoman government. Shaikh Mūsā al-Khalīdī, the *qāḍī 'askar* of Anatolia, sent a proclamation to the people of Palestine calling upon them to fight Napoleon,[169] and Shaikh Muḥammad b. Budair, the Jerusalem *'ālim*, composed a poem commemorating Jazzār's victory over the French.[170]

When Jazzār died in 1804, he was succeeded by Sulaimān Pāshā (1804–1818), who was in turn succeeded by 'Abdullāh Pāshā (1818–

1831). Although Jerusalem normally belonged at this time to the *wālī* of Damascus, it was actually governed in the greater part of the first third of the 19th century by the *wālī* of Ṣaida. In 1830/1831, the year that preceded the Egyptian occupation, the city was under the formal and actual rule of ʿAbdullāh Pāshā, the *wālī* of Ṣaida.[171] During this period Jerusalem had some more native governors (*mutasallimūn*). From 1802 to 1803 and from 1805 to 1807 the city was governed by the *mutasallim* of Jaffa, Muḥammad Abū Maraq, who was notorious for his tyrannical rule and his high handed treatment of the people of Jaffa, Jerusalem, Hebron, Ramla and Gaza. He also harassed Christian pilgrims and subjected them to heavy tolls.[172]

From 1808 to 1831 (the end of the first phase of Ottoman rule) Jerusalem experienced a series of riots and uprisings. In 1808 a fire destroyed the western part of the Holy Sepulchre. The Armenians were accused of starting the fire in their part of the church in an attempt to change the *status quo*. All communities made bids for rebuilding the church. After many representations the Greek Orthodox succeeded in getting permission to do the work. However, the Janissaries, who were angry that the citadel was garrisoned by other troops, incited the Muslim population to obstruct the repairs.[173] A general uprising ensued. The insurgents expelled the *mutasallim*, and occupied the citadel. Sulaimān Pāshā was ordered to take immediate action against insurgents. So he sent a detachment of soldiers under a Maghribī officer, named Abū Dharīʿa. The citadel was besieged and the insurgents were forced to surrender. Abū Dharīʿa cut off with his own hands the necks of 46 insurgents and sent their heads to Sulaimān Pāshā.[174]

Developments in the Balkans were not without repercussions in Jerusalem, in particular the Greek revolution of 1821. When the news of the revolution reached the city all Muslims were ordered to take up arms, and weapons were collected from the Christians. The Greek monk Neophytos reports that the *mutasallim* of Jerusalem at that time, Sulaimān effendi, was a converted Jew who harboured ill feelings towards the Christians and levelled at them false accusations.[175] The Christians of Jerusalem were accused of conspiring with the Greeks, and the populace was aroused against them. But Darwīsh Pāshā, the *wālī* of Damascus, firmly opposed any mistreatment of the Christians and sent instructions to Jerusalem that no Christian should be killed without his consent.[176] A large meeting was held at the *sharīʿa* court of Jerusalem and the *qāḍī* also warned against any maltreatment of Christians: 'Do you not disturb the Rayas [i.e. *raʿiyya* (Ar.) = subjects] for they are faithful: evil done to them is a sin and an injustice against our God and our Prophet.'[177] Shortly thereafter, things were under control and no Christian was hurt.

Some three years after these incidents (in 1824) Jerusalem witnessed a revolution of larger dimensions. Its events were told in detail by Neophytos. The cause was similar to that of many other uprisings in various parts of the empire: the increasing burden of taxation. The new *wālī* of Damascus, Muṣṭafā Pāshā, demanded 'payment of greater tithes . . . as much as ten times the usual tithes.'[178] When the peasants (*fallāḥīn*) around Jerusalem revolted, the pāshā sent 100 soldiers to the citadel, and then set out himself from Damascus at the head of 5,000 men to punish the insurgents. On the approach of the pāshā the peasants deserted their villages, and some of them took shelter in the monasteries which were searched by soldiers. Fearing lest the monasteries be destroyed by artillery fire, the Christians mediated between the pāshā and the *fallāḥīn*. After the payment of a heavy fine by the *fallāḥīn* and the Christians an agreement was reached. As soon as the pāshā left for Damascus, the rising was resumed, this time inside Jerusalem itself. On 5 June 1825 the citadel was occupied by the people of Jerusalem, and the gates of the city were closely guarded. When the *mutasallim* returned from Bethlehem and the surrounding villages, he was not allowed to enter the city. The people of Jerusalem elected two of their number, Yūsuf 'Arab Jabajī al-Jā'ūnī and Aḥmad Āghā al-Duzdār al-'Asalī, as their leaders. One of the first measures of the new rulers was to reduce the taxes. The inhabitants of Bethlehem and the villagers, Muslims and Christians alike, were freed from most of the tithes.[179] The new state of affairs drew a sharp response from the sultan who instructed 'Abdullāh Pāshā to subdue the traitors. Thereupon the pāshā sent his *kekhyā* (deputy) to Jerusalem with 2,000 soldiers. In the initial negotiations the Jerusalem leaders refused to budge. They had repeatedly sworn never again to receive in their own town a foreigner or a stranger (i.e. Ottoman or Albanian).[180] After a brave stand, and only after artillery fire started to fall indiscriminately on the city from the Mount of Olives, they gave in. This time the revolution ended without bloodshed and its leaders were given safe conduct out of the city.

Six years later, in 1831, Ibrāhīm Pāshā, son of Muḥammad 'Alī Pāshā of Egypt, marched into Syria and occupied Jerusalem.

NOTES

1 Ahmad Feridun Bey, *Munsha'āt al-Salāṭīn*, I, 483. Feridun Bey is a Turkish scholar who lived in the 16th century and died in 1583.
2 Ibn Iyās, *Badā'i' al-Ẓuhūr*, V, 136.
3 Evliya Çelebi, 'Evliya Tschelebi's Travels in Palestine', tr. St H Stephan, *Quarterly of the Department of Antiquities in Palestine*, VIII, 147.
4 Feridun, *Munsha'āt*, I, 452–56.
5 Inscription near the northern gate of the Dome.
6 Jerusalem *sharī'a* court registers, henceforth referred to as *sijill*. *Sijill* no. 44, 577 (971 AH).
The *sijill* contains rich material for the whole Ottoman period in all fields of social, economic, religious, cultural and political activities. There are now about 650 registers with more than 100,000 folios. It is still unindexed.
7 See, inter alia, Ibn Taghribardī, *al-Nujūm al-Ẓāhira*, VI, 245; R al-Imam, *Madīnat al-Quds*, 164; and N Avigad, *Discovering Jerusalem*, 254.
8 The seventh gate, the New Gate (al-Bāb al-Jadīd), was built during the reign of 'Abd al-Ḥamīd II (1876–1909).
9 *Sijill*, no. 10, 16 (945/1538).
10 See K Asali, *Min Āthārinā fī Bait al-Maqdis*, 151–52.
11 Burak Sulaimān (Solomon's Pools). There were three pools in the early 16th century. Mujīr al-Dīn in the late 15th century mentions only two: *birkatā al-Marjī'* (*Al-Uns*, II, 99). The third pool seems to have been added by the Ottomans under Sulaimān.
12 Named after the Mamlūk sultan Barquq, who repaired it in 801/1398 (Mujīr, *Al-Uns*, II, 94).
13 'Ārif, *Al-Mufaṣṣal*, 504.
14 For details of the *waqfiyya* (endowment deed) of Khāṣṣekī Sulṭān, *Sijill*, no. 270, 18–49.
15 *Sijill*, no. 270, the *waqfiyya*.
16 *Sijill*, no. 270, 50.
17 The *tapu defters*, drawn up for the assessment of taxes in the 16th century, yield information about the population, its composition and distribution, the towns, their quarters, inhabitants and their various institutions (baths, inns, shops, etc.), the countryside, the agricultural crops, cattle animals, etc. There are several defters relating to Jerusalem (e.g. nos. 522, 342, 602, 427, 131, 1015, 289, 346 and 950).
18 See, for example, U Heyd, *Ottoman Documents*, no. 94, 146–47.
19 According to M S Ya'cub, *Nihāyat al-Quds al-Sharīf*, unpublished MA thesis, University of Jordan, 1986, 24–71, the number of villages was 169.
20 *Sijill*, no. 3 (1532), 428.
21 *Sijill*, no. 12 (1540), 672, and *Sijill*, no. *Sijill*, no. 31 (1555), 426.
22 *Sijill*, no. 15 (1542), 79.
23 Elite infantry troops of the Ottoman empire, organised as a professional army in the late 14th century. They were selected from the Ottoman subject peoples, especially from Christian families. During the 17th and 18th centuries they became riotous and murdered two sultans. In 1826 they were liquidated by Maḥmūd II.
24 The Ḥanafī school of jurisprudence was one of the four schools of Sunnī Islam. The others were the Shāfi'ī, the Mālikī and the Ḥanbalī.
25 A Gharaybeh, *Sūriyya fī 'l-Qarn al-Tāsi' 'Ashar*, 52.
26 See, for example, Heyd, *Ottoman Documents*, no. 9.
27 Gibb and Bowen, *Islamic Society and the West*, II, pt. II, 288.
28 According to a provisional list drawn up from various sources.
29 Cohen and Lewis, *Population*, 94. See also Hütteroth and Abdul Fattah, *Historical Geography*, 52.
30 A study by the present writer has revealed that Muslims from 22 countries lived in Jerusalem in the Mamlūk period (Asali, 'Al-Tāba' al-Islāmī al-Dawlī li-'Ulamā' al-Quds' in *al-Quds al-Sharīf*, 8, November 1985, 40–50.
31 *Sijill*, no. 55, 207.
32 Ya'cub, *Nihāyat al-Quds*, 125–33.
33 Ibid, 136.
34 Cohen and Lewis, *Population*, 55, 63, citing the tapu register for 961/1553–4.
35 Heyd, *Ottoman Documents*, nos. 79, 80 and 82; Ya'cub, *Nihāyat al-Quds*, 171.
36 Ya'cub, op. cit., 173; Heyd, op. cit., no. 82, 132.
37 Heyd, *Ottoman Documents*, no. 23.
38 For details see Cohen and Lewis, *Population*, 46–72; Ya'cub, op. cit., 177–94.

39 Unit of Ottoman silver currency.
40 *EI*[2], V, 334.
41 Ibid.
42 Cohen and Lewis, *Population*, 70.
43 Al-'Ārif, *Al-Massīḥiyya fi 'l-Quds*, 24.
44 F E Peters, *Jerusalem*, 506.
45 M Farid, *Tārīkh al-Daula al-'Aliyya*, 78.
46 R Khalidi, *Al-Muqaddima fi 'l-Mas'ala al-Sharqiyya*, 65.
47 See J Hurewitz, *The Modern East and North Africa in Modern Politics*, I, *European Expansion*, 2–3.
48 Peters, *Jerusalem*, 499.
49 Ibid, 484.
50 A Cohen, *Jewish Life Under Islam*, 223, 224.
51 Ibid, 224.
52 Ibid, 119.
53 Ibid, 225.
54 Heyd, op. cit., 28.
55 Ibid, 43 (1583).
56 Ibid, 44.
57 Sulaimān I entrusted the Abu Ghush family of Qaryat al-'Ināb with protecting the road from Jaffa to Jerusalem. The Banu Zaid, Banu Ḥasan and 'Ibidiyya tribes were given similar duties in their regions.
58 M Sharon, 'The Political Role of the Bedouins in Palestine' in M Ma'os, *Studies on Palestine during the Ottoman Period*, 23.
59 Heyd, op. cit., no. 28.
60 Ibid, nos. 61, 62, 66.
61 Evliya Çelebi, *Siyāhatnāmesi*, XIII, 255.
62 Reports of travellers reflect the sad state of insecurity on the roads: when the Turkish traveller Çelebi wished to visit Hebron in 1672, he had to be escorted by 26 cavalrymen (*Siyāhatnāmesi*, XIII, 253). At that time fief-holders used to convey Muslim pilgrims to Hebron, Bethlehem and Nabī Mūsā ('Evliya Tschelebi's Travels in Palestine', tr. St H Stephan, *QDAP*, VIII, 150). In 1670 the Egyptian traveller, al-Madanī al-Khiyārī, reported that his caravan from Ramla to Jerusalem had to be protected by soldiers from highway robbers (al-Khiyārī, *Tuḥfat al-Udabā'*, II, 172). In 1663 the Moroccan traveller, Abu Sālim al-'Ayyāshī, was unable to make his cherished visit to Nabī Mūsā, and the *qāḍī* of Jerusalem could not help him (Abu Sālim al-'Ayyāshī, *Al-Riḥla*, 318–19).
63 K Asali, *Wathā'iq Maqdisiyya*, I, 289–90.
64 *Sijill*, no. 79 (1598), 530–31.
65 Al-'Ārif, *Al-Massīḥiyya fi 'l-Quds*, 250.
66 Al-'Ārif, *Al-Mufaṣṣal*, 363.
67 Peters, *Jerusalem*, 521.
68 Ramaḍān 1082 AH ('Evliya Tschelebi's Travels in Palestine', tr. St H Stephan, IX, 95).
69 Çelebi, *Siyāhatnāmesi*, XIII, 253.
70 Ibid, 250.
71 In early Ottoman times there were no separate quarters for Christians and Jews. The names 'Christian quarter' and 'Jewish quarter' do not appear in Ottoman registers before the 19th century. Christians and Jews lived together with Muslims in the same quarters.
72 'Evliya Tschelebi's Travels in Palestine', tr. St H Stephan, VIII, 156.
73 H Maundrell, *A Journey from Aleppo to Jerusalem*, 61.
74 See the itineraries of Muṣṭafā al-Bakrī al-Siddīqī and Muṣṭafā As'ad al-Luqaimī in al-Khālidī, *Riḥlāt fī Diyār al-Shām*, 56, 100.
75 K Asali, *Min Āthārinā*, 238.
76 Ibid, 284.
77 Ibid, 153, 155.
78 *Sijill*, no. 205, 24.
79 Al-'Ārif, *Al-Mufaṣṣal*, 307.
80 See, op. cit., nos. 98, 100–105.
81 'Tschelebi's Travels in Palestine', tr. St H Stephan, VIII, 149.
The commander of the pilgrims' caravan of Damascus, *amīr al-ḥajj al-shāmī*, was an important public figure. His primary duty was to ensure the safety of pilgrims and to

administer the affairs of the caravan. In the late 16th century and the early 17th, local amīrs were appointed to this post. In the middle of the 17th century, janissary officers were sometimes appointed. After 1660 Ottoman officers, who were given the government of a *sanjac*, succeeded the janissaries as caravan commanders. From 1708 the wālī of Damascus regularly occupied this post. (A Rāfiq, *Bilād al-Shām wa-Miṣr, 213–15*; also Rāfiq, *Buḥūth fi 'l-Tārīkh al-Iqtiṣādī*, 197).

82 In the 16th century fief-holders of the *sanjaq* of Jerusalem and other Palestinian *sanjaqs* were ordered to take the field outside their provinces, especially against the Persians (Heyd, op. cit., no. 27).

83 'Tschelebi's Travels in Palestine', tr. St H Stephan, VIII, 150.

84 Ibid.

85 Ibid, 149.

86 Ibid, 150.

87 Ibid.

88 Muḥibbī, *Khulāṣat al-Āthār*, IV, 108; Peters, *Jerusalem*, 488.

89 Rāfiq, *Bilād al-Shām wa-Miṣr*, 214.

90 Shaikh Muḥammad al-Nafātī by name, see 'Ayyāshī, *Riḥla*, II, 53.

91 From a tentative list prepared by the present writer.

92 Al-Khiyārī, *Tuhfat al-'Udabā'*, II, 194.

93 Ibid, 195.

94 'Ayyāshī, loc. cit.

95 Al-Maqqarī, *Nafḥ al-Ṭīb*, I, 33.

96 Al-'Ārif, *Al-Mufaṣṣal*, 267, 269.

97 'Tschelebi's Travels in Palestine', IX, 100.

98 Ibid, 84.

99 *Sijill*, no. 57 (982/1574), 62.

100 Heyd, op. cit., no. 94.

101 Khair al-Dīn al-Ramlī, *Al-Fatāwa al-Khairiyya*, ms 442, Yehuda section, Princeton University Library, f. 117. See I 'Abbās, 'Al-Ḥayāt al-'Umrāniyya' in *Al-Mustaqbal al'Arabī*, VI, 1979, 143.

102 'Tschelebi's Travels in Palestine', IX, 95.

103 *Sijill*, no. 167 (1077/1666), 277.

104 Al-Manīnī, *Al-I'lām bi-faḍā'il al-Shām*, 46.

105 L d'Arvieux, *Mémoires*, II, 227–28.

106 Appointed in 1702.

107 For further details about the uprising, see the following sources: Kurd 'Alī, *Khiṭaṭ al-Shām*, II, 273; Ḥasan b. 'Abd al-Laṭīf al-Ḥusainī, *Tajārim Ahl al-Quds*, 335; *Sijill*, no. 203, 44; A Mannā', ''Umar effendī al-Ḥusainī wa-naqābat al-Ashrāf fi 'l-Quds' in *Majmū'at Buḥūth 'Arabiyya*, 127.

108 Ihsan al-Nimr, *Tārīkh Jabal Nablus*, I, 126.

109 *Sijill*, no. 270, 11, and no. 272, 21 and 25.

CHAPTER VIII

Jerusalem in the 19th Century (1831–1917 AD)

Alexander Schölch

THE HISTORICAL SETTING

The history of Jerusalem in the 19th century is the history of her emergence as a major administrative centre in Bilād al-Shām and, in a way, as the capital of Palestine, which became prominent as a political-administrative entity beneath the surface of fluctuating Ottoman provincial divisions. During the period we are studying, Jerusalem represented a special case among the inland towns of the Ottoman empire. Practically all other cities which emerged as new urban centres in the course of the 19th century lay on the Mediterranean coast (for instance, Alexandria, Haifa and Beirut). Unlike these cases, however, the rise of Jerusalem was not due to its importance for commerce, finance and communications. Rather it was a function of the various and growing religious and political interests focused on the city: Christian, Jewish and Muslim interests on the one hand; European, Ottoman and Arab on the other.

Though a special case, the stages of the rise and growth of Jerusalem, her demographic, socio-economic and political-administrative development, correspond to the phases of the historical evolution of the eastern Mediterranean region in the 19th century in general. The major forces of change which were at work in Palestine were the temporary Egyptian rule (1831–1840); Ottoman *tanẓīmāt* policies during the period of the reform edicts (of 1839 and 1856), of ʿAbd al-Ḥamīd and of the Young Turks; European religious-cultural and economic penetration (including Jewish immigration and colonization); the increased integration of the country into the world economy since the middle of the century; and the local responses to these challenges. The development of

Jerusalem was embedded in this wider context, which constituted the historical framework of the rise of the city.[1]

The ephemeral Napoleonic invasion of Palestine in 1799 left virtually no traces in the country. This was a military campaign which did not aim at Palestine as such. The French army bypassed Jerusalem, for at that time the town was not a centre of local or Ottoman power; Napoleon marched via Gaza and Jaffa towards Acre, only to be forced to beat a catastrophic retreat. Thus the first confrontation of Jerusalem with aggressive outside forces in the 19th century was the occupation by the Egyptian troops under Ibrāhīm Pāshā, the son of Muḥammad ʻAlī, in 1832.

In a long-term perspective, however, Ibrāhīm's rule affected Palestine in general and Jerusalem in particular more through the subsequent developments it induced than through direct measures. The Egyptians established a centralized administration in Bilād al-Shām after the example of their home country. It was centred on Damascus.[2] Thus Jerusalem did not yet become an outstanding administrative centre.

However, Muḥammad ʻAlī and Ibrāhīm Pāshā tried to win the support of the European powers for their control of Syria by a calculated policy of granting equality of status to members of religious minorities and by opening the country to European missionary and consular activities. This policy unleashed forces which were quickly to be felt in Jerusalem, as the Ottomans, upon their return to the city, could not reverse the Egyptian measures. Whereas before the Egyptian occupation, European consuls and Christian missions could not establish themselves in Jerusalem, and European pilgrims and visitors were not allowed to settle there permanently, the Ottomans had to continue the Egyptian open-door policy.

The first European consulate established in Jerusalem was the British in 1838. This was followed by the nomination of Prussian (1842), Sardinian (1843), French (1843), Austrian (1847), Spanish (1854), American (1856) and Russian (1857) consuls. On the highest level, the religious-missionary penetration found expression in the establishment of a joint Anglo-Prussian Protestant Bishopric (1841), in the restoration of the Latin Patriarchate (1847) and in the arrival of a Russian bishop (1858). In this context it should also be mentioned that after 1845, the Greek-Orthodox patriarchs of Jerusalem no longer resided in Constantinople, but in Jerusalem itself. On a lower level, a great number of Christian churches and congregations established several new missions and institutions in Jerusalem throughout the 19th century.

For a short period, during the 'Eastern Crisis' in connection with the expulsion of the Egyptians from Syria, various circles in Europe tried to create a 'Jerusalem Question'. All kinds of projects for an 'internationalization' of Jerusalem emerged, i.e. for constituting a separate 'Christian' administrative entity under European control. But with the re-entry of the Ottomans and the inauguration of the *tanẓīmāt* policy in the Syrian provinces, these projects went up in smoke.[3]

From the return of the Ottomans until World War I, the development of Jerusalem reflected the rhythm of the interaction between Ottoman policies, European penetration and regional responses. The Ottoman landmarks were the reform edicts of 1839 and 1856, the constitution of 1876 and the establishment of the Young Turk regime in 1908. The European penetration of Palestine took place on two interconnected levels. On the one hand, there was the 'state level' of great power diplomacy, competing political and commercial interests and the policy of the so-called 'protection' of religious minorities. On the other hand, there was the level of the activities of the various churches, associations, movements and groups, which propagated, for instance, a 'peaceful crusade' (the 'recovery' of the 'Holy Land' for Christianity by peaceful means); the 'restoration of the Jews' (combined with their conversion to Christianity); the 'redemption' of the land through European colonization; or the 'return' of the Jews to the 'Land of Israel' (i.e. pre-Zionist and Zionist aspirations of European Jews).

From the time of the Egyptian rule, Palestine in general and Jerusalem in particular were thus caught up in the whirlpool of European rivalries in the context of the 'Eastern Question'. As a dismemberment of the core region of the Ottoman Empire was out of the question in the 19th century, the European powers did not strive for territorial control in Palestine, but for 'influence'. The easiest way to establish 'influence' was the policy of the 'protection' of religious minorities. The Russians already had the Orthodox Christians and the French had the Catholics to 'protect'. To draw even, England and Prussia (later Germany) had to find or to create their own minorities to be 'protected'. From 1839 the British took the Jews under their wings, and a small Protestant community was created by way of conversion. The policy of religious-cultural penetration and of 'religious protectorates' thus made Jerusalem an arena of European rivalries.

POPULATION GROWTH

Most of the population figures we find in the literature on 19th century Jerusalem are based on estimates by European travellers, consuls and residents in the city. The most detailed statistical tables based on these sources have been drawn up by Ben-Arieh. Table 1 represents a summary of his findings.

Table 1: Estimates of the Population of Jerusalem 1800–1922 according to Ben-Arieh

Year	Muslims	Christians	Jews	Total
1800	4,000	2,750	2,000	8,750
1835	4,500	3,250	3,000	10,750
1840	4,650	3,350	3,000	10,750
1850	5,350	3,650	6,000	15,000
1860	6,000	4,000	8,000	18,000
1870	6,500	4,500	11,000	22,000
1880	8,000	6,000	17,000	31,000
1890	9,000	8,000	25,000	42,000
1900	10,000	10,000	35,000	55,000
1910	12,000	13,000	45,000	70,000
1922	13,500	14,700	34,400	62,600

Source: Y. Ben-Arieh, 'The Growth of Jerusalem in the Nineteenth Century' in *Annals of the Association of American Geographers*, 65, 1975, 262. Slightly different figures appear in Yehoshua Ben-Arieh, 'The Population of the Large Towns in Palestine During the First Eighty Years of the Nineteenth Century According to Western Sources' in Moshe Ma'oz (ed.), *Studies on Palestine During the Ottoman Period*, Jerusalem, 1975; for more details see Yehoshua Ben-Arieh, *Jerusalem in the 19th Century. The Old City*, Jerusalem, 1984, passim.

Let us contrast these estimates with data from the Ottoman population registers which have been increasingly made use of in recent years. Some of the available figures are summarized in table 2.

Table 2: The Population of the Town/*Qaḍā'* of Jerusalem 1849–1914 according to the Ottoman Sources

		Muslims	Christians	Jews	Total
Town of	1849	6,148	3,744	1,790	11,682
Jerusalem	1871–72	6,150	4,428	3,780	14,358
Qaḍā' of	1881–93	54,364	19,590	7,105	81,059
Jerusalem	1914	70,270	32,461	18,190	120,921

Sources: For the town of Jerusalem see Alexander Schölch, 'The Demographic Development of Palestine, 1850–1882' in *International Journal of Middle East Studies*, 17/4, 1985; for the *qaḍā'* (including the town) of Jerusalem see Kamal H Karpat, *Ottoman Population 1830–1914*, Madison, 1985, 144–145 and 184—185.

The figures for 1849 are based on the *Defter-i Nufūs*, those for 1871/72 on the *Sālnāme-i Vilāyet-i Sūriyye*. The data for 1881/82–1893 represent the results of the general census, those for 1914 are taken from the population statistics of the Ministry of the Interior. The figures for the *qaḍā'* of Jerusalem include the Muslim and Christian inhabitants of the villages of the Jabal al-Quds.[4] The Jews lived almost exclusively in the town of Jerusalem.

The most obvious discrepancy between tables 1 and 2 concerns the figures of the Jewish inhabitants of Jerusalem. If we leave aside the minor problems of general undercounting and possible evasion of registration, one reason for the difference is the fact that in the Ottoman statistics only Ottoman citizens are included, while a significant portion of the Jews were foreigners and protégés. However, according to Ottoman statistics for the years 1895 and 1899, there were only about 5,500 foreigners in the whole *sanjaq* of Jerusalem.[5] The discrepancy thus remains. In this context we should also keep in mind that part of the Jewish immigrant population was transient during the three decades before World War I. Many of them were foreigners who remained in Jerusalem illegally. It has been estimated that during this period half of the European Jews who came to Palestine with the intention of staying there left the country again because of the unexpected living conditions and of the attitude of the Ottoman authorities towards them.[6] Though we are able to reconstruct the general trend of population growth in Palestine in the 19th century, we must thus conclude that no reliable breakdown of the population of Jerusalem is possible, as long as the Ottoman population registers, and the registers of the European consulates concerned, have not been scrutinized carefully and in detail.

Despite this fact it can be said, however, that Jerusalem, a relatively minor provincial town of not more than 10,000 inhabitants on the eve of the Egyptian occupation, had definitely become the biggest city of Palestine and the political and cultural centre of the country on the eve of World War I. During that war it could no longer be bypassed by the invaders, as Napoleon, heading towards Acre, had done. The main target of the British offensive under the command of General Allenby was Jerusalem, which he entered on 11 December 1917.[7]

BUILDING ACTIVITIES AND URBAN EXPANSION[8]

By the middle of the 19th century, Jerusalem was still bounded by walls. There were half-ruined uninhabited houses, cultivated plots and mounds of rubbish within the town. Under the Egyptians some building activity had occurred. For instance, Ibrāhīm Pāshā had built two barracks within and two windmills outside the walls. The Christian and Jewish communities also undertook some repair and construction work during this period, especially of religious buildings and pilgrims' hospices.[9] In the forties and early fifties, English and German Protestants were the first foreigners to erect new buildings inside and outside the town, notably Christ Church, the Protestant 'cathedral', which was consecrated in 1849.

A veritable building boom set in after the Crimean War (1853–1856). Within one decade, twenty-four building projects inside and outside the walls were completed, among them the vast Russian compound on the Maidan to the north-west of the town.[10] The erection of new churches, monasteries, synagogues, mosques, schools, hospitals, orphanages, hospices, hotels, consulates, etc. continued without interruption until World War I. The German Protestant Church of the Redeemer was even consecrated in the presence of the German Emperor in 1898. By the end of the 19th century, Cuinet counted and described, for instance, 42 Christian convents, 28 hospices, 17 hospitals and 54 schools (excluding the Muslim mosque schools) in Jerusalem.[11]

Among these schools were eight *rushdiyye* schools, the first of which was opened in 1867–68 (see below). The more important European educational institutions included the schools for boys and girls founded by Bishop Gobat; the Syrian Orphanage for boys, established in 1860 by the German Protestant missionary Schneller;

Talitha Kumi, the girls' school of the German Deaconesses, inaugurated in 1868; the Lamel school, originally founded by Austrian Jews in 1856; the Evelina de Rothschild school for girls (1864); the school of the Alliance Israélite Universelle (1881); the Catholic boys' school of Père Ratisbonne (Saint-Pierre, 1870); the boys' school of Frère des Ecoles Chrétiennes who arrived in 1876; the schools of the White Fathers (arrived in 1878) at Sainte-Ann, especially for Greek Catholics.

From the late sixties, houses were enlarged and new ones built within the walls, and Jewish residential quarters sprang up to the northwest of the city, on either side of the Jaffa road. In the seventies, Jewish building societies were founded, which erected blocks and row houses – uniform and 'barrack-like' as some contemporaries felt – in order to provide homes for the growing number of Jewish immigrants. At the same time, new Arab neighbourhoods emerged north and south of the town. The pioneers of Arab residential expansion outside the walls were prominent and wealthy Muslim families.

Therefore, the town walls became somewhat obsolete. From the early seventies, the gates remained open both during the night and during the Muslim Friday prayer.

Once the carriage road between Jaffa and Jerusalem had been constructed, making it possible to transport imported building materials without difficulty on carts, new building methods were introduced in the residential quarters outside the old city from the 1880s onward. The walls of the new buildings became less massive; the rooms had board floors and a covering of wooden beams, and later of iron girders and stone slabs, while the roof frames were covered with red tiles. Thus a European-style new city emerged side by side with historical Jerusalem.

In the three decades before World War I, the establishment of new Jewish neighbourhoods to the northeast of the old city continued with accelerated speed. The Jewish Quarter within the walls was almost totally *waqf* property (Muslim endowments); the houses were only rented by their Jewish occupants.[12] Outside the city, it was relatively easy to acquire building ground, because land on the periphery of the city was predominantly *mulk* (freehold property), not *mīrī* (state land).[13] As is well known, most of the Jewish newcomers were from Eastern Europe, and most of them had entered the country with a limited visiting permit only. In 1881 and 1890 several hundred families came from the Yemen.[14]

To add to the rush on Jerusalem, the German Templar sect

founded a colony southwest of the city in 1873 (three others had already been established: Haifa and Jaffa in 1869 and Sarona in 1871). In 1882, 257 persons lived in the Jerusalem colony, mainly craftsmen and their families.[15]

ECONOMY AND COMMUNICATIONS[16]

From the 1850s the city expanded and the population grew considerably, but Jerusalem did not become an important centre of commerce and production. The city lived mainly off and for the Muslim, Jewish and Christian holy places, for the institutions which existed or were established for their sake, and from the pilgrims and travellers who visited them. The influx of European Jews during the last decades of Ottoman rule did not change the economic foundation of Jerusalem. The immigrants did not set in action important industrial or commercial developments. A significant part of the Jewish community continued to live on alms collected from Europe.

An important effect of urban growth, however, was the building boom from the middle of the century, from which surrounding villages and towns also profited. There was full employment for lime-burners and quarrymen. Long lines of camels approaching Jerusalem with heavy loads of lime and stones were a frequent spectacle. Masons and stone-cutters had first to be recruited from elsewhere. But in the early 1860s the demand for skilled labour could already be met locally. Especially in Bethlehem and Bait Jala, an occupational specialization took place. Thus in the early 1890s, 30 masons, 250 stone-cutters, 50 quarrymen, 6 plasterers and 40 cameliers (organizing, among other things, the transport of lime and stone) were counted among the 792 artisans, traders, and entrepreneurs of Bethlehem.[17] They worked above all in the Jerusalem building industry.

Apart from this, the main economic activities in Jerusalem centred around the supply of the city's inhabitants with essential commodities and around varied services for pilgrims and visitors. As in other Palestinian towns, the Jerusalem soap industry was of some importance during the first half of the 19th century; but it declined during the second half (whereas it grew considerably in Nablus). In the 1840s and 1850s the Lebanese example stimulated the introduction of silk production in Jerusalem, but the effort was given up in the early 1860s. To some extent devotional articles were manufactured in the city, yet the bulk of these articles, which were sold in and exported from Jerusalem in increasing quantities during the second half of the century, were manufactured in Bethlehem.

For the late 1860s and 1870s we have two interesting, though incomplete, statistics of those engaged in trades and crafts in Jerusalem.[18] In the late 1860s Warren[19] counted 1,932 'able-bodied working men' in 1,320 shops, among whom were 143 general shopkeepers, 88 greengrocers, 189 grocers, 101 bakers and bread sellers, 46 butchers and chicken sellers, 58 wine sellers, 30 coffee grinders, 37 tobacconists, 230 shoemakers, 62 tailors, 28 dyers, 32 *simsim* pressers, 76 soap factors, 151 smiths (various branches), 36 carpenters, 86 coffin makers, 56 barbers, 23 watchmakers and 22 moneychangers. This list was more complete for the Muslim (828) and Christian (601) employed persons than for the Jewish (503).

The reverse was the case with the statistics which Luncz established in 1877.[20] Obviously, Luncz was badly informed about the Muslim and Christian communities. He counted 2,190 men employed in trades and services: 1,425 Jews, 382 Muslims and 383 Christians. Among those he listed were 185 grocers, 55 greengrocers, 35 spice dealers, 49 bakers, 52 butchers and poultry dealers, 26 wine dealers, 18 coffee grinders and coffee roasters, 88 tobacconists, 170 shoemakers, 85 tailors, 115 textile merchants, 7 manufacturers of sesame oil, 73 smiths (various branches), 34 plumbers, 96 joiners and wood turners, 34 barbers, 11 watchmakers, 27 moneychangers, 42 scribes, 31 proprietors of coffeehouses and 51 proprietors of restaurants and public bars. Luncz added that there was a labour surplus in the craft sector, which led skilled Ashkenazi craftsmen, who were unable to support their families in Jerusalem, to emigrate to Egypt, while merchants and retailers were better off.

Thus throughout the 19th century, the economic structure reflected the character of Jerusalem as a holy city, as a religious and spiritual centre for the members of three holy religions. The economy of the city remained a consumer's economy, supported by supplies from outside and, in the case of the Christian and Jewish communities, by foreign funds.[21]

Similarly, the improvement of the system of communications (telegraph, roads, railway), an important aspect of the development of Jerusalem from the 1860s, was not a factor which stimulated the transformation of Jerusalem into an industrial or commercial centre. It rather facilitated access to and travel in the country, and it was a precondition for the rise of Jerusalem as an administrative centre.

In August 1864 the telegraph line reached Jaffa, and the extension to Jerusalem was completed in June 1865. Jerusalem was now connected by telegraph with Constantinople and Cairo, and via them with the European capitals. This was important for the later separation of Jerusalem from Damascus and the establishment of southern Palestine as an 'independent' *sanjaq*.

In 1867 the Ottoman authorities began work on the first carriage road between Jaffa and Jerusalem, using corvée labour. The Italian architect Pierotti was entrusted with the supervision of the project, which was completed in 1868. On the initiative of the mayor of Jerusalem, Yūsuf al-Khālidī, even a regular carriage service along the new road functioned for some time. In the seventies and early eighties the road was repaired several times and relocated in places. In 1875 the Templar colonists founded a transport company, which was able to maintain a regular daily service between Jaffa and Jerusalem. In 1879 they obtained a formal concession for that business which, however, they later lost to their Arab and Jewish competitors.

However, the transport situation changed with the inauguration of the Jaffa–Jerusalem railway line in 1892. Since the early sixties there had been various plans for the construction of a railroad to connect Jerusalem with Jaffa, her port on the Mediterranean. The main reason why none of these projects materialized was doubts about their profitability. In view of the growth of Jerusalem and of the population of Palestine as a whole, and of the growing stream of pilgrims and tourists, however, the question could be rethought. (Already in the 1870s the annual number of European pilgrims and visitors to Jerusalem was between 10,000 and 20,000; in 1910 it reached the figure of 40,000.[22]) In 1889 a French company acquired the concession for the railway line, which had been granted in 1888 to a certain Navon Effendi. Work started in 1890, and the line was completed in 1892. Profits, however, could only be realized after the turn of the century. There were 85,440 passengers altogether in 1893 and 149,200 in 1909.[23]

Parallel to this development, the Ottoman authorities in Jerusalem built a road network, which by the early 1890s connected the city with other towns in central and southern Palestine, notably with Ramallah and Nablus, with Bethlehem and Hebron, and with Jericho.[24]

THE RISE OF JERUSALEM AS AN ADMINISTRATIVE CENTRE[25]

One of the most important administrative developments in the 19th century was the fact that a Palestinian political entity became visible. In this context, Jerusalem became a centre of administration to which the Ottomans attached special importance. There were two lines to this development. One was represented by the attempts to unite the three Palestinian *sanjaqs* (Jerusalem, Nablus and Acre) under one governor. The other consisted of the efforts to give a special status to the city and *sanjaq* of Jerusalem.

In 1830, on the eve of the Egyptian occupation of Syria, the Porte united the three Palestinian *sanjaqs* under the governor of Acre. Palestine was to serve as a kind of buffer province against Muḥammad 'Alī's ambitions. Ten years later, in 1840 (in the context of the international negotiations for a solution to the 'Eastern Question'), the sultan offered to appoint Muḥammad 'Alī as governor of Acre for life, if he would accept the Ottoman peace conditions. The province which Muḥammad 'Alī would have had to administer had he accepted this offer would have been nearly identical with the territory of later Mandated Palestine.

Both in 1830 and 1840 Acre was seen as the capital of the united Palestinian *sanjaqs*. After the return of the Ottomans, however, it was Jerusalem which evolved as the capital of central and southern Palestine. The *qaḍā's* of Gaza and Jaffa were permanently attached to the *sanjaq* of Jerusalem, and until 1858 the *sanjaq* of Nablus was also under the authority of the governor of Jerusalem.

When the three *sanjaqs* were again united in 1872, albeit for a short period only, Jerusalem quite logically became the capital. The Europeans in the country enthusiastically applauded the creation of the province of Jerusalem, or, as they said, of the province of Palestine. It included all the Christian and Jewish holy places and institutions. As the consuls would have had to deal with one governor only, the European penetration of Palestine would have become easier. For exactly this reason, however, the Porte rescinded this administrative measure in the same year. The Ottoman authorities were not in a mood to pave the way for the Europeans.

Instead, to counterbalance European activities, the Porte tightened its own control over Palestine. Already in 1841 and 1854 the governor of Jerusalem had been made directly subject to the Porte for short periods. In 1874 the *sanjaq* of Jerusalem became again 'independent', i.e. the governor of Jerusalem was made directly responsible to Constantinople. Jerusalem and southern Palestine retained this special status until the British occupation.

It is quite obvious that in the course of the 19th century, the Ottoman authorities placed an increasing importance on Palestine, where they tried to strengthen their administrative presence vis-à-vis Egypt on the one hand and, more importantly, vis-à-vis Europe on the other. This meant the emergence of Jerusalem as a provincial capital with a privileged status.

THE COUNCILS: POLITICAL-ADMINISTRATIVE PARTICIPATION

There was another side to the administrative development. As a result of Ottoman *tanẓīmāt* policies, there was a marked change in the political life of Jerusalem. One factor was the establishment of various councils in the city: the municipal council, the administrative council and, on the eve of World War I, the general council of the *sanjaq*. The other factor was the representation of the city and *sanjaq* of Jerusalem in the Ottoman parliament in 1877/78 and during the Young Turk period.

This introduced the period of elections, political competition and representation into socio-political life. As a result, members of the notable families of the city became political leaders and spokesmen of the population of the *sanjaq*. Until the late 1850s the Palestinian mountains were the main arena of the struggle for power and fiscal resources, involving competing families of rural shaikhs and the Ottoman authorities. After the destruction of the system of local rule by the Ottomans, the cities, and particularly Jerusalem, became the real scene of political and financial competition.[26]

Already in 1863 a municipal council (*majlis baladī*) was introduced in Jerusalem by a special firman.[27] Jerusalem was probably the first Ottoman town after Constantinople to receive such an institution. In the early period of the municipality, its most prominent mayor (*ra'īs al-baladiyya*) was Yūsuf al-Khālidī, who served for nine years altogether. Until 1914 nearly all the mayors came from the Khālidī, Ḥusainī, 'Alamī and Dajānī families. The appointment of the mayor and the composition of the town council usually reflected the internal balance of power between the notable families of the city, especially between the Ḥusainīs and the Khālidīs.

Only in 1875 and 1877 were the elections of the town councils and the functions of the municipalities regulated in detail by law.

According to these legal provisions, every male Ottoman citizen from the age of 25 who paid an annual property tax of at least 50 Turkish pounds was entitled to vote for the town council. Candidates had to be at least 30 years old and to pay a property tax of not less than 150 Turkish pounds a year. The members of the town council were elected for four years, half of them being replaced every two years. In Jerusalem the council had ten members, six of whom were Muslims, two Christians and two Jews (in 1908). In the same year 1,200 citizens participated in the elections: 700 Muslims, 300 Christians and 200 Jews. The municipal budget, made up of government grants and income from taxes and fees, had to be approved by the administrative council. The mayor was nominated by the governor from among the elected members of the town council.

From the very beginning, the Jerusalem municipality tried to improve the infrastructure and the conditions of life in the city. The earliest activities included measures to clean and light the city, to pave the streets, to remove obstacles to traffic and to improve the water supply. The paving of the streets and the installation of a sewage system started in the 1870s. The sewage system was expanded continuously until 1914, and the water supply remained one of the major concerns of the municipality. From the 1890s the streets were sprinkled with water, at least at periods when the dust became too much of an annoyance. A regular collection of garbage was introduced, and public conveniences were built. In 1892 a city park on Jaffa Road was made open to the public; twice a week a military band performed music there, at least for some time. On the eve of the war, the municipality began planting trees along some streets. From the end of the 19th century thousands of kerosene lamps were installed to light the city, and in the years before the war, plans were discussed to introduce electricity, a telephone system and tramway lines (in the new suburbs).

In 1886 a city police force was introduced. In the same year the municipality appointed a municipal physician, who treated patients free of charge, and in 1891 a municipal hospital was inaugurated. The municipality also became responsible for issuing building permits. At least from the late 19th century, a register of these permits was kept. Among the building activities of the town council itself were the erection of a public drinking fountain near the Jaffa gate in 1900, and of a clock tower over this gate in 1907. The cultural activities included the foundation of a museum of antiquities and the opening of a theatre beside the Jaffa gate in 1901, where plays were performed in Arabic, Turkish and French.

The municipality thus took an active part in the development of Jerusalem, in the improvement of the infrastructure and in the embellishment of the city. There were not very many cities in the late Ottoman empire which could boast of municipal activities on a similar scale.

The administrative council (*majlis al-idāra*) had responsibilities with regard to the general administration of the *sanjaq*. It was composed of ex officio members, which included the *mutaṣarrif*, the *qāḍī*, the *muftī*, the treasurer, and representatives of the Greek Orthodox, Latin, Armenian and Jewish communities, as well as a handful of elected members. The latter usually came from the same prominent Muslim families of Jerusalem who also sat on the town council. According to the Vilāyet Law of 1864 and to the Law on Vilāyet Administration of 1871, the administrative council was authorized to deliberate and decide on matters concerning public works, agriculture, land registration, finance, tax collection and police. Its most important function was the organization of tax collection. The Jerusalem families represented in the council thus acquired considerable fiscal and economic influence in the *sanjaq*.

A general council (*majlis 'umūmī*) was established in Jerusalem only after the 1913 Vilāyet Law.[28] It was composed of representatives of the various *qaḍā's*, and its main function was to meet once a year in order to deliberate the budget of the *sanjaq*.[29]

A JERUSALEMITE REFORMER

The important role of these councils throws light upon the rise of Jerusalem from a local perspective. This development can be depicted even more vividly by portraying the career of Yūsuf al-Khālidī, the long-standing mayor of the city and member of the 1877/78 Ottoman parliament.[30]

Born in 1842 into one of the two most prominent families of 19th century Jerusalem, i.e. the Khālidīs and the Ḥusainīs,[31] Yūsuf Effendi spent the formative years of his life in a city which was heading towards a new future under the impact of the *tanẓīmāt* policy, especially after the promulgation of the reform edict of 1856. He was deeply aware of the changing situation, above all of European penetration, which, he thought, must be resisted.

The necessary strength had to be acquired through a modern education on the European model. Therefore Yūsuf Effendi asked his father to send him to one of the modern schools in Egypt, where he wished to imbibe 'useful knowledge'. When his father told him that an invitation from Egypt would be necessary for that purpose, he requested permission to study in Europe. This his father refused. Thereupon, together with his cousin, Yūsuf Effendi ran away from home and, through the help of Gobat, the Anglican bishop in Jerusalem, was able to enter the Protestant College in Malta. After two years, his brother Yāsīn brought him from there to Constantinople, where Yūsuf Effendi studied for one year in the imperial medical school and for one and a half years in the American Robert College. The death of his father called him back to Jerusalem.[32]

This had been a remarkable educational journey. Full of enthusiasm, Yūsuf Effendi returned to Jerusalem, where in 1866/67 he campaigned for the establishment of a *rushdiyye* school. He was disappointed that he neither became a teacher nor an administrator of this school when it was opened in 1284/1867–68. Instead, however, he was appointed *ra'īs al-baladiyya*. He devoted all his energies to this new task.

By that time, the Khālidīs had already become known as sincere supporters of the Ottoman *tanẓīmāt* policy. Early in 1874 the foreign minister Rāshid Pāshā, who had been governor in Damascus from 1866 to 1871, called Yūsuf Effendi to Constantinople, where he first served in the Porte's translation office and then as Ottoman consul in Poti on the Black Sea coast. When Rāshid Pāshā was removed from office, Yūsuf Effendi also lost his post. Being on Russian soil, he seized the opportunity to travel to St Petersburg and from there to Vienna, where Rāshid Pāshā had meanwhile become Ottoman ambassador. In Vienna Yūsuf Effendi accepted a position as teacher of Arabic and Ottoman Turkish in the Oriental Academy.

While on leave to settle some family affairs at home in Jerusalem, early in 1877, Yūsuf Effendi was elected by the administrative council of Jerusalem to represent the *sanjaq* in the first Ottoman parliament, which met in Constantinople from 19 March to 28 June 1877. He was re-elected for the second and last session as well (13 December 1877 to 14 February 1878).[33] In Jerusalem he received eight out of fourteen votes, including that of the governor. The rival candidate was 'Umar 'Abd al-Salām al-Ḥusainī.

In Constantinople Yūsuf Effendi became an ardent defender of the constitution against arbitrary measures by the sultan. On account of his courageous conduct he was regarded as one of the leaders of the opposition, and he was ranked among the four 'most dangerous' deputies by the authorities. When parliament was dissolved by the sultan on 14 February 1878, Yūsuf Effendi was among those ten deputies who had to leave the capital immediately.

It has to be stressed that Yūsuf al-Khālidī was and remained a liberal and loyal Ottoman reformer. His activities as a deputy were directed against corruption and arbitrary rule. Yūsuf Effendi's 'opposition' did not aim at Ottoman rule in the Arab provinces as such. He was an 'Ottomanist'. He demanded, however, an intellectual regeneration, a new political philosophy, in the centre of which he placed the concepts of personal freedom (*al-ḥurriyya al-shakhṣiyya*), the acquisition and diffusion of useful knowledge (*al-'ulūm al-mufīda*), patriotism and a sense of duty, a veritable 'bismarckian thinking' (*afkār bismarkiyya*), as he wrote in a long political statement.

Back in Jerusalem, Yūsuf Effendi resumed his duties as mayor. In autumn 1879, however, the *mutaṣṣarrif* (Ra'ūf Pāshā) made an attempt to reduce the 'rule of the Arab patricians' in the city, i.e. to subject the notables of Jerusalem more efficiently to Ottoman control. In this context, most of the Khālidīs and some of the Ḥusainīs lost their offices in the city. More especially, the Khālidīs were obviously to be punished for Yūsuf Effendi's role as a leader of the 'opposition' in Constantinople. Yūsuf Effendi was replaced as mayor by 'Umar 'Abd al-Salam al-Ḥusainī, and for some time the Khālidīs lost their political-administrative preponderance in Jerusalem. But Yūsuf Effendi remained in the service of the Empire, though outside his native town. During the following two decades he mainly served as *qā'im maqām* in various Syrian and Anatolian districts.

Yūsuf al-Khālidī's last, virtually prophetic, act of which we know was a letter he wrote in 1899 to the French chief rabbi Zadok Kahn, an acquaintance of the Zionist leader Theodor Herzl. Impelled by 'a sacred duty of conscience', and 'in the name of God', he implored the Zionists to leave Palestine in peace. If they insisted on their programme, he predicted a popular movement against the Jews which nobody would be able to quell.[34] This letter was forwarded to Herzl, who replied to it from Vienna. In his answer, Herzl stressed the benefit which would result from Jewish immigration for the Ottoman empire in general and for 'la population non juive en Palestine' in particular. He hoped, he wrote, that the sultan would understand this. Menacingly he added: 'S'il n'acceptera pas nous chercherons et croyez-moi nous trouverons ailleurs ce qu'il nous faut.'[35]

It seems to us that Yūsuf al-Khālidī's education, career and activities, including his appeal to the newly created Zionist movement, mirrored the administrative, political, and cultural development of Jerusalem in the 1860s and 1870s, and finally the new problem of Jewish immigration and Zionist political aspirations, with which Arab Palestinians were confronted.

A STORM IS BREWING

Yūsuf al-Khālidī was not the first Jerusalemite who directed public attention to this emerging problem. In 1891 as a large part of the Jewish immigrants from Europe streamed towards Jerusalem, and as the Ottoman authorities were incapable of putting into effect the restrictive immigration laws and of preventing the permanent establishment of the Jewish 'pilgrims' in the city, some leading Jerusalemite personalities sent a protest resolution to the grand vizier. It is said to have born the signatures of 500 inhabitants of the town, who remonstrated against Jewish immigration and land acquisition.[36]

This was probably the first act of this kind, which was preceded and followed, however, by other forms of protest throughout Palestine. New possibilities arose when newspapers sprang up and when the Ottoman parliament was summoned again after the Young Turks had taken power in 1908. In 1911 in particular, the issue of Zionism was a major concern of the Syrian deputies in the Ottoman chamber. They called for legislation to check Jewish immigration into Palestine more effectively. Quite naturally, the two deputies from Jerusalem, Rūḥī al-Khālidī (the vice-president of the chamber) and Sa'īd al-Ḥusainī,[37] were at the front of these activities.[38]

Very soon after the establishment of the Young Turk regime, the deputies from the *sanjaq* of Jerusalem (together with other deputies from Bilād al-Shām) had a double reason for becoming opponents of the new regime: because of its policy of 'Turkification', which increasingly alienated the Arabs from Constantinople, and because of the regime's failure to do something about one of the most pressing problems of the Palestinian Arabs, i.e. Jewish immigration and land acquisition.[39] Sa'īd al-Ḥusainī from Jerusalem and Ḥāfiẓ al-Sa'īd from Jaffa became outspoken critics of the Committee of Union and Progress and, consequently, lost their parliamentary seats in the 'big stick election' of 1912. Rūḥī al-Khālidī maintained his critical support of the regime, though in his opposition to Zionist aspirations, which he had studied thoroughly (he wrote an unpublished book on Zionism), he remained unfaltering. It should be added that personalities from Jerusalem were among the most active members of the various groups within the Arab movement after 1908.

CONCLUSION

If there was a watershed in the history of Jerusalem in the 19th century, it has to be seen in the change which took place during the 1860s and 1870s. This change was part of the decisive demographic, socio-economic and political-administrative transformation which Palestine as a whole witnessed during those decades under the impact of the Ottoman policy of reforms and of European penetration.[40]

With hindsight, however, i.e. in view of the developments after World War I, the year 1882 also appears as a turning point. The British occupation of Egypt and the beginning of the first Jewish *'aliyah*, both in 1882, were starting points of two lines of development, British imperialism on the one hand and Zionism on the other, which moved towards each other and finally met during the war. The results were the Balfour Declaration (2 November 1917) and the entry of Allenby into Jerusalem (11 December 1917).

NOTES

1 On the general history of Palestine during the period 1831–1917, compare A L Tibawi, *A Modern History of Syria including Lebanon and Palestine*, London, 1969; Bichara Khader, *Histoire de la Palestine*, 2 vols., Tunis and Algiers, 1976–77; Moshe Ma'oz, *Ottoman Reform in Syria and Palestine 1840–1861*, Oxford, 1968; Alexander Schölch, *Palästina im Umbruch 1856–1882. Untersuchungen zur wirtschaftlichen und sozio-politischen Entwicklung*, Stuttgart, 1986; 'Abd al-'Azīz Muḥammad 'Awad, *Mutaṣarrifiyyāt al-Quds fi 'l-'Ahd al-'Uthmānī 1874–1914*, PhD thesis, 'Ain Shams University, Cairo, 1970; Haim Gerber, *Ottoman Rule in Jerusalem 1890–1914*, Berlin, 1985; Neville J Mandel, *The Arabs and Zionism before World War I*, Berkeley, 1976.

See also the reports about events in Palestine in the weekly newspaper of the German Templar colonists, *Die Warte*; two volumes of selected articles from this paper have been published by Alex Carmel, *Palästina-Chronik 1853 bis 1882*, Ulm, 1978, and *Palästina-Chronik 1853 bis 1914*, Ulm, 1983.

On the history of Jerusalem during this period compare Philipp Wolff, 'Zur neueren Geschichte Jerusalems. Von 1843–1884', *Zeitschrift des Deutschen Palästina-Vereins*, VIII, 1885; Leonhard Bauer, *Volksleben im Lande der Bibel*, Leipzig, 1903, ch. 32 ('Jerusalem im 19. Jahrhundert); 'Ārif al-'Ārif, *Al-Mufaṣṣal fī Tārīkh al-Quds*, Jerusalem, 1961; Muṣṭafā Murād al-Dabbāgh, *Bilādunā Filisṭīn*, vol. 10/2, Beirut, 1976; Yehoshua Ben-Arieh, *Jerusalem in the 19th century. The Old City*, Jerusalem and New York, 1984.

2 Compare al-'Ārif, *Al-Mufaṣṣal*, 277–91; al-Dabbāgh, op. cit., 16–31; Yitzhak Hofman, 'The Administration of Syria and Palestine under Egyptian Rule (1831–1840)' in Moshe Ma'oz (ed.), *Studies on Palestine during the Ottoman Period*, Jerusalem, 1975; Laṭīfa Sālim, *Al-Ḥukm al-Miṣrī fi 'l-Shām 1831–1841*, Cairo, 1983.

For a lively contemporary account of the events in Jerusalem during the 1834 Palestinian uprising against Ibrāhīm Pāshā, see S N Spyridon, 'Annals of Palestine, 1821–1841', *Journal of the Palestine Oriental Society*, 18, 1938, 89–120; see also al-'Ārif, *Al-Mufaṣṣal*, 281–286.

3 Compare Joseph Hajjar, *L'Europe et les Destinées du Proche-Orient (1815–1848)*, n.p. 1970, 352–72.; Mayir Vereté, 'A Plan for the Internationalization of Jerusalem, 1840–1841', *Asian Affairs*, 12/1, 1978; Alexander Schölch, 'Europa und Palästina 1838–1917' in Helmut Mejcher and Alexander Schölch (eds.), *Die Palästina Frage 1917–1948*, Paderborn, 1981, 17–18.

4 There were 116 villages in the *qaḍā'* in 1871/72 (see Alexander Schölch, 'The Demographic Development of Palestine, 1850–1882', *International Journal of Middle East Studies*, 17/4, 1985, table 2, and 126 in 1903/04 (see al-'Ārif, *Al-Mufaṣṣal*, 329).

5 Kemal H Karpat, *Ottoman Population 1830–1914*, Madison, 1985, 157 and 161. According to Neumann, there were about 5,000 foreigners and protégés in Jerusalem in the second half of the 1870s; see Bernhard Neumann, *Die Heilige Stadt und deren Bewohner*, Hamburg, 1877, 217. The British consul spoke of only 3,000 foreigners and protégés in Jerusalem in 1874, *Public Record Office*, London, FO 195, vol. 1047 (Jerusalem, February 21, 1874).

6 Mandel, op. cit., pp. XXIV, n. 5, and 29.

7 Cf. al-'Ārif, *Al-Mufaṣṣal*, 271–73 and 374–84; Tibawi, *A Modern History*, 35–38 and 249–52.

8 On this aspect, see particularly Wolff, 'Zur neueren Geschichte Jerusalems'; C Schick, 'Die Baugeschichte der Stadt Jerusalem', pt. VII, *Zeitschrift des Deutschen Palästina-Vereins*, XVII, 1894.; Bauer, op. cit.; al-'Ārif, *Al-Mufaṣṣal*, 303–08; Y Ben-Arieh, 'The Growth of Jerusalem in the Nineteenth Century', *Annals of the Association of American Geographers*, 65/2, 1975; Ruth Kark and Shimon Landman, 'The Establishment of Muslim Neighbourhoods in Jerusalem, outside the Old City, during the Late Ottoman Period', *Palestine Exploration Quarterly*, 112, 1980; Ben-Arieh, *Jerusalem in the Nineteenth Century*; Schölch, *Palästina im Umbruch 1856–1882*, pt. II.

9 Cf. Spyridon, op. cit., 123–25.

10 On the development of Jerusalem during the late fifties and sixties, see the detailed accounts by Philipp Wolff, *Sieben Artikel über Jerusalem aus den Jahren 1859 bis 1869*, Stuttgart, 1869; *Flugblätter aus Jerusalem vom November und Dezember 1869*, Stuttgart, 1870; *Jerusalem*, Leipzig, 3rd edition, 1872.

11 Vital Cuinet, *Syrie, Liban et Palestine. Géographie Administrative, Statistique, Descriptive et Raisonée*, Paris, 1896–1901, 522, 535, 542, 553, 563.

12 According to Muḥammad Adīb al-'Āmirī, *Al-Quds al-'Arabiyya*, Amman, 1971, p. 12, 85 per cent of the Jewish quarter was *waqf*, according to 'Ārif al-'Ārif, *Al-Nabka*, vol. 2, Sidon and Beirut, 1957, 490, n. 3, 90 per cent was *waqf*.

See also A L Tibawi, *The Islamic Pious Foundations in Jerusalem*, London, 1978, 43–45. On the quarters of Jerusalem in general, see I W J Hopkins, 'The Four Quarters of Jerusalem', *Palestine Exploration Quarterly*, 103, 1971.

13 Mandel, op. cit., 78 and 105.

14 On the Yemenite Jews, see Martin Gilbert, *Jerusalem – Rebirth of a City*, London, 1985, 176–77 and 208.

15 Cf. Christopher Paulus, 'Die Tempelcolonien in Palästina', *Zeitschrift des Deutschen Palästina-Vereins*, VI, 1883; on the Templar colonies in Palestine in general, compare Muḥammad Rafiq and Muḥammad Bahjat, *Wilāyat Bairūt*, pt. 1, Beirut, 1335/1916–17, 238–40 and 253–57; Alex Carmel, *Die Siedlungen der würtembergischen Templer in Palästina 1868–1918*, Stuttgart, 1973; 'Alī Maḥāfẓa, *Al-'Alāqāt al-Almaniyya – al-Filasṭiniyya, 1841–1945*, Beirut, 1981, 100–133.

16 For the sources and for more details, see Alexander Schölch, 'European Penetration and the Economic Development of Palestine, 1856–82', in R Owen (ed.), *Studies in the Economic and Social History of Palestine in the Nineteenth and Twentieth Centuries*, London, 1982, 10–87; Schölch, *Palästina im Umbruch 1856–1882*, pt. II.

17 P Palmer, 'Das jetzige Bethlehem', *Zeitschrift des Deutschen Palästina-Vereins*, XVII, 1894, 91–94.

18 A detailed description of the occupations in Jerusalem in the second half of the 1840s, though without satisfactory statistical data, can be found in Titus Tobler, *Denkblätter aus Jerusalem*, St Gallen and Constanz, 1853, 228–76. This book of 759 pages is an almost encyclopedic description of Jerusalem and of life in the city at that time..

19 Charles Warren, *Underground Jerusalem*, London, 1876, 490–522.

20 A M Luncz, *Jerusalem, Jahrbuch zur Beförderung einer wissenschaftlich genauen Kenntnis des jetzigen und des alten Palästinas*, I, 1881, Vienna, 1882, 33–60 (from 1882 to 1919, Luncz published 13 volumes of his *Jerusalem Yearbook* in Hebrew, and from 1896 to 1916, 21 volumes of his *Palestine Almanac* also in Hebrew).

On Jerusalem in the 1870s, see also Neumann, op. cit., and G Gatt, *Beschreibung über Jerusalem und seine Umgebung*, Waldsee, 1877.

21 This remained so well into the period of the Mandate: 'The first census of industry taken by the Government of Palestine revealed that in 1928, in the 658 "industrial" establishments in the city, only 3316 persons were employed, including owners. Only 80 workshops possessed some kind of power-driven machinery.' Alfred E Lieber, 'An Economic History of Jerusalem' in John M Oesterreicher and Anne Sinai (eds.), *Jerusalem*, New York, 1974, 40.

22 Schölch, 'European Penetration', 27; Gerber, op. cit., 241.

23 Gerber, op. cit., 241.

24 Cuinet, op. cit., 610–13; Bauer, op. cit., 340; Gerber, op. cit., 242.

25 For the details of this administrative development, compare Schölch, *Palästina im Umbruch 1856–1882*, pt. I; B Abu Manneh, 'The Rise of the Sanjak of Jerusalem in the Late 19th Century' in Gabriel Ben-Dor (ed.), *The Palestinians and the Middle East Conflicts*, Ramat Gan, 1978; 'Awad, *Mutaṣarrifiyyāt al-Quds*, 1–5, 24–28.

26 Schölch, *Palästina im Umbruch 1856–1882*, pt. III.

27 On the establishment of the municipality and its activities, see above all Ruth Kark, 'The Jerusalem Municipality at the End of the Ottoman Rule', *Asian Affairs*, 14, 1980. Compare also Daniel Rubenstein, 'The Jerusalem Municipality under the Ottomans, British and Jordanians' in Joel L Kraemer (ed.), *Jerusalem – Problems and Prospects*, New York, 1980, 72–74; al-Dabbāgh, op. cit., 201–02; Ben Arieh, *Jerusalem in the 19th Century*, 122–25; Gerber, op. cit., 113–17.

28 The list of members in 1332/1913–14 is to be found in al-'Ārif, *Al-Mufaṣṣal*, 316. The general council had three members for the *qaḍā'* of Jerusalem, three for Jaffa, four for Gaza and Beersheba and two for Hebron.

29 On the administrative council and the general council, see above all Gerber, op. cit., ch. 5 and passim. This study is based on three registers of the administrative council and one of the general council from the last decade of Ottoman rule.

30 On the biography of Yūsuf al-Khālidī, see my article, 'Ein palästinensischer Repräsentant der Tanẓīmāt-Periode: Yūsuf Ḍiyā'addīn al-Khālidī (1842–1906)', *Der Islam*, 57, 1980. This study is based, among other sources, on Yūsuf al-Khālidī's autobiography (a manuscript kept in the family library in Jerusalem) and on a long political letter, which he wrote to the orientalist, Wahrmund. See also 'Ādil Mannā', 'Yūsuf Ḍiyā'addīn al-Khālidī', *Al-Fajr al-Adabī*, 35/36, 1983.

31 Traditionally, members of the Khālidī family had held the post of *bāshkātib* and *nā'ib* of the *sharī'a* court, members of the Ḥusainī family had been *muftīs* and *nuqabā' al-ashrāf*.

32 It seems that Yūsuf al-Khālidī was one of the first Jerusalemite scholars who wished to be educated in one of the modern schools in Egypt and who then studied in similar colleges in Istanbul. In the 19th century, the strongest cultural ties of Jerusalem notables and *'ulamā'* continued to be those with al-Azhar in Cairo. However, during the *tanẓīmāt* period, Istanbul gradually became Cairo's rival as a centre of cultural attraction. Damascus was and remained much less important for the Jerusalem families in this respect. On the cultural ties and orientations of Jerusalem notables and *'ulamā'*, compare Uri M Kupferschmidt, 'Connections of the Palestinian 'Ulamā' with Egypt and Other Parts of the Ottoman Empire' in Amnon Cohen and Gabriel Baer (eds.), *Egypt and Palestine*, Jerusalem and New York, 1984; Gabriel Baer, 'Jerusalem Notables in Ottoman Cairo' in ibid; 'Ādil Mannā', 'Cultural Relations between Egyptian and Jerusalem 'Ulamā' in the Early Nineteenth Century' in Gabriel R Warburg and Gad G Gilbar (eds.), *Studies in Islamic Society. Contributions in Memory of Gabriel Baer*, Haifa, 1984.

33 For the dates of the two sessions, see Robert Devereux, *The First Ottoman Constitutional Period*, Baltimore, 1963, 16.

34 Mandel, op. cit., 47–49.

35 Theodor Herzl, *Gesammelte zionistische Werke*, vol. 5, Tel Aviv, 1935, 484–86.

36 Cf. A L Tibawi, *Jerusalem. Its Place in Islam and Arab History*, Beirut, 1969, 28; Maḥmūd al-'Ābidī, *Qudsunā*, Cairo, 1972, 134; 'Abd al-'Azīz Muḥammad 'Awad, 'Al-Haraka al-'Arabiyya fī mutaṣarrifiyyat al-Quds', *Majallat al-Sharq al-Awsaṭ*, 1, 1974, 145; al-Dabbāgh, op. cit., 49; Mandel, op. cit., 39–40.

37 In many ways Rūḥī Khālidī (1864–1913) was a worthy successor of Yūsuf Effendi as a leading Arab intellectual and politician in Jerusalem. On his biography, compare Rūḥī Khālidī, *Al-Muqaddima fī 'l-Mas'ala al-Sharqiyya*, Jerusalem, n.d., i–iv; Nāṣir al-Dīn al-Asad, *Muḥammad Rūḥī Khālidī – rā'id al-baḥth al-tārīkhī al-ḥadīth fī Filasṭīn*, Cairo, 1970, 35–46; Zakī Muḥammad Mujāhid, *Al-a'lām al-sharqiyya fī 'l-mi'a al-rābi'a 'ashra al-hijriyya*, 4 vols, Cairo, 1949–1963, no. 1071; Ya'qūb al-'Audāt, *Min a'lām al-fikr wa-'l-adab fī Filasṭīn*, Amman, 1976, 155–60; 'Irfān Sa'īd Abū Ḥamad al-Hawārī, *A'lām min arḍ al-salām*, Haifa, 1979, 545; al-Dabbāgh, op. cit., 363–69. On Sa'īd al-Ḥusainī, see al-Dabbāgh, op. cit., 379–81.

38 The deputies, who were elected to the Ottoman parliament in the *sanjaq* of Jerusalem, were in 1908: Rūḥī Khālidī, Sa'īd al-Ḥusainī, Ḥāfiẓ al-Sa'īd (Jaffa); in 1912: Rūḥī Khālidī, 'Uthmān al-Nashāshībī, Aḥmad 'Ārif al-Ḥusainī (Gaza); in 1914: Sa'īd al-Ḥusainī, Rāghib al-Nashāshībī, Faiḍī al-'Alamī. Compare the lists in al-'Ārif, *Al-Mufaṣṣal*, 316; al-Dabbāgh, op. cit., 51–52; Mandel, op. cit., 65–66, 119–20 and 181–82; Rashid Ismail Khalidi, *British Policy towards Syria and Palestine 1906–1914*, London, 1980, chart between pages 258 and 259.

39 On the policy of the Jerusalem deputies and on Palestinian protests against Zionist penetration in general, compare 'Awad, 'Al-Ḥaraka al-'Arabiyya'; Mandel, op. cit.;, Khalidi, *British Policy*, ch. 4–6; Rashid Ismail Khalidi, 'The 1912 Election Campaign in the Cities of Bilad al-Sham', *International Journal of Middle East Studies*, 16/4, 1984.

40 This is the main theme of my book *Palästina im Umbruch 1856–1882*.

CHAPTER IX

The Transformation of Jerusalem 1917–1987 AD

Michael C Hudson

The year 1917 was fateful for the inhabitants of Jerusalem – both Arab and Jewish – not only because of the issuance of the Balfour Declaration but also because it marked the end of over 1,200 years of Arab and Turkish Muslim rule, interrupted only briefly by the Crusaders. The transformation of Jerusalem that has occurred since General Edmund Allenby entered the city on 9 December 1917 surely exceeds that of any period in its eventful history. It has been a double transformation: on the political level, the total replacement of indigenous Arab and Turkish Muslim rule by that of Zionist-Jewish newcomers; and on the social level, the establishment of a modern fortress city, whose physical aspects, demographic 'revolution' and Western acculturation have enveloped and almost overshadowed the Arab character of the city.

The Arab character of Jerusalem in the 1980s is a shadow of what it was in 1917, 1948, or even 1967. In 1987 Arabs comprised only 28 per cent of the city's 475,000 inhabitants, compared to 73 per cent in 1873 (before the first wave of European Jewish immigration), 46 per cent in 1922 and 40 per cent in 1944.[1] The Arab Old City is in danger of becoming a museum-piece for tourists instead of being a vital part of the city, and the Arab quarters built up outside the Old City during the Jordanian rule are now dwarfed by the surrounding high-density Jewish developments. Few people now remember that there were many thousands of Arabs living in West Jerusalem until they were driven out in 1948. And as religious fanaticism has intensified in Israel in the last several years there is now a growing danger to the sanctity and physical security of the Ḥaram al-Sharīf, with its most sacred mosques. For Arab Jerusalemites, Palestinians, Arabs elsewhere, and Muslims the world over, the condition of the Holy

City and its prospects must give rise to feelings of concern. Indeed, for everyone for whom Jerusalem is important, the inflamed political environment in the region should arouse worry for the city's future.

Ironically, the period of the loss of Jerusalem coincides with the emergence of the Arab world as a whole into an age of political independence and modernity. Other things equal, Jerusalem would not only have remained under Arab control, but it might also have been the capital of an independent Palestinian state with an Arab majority and a Jewish minority. Palestine, however, was not fated to experience the 'normal' liberation from European colonialism as did other parts of the Arab world. Instead, under the umbrella of Great Britain's mandate, a European-rooted Jewish national movement – Zionism – was able to reproduce itself in Palestine and develop the institutions of statehood. Zionist literature depicts this achievement as little short of miraculous, considering the demographic odds; while Arab accounts reflect a kind of mirror-image amazement that such a catastrophe could have befallen a people whose presence and historical rights to the land were so overwhelming. In the popular histories of both sides, therefore, one is not surprised to find simplistic 'black and white' explanations in which the outcome is determined by heroes or villains, by courage or treachery, by God's grace or wrath.

But simplistic answers do not adequately explain how over the following 50 years Palestine, and with it Jerusalem, fell bit by bit to the Zionist conquerors. Certainly part of the explanation lies in the leadership, organizational skills and economic resource base of the Zionist movement. It demonstrated the ability both to influence the British and later the American government; it also managed to expand a relative toehold in Palestine itself into a settler-colonial para-state and then a formal state. It also somehow achieved enough internal coherence to overcome deep ideological cleavages and organizational rivalries, so that it could successfully confront what was seen as the common Arab enemy. Another element undoubtedly is the relative incoherence and weakness in Arab politics at the time. The Arab nationalist movement, striving to come to terms with the confusion created by the departure of Turkey and the arrival of Britain and France, lacked the unity of purpose and unity of ranks that would have been necessary to cope with the Europeans and, in Palestine, with the Zionists as well. Unlike their Zionist counterparts the Arab leadership in Palestine could not close ranks sufficiently to mount a sustained political and armed resistance.

For their part, the British and French, and later the Americans, had larger economic and strategic interests in the region to pursue. Owing mainly to domestic pro-Zionist influences British and, later, American leaders eventually were persuaded (but not easily) that a Jewish state in Palestine and even a Jewish-controlled Jerusalem were supportive of these interests, as well as morally desirable. It is a mark of the proficiency of British and American diplomacy that this basic acceptance of the Zionist claim, and America's subsequent lavish support for it, was achieved without arousing genuinely effective Arab protest. After Britain successfully crushed Palestinian Arab resistance and decimated its leadership in the late 1930s, the primary Arab leadership role for Palestine fell to the Hashemites of Transjordan. But caught between the policies of Great Britain and America on the one hand and the frustrated aspirations of Arab nationalism on the other, the Hashemites found themselves playing custodian of the rump Arab territories remaining in Palestine, including Jerusalem, without being able to protect them from further Zionist expansion.

It is within this larger framework that one must try to understand the struggle for Jerusalem. To Jews and Zionists the city was both a religious and a national symbol. To Arab Muslims and Christians it was no less significant on both grounds. And to practical politicians and fighters on both sides Jerusalem was a strategic prize. Each side used extraordinary means to influence the external arbiters, and each has scored some successes; but finally in 1967 it was Jewish power that carried the day. Nevertheless, two decades after the fall of Arab Jerusalem Israel still has not achieved *de jure* recognition of its conquest either from the Arabs or the international community. The struggle continues.

BRITISH JERUSALEM

'Neither the Jews nor the Arabs conquered Palestine from the Turks, but the British . . .'

Ronald Storrs

Ḥājj Amīn al-Ḥusainī, the Muftī of Jerusalem, once warned Lord Plumer, Britain's second High Commissioner in Palestine, that if England continued favouring the Zionists then he (the Muftī) could not be responsible for the safety of Palestine; to which Lord Plumer retorted, 'You responsible? Who asked you to be responsible for the peace of this place? I am!' It is said that he addressed the Zionist

Commission in the same brusque manner.[2] The British were imbued in part by philo-Semitic zeal: Vester observes Lord Balfour at the opening of the Hebrew University 'profoundly moved . . . tears running down his face.'[3] They also felt a certain sympathy for the native Palestinian Arabs and hoped to elevate their way of life now that they were unburdened of what the English viewed as corrupt, backward Turkish rule. One cannot read the accounts of Palestine Mandate officials like Storrs or Herbert Samuel without perceiving a sense of English-style *mission civilisatrice.*

From the beginning, however, the British found that implanting law and order would not be easy. This was because of a contradiction in the mandate for Palestine. Article 22 of the League of Nations Covenant required the Mandatory to apply 'the principle that the well-being and development [of the people of Palestine] form a sacred trust of civilization'. In 1917 the Arabs constituted around 90 per cent of the population of Palestine and just about half the population of Jerusalem. At the same time, however, the Balfour Declaration committing Britain and the other victorious powers to the establishment of a Jewish National Home in Palestine was also written into the Mandate. Moreover, the Mandate also provided for a Jewish Agency (designated as the Zionist organization) to be established as a public body to facilitate development of the National Home, and the country in general (Art. 4), and it was enjoined 'to facilitate Jewish immigration under suitable conditions' (Art. 6) and 'facilitate the acquisition of Palestinian citizenship by Jews . . .' (Art. 7). The Palestinian Arabs rightly suspected the political intentions of the Zionist movement, but their leaders, for the most part, remained naively convinced until the mid-1930s of Britain's good intentions toward them.

Palestine, and Jerusalem, were under British military administration (the Occupied Enemy Territories Administration) until July 1920. During this time the main preoccupation of the authorities was alleviating the dislocations resulting from the war and organizing economic and administrative affairs. Religious affairs and the holy places were sensitive issues and required much attention from the Military Governor of Jerusalem, Lt Col Ronald Storrs. In order to help preserve and advance the city's patrimony he established the Pro-Jerusalem Society, which was composed of Christian, Muslim, and Jewish religious leaders and civic notables. Under the technical supervision of the planner and architect C R Ashbee, the Society sought to organize repairs and renovation of public buildings and monuments.[4] While adhering to the customary procedures on intercommunal relations from Ottoman times known as *status quo*, the High Commissioner and his staff immediately began to implement the spirit of the Balfour Declaration by introducing Hebrew into official notices and documents, along with English and Arabic, and employing Jewish bureaucrats and translators.[5]

The first civilian High Commissioner of Palestine was Herbert Samuel, a former cabinet secretary. In 1918 and 1919 Samuel wrote that he was ' . . . closely co-operating with its leaders'.[6] Despite his skills and tact, Samuel was embarking on an undertaking that eventually would fail because of its fundamental contradictions.[7] Fair as he may have tried to be, Samuel nonetheless was deeply committed to implementation of the Balfour Declaration. Inevitably, he would run foul of the aspirations of the Arab majority in Palestine.

A year before his appointment (July 1920) the General Syrian Congress meeting in Damascus (with Palestinian participants) had rejected the Balfour Declaration, and only three months before his appointment major demonstrations had erupted in April, the culmination of several months of growing protest against the Zionist enterprise and a demonstration of support for the new (but shortlived) independent Arab government of the Hashemite Amīr Faiṣal in Damascus. On this and subsequent occasions the traditional Arab leadership urged moderation and patience on their outraged rank-and-file. But these leaders did not fully comprehend the structural commitment of the Mandate authorities toward facilitating the development of an autonomous Jewish community, nor were they willing to accept the discriminatory offers of the British to participate in local government. The White Paper of 1922, written by Colonial Secretary Winston Churchill, tried to allay Arab apprehensions, yet by reaffirming Jewish 'rights' to a homeland and further immigration failed to do so. Proposals by the Mandatory in 1922 and 1923 to establish a legislative council were rejected both by the Zionists because they were in a minority and by the Arab leadership because the proposed 'Arab Agency' reduced them to the same status as the Jewish minority and also did not allow for the same autonomy as the Jewish Agency. In 1925 the Religious Communities Ordinance not only perpetuated the Ottoman distinction between Muslim and Christian Arabs but also enhanced the autonomy of the Jewish community in education and other organizational aspects.[8]

Herbert Samuel's successor in 1925, Lord Plumer, enjoyed a

relatively tranquil tenure, until September 1928. But during this period of deceptive calm, the Jewish community, or *Yishuv*, was organizing itself as a para-state, with an army (the Haganah), taxation and financial institutions, and an array of educational, cultural, and charitable organizations. The Arabs on the other hand remained largely unorganized, led by traditional religious and commercial notables, cultured but untutored in the ways of *Realpolitik*. Their ability to lead was hampered by their ambivalence toward the British – the tension between their interests and their national commitment – and also by their personal and factional rivalry, exemplified in the frictions between members of the Ḥusainī and Nashāshībī families.

The first decade of British rule had been exasperating, no doubt, but Palestine was under control. In Jerusalem, the Mandatory had apparently stabilized intercommunal relations and had undertaken many municipal improvements. The fact remained, however, that the Mandate was not regarded as legitimate by the Arabs; they had not been consulted and they saw, increasingly, that it was not evenhanded. The gentility of Palestinian leadership and the passivity of the people were about to give way to militancy and violence even as more extreme tendencies in the *Yishuv* began to gain strength.

British exasperation gave way to alarm with the Wailing Wall violence of 1929; and by the early 1930s, as accelerated Jewish immigration stimulated the Arabs to organize themselves for forceful resistance. By then even Storrs was moved to comment that 'Zion and England', having created the Jewish National Home enterprise, had thus far failed, the result being 'an explosion of feeling so momentous that the greatest Power in the world, after near twenty years' experiment and experience, required, in full peace time, an Army Corps and all the panoply of war to control the "liberated" civil population . . .'[9]

In truth, the Wailing Wall disturbances, which both Arab and Zionist historians have seen as a catalyst for the impending cataclysm, went back well beyond 1928–29.[10] And while the modern history of Jerusalem is inextricably a part of that of Palestine as a whole, they demonstrate how the Holy City became a focus of conflict because of its dual religious and national importance to both sides. Under the Ottoman *status quo* arrangements, Jews had been allowed to pray at the wall, but they were there by sufferance not by right because the entire Ḥaram al-Sharīf and much neighbouring territory were Islamic *waqf* properties. After Jerusalem fell under British rule (and with the Balfour Declaration written into the

Mandate) Zionists not only began vigorously contesting the *status quo* but also began receiving a more sympathetic hearing from the British authorities than they had from the Turks. Efforts by Zionists to purchase the wall had been made as early as the 1850s. They were renewed with vigour almost immediately after the British occupation. In 1918 Jews praying at the wall intensified their efforts to bring chairs, benches, and other accoutrements for worshippers. Such activities raised Muslim fears that they were attempting to establish an open synagogue, in violation of the *status quo*, that would prejudice Muslim rights.

It was a particularly bold attempt of this kind on Yom Kippur in September 1928 that set in motion the chain of disturbances which by the end of August 1929 had caused the deaths of 113 Jews and 116 Arabs. According to Mattar, the initial incidents were magnified and exaggerated by Jewish organizations and media both in Palestine and Europe, provoking to justified alarm the Muslim Arab religious leaders (the most important being the Muftī, Ḥājj Amīn al-Ḥusainī). The Arabs abandoned their initial efforts to co-operate with the British in calming the situation and instead began to mobilize violent protest.[11]

The Palestinians in a sense won the 'battle' for the Wailing Wall inasmuch as Great Britain through the Shaw Commission and the International Wailing Wall Commission confirmed the *status quo* arrangements there. They also now began enlisting much stronger support from the Arab and Islamic world. But the victory was hollow; indeed the violence at the Wailing Wall and elsewhere in Palestine only accelerated the tendency toward confrontation on both sides. Rebounding from the stagnation of the late 1920s, the Zionist movement came under more extremist influences. Furthermore, the revival of heavy immigration in the early 1930s raised Arab political fears anew and also created economic and unemployment pressures.

New violence erupted in 1933, and the Jerusalem-dominated traditional Arab leadership, reluctant to encourage such tactics, began to lose control of its own followers. The Arab Executive Committee, which had been the main political organization since 1920, was seen as too conservative and accommodating in light of the new violence, and faded from the scene. In response to growing mass pressures for action new political parties appeared, though still dominated by the elite: the pan-Arab Istiqlāl, the Defence Party, the Reform Party, and the National Bloc Party. But party activity could not contain the feelings that had by now been aroused, and organizations began to form committed to armed struggle both against the British and Zionists. Shaikh ʻIzz al-Dīn al-Qassām's guerrillas staged a shortlived revolt in November 1935 near Jenin, in which the Shaikh was killed and instantly honoured as a martyr, heralding a new phase in the Palestinian struggle.

On 25 April 1936 the Arab Higher Committee was established in Jerusalem under the leadership of Ḥājj Amīn al-Ḥusainī and composed of leaders of the new parties. If the faces were the same (and Jerusalemites continued to dominate) the strategy and tactics were different: now there was a call for civil disobedience, setting the stage for the general strike of 1936 and the rebellion in 1937–38.[12]

Jerusalem figured all too prominently in the bloody events of 1936–39. It was the scene of numerous incidents of violence and terrorism, with the Irgun Zvai Leumi responsible for a wave of bombings beginning in the fall of 1937 until the outbreak of World War II two years later. Even though Palestinian rebels controlled major rural and hilly portions of Palestine during the revolt, they were not able to gain or maintain footholds in the main towns. Palestinian fighters briefly seized control of Jerusalem's Old City, however, in October 1938. The increasing violence of the Arab-Jewish-British confrontation led the British to intervene massively but not evenhandedly. The British largely ignored the arming of the Jewish community, and a British officer, Orde Wingate, even trained Jewish guerrillas. But they cracked down hard on the Palestinians in every way; arms were diligently confiscated and suspects harshly treated. The Arab Higher Committee was disbanded in October 1937 and exiled. Despite the militancy of its chairman Ḥājj Amīn, its members largely represented the relatively moderate well-to-do traditional elite. By default, Palestinian leadership fell into the hands of rural chieftains for many of whom 'moderation' was not a virtue. At the same time Jerusalem lost its pre-eminent place in the Palestinian political scene; according to the data compiled by Porath, of 281 'officers' in the Palestinian revolt only 10 (3.5 per cent) were from Jerusalem (seven of them were from the Ḥusainī family), and only 23 (8 per cent) were from Jerusalem and surrounding villages.[13]

Defeated militarily by the British, the Palestinians by 1939 nevertheless had won a substantial diplomatic victory. With help from several Arab governments they managed to convince the British, mindful of their broader Arab and Muslim interests in the impending world war, to downgrade significantly their commitments to the Zionists. The White Paper of 1939 marked a severe setback for Zionist aspirations. Unfortunately, the Palestinian leadership – Ḥājj Amīn in particular – failed to take advantage of this windfall, even though some appreciated its potential. It remained unbending, but it was incapable of reorganizing itself for renewed armed confrontation. The Zionists, however, redoubled their efforts, realizing that Britain's power was fading. They continued to organize their indigenous military organization, the Haganah, and their 'unofficial' terrorist groups, the Irgun and the Stern Gang. After a lull in local violence during World War II, the conflict resumed in 1944 and 1945. Organized Jewish violence against the British and Arabs (exemplified by the Irgun's bombing of the King David Hotel in 1946), however, was far more systematic and successful than that of the Palestinians, and the latter were unable to play a significant role in the final years of the Mandate. On 29 November 1947 the UN Special Committee on Palestine's majority report was adopted by the General Assembly: partition was recommended, but now on terms much more favourable to the Jews than in the 1936 Peel Commission report, and Jerusalem was to be an international zone, a *corpus separatum*.

The idea of Jewish sovereignty in Jerusalem (or even a part of it) never figured in the political and diplomatic discussions almost until it became a reality by force of Zionist arms in 1948. None of the royal commission reports for Palestine envisioned it. Even the Zionists themselves as late as November 1947 were prepared to accept internationalization, although the notion of Jewish sovereign statehood (as opposed to the Balfour Declaration's ambiguous 'National Home') was filtering into their planning by the early 1940s. Indeed, long after Israel's seizure of the western part of the city in 1948 and the rest of it in 1967 the prevailing international legal position is *corpus separatum*. Today, when we are accustomed to thinking of Jerusalem as an overwhelmingly Jewish-Israeli city, it may seem strange that Jewish control of the city was so strongly resisted. But at the time the UN passed its famous partition resolution, calling for Jerusalem as a *corpus separatum*, the Arab presence – demographic, economic, and social – was inescapable. True, within the narrowly defined municipal boundaries there was a clear Jewish majority – roughly 100,000 Jews to 60,000 Arab Muslims and Christians. But Jerusalem, by virtue of geography and topography, was the economic and administrative centre for central Palestine; as such, it extended organically as a metropolitan area beyond these boundaries. This is why the British had established an extensive Jerusalem sub-district and why the proposed UN international zone included surrounding 'satellite' areas. In this zone the Arab population constituted slightly more than half the total population (around 105,000 Arabs to around 100,000 Jews); and Arabs owned over 80 per cent of the property, while Jews owned only 7 per cent (the remainder belonging either to others or to the State). In the municipality Jewish ownership was still only around 18 per cent.[14] Moreover, owing to the dramatic Jewish influx into Jerusalem during the Mandate, it is sometimes forgotten that the Arab population of the city had also grown considerably. According to data compiled for the Anglo-American Committee of Inquiry in 1945, the Arab population of the Jerusalem municipality increased by 37 per cent between 1922 and 1931, and by 53 per cent between 1931 and 1944 (the comparable Jewish increases were 51 and 89 per cent, respectively).[15] Particularly significant was the growth of a middle and upper class educated Arab community – merchants and professionals – in the modern quarters outside the Old City: Katamon, Muṣrārah, Ṭalbiyya, Upper and Lower Bak'a, the Greek and German colonies, Shaikh Jarrāḥ, Dair Abū Tor, Māmillā, Nabī Dā'ūd, and Shaikh Badr. Economic growth was similar between the two communities: for example, the statistics on new construction between 1936 and 1945 show that Jews accounted for 60 per cent of new rooms, and the Arabs 40 per cent, roughly proportional to their share of population.[16] When the Israelis eventually seized western Jerusalem they acquired whole neighbourhoods of valuable Arab-owned real estate and 'a rich haul' of movable property as well.[17]

Following Britain's decision in February 1947 to transfer its Mandate responsibilities to the UN and the Security Council's approval of the Partition Resolution in November, Zionist military planners appear to have begun actively to prepare to seize by force the Holy City, even though it was far outside the boundaries of the territory allocated for a Jewish state. At the beginning of April, six weeks before the date fixed for termination of the Mandate, the Zionists began to execute military 'Plan Dalet'. The object was to open a corridor from the coast up to Jerusalem and to annex as much of the city as possible to the Jewish state. Cynical psychological warfare conducted against poorly led, unorganized Arab civilian populations was underscored by one of the most infamous terrorist acts of modern times: the Irgun's massacre of over 250 civilians at the village of Deir Yassin on the western outskirts of Jerusalem on 9 April 1948. Following immediately upon the death of 'Abd al-Qādir al-Ḥusainī, the strongest of the Palestinian guerrilla leaders at the nearby village of Qastel, the morale of the civilian population of

Jerusalem and other cities plummeted.

On 26 April the Haganah launched 'Operation Jevussi' against the large, middle-class Arab quarters in western Jerusalem, driving out all of the inhabitants. UN representatives dispatched early in May to establish the city's new international administration were simply ignored by the British and the contesting forces. By 15 May, as the British High Commissioner left the city, the Jewish forces were poised from three directions for an assault on the old walled city. Only with the last-minute intervention of the Transjordanian Arab Legion was the Old City and the adjacent modern quarters to the north and east saved. Tibawi reports that during the fighting the Ḥaram al-Sharīf sustained some shelling, mortar and small arms fire; the Dome of the Rock was hit in several places, and several worshippers were killed or wounded.[18] Glubb Pasha, commander of the Arab legion, later wrote of a revealing incident: a Haganah officer had warned a senior Arab Legion officer some weeks before the end of the Mandate not to interfere with the Haganah in Jerusalem. '"And what will happen if we do?" our officer had enquired. "You will enter Jerusalem only over our dead bodies", the Jewish officer had replied. Perhaps the Jews had long beforehand determined to seize the whole of Jerusalem.'[19]

Despite the UN's reaffirmation of the internationalization plan in December 1948, and indeed on many occasions since then, the city was effectively partitioned along the battle lines established by the second truce of 18 July – the western ramparts of the walled city and a band of deserted buildings and no-man's land. The dislocations wreaked upon the Arabs of Jerusalem were enormous. The western part of the city, where Arabs had owned up to 40 per cent of the property,[20] was now emptied of Arabs. By conservative estimates more than 30,000 people – the entire Arab population of 'new' (western) Jerusalem – had been driven out permanently.[21] By other estimates the number of displaced Arabs was far higher, perhaps 60,000, counting those who fled from the Old City as well or from villages just adjacent to the municipal boundaries.[22] If one includes as well the many villages of the Jerusalem sub-district to the west of the city, which were also largely emptied of Arabs, the figure may be as high as 80,000.[23] It must also be recorded that in the fight to save the Old City, some 2,000 Jews who had lived in the Jewish Quarter were driven out by the Arab Legion.

Neither the Israelis nor King 'Abdullāh of Transjordan, who had emerged over the dispersed local Palestinian leadership as the effective ruler of East Jerusalem, paid heed to the calls from abroad for internationalization. Israel made West Jerusalem its capital in January 1950. Transjordan undertook a series of steps to legitimize its authority in the West Bank, including East Jerusalem, changing the country's name to Jordan and convening a congress of Palestinian notables to ratify the King's authority. Neighbouring Arab states that had vehemently opposed Jordan's assertion of sovereignty in Jerusalem gradually came to accept the *fait accompli*.

THE DIVIDED CITY, 1948–1967

After the guns fell silent, there were two Jerusalems separated only by walls and barbed wire, but as Malcolm Kerr observed they were '. . . politically, economically, socially, and psychologically as far removed as New York and Peking.'[24] The socially and ethnically diverse city was now polarized: the bi-cultural Arab and Jewish western side was all Jewish; and the old Jewish Quarter of the Old City, with its traditional Orthodox community, was a shambles, the surviving Jews expelled and replaced by displaced Arabs. Only foreigners, diplomats and occasionally local Christian pilgrims crossed through the single crossing-point, the so-called Mandelbaum Gate. Jews were now definitively cut off from the Wailing Wall as Jordan refused to allow them through, given the continuing state of war and Israel's refusal to allow Arab refugees to return to their homes. Each side was to accuse the other of desecrating its holy places: Israelis blamed Jordan for allowing the Jewish cemetery on the Mount of Olives to be defiled and neglected; while Arabs were outraged at Israel's destruction of the historic Muslim cemetery in Māmillā that dated back to the Arab conquest and was the burial ground for many famous scholars, mystics, and warriors.[25]

The fortunes of war – which had smiled on the Zionists – had carved out a *de facto* partition unlike anything envisioned by any of the British or international commissions. Even during the episodic course of the 1948 fighting the UN Special Mediator, Count Folke Bernadotte, continued to work for a united city: in his initial proposal issued on 28 June, Jerusalem would have fallen under Arab authority but with strong local autonomy and guarantees for Jewish access to holy places. His revised plan of 16 September (written the day before his assassination by the Zionist Stern Gang) called for internationalization of the entire city under UN auspices, in conformity with the 1947 Partition Resolution. But as the Arab military position weakened, and the rift deepened between Transjordan's King 'Abdullāh and the other Arab states over future control of what remained of Arab Palestine, the Zionists' strength increased; and so did their determination to hold as much of the city as possible and, indeed, make it the capital of the Jewish state.

There were subsequent efforts by the world community to implement internationalization, but these were ineffective. In December 1948 the UN General Assembly reiterated its stand, and Israel's admission to the UN in May 1949 was granted only after Israel agreed to abide by the UN position; but upon admission Israel failed to honour its commitment. The Conciliation Commission for Palestine, created by the General Assembly in December 1948 and composed of representatives from Turkey, France and the United States, tried its hand at engineering a compromise between the *de facto* partition and the UN's decision on internationalization in a plan presented in September 1949; but Israel and Transjordan each opposed it, and other concerned governments were at best lukewarm toward it.[26] King 'Abdullāh explained his opposition thus:

> The demand for the internationalization of Jerusalem was the strangest and most unbalanced of the Arab national aims. It was one that disregarded Arab rights and interests by handing the Holy Places over to international control and wrenching Jerusalem from the possession of the Arabs. It was my duty to stand resolutely and firmly in the defence of the Arab character of the Holy City and resist internationalization in all its aspects.[27]

By the end of 1949 the CCP had removed the Jerusalem question from its agenda. In April 1950 the UN Trusteeship Council made yet another attempt at a workable formulation, again taking internationalization as the basic model, but strong opposition from both Israel and Jordan condemned it to languish. After that effort, there were no further active efforts to implement internationalization or indeed to alter Jerusalem's new situation in any way until Israel's capture of the remaining Arab section in 1967. The UN nevertheless regularly has reiterated its position on Jerusalem and condemned Israel's actions to change the character of the city. So has the United States, despite persistent domestic political pressures to accept Israel's rule as legal.

The Israeli Sector

Even in the days just before the end of the Mandate the Zionist organizations in Jerusalem had refused to co-operate with the UN officials charged with organizing the international municipality for Jerusalem.[28] On 2 August 1948, after it had become clear to the Israelis that they could go no farther in the Holy City, Prime Minister David Ben Gurion declared that the laws of Israel would henceforth apply to Jerusalem. He appointed a military governor for the area, Dov Joseph, and by the end of September the government had definitively renounced internationalization, even though this risked future access to the most important religious and historical parts of the city. In quick succession Israel made other moves to cement its authority in West Jerusalem: the Supreme Court moved there, government offices were transferred; a municipal council was established, West Jerusalemites voted in elections for an Israeli constituent assembly, and finally in December 1949 the Israeli parliament began to meet in Jerusalem. On 23 January 1950 the Knesset (parliament) proclaimed West Jerusalem the capital of the State of Israel.[29] Three years later when the Foreign Ministry was moved there, most countries (including the United States) refused to transfer their embassies from Tel Aviv in order to demonstrate the unacceptability of Israel's unilateral assertion of authority over Jerusalem.

Israeli Jerusalem, according to a former deputy mayor and urban specialist, became a somewhat provincial city over the 1948–67 period. Cut off from the historic Muslim city astride the hilly spine of Palestine, it became the terminus for transport and communications from the sea rather than a meeting point of east–west and north–south axes.[30] It enjoyed modest economic growth, somewhat less than for Israel as a whole, and it lost its former social pre-eminence. Eight out of some twenty-four neighbourhoods could be classified as poor, indicative of considerable income inequality. Tourism did not develop according to expectations. Now too, of course, the Israeli city was cut off from historic Jerusalem, with the Arab and Islamic dimensions almost totally removed; if it was a 'mosaic' it was so entirely in terms of the variegated Jewish communities from different parts of the world that had settled there. The city's educational curriculum, observes Benvenisti, was largely devoid of studies about the Arabs or their history.

The Jewish population of Jerusalem on the eve of the 1948 war was around 100,000; by 1967 Israeli Jerusalem's population was around 197,000. Inadequate housing, red tape, frictions between orthodox and secular communities, and poor public services were among the more important municipal problems; one senses also, at least in reading the autobiography of Mayor Teddy Kollek, that those officials who came before him did not exhibit very effective leadership.[31] Benvenisti criticizes the politicians of the time for neglecting the city's commercial centre and those areas to the east near the armistice line, for allowing slums to develop, and for orienting future development too much to the west.[32] Nevertheless, there were important municipal improvements: the water supply problem was solved when Jerusalem was connected into Israel's National Water Carrier, the pipeline (built by Israel over Arab protests) that tapped the headwaters of the Jordan River in Syria and Lebanon. Important public buildings – libraries, museums, the Knesset building, and a new Hadassah Hospital – were built. A comprehensive urban plan was drawn up in 1950 and revised in 1959.[33] Shaped by European urban sensibilities, albeit with an effort at harmonizing with the local physical environment, the new Israeli Jerusalem displayed a certain Western urban anonymity and little sense of the indigenous Middle Eastern spirit; but certainly it could have been worse. To many residents and visitors the most aesthetically pleasing neighbourhoods were the former Arab quarters like Katamon and Talbiyya, where the fine stone houses stood in sharp contrast to the new jerrybuilt apartment blocks. Without denigrating the efforts which the Israelis made at municipal improvement one must ask, was it really Jerusalem? Disconnected as it was from historical Jerusalem – an Arab-Islamic city – how could it be?

The Jordanian Sector

Jordan meanwhile moved to assert its claim to govern East Jerusalem, which had been saved from the Zionists by its Arab Legion. Assemblies of Palestinian notables convened by King 'Abdullāh in December 1948 ratified Jordan's authority, and in April 1950 the parliament officially approved the annexation of what remained of Arab-controlled Palestine – including of course East Jerusalem – into the Hashemite Kingdom of Jordan.[34] Jordan's justification for taking control of the Palestinian territories has rested in large part on the apparent lack of effective alternative Arab leadership. Similar motivations presumably explained Jordan's attempt after the war to acquire the Arab parts of West Jerusalem and the Bethlehem Road in exchange for ceding the Jewish Quarter of the Old City to Israel.[35]

By the autumn of 1948 it was clear that the Zionists had military superiority and were in a position to acquire additional territory such as the Negev desert and strategically important slivers in the West Bank. The indigenous Palestinian leadership had never recovered from its dispersion by the British during the 1937–38 uprising even though the Arab Higher Committee was reconstituted in 1945. Notables who flocked to form an All-Palestine Government under Egyptian auspices eventually found that the Egyptian connection was not very efficacious – at least not until Gamal Abdel Nasser seized power in Cairo. So with the collapse of indigenous Palestinian capabilities, the centre of Arab power shifted to Amman, and before long many of the Jerusalem notables were aligning themselves with the new order – sitting in the Jordanian parliament, accepting high political and administrative positions.

Some writers have been unduly critical of the Hashemite custodianship of Jerusalem and the West Bank.[36] Certainly there were many flaws, but one should not lose sight of the fundamental legitimizing asset of Jordan's rule and role: it was an Arab government and it was the only Arab government with the capability to contain further Israeli expansion. For two decades it performed this most vital of all functions. On the positive side there was also the imposition of internal order. After the post-war chaos had settled, Jordan worked within its financial and political limits to administer the city, to care for its Muslim and Christian shrines, and to promote tourism and commerce. By respecting *waqf* property inside and outside the old city, writes Schleifer, Jordan 'enabled the city's architectural fabric to survive . . .'[37] A major renovation of the Ḥaram al-Sharīf, supported by several Arab governments and Islamic organizations, was begun in 1958. A new commercial district to the north and east of the Old City was developed.

But various constraints – financial, political, even geographical – inhibited any major development planning effort for eastern Jerusalem. The displacement of tens of thousands of Palestinians in the Jerusalem area during and after the fighting also complicated reconstruction and development. In time, however, Arab Jerusalem recovered. Whatever political problems there may have been, the Jordanian administration brought order and economic growth to both parts of the country. Jerusalem prospered as a tourist centre and benefited in general from the foreign aid and investment that Amman was able to attract and from remittances sent home by Palestinians working in the Arab oil-exporting countries. While income inequality remained a feature of the social scene, the middle and upper classes on the Arab side probably enjoyed a higher quality of life than their counterparts on the Jewish side. Israeli Jerusalemites reportedly were shocked in 1967 when they discovered the quantity and quality of foodstuffs, housing, and foreign-made consumer goods available in East Jerusalem.[38] By the 1960s Arab Jerusalem had recovered to the point where it was a pleasant place to live and certainly a special place to visit: its historical Arab character remained vital, its religious ambience and traditional society intact, and its modernization mercifully moderate.

Nevertheless, the Hashemite tenure over Jerusalem's fortunes had negative as well as positive attributes. The transition from British to Jordanian rule was not without its problems. Some were administrative, others political. On the administrative side were problems in recovery, development, and planning. Jordan's capabilities had been stretched to the limit simply trying to defend Jerusalem; it was hardly in a position to alleviate the enormous distress caused by the uprooting of hundreds of thousands of Palestinians in the Jerusalem area and elsewhere. Even with the substantial assistance rendered by the international community through the UN Relief and Works Agency (UNRWA), living conditions in the city were very difficult for many months. Putting in place an orderly administration to replace the British-run municipality also took time, and differences arose with Amman about a host of administrative issues.

The long-range city planning effort also encountered difficulties, now that the city had split in two. The town planner in the last years of the Mandate, Henry Kendall, had designed a plan for the whole city in 1944;[39] Kendall stayed on after 1948 in Arab Jerusalem, but his conception was steadily eroded by political and commercial pressures. Much the same thing occurred on the Israeli side adjacent to the Old City.

The political problems revolved around the differences between Palestinians and Jordanians. Jerusalem had been the heart and nerve centre of the Palestinian body politic. Palestinian society in the early 1950s was more modern in orientation and better educated than the smaller, poorer society east of the Jordan river. The fact that Amman was the locus of major decision making was unacceptable to many Jerusalemites. In the immediate post-war period, Jerusalem leaders

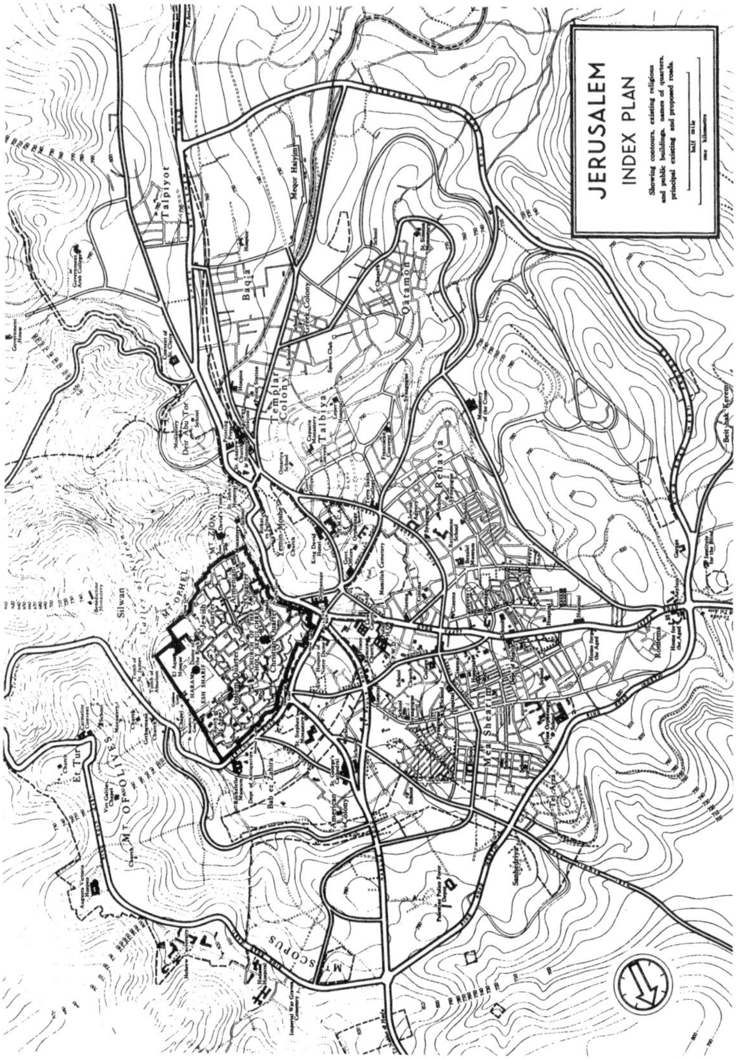

Fig. 14 Jerusalem: Index Plan (source: Henry Kendall, *Jerusalem: The City Plan; Preservation and Development during the British Mandate 1918–1948*, London, 1948. Crown copyright, reproduced by permission of the Controller of Her Majesty's Stationery Office).

complained that the city was not getting enough reconstruction support from Amman; and the assassination of King 'Abdullāh in the Ḥaram al-Sharīf could hardly have improved Amman's relations with the city. In the late 1950s Jerusalem along with the other West Bank towns was the site of numerous protest demonstrations. With the resurgence of Palestinian nationalism in the early 1960s a new, albeit veiled, challenge arose to the relationship between the two parts of the Kingdom. The first meeting of the Palestine Liberation Organization took place in 1964 in East Jerusalem in a building hardly a stone's throw from the armistice line. Looking back over the two decades of Jordanian rule, it seems clear that the East Bank was chosen to receive the bulk of investment and development resources. Certainly the growth of the Amman area was far more extensive than that of Jerusalem or other West Bank towns. It is widely believed that the Jordanian authorities feared that sooner or later Israel would strike again and so had this security incentive to give priority to the East Bank.

Yet at the same time Jordan was becoming more integrated, as demographic, social and economic ties increased between the two banks of the river. Circumstances had driven hundreds of thousands of Palestinians toward Amman, among them some of the most influential Jerusalem families; and King Hussein was going to great lengths to include Palestinian leaders in the government. Under Mayor Rūḥī al-Khaṭīb, who governed from 1957 until 1967, the city experienced stable administration and improved relations with Amman. By 1959 Jerusalem's administrative status was upgraded from *baladiyya* (municipality) to *amāna* ('trusteeship'), a special status equivalent to that of Amman. The king planned to build a palace north of the city to symbolize his presence, and he visited Jerusalem from time to time. The gradual extension of government services and the growing dependence of Jerusalem on Amman all contributed to 'state-building' and integration. On the eve of the 1967 war, despite the political cleavages, Arab Jerusalem and the West Bank for all practical purposes were highly integrated into the Jordanian state.

The Fall of Arab Jerusalem

A traveller just outside Jerusalem on the old winding road to Bethlehem in the summer of 1966 noticed a new and curious sight: at the top of a steep hill a hotel was under construction – what made the sight curious was that the building was in the no-man's land between the Israeli-Jordanian armistice line. This little test of Jordanian and UN resistance was a sign of Israeli confidence and pressure on the *status quo*. It was also a sign of things to come.

Israel's attack on Egypt on 5 June 1967 inexorably pulled Jordan into the conflict, owing to belated inter-Arab agreements and a prevailing assumption that Arab armies could now teach Israel some lessons. Yet in retrospect it is difficult to understand how a commitment to war could have been made when there had been so little military planning. A partial explanation may be that Egyptian and Jordanian leaders were lulled by a flurry of hopeful US-Egyptian diplomatic activity just days before the war and did not actually expect hostilities to commence. By a reliable local account, Jerusalem was only thinly defended on 5 June – by perhaps 5,000 soldiers, with no hope of adequate or timely armoured or air support.[40] By noon on Wednesday, 7 June the Israelis had captured Arab Jerusalem. The Jordanian defenders had done the best they could – some 200 were killed – but neither they nor the civilian population were prepared to give the Israelis really serious resistance.

In the course of the fighting the Israelis had fired shells into the Ḥaram al-Sharīf and bombed a hospice in the Old City. Although atrocities apparently were few, looters followed close behind the advancing troops, and there were cases of mosques being robbed, and the Dead Sea Scrolls were removed from the Palestine Archaeological Museum. The first major act of post-war destruction was the bulldozing of the Maghāriba Quarter next to the Wailing Wall beginning on the evening of 8 June; within a few days this historic *waqf* property was rubble. This action, in contravention of the Geneva Conventions, was only the first step in a massive process of 'urban renewal' that would change the face and skyline of the city within a few years. On 28 June Israel annexed eastern Jerusalem (avoiding, however, the bald term 'annexation'), even though this was in clear violation of international law (the Hague Convention of 1907). At the same time it vastly enlarged the boundaries of the 'reunited' city. Then it dissolved the Arab municipal council and later exiled Mayor Rūḥī al-Khaṭīb to Jordan. Other leaders were to follow him into exile. Defence Minister Moshe Dayan wasted no time in integrating the two parts of the city: walls and barbed wire came down, utility lines were joined, Israeli identity cards issued, and taxes assessed.[41] Although the United States protested the annexation and other illegal measures, the Israelis went right ahead 'creating new facts' to ensure their permanent sovereignty over the entire city.

ISRAELI JERUSALEM AND PROSPECTS FOR THE FUTURE

Israel lost no time in what its leaders liked to call 'creating new facts' in order to cement their control over all Jerusalem, mindful that their title to the city was far from clear. As Crown Prince Hassan of Jordan pointed out in a detailed critique of Israel's legal claims to the city, neither the Hague Regulations of 1907 nor the Geneva Conventions of 1949 support such claims; nor is King David's declaration of 1000 BC an acceptable basis. Similarl, Israels' claims that it had neither occupied nor annexed the city (illegally) but simply was engaging in 'municipal unification' were hardly credible to unbiased students of international law.[42]

The 'reunited' city now contained around 200,000 Jews and 70,000 Arabs. Owing to population flight and gerrymandered boundaries, Arabs now accounted for about a quarter of the city's population. By comparison, in 1947 the population of the Jerusalem area envisaged by the UN as the *corpus separatum* would have been almost equally distributed between Arabs (51 per cent) and Jews (49 per cent), and the distribution in the municipality itself was about 40 per cent Arab.[43] According to the deposed mayor, Rūḥī al-Khaṭīb, some 60,000 fled in 1948, and 5,000 were 'absent' in June 1967, either having fled or been out of the country;[44] estimating some 35,000 offspring from the 1948 exiles, he concluded that there were around 100,000 Jerusalemites in exile.[45] Meanwhile, between 1967 and 1975 Israel succeeded in bringing 35,000 new Jewish immigrants into the city.[46]

Israel also undertook a programme to surround the eastern part of the city with a 'security belt', (euphemistically described as 'urban development') of high rise apartment complexes – French Hill, Ramat Eshkol, Ramot, East Talpiot, and Gilo. These 'housing estates' either displaced, engulfed, or crowded long-established Arab settlements.[47] Several miles farther east, on the slopes down to the Jordan valley, a massive project of urban settlement – Ma'alot Adumim – was constructed, part of Jerusalem's 'outer security belt'. International architects and city planners deplored the new Master Plan for the city, as indeed did some Israeli experts, and some of the more atrocious plans (involving West as well as East Jerusalem) were scrapped or modified.[48] Nevertheless, in what a British journalist described as 'a frenzy of construction'[49] the new masters of Jerusalem began changing the physiognomy of the city more drastically than ever before in its history. In the two decades following the occupation Israel built 26,000 new apartments for Jews in the city, but only 450 for Arabs.[50]

Notwithstanding some significant improvements in the quality of life – more roads, sewage lines, classrooms, and the like – the situation of Arab Jerusalemites remained clearly inferior to that of Jews. For those Arabs determined to remain in the city, life under occupation was onerous, especially for the educated middle class. The conquering state exercised its power of eminent domain, claiming 'public purpose' or security grounds, to expropriate Arab private property. To be sure, it came to be done cloaked in legal form rather than by outright forcible eviction as had been practised on the thousand or so luckless inhabitants of the demolished Maghāriba Quarter. There were large expropriations such as the seizure of 840 acres along the Ramallah Road in 1969, and smaller ones directed at individual Arab owners of desirable plots, such as in the Government Hill area. Between 1967 and 1977 it was estimated that they had seized some 15,000 dunums.[51] Excavations and other intrusions into the Ḥaram al-Sharīf and the expropriation of other *waqf* properties brought many protests from the Muslim Council and from international bodies, notably UNESCO. The Muslim custodians of al-Aqṣā Mosque feared that the Israeli excavations might undermine its foundations.[52]

Beginning in 1978 an orthodox Jewish *yeshiva* called Ateret Cohanim, funded largely by American Jews, began acquiring Arab property in the Muslim quarter of the Old City: within ten years it owned more than 70 buildings.[53]

The crackdown on political expression took the form of expulsions of prominent Palestinians, such as the mayor and the chief Muslim *qāḍī*, Shaikh 'Abd al-Ḥamīd al-Sāyiḥ; and the practice continues to the present day as indicated by the expulsion of Akram Haniye, editor of the Jerusalem newspaper *Al-Sha'b* in December 1986. Resistance to occupation was harshly punished. The practice of blowing up houses of suspects, Benvenisti assures us, came to an end in March 1969. But Jerusalem Arabs (especially the youth), like their compatriots elsewhere in the West Bank, and notwithstanding their Israeli 'citizenship', lived – and still live – with the lurking fear of being detained by the security police and abused. Such fears are particularly acute whenever a violent incident occurs – and they have been occurring, with greater or lesser frequency, up to the present. In 1977 *The Sunday Times* of London published an extensive investigative report on Israel's use of torture against the Arabs in the occupied territories, and it singled out Jerusalem's infamous Russian Compound detention centre as the site of some particularly brutal interrogation practices, employed on female as well as male detainees.[54] In 1979 US consular officials in Jerusalem reported similar practices.[55]

Israelization of the educational curriculum created problems for young Jerusalem Arabs whose chances of going on to higher education in Israel were very poor but who were now ill-prepared and even stigmatized when trying to advance to universities in Arab countries. The integration of East Jerusalem into the Israeli economy also created hardships for Arab businessmen. The hotel and tourist trade, backbone of the local economy, suffered heavily from the privileged competition of Jewish enterprises and, of course, from the loss of business from the Arab world. Construction activities were severely constricted by Israeli regulations and the shortage of investment capital. The Arab-owned Jerusalem Electricity Company was threatened with takeover by the Israelis. The professions – law, medicine, education, and engineering – could offer few career opportunities. For local merchants and consumers the 'new economic order' meant restrictions on imports, new and higher taxes, and the necessity of coping with Israel's high inflation and its weak currency.

Jerusalem's Arabs also complained of a deterioration in the moral climate as bars, disrespectful tourists and even prostitutes began to appear for the first time in or around the Old City. Certainly 1967 brought some benefits in terms of improved municipal services and social welfare benefits; yet the sense of being second-class citizens (the right to vote in Israeli elections hardly compensates for the loss of Arab authority) is as pervasive in the 1980s as it was immediately after the occupation.[56] Finally, it might be remarked that Israel's occupation effectively prevented Arab Muslims or Christians (except those Palestinian-Jordanians able to obtain permits to visit relatives; and after 1979, Egyptians) from visiting the holy places – a condition little noted in the West, where Jordan's previous denial of Israeli access to the Wailing Wall was widely criticized, despite the state of war between the two countries.

Israel's conduct in Jerusalem continues to disturb the international community. In 1979 the Security Council created a commission to investigate the problem of settlements and other alterations in the occupied territories, including Jerusalem, in violation of the Geneva Conventions. The commission carried out its investigations without Israel's co-operation and a year later the Security Council passed a resolution determining:

> that all measures taken by Israel to change the physical character, demographic composition, institutional structure or status of the Palestinian and other Arab territories occupied since 1967, including Jerusalem, or any part thereof, have no legal validity . . .[57]

The resolution was passed unanimously but later the United States declared that its affirmative vote had been a mistake and that it really had meant to abstain. On 30 July 1980 the Israeli Knesset passed a 'basic law' proclaiming all Jerusalem (east and west) the capital of Israel. This highly symbolic and provocative move appeared to be a defiant riposte to the Security Council's censure resolution and was yet another reflection of the rise of the militant right-wing in Israeli politics. Israel's action generated international protests, including new censure resolutions from the Security Council and the General Assembly. Of the only thirteen states that had established embassies in Jerusalem, eleven removed them to Tel Aviv, where the other embassies are located out of refusal to accept Israel's control of Jerusalem as legitimate. In the United States, however, pro-Israel congressmen renewed their campaign to require the State Department to move the US embassy in Tel Aviv to Jerusalem.

Jerusalem's Future

In 1985 the Israel correspondent of *The New York Times* wrote a lengthy assessment of the twenty-year tenure of Teddy Kollek as mayor of Jerusalem. It is a laudatory piece, and Mayor Kollek comes across as an able politician, quite successful in administration, development, and most importantly the management of intercommunal tensions – between Jews and Arabs, and between orthodox and secular Jews. Kollek is popular with the Arabs and he receives their votes, and he acts to temper the growing extremism of some groups within Israel. The city itself after nearly two decades of Israeli rule appears prosperous and orderly. But *The Times*'s correspondent observes that it will be difficult to find a successor to the seventy-four-year-old mayor who possesses his conflict-management skills, and he quotes a rabbi who warns that unless 'a pluralistic sensibility takes hold' then 'there will come an explosion of fantasy that will wash this city with blood'.[58]

Despite its present image of normality and prosperity, to anyone with a sense of history Jerusalem is a city in danger. First, it is endangered with the further dilution of its Arab-Islamic heritage. A one-time resident of the Old City illustrated the matter by drawing a comparison between Jaffa and Jerusalem:

> I must confess that I now fear for Islamic Jerusalem what has happened to the traditional quarter of Jaffa – a brilliant restoration job and technically worthy of study – the physical frame of Jaffa's Islamic core brilliantly preserved, the inner structure rewired, reinforced and replastered. But the moral implications are, to say the least, deeply disturbing – the transfer of a once vital but morally conservative Arab quarter into a Muslim-free bohemian artistic quarter and red light district. May God spare Jerusalem such a restoration.[59]

Second, it is endangered by the failure of all those concerned with and for the city to solve the deep political conflict of which Jerusalem is both symbol and victim. In the distance looms the probability of new Arab-Israeli wars, in which Jerusalem might endure far more destruction than it has in past conflicts. But in the more immediate future another kind of physical threat exists. This is the threat of localized violence between Arabs and Jews. The Palestinian uprising that began in December 1987 (and was still underway a year later) shocked Israel, especially when it spread to Arab Jerusalem. It also reminded the Arab countries and the rest of the world of the continuing volatility of the Palestine problem. From the beginning of the occupation, localized violent protest by Palestinians had occurred throughout the territories but not at a level that involved a serious challenge to the Israeli security apparatus. Bombings and sabotage by Palestinian guerrillas or local groups took place in Jerusalem sporadically after 1967, particularly in the early years of occupation, and up to the beginning of the *intifāḍa*, as marked by the grenade explosions near the Wailing Wall in 1986. Violent acts by individual Arabs also occurred, such as the stabbing of an Israeli in the Old City in November 1986, which triggered a week of anti-Arab rioting.

At the same time another and more potent kind of violence –

attacks by militant Jews on Islamic holy places and on Palestinian Arabs – was taking place and, indeed, gathering momentum.

The *Intifāḍa*

The *intifāḍa* erupted on 9 December 1987, seventy years to the day from Allenby's entry into Jerusalem. Triggered by an incident in Gaza, the uprising was the product of an accumulation of Palestinian tensions and grievances. Less than a week later General Ariel Sharon inaugurated his newly acquired apartment in the Muslim quarter of Jerusalem's Old City – a highly provocative and symbolic act by a man regarded as the *bête noire* of Palestinian nationalism. In mid-January the *intifāḍa* broke out in the heart of Arab Jerusalem itself, as Israeli security forces used tear gas around the two especially sacred mosques in the Ḥaram al-Sharīf, trying to disperse Palestinian demonstrators. Accustomed to thinking of Jerusalem and its Arab population as an integral part of Israel, Israelis were shocked by the solidarity with the *intifāḍa* being demonstrated in East Jerusalem. The Jerusalem merchants and professional people observed the authority of the clandestine Unified Command in adhering to the rules for opening, closing and strikes. Although less intense than in Gaza and the other West Bank towns, Jerusalem continued to experience violence and protest; in July 1988 the first Arab Jerusalemite – a 15 year-old boy – was killed by Israeli troops in the Old City.

By the time the *intifāḍa* marked its first anniversary, it had already had a profound impact on the politics and diplomacy of the Arab-Israeli conflict. Spurred largely by the uprising, Jordan definitively renounced its theoretical role as agent for the Palestinians; the Palestinian Liberation Organization declared itself definitively in favour of a two-state solution, recognizing Israel's right to exist, accepted UN Resolution 242, and renounced terrorism; and the United States agreed to open official contacts with the PLO. The effect of the *intifāḍa* on Israel, however, appears to be a hardening of the attitudes toward Palestinian aspirations, as indicated by the 1988 election results which eventually led to a renewal of the leadership of Prime Minister Yitzhak Shamir.

The Palestinian Declaration of Independence of 15 November 1988 proclaimed 'the establishment of the State of Palestine on our Palestinian territory with its capital Jerusalem (Al-Quds al-Sharīf).' For their part, Israel's leaders categorically refused to negotiate with the PLO, refused to countenance the idea of a Palestinian state, and rejected totally the idea of surrendering sovereignty over any part of Jerusalem, let alone allowing the Palestinians to declare it their capital. But the impasse on the international level seemed to have been broken as the idea of a two-state solution gained acceptance. And the *intifāḍa* continued. In the absence of movement toward an overall settlement that would take account of Palestinian political rights and religious sensibilities, it seemed unlikely that the disturbances would die down. Whether Israel might then seek forcibly to expel tens or hundreds of thousands of Palestinians, including Arab Jerusalemites, whether it would succeed in doing so, and whether this 'solution' would succeed in pacifying the occupied territories, remained to be seen.

Conclusion

The problem of Jerusalem is often said to be the most difficult aspect of the Arab-Israeli conflict, and diplomats have argued that therefore it should not be tackled until easier issues have been dealt with. If nothing else, this narrative should have shown that the problem is indeed difficult, but that does not mean that it should be 'put on the back burner', in the phraseology of American foreign policy planners. If a Jerusalem solution is dependent upon a larger Arab-Israeli settlement, it is hard to imagine the latter being achieved without an agreement on Jerusalem. The present situation of Israel's *de facto* total control is neither just nor, in the long run, a stable solution. The Palestinian claim to total control, although strongly supported by history and until recently demography, is probably negotiable, mainly because of today's power realities; and the Palestine Liberation Organization appears to have accepted the idea of settling only for eastern Jerusalem as part of the two-state solution to the whole conflict. The *corpus separatum* 'internationalization' solution remains the position of the world community and has been regularly reaffirmed since 1947. Although the Soviet Union no longer supports internationalization the other major powers do, along with the Vatican and other Christian churches. Yet since 1967, and the promulgation of UN Security Council Resolution 242, the emphasis has shifted toward the illegality of Israel's continued occupation of territories seized in 1967 – meaning eastern Jerusalem – rather than the western part which Israel seized in 1948. Nevertheless, *corpus separatum* has 'continuing relevance'.[64] The Vatican's position too has softened, having moved from advocating an international regime for the city (in 1948) to international supervision for the holy places in a city that could be under national sovereignty.[65]

It is true that Israel's official position is totally unyielding in its insistence on total control of the city; but many thoughtful Israelis have discussed various kinds of power-sharing arrangements that might be possible in the context of an overall Arab-Israeli settlement.[66] The Palestinians, having now accepted the two-state solution, seem more disposed to accept sharing Jerusalem. Walid Khalidi, a prominent Palestinian figure, has proposed:

> – the designation of West Jerusalem as the capital of Israel, East Jerusalem as the capital of Palestine. Extraterritorial status and access to the Jewish holy places would be assured, and a Grand Ecumenical Council formed to represent the three monotheistic faiths (with rotating chairmanship), to oversee interreligious harmony. Reciprocal rights of movement and residence between the two capitals with agreed-upon limits would be negotiated.[67]

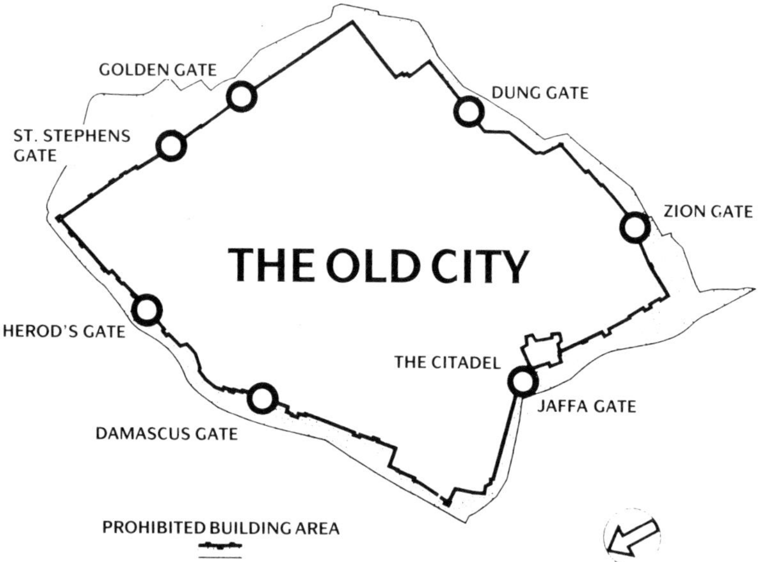

Fig. 15 The 1929 Scheme

Clearly there are no simple answers to the Jerusalem problem. Yet the dangers to the city are too serious to permit it to fester unattended. The many friends of Jerusalem in the world would be doing a service if they would promote active and creative discussion about the city's future. These include those who can speak for the three religions for whom the city is so holy as well as those who can influence the policies of the states and political communities directly involved – Israel, the Palestinians, Jordan and the other Arab states. In the search for an overall settlement ideas such as shared or dual sovereignty,[68] cantonization, or even re-partition without walls might – if properly developed – help solve not only the Jerusalem problem but the entire conflict.

NOTES

The writer would like to acknowledge the help of his research assistant, Emily Rayyes, a student in the Master's Degree Program in Arab Studies at Georgetown University. See the bibliography for full details of works cited.

1 *Survey of Palestine*, I, 151; Frankel, *The Washington Post*, June 2, 1987.
2 The anecdote is told by Bertha Spafford Vester, the proprietor of the American Colony Hotel in *Our Jerusalem*, 319.
3 Vester, 318; but he does not see the Arab residences and buildings draped with black flags, she adds.
4 See Ashbee, *Jerusalem, 1918–1920* and *Jerusalem, 1920–1922*.
5 Storrs, 301.
6 Samuel, 181.
7 To mark the transfer from military to civilian government the retiring governor asked Samuel for a receipt which read 'Received from Major-General Sir Louis Bols one Palestine complete.' Vester, 303.
8 Lesch, 40–41.
9 Storrs, 372.
10 On the history of the Wailing Wall controversy, see Tibawi, 'Jerusalem: Its Place in Islam and Arab History', 35–42.
11 Mattar, ch. 3, 60–75; see also Porath, I, ch. 7.
12 On the slide towards armed resistance, see Lesch, ch. 9, esp. 208–27; Porath, II, chs. 7–9; and the chapters by David Waines, Barbara Kalkas, and Richard Verdery in I Abu-Lughod, part III, 203–304.
13 Porath, II, appendix B.
14 John and Hadawi, II, 271, citing Government of Palestine data; see also Hirst, 232, citing UN data, and Aamiry, 9.
15 *Survey of Palestine*, I, 148, 151.
16 *Survey of Palestine*, II, 789.
17 Hirst, 232–34.
18 Tibawi, 'Jerusalem . . .', 44.
19 Glubb, 107.
20 Cattan, 98.
21 From British Mandate population estimates for November 1947 cited in al-'Ārif, 191; see also Benvenisti, 43–44.
22 See, e.g. Hirst, 237, quoting Rūḥī al-Khaṭīb; and Schleifer, 43.
23 Janet Abu Lughod, 159, arrives at this figure, projecting from 1946 Mandate census data and 1944 data from the Anglo-American Committee of Inquiry.
24 Kerr, in Abu Lughod (ed.), 358.
25 Tibawi, *Islamic Pious Foundations in Jerusalem*, 49.
26 Forsythe, 65–67.
27 King 'Abdullāh of Jordan, *My Memoirs Completed*, 13.

28 Kerr, 356.
29 Benvenisti, *Jerusalem: The Torn City*, 6–15; Mallison, 214.
30 Benvenisti, 39 and ch. 3, passim.
31 Teddy Kollek, *For Jerusalem*, ch. 12.
32 Benvenisti, *Jerusalem: The Torn City*, 39.
33 Sharon, 132–33.
34 Crown Prince Hassan, *Palestine Self-Determination*, 40–41.
35 Cattan, 131–32; cf. Benvenisti, *Jerusalem: The Torn City*, 10.
36 See, e.g., Daniel Rubenstein, 'The Jerusalem Municipality under the Ottomans, British, and Jordanians', ch. 4 in Kraemer, 72–99.
37 Schleifer, 'Islamic Jerusalem . . .', 173.
38 Benvenisti, *Jerusalem: The Torn City*, 60–62, argues strongly to the contrary, but then is forced to qualify his findings.
39 See Henry Kendall, *Jerusalem: The City Plan*, ch. 5.
40 Schleifer, 166 and passim.
41 Neff, 311–14.
42 HRH Hassan bin Talal, *A Study on Jerusalem*, 27–39.
43 One might also note that Arabs comprised 62 per cent of the *subdistrict* of Jerusalem (the city and surrounding villages) at the end of the Mandate. See Cattan, *Jerusalem*, 96.
44 Cattan, *Jerusalem*, 71, cites an International Red Cross estimate of 7,000 and other estimates of up to 30,000.
45 Al-Khaṭīb, quoted in Hirst, *The Gun and Olive Branch*, 237.
46 Benvenisti, *Jerusalem: The Torn City*, 253.
47 Benvenisti claims that 'the Arab mind' did not see a close connection between these housing projects and Jerusalem. *Jerusalem: The Torn City*, 247.
48 See the informed critique by Arthus Kutcher, esp. 54–55 and ch. IV.
49 David Hirst, 'Israel in Jerusalem', 29.
50 Frankel, *The Washington Post*, June 2, 1987.
51 Hirst, *The Gun and the Olive Branch*, 232. A dunum equals about a quarter acre.
52 For details about the Israeli depredations, see Tibawi, 35–41.
53 Robert I Friedman, *The Washington Post*, January 10, 1988
54 'Israel and Torture', *The Sunday Times* (London), 19 June, 1977.
55 *The Washington Post*, 7 February, 1979; and *The Christian Science Monitor*, 4 April, 1979.
56 For vignettes that convey these feelings, see Halsell, *Journey to Jerusalem*, 12–36 and passim; also Hudson, 'Jerusalem: A City Still Divided', 1969.
57 SC Res. 465, March 1, 1980; cited in Mallinson, 224.
58 Thomas L Friedman, 'Teddy Kollek's Jerusalem', *The New York Times Magazine*, 4 August, 1985.
59 Abdallah Schleifer, 'Islamic Jerusalem as Archetype of a Harmonious Urban Development', *Saqqaf*, 149–75, 172.
60 Cattan, 74.
61 Halsell, 'Shrine Under Siege', 10–12.
62 *The Washington Post*, 12 April and 15 April, 1982.
63 *The New York Times Magazine*, 15 January, 1986, and 6 August, 1986.
64 See the Mallisons' informed analysis, 209–29, 228.
65 See Irani, ch. 2.
66 See, e.g., the interesting ideas of Heller, 116–26.
67 Walid Khalidi, 'Toward Peace in the Holy Land', 788.
68 See, e.g., the interesting ideas of Heller, 116–26.

BIBLIOGRAPHY

Chapter I

Albright, W F, 'The Amarna Letters from Palestine', *CAH*, vol. II, ch. XX.
'The Egyptian Empire in Asia in the Twenty-first Century BC', *JPOS*, vol. III, 1928.
Bottero, J, 'Syria during the third dynasty at Ur', *CAH*, vol. I, ch. XXI, part 4.
de Vaux, R, 'Les Patriarches hébreux et les découvertes modernes', *RB*, 55, 1948.
Eggers, H J, *Einführung in die Vorgeschichte*, Munich, 1959.
Galling, K, 'Die Nekropole von Jerusalem', *PJB*, 32, 1936.
Biblisches Reallexicon^2, 1977.
Gunkel, H, 'Mythus und Mythologie', *Die Religion in Geschichte und Gegenwart*, IV, 2nd ed.
Hauer, C, 'Who was Zadok?', *JBL*, 1963.
Hayes, J H and J Maxwell Miller, *Israelite and Judaean History*, London, 1984.
Hayes, W C, 'Chronology, Egypt – to end of twentieth dynasty', *CAH*, vol. I, ch. VI, part 1.
Henton Davies, G, 'An approach to the problem of Old Testament Mythology', *PEQ*, 88, 1956.
Kenyon, K M, *Digging up Jerusalem*, London, 1974.
Amorites and Canaanites, London, 1963.
Archaeology in the Holy Land, London, 1979.
Knudzon, J A, *Die El-Amarna-Tafeln*, Leipzig, 1907.
Macalister, R A S and J G Duncan, 'Excavations on the Hill of Ophel, Jerusalem 1923–1925', *Palestine Exploration Fund Annual*, London, 1926.
Maisler, B, 'Das vordavidische Jerusalem', *JPOS*, vol. X, 1930.
Mallon, A, 'Jérusalem et les documents égyptiens', *JPOS*, vol. VIII, 1928.
Neuville, I, 'Le Préhistorique de Palestine', *RB*, 1934.
Noth, M, *The Old Testament World*, London, 1966.
Peter, M, 'Wer sprach den Segen nach Genesis xiv 19 über Abraham aus?' *VT*, vol. XXIX, 1979.
Posener, G, 'Syria and Palestine during the twelfth dynasty', *CAH*, vol. 1, ch. XXI, part 2.
Saller, S J, *The excavations at Dominus Flevit*, part II, 'The Jebusite burial place', Jerusalem, 1964.
Schmitt, J J, 'Pre-Israelite Jerusalem' in C D Evans, W W Hallo and J B White, *Scripture in context, essays on the comparative method*, Pittsburg, 1980.
Seters, J V, 'The terms "Amorite" and "Hittite" ', *VT*, vol. XXII, 1972.
Sethe, N, *Die Ächtung feindlicher Fürsten, Völker und Dingen auf altägyptischen Tongefäßscherben des Mittleren Reiches*, Berlin, 1926.
Shiloh, Y, 'Excavations at the City of David I, 1978–1982', *Qedem*, 1984.
Simons, J, *Jerusalem in the Old Testament*, Leiden, 1952.
Skinner, J, 'Genesis', *ICC*, 1930.
Smith, R H, 'Abraham and Melchizedek', *ZAW*, LXXVII, 1965.
Stoltz, F, 'Strukturen und Figuren im Kult von Jerusalem', *BZAW*, 118, Berlin, 1970.
Terrien, S, 'The Omphalos Myth and Hebrew Religion', *VT*, vol. XX, 1970.
Thompson, Th. L, 'The Historicity of the patriarchal Narratives', *BZAW* 133, Berlin, 1974.
Vandermeersch, B, *De Evolutie van de mens*, Natuur en Techniek, 1982.
Vincent, L-H and A M Steve, *Jérusalem de l'ancien Testament*, IIIème partie, Paris, 1956.
Wensinck, A J, *The ideas of the Western Semites concerning the Navel of the Earth*, Amsterdam, 1916.

Chapter II

The Physical History of Jerusalem
The physical history of Jerusalem has been clarified to a great extent by archaeological excavations since the 1960s. An excellent brief summary with maps is given by A D Tushingham in *Atlas of the Biblical World*, by Tushingham and Denis Baly, New York, 1971, ch. 6. Some modification of

this description, which was largely based on the excavations of Kathleen Kenyon (see *Digging up Jerusalem*, London, 1974), was made necessary by further excavations. More recent discoveries and modifications of earlier conclusions are given by N Avigad in *Discovering Jerusalem*, Nashville, 1983. A valuable compendium of older information is found in J Simons, *Jerusalem in the Old Testament*, Leiden, 1952, and in *Jérusalem de l'ancien Testament*, I–III, Paris, 1954–56, by L-H Vincent and M-A Steve. The standard biblical histories, for example, by John Bright, *A History of Israel*, 3rd ed., Philadelphia, 1981, and J Alberto Soggin, *A History of Ancient Israel*, Philadelphia, 1985, mention, but do not go into detail, the fact that the population of Jerusalem was non-Israelite and polytheistic, nor do they discuss the cultural and religious consequences of that incorporation of pagan urban populations into the political state of Judah that took place with the empire of David, not only in Jerusalem, but also in most parts of ancient Palestine.

The History of Biblical Jerusalem

From the time of King David the history of Jerusalem was inextricably bound up with the history of the monarchy and its various successors. Only recently has it been realised that there was a difference between that monarchy and the religious tradition that the monarchy claimed as the basis for its legitimacy, in spite of the fact that both the histories and the prophetic writings condemn almost all of the kings of Judah and all of the kings of 'Israel'. Therefore, the following histories of Judah and the schismatic state of Israel in the biblical period will exhibit considerable differences in treatment, and often considerable success in ignoring fundamental issues. A major part of the problem is the fact that with very few exceptions the authors are innocent of any understanding of peoples and cultures other than of Europe and North America.

Bright, John, *A History of Israel*, 3rd ed., Philadelphia, 1981.

Maxwell Miller, J and John H Hayes, *A History of Ancient Israel and Judah*, Philadelphia, 1986.

Soggin, J Alberto, *A History of Ancient Israel: From the Beginnings to the Bar Kochba Revolt, AD 135*, Philadelphia, 1985.

Herrmann, S, *History of Israel in Old Testament Times*, 2nd ed., Philadelphia, 1980.

Noth, Martin, *The History of Israel*, 2nd ed., Philadelphia, 1959. An old classic still followed in main outline by much of European scholarship.

Hayes, J H and J Maxwell Miller, *Israelite and Judaean History*, Philadelphia and London, 1977. A collection of essays by various scholars almost none of whom are historically orientated. It is useful primarily for the voluminous bibliography included in each chapter.

The following works (to which the history of John Bright should be added) have broken away from old 19th century theories and methods in favour of a more adequate historical and cultural understanding of ancient Near Eastern social processes.

Mendenhall, George E, *The Tenth Generation: The Origins of the Biblical Tradition*, Baltimore, 1973.

Herlon, Gary, *The Social Organization of Tradition in Monarchic Judah*, unpublished dissertation, Ann Arbor, Michigan, 1982. Demonstrates the great contrast between the ideology of the monarchy and the authentic Yahwistic tradition.

Freedman, D N and David F Graf, eds., *Palestine in Transition: The Emergence of Ancient Israel*, Sheffield, 1983. A collection of essays by six scholars centering on new views of the origins of the biblical community and the controversial application of modern social science methodology.

Gottwald, Norman K, *The Tribes of Yahweh: A Sociology of the Religion of Liberated Israel, 1250–1050 BCE*, Maryknoll, New York, 1979. A ludicrous and irresponsible attempt to force biblical history into the categories of 19th century Marxism. Mentioned here only because it is receiving attention from some socialist-oriented circles.

Chapter III

Abel, F M, *Histoire de la Palestine*, Paris, 1952.

Avi-Yonah, Michael, *The Jews of Palestine*, Oxford, 1976.

Avigad, N, *Discovering Jerusalem*, Nashville, Tennessee, 1983.

Blomme, R, 'Faut-il revenir sur la datation de l'Arc de l'"Ecce Homo"?', *Revue Biblique*, 1979.

Cyril of Scythopolis, *Life of Euthymius* (tr. Festugière).

Dio Cassius, *Roman History* (Loeb vol. VII).
Eusebius, *Ecclesiastical History*, 4, 6 (tr. McGiffert in series *Nicene and Post-Nicene Fathers*).
Life of Constantine (tr. McGiffert, *NPNF*).
Onomasticon, *GCS*.
Gregory of Nazianzus, *Or. V. contra Julianum*, (*GCS*).
The History of Barsauma of Nisibis, ed. F Nau, *Resumé de Monographies Syriacques*, 8(18), 1913.
Hüttenmeister, F and G Reeg, *Die antiken Synagogen in Israel, (BTAVO)*, Wiesbaden, 1977.
Itinerarium Burdigalense in *Corpus Christianorum*.
James, M R, *The Apocryphal New Testament*, Oxford, 1924.
Jerome, *Epistles* (tr. W H Fremantle, *NPNF*).
Josephus, *Antiquities of the Jews*.
War of the Jews.
Junior, Philosophus, ed. A Riese, *Geographi Latini Minores*, Heilbron, 1878.
Libanius, *Letter*.
Melito of Sardis, *On Pascha*, ed. S G Hall.
Paschal Chronicle in *Patrologia Graeca*.
Philostorgius, ed. J Bidez, *GCS*.
Procopius of Caesarea, *The Buildings of Justinian* (Loeb vol. VII, p. 347).
Sebeos, *Histoire d'Heraclius*, tr. F Macler, Paris, 1904.
Sophronius, *On the Birthday of Christ*, ed. H Usener, *Kleine Schriften*, Leipzig, 1913.
Strabo, *Geography*, XVI (Loeb vol. VII).
Strategius, *Capture of Jerusalem*, ed. and tr. G Garitte, *CSCO*.
Wilkinson, J, *Egeria's Travels*, Warminster, 1981.
Jerusalem Pilgrims before the Crusades, Warminster, 1977.

Chapter IV

Abu 'Ubayd, *Kitāb al-Amwāl*, Cairo, 1968.
Abu Zurā'a, *Tārīkh*, ed. Sh. N al-Qujani, Damascus, 1980, 2 vols.
Anon, *Arabische Chronik*, Band XI (von elbaladori elbagdadi), ed. W Ahlwardt, Griefeswald, 1883.
'Ārif, 'Ārif al-, *Al Mufaṣṣal fī Tārīkh al-Quds*, 1961.
'Asali, K J al-, *Ajdādunā fī Tharā Bait al-Maqdis*, Amman, 1981.
Makhṭūṭāt Faḍā'il Bait al-Maqdis, Amman, 1981.
Azdī, al-, *Futūḥ al-Shām*, ed. A M 'Amir, Cairo, 1970.
Tārīkh al-Mawṣil, ed. A Ḥabība, vol. II, Cairo, 1967.
Balādhurī, al-, *Ansāb al-Ashrāf*, I, ed. M Hamidullah, Cairo, 1959.
Ansāb, IV, pt. 1, ed. Schlessinger and Kister, Jerusalem, 1971.
Futūḥ al-Buldān, ed. de Goeje, Leiden, 1968.
Basawī, al-, *Kitāb al-Ma'rifa wa-'l-Tārīkh*, ed. A Z al-'Umari, Baghdad, 1974–76, 3 vols.
Baihaqī, al-, *Sunan*, Hyderabad, 1344–55 AH, 10 vols.
Bukhārī, al-, *Ṣaḥīḥ*, ed. M A Sabih, Cairo (n.d.), 9 pts in 3 vols.
Bustī, al-, Muḥammad b. Ḥibbān, *Mashāhīr 'Ulamā' al-Amṣār*, ed. Fleischhammer, Cairo, 1959.
Creswell, K A C, *Early Muslim Architecture. Umayyads, 622–750*, 2nd ed., Oxford, 1969.
Donner, F, *The Early Muslim Conquest*, Princeton, 1981.
Duri, A A, *The Rise of Historical Writing among Arabs*, tr. C I Conrad, Princeton, 1983.
Eutychius, *History*, ed. L Cheikho, Beirut, 1905, 1909, 2 vols.
Goitein, S D F, *Studies in Islamic History and Institutions*, Leiden, 1966.
Goldziher, I, *Muslim Studies*, tr. C R Barber and S M Stern, London, 1967.
Ḥanbalī, al-, Mujīr al-Dīn, *Al-Uns al-Jalīl*, Beirut, 1973, 2 vols.
Harawī, al-, *Al-Ishārāt ilā Ma'rifat al-Ziyārāt*, ed. Janine Sourdel-Thomine, Damascus, 1953.
Ḥimyarī, al-, *Al-Rawḍ al-Mi'tar*, ed. Iḥsān 'Abbās, Beirut, 1975.
Ibn 'Abd al-Ḥakam, *Sīrat 'Umar b. 'Abd al-'Azīz*, ed. A 'Ubaid, Damascus, 5th ed., 1967.
Ibn 'Abd Rabbihi, *Al-'Iqd al-Farīd*, ed. A Amin et al., Cairo, 1940–49, 6 vols.
Ibn 'Asākir, *Tahdhīb Tārīkh Ibn 'Asākir*, ed. A Q Badran, Damascus, 1329/1911, 2 vols.
Tārīkh Dimashq, I, ed. S al-Munajjid, Damascus, 1951.

Ibn A'tham al-Kūfī, *Futūḥ*, I, Hyderabad, 1968.
Ibn al-Athīr, *Al-Kāmil fī 'l-Tārīkh*, Beirut, 1979, 13 vols.
Ibn al-Faqīh, *Al-Buldān, BGA*, V, ed. de Goeje, Leiden, 1885.
Ibn Ḥajar, *Al-Isāba*, Cairo, 1934, 4 vols.
Ibn Ḥanbal, *Musnad*, Beirut, 19XX, 6 vols.
Ibn Isḥāq, *Sīra*, ed. M Hamidullah, Rabat, 1976.
Ibn al-Jawzī, *Faḍā'il al-Quds*, ed. J Jabbur, Beirut, 1979.
Ibn Kathīr, *Al-Bidāya wa-'l-Nihāya*, Dār al-Fikr al-'Arabī, 1932, 13 vols.
Ibn Khaldūn, *Kitāb al-'Ibar, I, (Muqaddima)*, reprint of Bulaq ed., Beirut, 1970.
Ibn Māja, *Sunan*, ed. M F 'Abd al-Baqi, Cairo, 1952–3, 2 vols.
Ibn al-Qalānisī, *Dhail Tārīkh Dimashq*, ed. F Amedroz, Beirut, 1908.
Ibn Qayyim al-Jawziyya, *Aḥkām Ahl al-Dhimma*, ed. Subhi al-Salih, Damascus, 1961.
Ibn Sa'd, *Kitāb al-Ṭabaqāt*, ed Wüstenfeld, Leiden, 1866–76, 9 vols.
Ibn Taghribardī, *Al-Nujūm al-Zāhira*, Cairo, 1929, 12 vols.
'Imara b. Wāthima, *Kitāb Bad' al-Khalq wa-Qaṣaṣ al-Anbiyā'*, R G Khoury, Wiesbaden, 1978.
Jahshiyārī, al-, *Kitāb al-Wuzarā' wa-'l-Kuttāb*, ed. al-Saqqa et al., Cairo, 1938.
Khalīfa b. Khayyāṭ, *Tārīkh*, ed. S Zakkar, Damascus, 1968, 2 vols.
Khaṭīb, al-, al-Baghdādī, *Tārīkh Baghdād*, Cairo, 1931, 14 vols.
Kindī, al-, *Kitāb al-Wulāt wa-Kitāb al-Quḍāt*, ed. R Guest, Beirut, 1908.
Maqdisī, al-, al-Muṭahhar b. Ṭāhir, *Kitāb al-Bad' wa-'l-Tārīkh*, ed. C Huart, Paris, 1899–1918, 6 vols.
Aḥsan al-Taqāsim, reprint of de Goeje, Leiden, 1906, Beirut; also Philadelphia, 1982.
Muthīr al-Gharām, ed. A S Khalidi, Yaffa, 1365 AH.
Mas'ūdī, *Murūj al-Dhahab*, ed. and tr. Barbier de Meynard and Pavet de Corteille, Paris, 1861–77, 9 vols.
Michael I, Jacobite Patriarch of Antioch, *Chronique de Michael le Syrien*, ed. and tr. J B Chabot, Brussels, 1963, 4 vols.
Muhallabī, *Al-Masālik wa-'l-Mamālik*, a fragment ed. by Munajjid in *Majallat Ma'had al-Makhṭūṭāt al-'Arabiyya*, I, 1958.
Mukhliṣ, 'Abdullāh, 'Al-Ṭarīq min Dimashq ilā Bait al-Maqdis', *Majallat al-Khashshāf*, vol. 2, no. 1, 1928.
Munajjid, S, *Mu'jam Banī Umayya*, Beirut, 1970.
Muqātil b. Sulaimān, *Tafsīr*, vol. 1, ed. M Shihata, Cairo, 1969.
Musharraf, al-, b. al-Murajja' al-Maqdisī, *Faḍā'il Bayt al-Maqdis wa-'l-Khalīl wa-Faḍā'il al-Shām*, ms, Tübingen University Library no. 381.
Muslim, *Ṣaḥīḥ*, ed. 'Abd al-Baqi, Cairo, 1955, 5 vols.
Mutaqqī al-Hindī, 'Alī, *Kanz al-'Ummāl*, Hyderabad, 1364–85 AH, 13 vols.
Na'nā'a, R, *Al-Isrā'ilyyāt*, Beirut, 1970.
Nasā'ī, al-, *Sunan*, Beirut, 1930, 8 pts. in 4 vols.
Nāṣir-i Khusrau, *Riḥla (Safarnāma)*, Ar. tr. Y al-Khashshab, Cairo, 1945.
Naṣr b. Muzāhim, *Wa'qat Siffīn*, ed. A S M Harun, 2nd ed., Cairo, 1382 AH.
Qalqashandī, al-, *Ṣubḥ al-A'sha*, Cairo, 1919–22, 14 vols.
Al-Ināfa fī Ma'athir al-Khilāfa, ed. A S Farraj, Kuwait, 1964, 3 vols.
Ṣan'ānī, al-, *Al- Musannaf*, ed. Habib al-Rahman al-Azami, Beirut, 1970, 11 vols.
Shamma, Samīr, 'Al-Nuqūd wa-'Urubat al-Quds', *Majallat al-Quds al-Sharif*, no. 10, Jan 1986.
Suyūṭī, Shams al-Dīn, *Itḥāf al-Akhiṣṣa bi-Faḍā'il al-Masjid al-Aqṣā*, ed. A R Muhammad, Cairo, 1984, 2 vols.
Ṭabarī, *Jami' al-Bayān*, ed. A M Shakir, Cairo, 1960–61, 16 vols., and Cairo, 1323–29 AH, 30 pts.
Tārīkh, ed. de Goeje et al., Leiden, 1879–1901, 15 vols.
Ṭarṭūshī, *Kitāb al-Ḥawādith wa-'l-Bida'*, ed. M Talbi, Tunis, 1959.
Theophanes, *The Chronicle of Theophanes*, tr. H Turtledove, Philadelphia, 1982.
Tritton, A S, *The Caliphs and their Non-Muslim Subjects*, repr. London, 1970.
van Berchem, M, *Materiaux pour un Corpus Inscriptionum Arabicarum*, IIème, Jerusalem 'Ḥaram', 1922.
Wāqidī (pseudo), *Futūḥ al-Shām*, Cairo, (n.d.), 2 vols.

Wāṣitī, *Faḍā'il al-Bait al-Muqaddas*, ed. A Hasson, Jerusalem, 1979.
Wellhausen, J, *The Arab Kingdom and its Fall*, Ar. tr. Abu Rida, Cairo, 1968.
Wensinck. A J et al., *Concordance et Indices de la Tradition Musulmane*, Leiden, 1936–69, 7 vols.
Ya'qūbī, *Tārīkh*, ed. Houtsma, Leiden, 1969, 2 vols.

Chapter V

'Abbās, Iḥsān 'Riḥla-t Ibn al-'Arabī ilā Mashriq kamā sawwarahā Qānūn al-Ta'wīl', *al-Abḥath*, vol. 21, pt. 1, March 1968.
'Abd al-Laṭīf al-Baghdādī, *Al-Ifāda wa-'l-I'tibār*, ed. Ahmad Gh Sabana, Damascus, 1983.
Abu 'l-Fidā, *Al-Mukhtaṣar fī Akhbār al-Bashar*, III, Beirut, n.d..
Anon, *Akhbār al-Dawla al-Saljūqiyya min Mir'at al-Zamān*, ed. A Savim, Ankara, 1968.
Anon, *Anonymous Pilgrims* in *PPTS*, IV, New York, 1971 (reprint of 1894 ed.).
Anon, *The Pilgrim of the Russian Abbot Daniel in the Holy Land*, 1106–1107 AD, tr. C W Wilson, New York, 1971 (reprint of 1895 ed.), in *PPTS*, IV.
Anon, [?]*Cartulaire Sepulchre*, 1849, 83–85, as tr. in Peters, *Jerusalem, the Holy City in the Eyes of Chroniclers . . .*, Princeton, 1985.
Anon, [?]*Description of the Holy Land*, tr. Aubrey Stewart, *PPTS*, V, New York, 1971.
'Asali, Kamal al-, *Wathā'iq Maqdisiyya Tārīkhiyya*, I, Amman, 1983.
Burgoyne, M H and Amal Abul Hajj, 'Twenty-four Medieval Arabic Inscriptions from Jerusalem', *Levant*, vol. XI, 1979.
Burgoyne, M H, 'A recently discovered Marwānid inscription in Jerusalem', *Levant*, vol. XIV, 1982.
Mamlūk Jerusalem, London, 1987.
Canard, M, 'Djarrāḥids', EI^2.
Finucane, Roland, *Soldiers of the Faith*, London and Melbourne, 1983.
Fulcher of Chartres, *A History of the Expedition to Jerusalem*, 1095–1127, tr. S Fink, New York.
Hiyari, Mustafa A, *al-Imāra al-Ta'iyyah*, Amman, 1977.
Howarth, Stephen, *The Knights Templar*, London, 1982.
Ibn al-Athīr, *al-Kāmil fī 'l-Tārīkh*, X, Beirut, 1979.
Ibn al-Qalānisī, *Tārīkh Dimashq*, ed. S Zakkar, Damascus, 1983.
Ibn Myassar, *al-Muntaqa min akhbār Miṣr*, ed. Ayman F al-Sayyid, Cairo, 1981.
Ibn Shaddād, *al-Nawādir al-Sulṭāniyya fī 'l-Maḥāsin al-Yūsufiyya*, ed. M J al-Shayyal, Cairo, 1964.
Ibn Taghribardī, *Al-Nujūm al-Ẓāhira fī Mulūk Miṣr wa-'l-Qāhira*, VI (reprint).
Ibn Wāṣil, *Mufarrij al-Kurūb fī Akhbār Banī Ayyūb*, IV, ed. Hasanien Rabi', Cairo, 1972.
Ipşirli, M and M D Tamimi, (eds.), *Awqāf wa-amlāk al-Muslimīn fī Filasṭīn*, Istanbul, 1982.
Iṣfahanī, al-, *al-Fatḥ al-Quṣṣī fī 'l-Fatḥ al-Qudsī*, ed. M M Subuh, Cairo, (n.d.).
Join-Lambert, Michel, *Jerusalem*, tr. Charlotte Haldane, London, 1966.
La Monte, John, *Feudal Monarchy in the Latin Kingdom of Jerusalem*, New York, 1970 (reprint of 1932 ed.).
Maqrīzī, al-, *Itti'āz al-Ḥunafā' bi-akhbār al-a'immah al-Fāṭimiyyīn al-Khulafā'*, vol. II, ed. Muhammad H M Ahmad, Cairo, 1971, III, ed. M H Ahmad, Cairo, 1973.
Mayer, Hans E, *The Crusades*, tr. John Gillingham, Oxford, 1972.
Mujīr al-Dīn, *Al-Uns al-Jalīl bi-Tārīkh al-Quds wa-'l-Khalīl*, Amman, 1973.
Nāṣir-i Khusrau, *Diary of a journey through Syria and Palestine*, tr. Guy Le Strange, *PPTS*, vol. 4, London, 1893 (reprint, New York, 1971).
Safarnāma, Ar. tr. Yahya al-Khashshab, 3rd ed., Beirut, 1983.
Prawer, J, *The Latin Kingdom of Jerusalem*, London, 1972.
' "Minorities" in the Crusader States', *A History of the Crusades*, V, ed. Zacour and Hazard, Madison, 1985.
'Social Classes in the Latin Kingdom: the Franks', *A History of the Crusades*, V, ed. Zacour and Hazard, Madison, 1985.
'The Origin of the Court of Burgesses', *Crusader Institutions*, Oxford, 1980.
'The Patriarch's Lordship in Jerusalem', *Crusader Institutions*, Oxford, 1980.
Richard, J, *The Latin Kingdom of Jerusalem*, tr. Janet Shirley, Amsterdam, 1979.
Riley-Smith, J, *The Knights of St John in Jerusalem and Cyprus, c. 1050–1310*, London, 1967.

Runciman, S, *A History of the Crusades, vol. I: The First Crusade and the Foundation of the Kingdom of Jerusalem*, New York, 1964.
Russel, Josiah C, 'The Population of the Crusader States', *A History of the Crusades*, vol. V *The Impact of the Crusades on the Near East*, ed. Norman P Zacour and Harry W Hazard, Madison, 1985.
Setton, K, (ed), *A History of the Crusades vol. 1: The First Hundred Years*, ed. Harry W Hazard.
Sibṭ Ibn al-Jawzi, *Mir'at al-Zamān*, Bibliothèque Nationale Ms., VIII, Hyderabad, 1370 AH.
Tibawi, A L, *The Extant Pious Foundations in Jerusalem*, London, 1987.
'Umarī, al-, *Masālik al-Abṣār fī Mamālik al-Amṣār*, section ed. Ayman F Sayyid, Cairo.
William of Tyre, *A History of Deeds Done Beyond the Seas*, 2 vols., tr. Emily A Babcock and A C Krey, New York, 1976, reprint of 1941 ed., I.
Yahya b. Sa'id, *Tārīkh*, Beirut, 1909.

Chapter VI

'Ārif al-'Ārif, *Al-Mufaṣṣal fī Tārīkh al-Quds*, Jerusalem, 1961.
Asali, K J, *Ma'āhid al-'Ilm fī Bayt al-Maqdis*, Amman, 1981.
Makhṭūṭāt Faḍā'il Bait al-Maqdis: Dirāsa wa-Bīblīyughrāfiyā, 2nd ed., Amman, 1984.
Wathā'iq Maqdisiyya Tārīkhiyya, I, Amman, 1983.
Ayalon, David, 'Discharges from Service, Banishments and Imprisonments in Mamluk Society', *Israel Oriental Studies*, 1972, II.
Berchem, Max van, *Matériaux pour un corpus inscriptionum arabicarum, Jérusalem 'Ville'*, Cairo, 1922-23, *Jérusalem 'Ḥaram'*, Cairo, 1925-27.
Butrus Abu-Manneh, 'The Georgians in Jerusalem in the Mamluk Period', *Egypt and Palestine*, ed. Cohen and Baer.
Cahen, Claude, and Ibrahim Chabbouh, 'Le testament d'al-Malik aṣ-Ṣāliḥ Ayyūb', *Bulletin d'Etudes Orientales*, XXIX, 1977.
Cleve, Thomas C van, 'The Crusade of Frederick II', *A History of the Crusades*, ed. Kenneth Setton, II.
'The Fifth Crusade', *A History of the Crusades*, ed. Setton, II.
Darrāj, Ahmad, *Wathā'iq Dayr Ṣayhūn bi'l-Quds al-Sharīf*, Cairo, 1968.
Drory, Joseph, 'Jerusalem during the Mamluk Period (1250–1517)', *The Jerusalem Cathedre*, Jerusalem, 1981.
Gibb, H A R, 'The Aiyūbids', *A History of the Crusades*, ed. Setton, II.
Goitein, S D, 'al-Ḳuds', *EI²*, V.
Gottschalk, Hans L, *Al-Malik al-Kāmil von Ägypten und seine Zeit*, Wiesbaden, 1958
Hasson, Issac, 'Muslim Literature in Praise of Jerusalem: Faḍā'il Bayt al-Maqdis', *The Jerusalem Cathedre*, Jerusalem, 1981.
Humphreys, R Stephen, *From Saladin to the Mongols: The Ayyubids of Damascus, 1193–1260*, Albany, 1977.
Ibn Shaddād, *Al-Nawādir al-Sulṭāniyya wa-'l-Maḥāsin al-Yūsufiyya, Recueil des historiens des Croisades: Historiens orientaux*, Paris, 1884, III.
Kessler, Christel M and Michael H Burgoyne, 'The Fountain of Sultan Qāytbāy in the Sacred Precinct of Jerusalem', *Archaeology in the Levant, Essays for Kathleen Kenyon*, ed. by P R S Moorey and P J Parr, Warminster, 1978.
Lane-Poole, Stanley, *Saladin and the Fall of the Kingdom of Jerusalem*, reprint Beirut, 1964.
Little, D P, *A Catalogue of the Islamic Documents from al-Ḥaram aš-Šarīf in Jerusalem*, Wiesbaden, 1984.
'Ḥaram Documents Related to the Jews of Late Fourteenth Century Jerusalem', *Journal of Semitic Studies*, vol. 30, no. 2, 1985, 227–264.
'Jerusalem and Egypt during the Mamluk Period', *Egypt and Palestine*, ed. Ammon Cohen and Gabriel Baer, New York, 1984.
Lutfi, Huda A, *A Study of al-Quds during the Late Fourteenth Century Based Primarily on the Haram Estate Inventories*, unpublished McGill University dissertation, 1983. (This dissertation was published in 1985 in Berlin.)

Maqrīzī, al-, *A History of the Ayyūbid Sultans of Egypt Translated from the Arabic of al-Maqrīzī*, by R J C Broadhurst, Boston, 1980.
Matthews, Charles D, 'A Muslim Iconoclast (Ibn Taimiya and the 'Merits' of Jerusalem and Palestine)', *Journal of the American Oriental Society*, LVIC, 1936.
Mitchell, R J, *The Spring Voyage: The Jerusalem Pilgrimage in 1458*, London, 1964.
Muhammad Umar Memon, *Ibn Taimiya's Struggle against Popular Religion*, The Hague, 1976.
Mujīr al-Dīn al-'Ulaimī, *Al-Uns al-Jalīl bi-Tārīkh al-Quds wa-'l-Khalīl*, Amman, 1973.
Oleg Grabar, 'al-Ḳuds: Monuments', EI^2, V.
Painter, Sidney, 'The Third Crusade: Richard the Lionhearted and Philip Augustus', *A History of the Crusades*, ed. Setton, 2nd ed., Madison, 1969.
Prescott, H F M, *Jerusalem Journey: Pilgrimage to the Holy Land in the Fifteenth Century*, London, 1954.
Qalqashandī, al-, *Ṣubḥ al-A'shā fī Sinā'at al-Inshā'*, Cairo, 1913–19.
Rashād al-Imām, *Madīnat al-Quds fī 'l-'Aṣr al-Wasīṭ (1253–1516 m.)*, Tunis, 1976.
Risciani, Noderto, *Documenti e Firmani*, Jerusalem, 1931.
Runciman, Steven, *A History of the Crusades*, London, 1965, 3 vols.
Shoshan, Boaz, 'On the Relations between Egypt and Palestine: 1382–1517 AD', *Egypt and Palestine*, ed. Ammon Cohen and Gabriel Baer, New York, 1984.
Sivan, E, 'Le caractère sacré de Jérusalem dans l'Islam aux XIIè–XIIIè siècles', *Studia Islamica*, XVII, 1967.
'The Beginnings of the *Faḍā'il al-Quds* Literature', *Israel Oriental Series*, 1971.
Slane, W M de, *Ibn Khallikan's Biographical Dictionary Translated from the Arabic*. Paris, 1843, II.
Ziada, Mustafa M, 'The Mamluk Sultans to 1293', *A History of the Crusades*, ed. Setton, II.

Chapter VII

'Abbās, Iḥsān, 'Al-Ḥayāt al-'Umrāniyya wa-Thaqāfiyya fī Filisṭīn fi 'l-Qarn al-Sābi' 'Ashar (1010–1112 AH)' in *Al-Mustaqbal al'Arabī*, VI, March 1979.
Abu Manneh, Butrus, 'The Hussainis, the Rise of a Notable Family in the 18th Century' in *Palestine in the Late Ottoman Period*, ed. D Kuschner, Jerusalem, 1986.
'Ārif al-'Ārif, *Al-Massīḥiyya fī 'l-Quds*, Jerusalem, 1951.
Al-Mufaṣṣal fī Tārīkh al-Quds, Jerusalem, 1961,
Tārīkh Qubbat al-Ṣakhra al-Musharrafa wa-'l-Masjid al-Aqṣā al-Mubārak, Jerusalem, 1955.
Akademie der Wissenschaft der UdSSR, *Weltgeschichte*, vol. 4 and 5, German translation, Berlin, 1964, 1966.
'Asalī, K J al-, *Ma'āhid al-'Ilm fī ait al-Maqdis*, Amman, 1981.
Makānāt al-Quds 'Arabiyyan wa-Islāmiyyan 'abr al-Tārīkh, manuscript.
Min Āthārinā fī Bait al-Maqdis, Amman, 1982.
'Al-Tāba' al-Islāmī al-Dawlī li'-l-'Ulamā' allādhīna 'ammu al-Quds wa-'āshu fihā', *al-Quds al-Sharīf*, 8, Amman, November 1985.
Wathā'iq Maqdisiyya Tārīkhiyya, I, Amman, 1983, II, Beirut, 1985.
'Al-Ta'līm fī Filasṭīn' in *Encyclopaedia Palaestina (Al-Mawsū'a al-Filisṭīniyya*, forthcoming.
Arvieux, Laurent d', *Mémoires du Chevalier d'Arvieux*, II, Paris, 1775.
Avigad, Nahman, *Discovering Jerusalem*, Nashville, Tennessee, 1983.
'Awra, al-, Ibrāhīm, *Tārīkh Wilāyat Sulaimān Pāshā al-'Ādil*, Sidon, 1936.
'Ayyāshī, al-, Abu Sālim 'Abdullāh, *Riḥlat al-Shaikh al-Imām al-'Allāmah al-Qudwa al-Humām, al-'Ārif al-Kabīr wa-'l-Muḥaqqiq al-Shahīr Abi Sālim Sīdī 'Abdullāh al-'Ayyāshī*, Fez, n.d.
Baer, Gabriel, 'The Dismemberment of Awqaf in Early 19th century Jerusalem', *Asian and African Studies*, XIII, no. 3, 1979.
'Jerusalem's Families of Notables and the Waqf in the Early 19th Century', *Palestine in the Late Ottoman Period*, ed. D Kuschner, Jerusalem, 1986.
Bakhīt, M Adnān, *The Ottoman Province of Syria in the 16th Century*, Beirut, 1982.
Buraik al-Dimashqī, Mikhā'il, *Tārīkh al-Shām, 1720–1782*, ed. A Ghassān Sibano, Damascus, 1402/1982.
Burinī, al-, Ḥassan b. Muḥammad, *Tarājim al-A'yān min Abnā' al-Zamān*, vol. 2, ed. al-Munajjid, Damascus, 1963.

Çelebi, Evliya (Mehmed Zilli oğlu), *Evliya Çelebi Siyāhatnāmesi*, vol. 13, Özyadin Matbaasi, Istanbul, 1971.
Chateaubriand, F R de, *Oeuvres romanesques et voyages*, vol. 2, Paris, 1969.
Cohen, Amnon and Gabriel Baer, *Egypt and Palestine*, Jerusalem, 1984.
Cohen, Amnon, *Jewish Life under Islam: Jerusalem in the Sixteenth Century*, Cambridge, Mass., and London, 1984.
Cohen, Amnon and Bernard Lewis, *Population and Revenue in the Towns of Palestine in the 16th Century*, Princeton, 1978.
Dabbāgh, al-, Muṣṭafā, *Bilādunā Filisṭīn – Fī Bait al-Maqdis*, pt. 10, Beirut, 1376/1976.
Encylopaedia of Islam, 2nd ed., vol. V, article 'al-Ḳuds', Leiden, 1980.
Farīd Bey, Muḥammad, *Tārīkh al-Dawla al-'Aliyya al-'Uthmāniyya* (offset), Beirut, 1977.
Feridun Bey, Ahmed (d. 1583), *Munsha'āt al-Salāṭīn*, pt. I, Istanbul, 1274–75/1857–58.
Gerber, Haim, *Ottoman Rule in Jerusalem (1890–1914)*, Berlin, 1985.
Gharaybah, 'Abd al-Karīm, *Sūrriya fī 'l-Qarn al-Tāsi' 'Ashar*, (1840–76), Cairo, n.d.
Gibb, Sir H A R and Harold Bowen, *Islamic Society and the West*, vol. I, pt. 1 and pt. 2, London, 1967, 1969.
Gilbert, Martin, *Jerusalem, Rebirth of a City*, London, 1985.
Ḥanbalī, al-, Mujīr al-Dīn, *Al-Uns al-Jalīl bi-Tārīkh al-Quds wa-'l-Khalīl*, Amman, 1973.
Heyd, V, *Ottoman Documents on Palestine 1552–1615*, Oxford, 1960.
Hitti, P K, *History of the Arabs*, London, 1970.
co-authors: Edward Jurji and Gibra'il Jabbur: *Tārīkh al-'Arab (Muṭawwal)*, pt. II, 4th ed., Beirut, 1965.
Hourani, Albert, *The Emergence of the Modern Middle East*, London, 1981.
Hurewitz, J, *The Middle East and North Africa in Modern Politics*, vol. I, *European Expansion 1535–1914*, 2nd ed., New York, 1975.
Ḥusainī, al-, Ḥasan b. 'Abd al-Laṭīf, *Tajārim Ahl al-Quds fī Qarn al-Thānī 'Ashar*, ed. S S Nu'aimat, Amman, 1985.
Hütteroth, D and K Abdulfattah, *Historical Geography of Palestine, Transjordan and Southern Syria*, Erlangen, 1977.
Imām, al-, Rashād, *Madīnat al-Quds fī 'l-'Aṣr al-Wasīṭ*, Tunis, 1976.
Ipşirli, Mehmed and Mohammad Da'oud al-Tamīmī (eds.), *Awqāf wa-Amlāk al-Muslimīn fī Filasṭīn*, Istanbul, 1982.
Ibn Iyās al-Ḥanafī, Muḥammad b. Aḥmad, *Badā'i' al-Ẓuhūr fī Waqā'i' al-Duhūr*, 2nd ed., M Muṣṭafā, pt. V, Cairo, 1380/1961.
Khairallah, Shereen, 'The Chevalier d'Arvieux, Remarks on his Trips to Palestine (1660),' *The Third Conference on Bilād al-Shām*, vol. II, Amman, 1984.
Khalīdī, al-, Rūḥī, *Al-Muqaddima fī 'l-Mas'alah al-Sharqiyya*, Jerusalem, n.d.
Khalīdī, al-, A S, *Ahl al-'Ilm baina Miṣr wa-Filisṭīn*, Jerusalem, n.d.
Riḥlāt fī Diyār al-Shām, Jaffa, 1946.
Khalīlī, al-, M, *Wathīqa Maqdisiyya Tārīkhiyya*, ed. I M Husseini and A S Abu Lail, Jerusalem, 1979.
Khiyārī, al-, al-Madanī, Ibrāhīm b. 'Abd al-Raḥmān (d. 1083/1672), *Tuḥfat al-Udabā' wa-Salwat al-Ghurabā'*, pt. II, ed. R Samirrā'ī, Baghdad, 1979.
Kupferschmidt, Uri, 'Connections of the Palestinian 'Ulamā' with Egypt', *Egypt and Palestine*, ed. A Cohen and G Baer, New York, 1984.
Kurd 'Alī, Muḥammad, *Khiṭaṭ al-Shām*, pt. II, 3rd ed., Beirut–Damascus, 1403/1983.
Landmann, Sh, *Aḥyā' A'yān al-Quds khārij Aswārihā fī'l-Qarn al-Tāsi' 'Ashar*, Tel Aviv, n.d.
Leyblich, Badia Y, *Travels of Ali Bey (between the years 1803–1807)*, 2 vols., London, 1861.
Luqaimī, Muṣṭafā Aḥmad, *Mawānih al-Uns fī Riḥlati li-wādi 'l-Quds*, ms, University of Jordan Library, cat. no. 915, 642 104
Manīnī, al-, *Al-I'lām bi-Faḍā'il al-Shām*, ed. A S Khalīdī, Jerusalem, n.d.
Mannā', A, *A'lām Filisṭīn fī Awākhir al-'Ahd al-'Uthmānī (1800–1918)*, Jerusalem, 1986.
"Umar effendī al-Naqīb al-Ḥusainī wa-Naqābat al-Ashrāf fi 'l-Quds', *Majmū'at Buḥūth 'Arabiyya Muhdāt ila 'l-Duktur I M Ḥusainī*, , no date or place.
'The Sijill as Source for the Study of Palestine during the Ottoman Period with special reference to the French Invasion', *Palestine in the Late Ottoman Period*, ed. David Kushner, Jerusalem, 1986.

Maqqarī, al-, Aḥmad b. Muḥammad, *Nafḥ al-Ṭīb min Ghusn al-Andalus al-Ratīb*, vol. I, Cairo.

Maundrell, H, *A Journey from Aleppo to Jerusalem*, Beirut, 1963.

Muḥibbī, Muḥammad, *Khulāṣat al-Athar fī A'yān al-Qarn al-Ḥādī 'Ashar*, Cairo, 1284 AH.

Muradī, Muḥammad Khalīl, *Silk al-Durar fī A'yān al-Qarn al-Thānī 'Ashar*, vols. 1–4, Baghdad.

Nabulsī, al-, 'Abd al-Ghānī, *Al-Mukhtār min Kitāb al-Ḥaḍra al-Unsiyya fī 'l-Riḥla al-Qudsiyya*, ed. and abbrev. I Nimr, Nablus, 1972.

  Riḥlatī ila 'l-Quds al-Mussamat al-Ḥaḍra al-Unsiyya fī 'l-Riḥlat al-Qudsiyya, Cairo, 1902.

Neophytos of Cyprus, *Annals of Palestine 1821–1841*, tr. S N Spyridon, *JPOS*, vol. 18, Jerusalem, 1938.

Nimr, al-, Iḥsān, *Tārīkh Jabal Nablus wa-'l-Balqa'*, pt. I, 2nd ed., Nablus, 1395/1975, pt. II, Nablus, 1961.

Perlmann, Moshe, *'A Seventeenth Century Exhortation Concerning al-Aqṣā"* Israel Oriental Studies, 3, 1973.

Peters, F E, *Jerusalem, the Holy City in the Eyes of Chroniclers, Visitors, Pilgrims and Prophets*, Princeton, 1985.

Philipp, Thomas, 'Jews and Arab Christians, their Changing Position in Politics and Economy in Eighteenth Century Syria and Egypt', *Egypt and Palestine*, ed. A Cohen and G Baer, Jerusalem, 1984.

Rāfiq, 'Abd al-Karīm, *Al-'Arab wa-'l-'Uthmāniyyūn(1516–1914)*, 1st ed., Damascus, 1974.

  Bilād al-Shām wa-Miṣr min al-Fatḥ al-'Uthmānī ilā Ḥamlat Napoleon (1516–1798), Damascus, 1967.

  Buḥuth fī 'l-Tārīkh al-Iqtiṣādī wa-'l-Ijtimā' li-Bilād al-Shām fī 'l-'Aṣr al-Ḥadīth, Damascus, 1985.

Registers of the Sharī'a Court in Jerusalem.

Rustum, A, *Al-Uṣūl al-'Arabiyya li-Tārīkh Sūrriyya fī 'Ahd Muḥammad 'Alī Pasha*, vol. I, Beirut, n.d.

Seetzen, U J, *Reisen durch Syrien, Palästina etc.*, ed. F Krause, 4 vols., Berlin, 1854–59.

Sharon, Moshe, 'The Political Role of the Bedouins in Palestine in the Sixteenth and Seventeenth Centuries', *Studies on Palestine during the Ottoman Period*, ed. N Ma'oz, Jerusalem, 1975.

Stephan, St H, tr., 'Evliya Tschelebi's Travels in Palestine', *Quarterly of the Department of Antiquities in Palestine*, VIII, 1938, and IX, 1939.

Taghribardī, Ibn, Jamāl al-Dīn Abu'l-Maḥāsin, *Al-Nujūm al-Zāhira fī Mulūk Miṣr wa-'l-Qāhira*, pt. 6, Cairo, 1936.

Tapu Tahrir Defteri (Ottoman Land Register).

Volney, M C F, *Travels through Syria and Egypt in the Years 1783, 1784, and 1785*, tr. from French in 2 vols., republished London, 1972.

Ya'cub, M S, *Nāḥiyat al-Quds al-Sharīf fī 'l-Qarn al-'Ashir al-Hijrī/al-Sādis 'Ashar al-Mīlīdī*, unpublished MA thesis, University of Jordan, 1986.

Chapter VIII

'Ābidī, al-, Maḥmūd, *Qudsunā*, Cairo, 1972.

Abu Manneh, B, 'The Rise of the Sanjak of Jerusalem in the Late 19th Century', in Gabriel Ben-Dor (ed.), *The Palestinians and the Middle East Conflicts*, Ramat Gan, 1978.

'Ārif al-'Ārif, *Al-Mufaṣṣal fī Tārīkh al-Quds*, Jerusalem, 1961.

  Al-Nakba, vol. 2, Sidon and Beirut, 1957.

Asad, al-, Nāṣir al-Dīn, *Muḥammad Rūḥī al-Khālidī – rā'id al-baḥth al-tārīkhī al-ḥadīth fī Filasṭīn*, Cairo, 1970.

'Audāt, al-, Ya'qūb, *dMin a'lām al-fikr wa-'l-adab fī Filasṭīn*, Amman, 1976.

'Awad, 'Abd al-'Azīz Muḥammad, *Mutaṣarrifiyyāt al-Quds fī 'l-'Ahd al-'Uthmānī 1874–1914*, PhD. thesis, 'Ain Shams University, Cairo, 1970.

'Awad, 'Abd al-'Azīz Muḥammad, 'Al-Haraka al-'Arabiyya fī Mutaṣarrifiyyat al-Quds', *Majallat al-Sharq al-Awsaṭ*, 1, 1974.

Bauer, Leonhard, *Volksleben im Lande der Bibel*, Leipzig, 1903, ch. 32 ('Jerusalem im 19. Jahrhundert')

Ben-Arieh, Y, 'The Growth of Jerusalem in the Nineteenth Century', *Annals of the Association of American Geographers*, 65/2, 1975.
Jerusalem in the 19th century. The Old City, Jerusalem and New York, 1984.
Carmel, Alex, *Die Siedlungen der würtembergischen Templer in Palästina 1868–1918*, Stuttgart, 1973.
Palästina-Chronik 1853 bis 1882, Ulm, 1978, and *Palästina-Chronik 1853 bis 1914*, Ulm, 1983.
Cuinet, Vital, *Syrie, Liban et Palestine. Géographie Administrative, Statistique, Descriptive et Raisonée*, Paris, 1896–1901.
Devereux, Robert, *The First Ottoman Constitutional Period*, Baltimore, 1963.
Gatt, G, *Beschreibung über Jerusalem und seine Umgebung*, Waldsee, 1877.
Gerber, Haim, *Ottoman Rule in Jerusalem 1890–1914*, Berlin, 1985.
Gilbert, Martin, *Jerusalem – Rebirth of a City*, London, 1985.
Hajjar, Joseph, *L'Europe et les Destinées du Proche-Orient (1815–1848)*, n.p. 1970.
Hawārī, al-, Irfān Sa'īd Abū Ḥamad, *A'lām min arḍ al-salām*, Haifa, 1979.
Herzl, Theodor, *Gesammelte zionistische Werke*, vol. 5, Tel Aviv, 1935.
Hofman, Yitzhak, 'The Administration of Syria and Palestine under Egyptian Rule (1831–1840)' in Moshe Ma'oz (ed.), *Studies on Palestine during the Ottoman Period*, Jerusalem, 1975.
Hopkins, I W J, 'The Four Quarters of Jerusalem', *Palestine Exploration Quarterly*, 103, 1971.
Kark, Ruth and Shimon Landman, 'The Establishment of Muslim Neighbourhoods in Jerusalem, outside the Old City, during the Late Ottoman Period', *Palestine Exploration Quarterly*, 112, 1980.
Kark, Ruth, 'The Jerusalem Municipality at the End of the Ottoman Rule', *Asian Affairs*, 14, 1980.
Karpat, Kemal H, *Ottoman Population 1830–1914*, Madison, 1985.
Khader, Bichara, *Histoire de la Palestine*, 2 vols., Tunis and Algiers, 1976–77.
Khalidi, Rashid Ismail, *British Policy towards Syria and Palestine 1906–1914*, London, 1980.
'The 1912 Election Campaign in the Cities of Bilad al-Sham', *International Journal of Middle East Studies*, 16/4, 1984.
Khālidī, Rūḥī, *Al-Muqaddima fī 'l-Mas'ala al-Sharqiyya*, Jerusalem, n.d.
Kupferschmidt, Uri M, 'Connections of the Palestinian 'Ulamā' with Egypt and Other Parts of the Ottoman Empire' in Amnon Cohen and Gabriel Baer (eds.), *Egypt and Palestine*, Jerusalem and New York, 1984.
Lieber, Alfred E, 'An Economic History of Jerusalem' in John M Oesterreicher and Anne Sinai (eds.), *Jerusalem*, New York, 1974.
Luncz, A M, *Jerusalem, Jahrbuch zur Beförderung einer wissenschaftlich genauen Kenntnis des jetzigen und des alten Palästinas*, I, 1881, Vienna, 1882.
Ma'oz, Moshe, *Ottoman Reform in Syria and Palestine 1840–1861*, Oxford, 1968.
Mandel, Neville J, *The Arabs and Zionism before World War I*, Berkeley, 1976.
Mannā', 'Ādil, 'Cultural Relations between Egyptian and Jerusalem 'Ulamā' in the Early Nineteenth Century, in Gabriel R Warburg and Gad G Gilbar (eds.), *Studies in Islamic Society. Contributions in Memory of Gabriel Baer*, Haifa, 1984.
Mannā', 'Ādil, 'Yūsuf Ḍiyā'addīn al-Khālidī', *Al-Fajr al-Adabī*, 35/36, 1983.
Maḥāfẓa, 'Alī, *Al-'Alāqāt al-Almāniyya – al-Filasṭiniyya, 1841–1945*, Beirut, 1981.
Mujāhid, Zakī Muḥammad, *Al-a'lām al-sharqiyya fī 'l-mi'a al-rābi'a 'ashra al-hijriyya*, 4 vols, Cairo, 1949–1963.
Muḥammad Adīb al-'Āmirī, *Al-Quds al-'Arabiyya*, Amman, 1971.
Muṣṭafā Murād al-Dabbāgh, *Biladunā Filisṭīn*, vol. 10/2, Beirut, 1976.
Neumann, Bernhard, *Die Heilige Stadt und deren Bewohner*, Hamburg, 1877.
Palmer, P, 'Das jetzige Bethlehem', *Zeitschrift des Deutschen Palästina-Vereins*, XVII, 1894.
Paulus, Christopher, 'Die Tempelcolonien in Palästina', *Zeitschrift des Deutschen Palästina-Vereins*, VI, 1883.
Rafīq, Muḥammad and Muḥammad Bahjat, *Wilāyat Bairūt*, pt. 1, Beirut, 1335/1916–17.
Rubenstein, Daniel, 'The Jerusalem Municipality under the Ottomans, British and Jordanians' in Joel L Kraemer (ed.), *Jerusalem – Problems and Prospects*, New York, 1980.
Schick, C, 'Die Baugeschichte der Stadt Jerusalem', pt. VII, *Zeitschrift des Deutschen Palästina-Vereins*, XVII, 1894.
Schölch, A, 'Ein palästinensischer Repräsentant der Tanẓimāt-Periode: Yūsuf Ḍiyā'addīn al-Khālidī (1842–1906)', *Der Islam*, 57, 1980.

Palästina im Umbruch 1856–1882. Untersuchungen zur wirtschaftlichen und sozio-politischen Entwicklung, Stuttgart, 1986.
'Europa und Palästina 1838–1917' in Helmut Mejcher and Alexander Schölch (eds.), *Die Palästina Frage 1917–1948*, Paderborn, 1981.
'European Penetration and the Economic Development of Palestine, 1856–82' in R Owen (ed.), *Studies in the Economic and Social History of Palestine in the Nineteenth and Twentieth Centuries*, London, 1982.
'The Demographic Development of Palestine, 1850–1882', *International Journal of Middle East Studies*, 17/4, 1985.
Spyridon, S N, 'Annals of Palestine, 1821–1841', *Journal of the Palestine Oriental Society*, 18, 1938.
Sālim, Laṭīfa, *Al-Ḥukm al-Miṣrī fi 'l-Shām 1831–1841*, Cairo, 1983.
Tibawi, A L, *A Modern History of Syria including Lebanon and Palestine*, London, 1969.
Jerusalem. Its Place in Islam and Arab History, Beirut, 1969.
The Islamic Pious Foundations in Jerusalem, London, 1978.
Tobler, Titus, *Denkblätter aus Jerusalem*, St Gallen and Constanz, 1853.
Vereté, Mayir, 'A Plan for the Internationalization of Jerusalem, 1840–1841', *Asian Affairs*, 12/1, 1978.
Warren, Charles, *Underground Jerusalem*, London, 1876.
Wolff, Philipp, *Sieben Artikel über Jerusalem aus den Jahren 1859 bis 1869*, Stuttgart, 1869.
'Zur neueren Geschichte Jerusalems. Von 1843–1884', *Zeitschrift des Deutschen Palästina-Vereins*, VIII, 1885.

Chapter IX

Aamiry, M A, *Jersulem: Arab Origin and Heritage*, London, 1978.
'Abdallāh b. al-Ḥusain, King of Jordan, *My Memoirs Completed ('Al-Takmīlah)*, with a foreword by His Majesty King Hussein ibn Talal of Jordan, London, 1971.
Abu-Lughod, Ibrahim, *The Transformation of Palestine,* Evanston, Ill., 1971.
Abu-Lughod, Janet, 'The Demographic Transformation of Palestine' in Ibrahim Abu-Lughod (ed.), *The Transformation of Palestine*, Evanston, Ill., 1971, 139–63.
Al-'Ārif, 'Ārif Pasha, *Tārīkh al-Quds*, Cairo, 1951.
Asadi, Fawzi, 'Geographic Elements in the Arab-Israeli Conflict', *Journal of Palestine Studies*, 5, 1, autumn, 1976, 79–91.
Ashbee, C R, *Jerusalem, 1918–1920.* Published for the Council of the Pro-Jerusalem Society, London, 1921.
Jerusalem, 1920–1922. Published for the Council of the Pro-Jerusalem Society, London, 1924.
Bentwich, Norman and Helen, *Mandate Memories, 1918–1948*, New York, 1965.
Benvenisti, Meron, *Jerusalem: The Torn City*, Minneapolis, 1976.
The West Bank Data Project: A Survey of Israel's Policies, Washington: American Enterprise Institute, 1984.
The West Bank Data Base Project: 1986 Report, Washington: American Enterprise Institute, 1986.
Bovis, H Eugene, *The Jerusalem Question 1917–1968*, Stanford, 1971.
Cattan, Henry, *Jerusalem*, New York, 1981.
Cobban, Helena, *The Palestinian Liberation Organization: People, Power and Politics*, Cambridge, 1984.
Collins, Larry and Dominique La Pierre, *O Jerusalem!*, New York, 1972.
Dakkak, Ibrahim, 'Jerusalem's Via Dolorosa', *Journal of Palestinian Studies*, 11, 1, autumn 1981, 136–49.
Forsythe, David P, *United Nations Peacekeeping: The Conciliation Commission for Palestine*, Baltimore, 1972.
Frankel, Glenn, 'Golden Jerusalem: The Grand Prize', *The Washington Post*, June 2, 1987, 1 ff.
Friedman, Thomas L, 'Teddy Kollek's Jerusalem', *The New York Times Magazine*, 4 August, 1985, 16–22 ff.
Glubb, Sir John Bagot, *A Soldier With the Arabs*, London, 1957.
Gubser, Peter, *Jordan: Crossroads of Middle Eastern Events,* Boulder, Colorado, 1983.

Hadawi, Sami, *Bitter Harvest*, New York, 1967.
Halsell, Grace, *Journey to Jerusalem*, New York, 1981.
'Shrine under Siege', *The Link*, 17, 3, August/September, 1984.
Hassan bin Talal, *A Study on Jerusalem*, London, 1979.
Palestinian Self-Determination, New York, 1981.
Heller, Mark A, *A Palestinian State*, Cambridge, Mass., 1983.
Hirst, David, *The Gun and the Olive Branch*, London, 1977.
'Rush to Annexation: Israel in Jerusalem', *Journal of Palestinian Studies*, III, 4, summer 1974, 3–31.
Hudson, Michael C, 'Jerusalem: A City Still Divided', *Mid-East*, Washington, VIII, 4, September, 1968, 20–25.
Hurewitz, J C, *The Struggle for Palestine*, New York, 1950.
Irani, George E, *The Papacy and the Middle East: The Role of the Holy See in the Arab-Israeli Conflict 1962–1984,* Notre Dame, Indiana, 1986.
'Israel and Torture', *The Sunday Times*, London, 19 June, 1977.
John, Robert and Sami Hadawi, *The Palestinian Diary*, 2 vols., New York, 1970.
Kendall, Henry, *Jerusalem, The City Plan, Preservation and Development during the British Mandate, 1918–1948*, London, HMSO, 1948.
Kerr, Malcolm H, 'The Changing Political Status of Jerusalem' in Abu-Lughod, Ibrahim, *The Transformation of Palestine,* Evanston, Ill., 1971, 355–77.
Khader, Bishara, 'Palestinian Demography 1900–2000: The Stake and the Challenge', paper presented to the symposium on 'The Demographic Characteristics of the Palestinian People', Tunis, 1984.
Khālidī, Walīd, *Before Their Diaspora: A Photographic History of the Palestinians, 1876–1948*, Washington, Institute for Palestinian Studies, 1984.
(ed.) *From Haven to Conquest: Readings in Zionism and the Palestine Problem until 1948*, Beirut, Institute for Palestinian Studies, 1971.
'Toward Peace in the Holy Land', *Foriegn Affairs*, vol. 66, no.4, (spring 1988), 771–89.
Kollek, Teddy, *For Jerusalem*, New York, 1978.
Kraemer, Joel (ed.), *Jerusalem: Problems and Prospects*, New York, 1981.
Kroyanker, David, *Jerusalem Planning and Development, 1979–1982*, Jerusalem, 1982.
Kutcher, Arthur, *The New Jerusalem: Planning and Politics*, London, 1973.
Lesch, Ann Mosely, *Arab Politics in Palestine 1917–1939*, Ithaca, NY, 1979.
Louis, William Roger, *The British Empire in the Middle East, 1945–1951*, London and New York, 1984.
Mallison, W Thomas and Sally V Mallison, *The Palestine Problem in International Law and World Order*, London, 1986.
Mattar, Philip, 'The Mufti of Jerusalem: Muhammad Amin Al-Husayni, A Founder of Palestinian Nationalism', PhD dissertation, Columbia University, n.d.
Palestine Partition Commission, *Report*, Cmd. 5854, October, 1938, London, HMSO, 1938, ('The Woodhead Report').
Palestine Royal Commission, *Report*, Cmd. 5479, July, 1937, London, HMSO, 1937 ('The Peel Report').
Palestine, A Survey of, prepared in December 1945 and January 1946 for the Anglo-American Committee of Inquiry, 2 vols., Palestine: The Government Printer, 1946.
Porath, Yehoshua, *The Emergence of the Palestinian-Arab National Movement*, vol. 1 (1919–1929), London, 1977.
The Palestinian Arab National Movement: From Riots to Rebellion, vol. 2 (1929–1939), London, 1977.
'Al-Quds' (Jerusalem), *Al-Mawsū'ah al-Filasṭīniyyah (The Palestinian Encyclopaedia)*, vol. 3, Damascus, 1984.
Resolutions and Decisions of the Grand Assembly and the Security Council Relating to the Question of Palestine, 1947–1975, United Nations, General Assembly, Committee on the Exercise of the Inalienable Rights of the Palestinian People, A/AC. 183/L.2 (5 March 1976).
Samuel, The Rt. Hon. Viscount (Herbert), *Grooves of Change: A Book of Memoirs*, Indianapolis, 1946.

Saqqaf, Abdalaziz Y, *The Middle East City: Ancient Traditions Confront a Modern World*, New York, 1987.
Schleifer, Abdallah, *The Fall of Jerusalem*, New York, 1972.
Sharon, Arieh, *Planning Jerusalem: The Master Plan for the Old City of Jerusalem and Its Environs*, New York, 1973.
Shiber, Saba George, *Recent Arab City Growth*, Kuwait, 1967.
Storrs, Ronald, *Orientations*, London, 1943.
Sykes, Christopher, *Crossroads to Israel*, London, 1965.
Tibawi, A L, *Anglo-Arab Relations and the Question of Palestine, 1914–1921*, London, 1978.
The Islamic Pious Foundations in Jerusalem: Origins, History and Usurpation by Israel, London, 1978.
'Jerusalem: Its Place in Islam and Arab History' in Ibrahim Abu-Lughod (ed.), *The Arab-Israeli Confrontation: An Arab Perspective*, Evanston, Ill., 1970, 10–48.
Tsimhoni, Daphne, 'Demographic Trends of the Christian Population in Jerusalem and the West Bank 1948–1978', *Middle East Journal*, 37, 1, winter, 1983, 54–64.

Index